FILM ADAPTATIONS OF RUSSIAN CLASSICS

FILM ADAPTATIONS OF RUSSIAN CLASSICS

Dialogism and Authorship

Edited by Alexandra Smith and
Olga Sobolev

EDINBURGH
University Press

Edinburgh University Press is one of the leading university presses in the UK. We publish academic books and journals in our selected subject areas across the humanities and social sciences, combining cutting-edge scholarship with high editorial and production values to produce academic works of lasting importance. For more information visit our website: edinburghuniversitypress.com

© editorial matter and organisation Alexandra Smith and Olga Sobolev, 2023, 2024
© the chapters their several authors, 2023, 2024

Edinburgh University Press Ltd
13 Infirmary Street
Edinburgh EH1 1LT

First published in hardback by Edinburgh University Press 2023

Typeset in 10/12.5 pt Sabon
by IDSUK (DataConnection) Ltd

A CIP record for this book is available from the British Library

ISBN 978 1 4744 9913 2 (hardback)
ISBN 978 1 4744 9914 9 (paperback)
ISBN 978 1 4744 9915 6 (webready PDF)
ISBN 978 1 4744 9916 3 (epub)

The right of Alexandra Smith and Olga Sobolev to be identified as editors of this work has been asserted in accordance with the Copyright, Designs and Patents Act 1988 and the Copyright and Related Rights Regulations 2003 (SI No. 2498).

CONTENTS

List of Figures vii
Notes on Contributors ix
Acknowledgements xii

Introduction: On the Text–Film Relationship – The Question of Apt and Inapt Adaptations 1
Alexandra Smith and Olga Sobolev

PART ONE   GONCHAROV AND TURGENEV: ADAPTATION AS NOSTALGIA

1. The Politics of Nostalgia: Ivan Goncharov's *Oblomov* and Nikita Mikhalkov's Film Adaptation 31
   Henrietta Mondry

2. Adapting Turgenev's Novel as a Pastorale: Avdotya Smirnova's *Fathers and Sons* 52
   Alexandra Smith

PART TWO   REIMAGINING DOSTOEVSKY

3. Dostoevsky and Bresson: From 'A Meek Creature' to *Une femme douce* 79
   Olga Peters Hasty

4. Funny and Frightening: Dostoyevsky's *The Double* in Richard Ayoade's Interpretation   100
   Tine Roesen

PART THREE   COLLABORATING WITH CHEKHOV

5. 'The Paths I Have Established . . .': Chekhov on the Russian and American Screen   123
   Radislav Lapushin

6. Louis Malle and *Uncle Vanya*   144
   Angus Wrenn

7. Reinventing Chekhov for the American Screen: Michael Mayer's *The Seagull*   165
   Olga Partan

PART FOUR   ENGAGING WITH TOLSTOY

8. Thanatophobia on the Soviet Screen: Tolstoy's *Death of Ivan Il'ich* and Aleksandr Kaidanovsky's *A Simple Death*   183
   Otto Boele

9. Forged Network Narratives: Tolstoy's *The Forged Coupon* and a Cycle of Adaptations in World Cinema   205
   Greg Dolgopolov

10. *War and Peace*: A New Visual Dimension   226
    Olga Sobolev

Index   248

FIGURES

1.1	Oblomov tells Stolz that he refuses to go (away), *A Few Days from the Life of I. I. Oblomov*	40
1.2	Little Andrei Oblomov amidst the rural scenery, *A Few Days from the Life of I. I. Oblomov*	48
2.1	Andrei Ustiugov as Bazarov, *Fathers and Sons*	60
2.2	Natal'ia Rogozhkina as Odintsova, *Fathers and Sons*	65
3.1	Pawnbroker and Douce in front of the monkey cage at the Jardin des Plantes, *Une femme douce*	88
3.2	Douce shown dead on the pavement after her leap from the balcony, *Une femme douce*	97
4.1	Simon and James, *The Double*	108
4.2	Simon and Hannah, *The Double*	110
5.1	Marcia and Vincent, *The Sisters*	132
5.2	Ragin, *Ward No. 6*	136
6.1	Julianne Moore, Larry Pine and Wallace Shawn, *Vanya on 42nd Street*	148
6.2	Vanya and Yelena, *Vanya on 42nd Street*	158
7.1	Nina Zarechnaia, *The Seagull*	170
7.2	Arkadina and Masha, *The Seagull*	173
8.1	Ivan Il'ích as a corpse, *A Simple Death*	196
8.2	Ivan Il'ích's nurse: 'Kto ty ? Chto ty ?' ('Who are you?', 'What are you?'), *A Simple Death*	200
9.1	Kakha and Vazha, *Loot*	215

9.2 Niko Smolander teaching, *Frozen Land* 218
10.1 Natasha Rostova and Prince Andrei Bolkonsky at Natasha's first ball, *War and Peace* 229
10.2 Pierre Bezukhov at the Battle of Borodino, *War and Peace* 240

NOTES ON CONTRIBUTORS

Otto Boele is Senior Lecturer in Slavonic Languages and Cultures at the University of Leiden. He specialises in Russian literature and film. His numerous publications include the following: *Sluzhiv otlichno blagorodno/ Having Served Excellently, Nobly: Festschrift for Sander Brouwer* (edited with B. Noordenbos, 2019); *Post-Soviet Nostalgia. Confronting the Empire's Legacies* (edited with B. Noordenbos and K. Robbe, 2019); and *Erotic Nihilism in Late Imperial Russia. The Case of Mikhail Artsybashev's 'Sanin'* (2009).

Greg Dolgopolov is Senior Lecturer in Film Studies at the University of New South Wales. His research interests include film festivals, short films, film distribution, Australian and post-Soviet cinema, and the crime genre. He has published extensively on Russian and Australian cinema, as well as on film festivals. Greg is the artistic director of the Vision Splendid Outback Film Festival (2013–), Short+Sweet Film Festival (2017–), the Russian Resurrection Film Festival (2008–), and The Best of Australian Shorts Festival that screens throughout Russia (2018–19).

Olga Peters Hasty is Professor of Russian Literature in the Department of Slavic Languages and Literatures at Princeton University. She has published extensively on Russian nineteenth- and twentieth-century literature and authored the following books: *America Through Russian Eyes* (with Susanne Fusso, 1988); *Tsvetaeva's Orphic Journeys in the Worlds of the Word* (1996); *Pushkin's Tatiana* (1999); and *How Women Must Write* (2019).

Radislav Lapushin is Associate Professor of Russian Literature in the Department of Germanic and Slavic Languages and Literatures at the University of North Carolina at Chapel Hill. His numerous publications on Russian literature include the following: *'Dew on the Grass': The Poetics of Inbetweenness in Chekhov* (2010); *An Incomprehensible Existence: A Reading of Chekhov* (1998); and *Chekhov's Letters: Biography, Context, Poetics* (edited with Carol Apollonio, 2018).

Henrietta Mondry is Professor of Russian literature at the University of Canterbury. She has published extensively on Russian and European literature and the history of ideas. Her recent publications include the following: *Political Animals: Representing Dogs in Modern Russian Culture* (2015); *Vasily Rozanov and the Body of Russian Literature* (2010); *Exemplary Bodies: Constructing the Jew in Russian Culture, since the 1880s* (2009); and *Pure, Strong and Sexless: The Peasant Woman's Body and Gleb Uspensky* (2006).

Olga Partan is Associate Professor of Russian in the Department of World Languages, Literatures, and Cultures at the College of the Holy Cross. Her publications on Russian literature and culture include the monograph *Vagabonding Masks: The Italian Commedia dell'Arte in the Russian Artistic Imagination* (2017). Currently, Olga is preparing for publication a collection of essays (together with Sibelan Forrester) on the Russian creative intelligentsia.

Tine Roesen is Associate Professor in Russian in the Department of Cross-Cultural and Regional Studies at the University of Copenhagen. She has published extensively on Dostoevsky, Bakhtin, and Russian contemporary literature. Tine has translated several works written by Dostoevsky, Sorokin, and Aleksievich into Danish. Her list of publications includes the following: *Vladimir Sorokin's Languages.* (edited with D. Uffelmann, 2013); *Landslide of the Norm: Language Culture in Post-Soviet Russia* (edited with I. Lunde, 2006); and *Dostojevskij. En introduktion* (2021).

Alexandra Smith is Reader in Russian Studies at the University of Edinburgh. She has published extensively on Russian literature and culture and authored the following books: *Poetic Canons, Cultural Memory and Russian National Identity after 1991* (co-authored with Katharine Hodgson, 2020); *Twentieth-Century Russian Poetry: Reinventing the Canon* (co-edited with Katharine Hodgson and Joanne Shelton, 2017); *Montaging Pushkin: Pushkin and Visions of Modernity in Russian 20th-century Poetry* (2006); *Pesn´ peresmeshnika: Pushkin v tvorchestve Mariny Tsvetaevoi* (1998); and *The Song of the Mockingbird: Pushkin in the Work of Marina Tsvetaeva* (1994).

Olga Sobolev is Director of the Language, Culture and Society Programme at the London School of Economics and Political Science. Her research interests lie in comparative studies and concern nineteenth- and twentieth-century Russian and European culture. Her recent publications include: 'Anna Karenina: The Ways of Seeing' in *Critical Insights: Anna Karenina* (ed. Bob Evans, 2021); *From Orientalism to Cultural Capital: The Myth of Russia in British Literature of the 1920s* (co-authored with Angus Wrenn, 2017); 'Representation of H. G. Wells on the Russian Stage and Screen' in *H. G. Wells and All Things Russian* (2019); *The Only Hope of the World: G. B. Shaw and Russia* (with Angus Wrenn, 2012); and *The Silver Mask: Harlequinade in the Symbolist Poetry of Blok and Belyi* (2008).

Angus Wrenn teaches at the Language Centre at the London School of Economics and Political Science. He specialises in English and comparative literature, and in Anglo-Russian cultural relations. Angus is one of the editors of the ongoing Cambridge University Press edition of the complete fiction of Henry James. His recent publications include the following: *From Orientalism to Cultural Capital: The Myth of Russia in British Literature of the 1920s* (co-authored with Olga Sobolev, 2017); *The Only Hope of the World: G. B. Shaw and Russia* (co-authored with Olga Sobolev, 2012), and *Henry James and the Second Empire* (2009).

ACKNOWLEDGEMENTS

Our gratitude goes to all contributors to this volume for their dedication, and deep interest in this project, and for constructive and thought-provoking discussions carried out virtually over these months of pandemic.

We also would like to thank everyone who took part in the *Overcoming the Anxiety of Authorship: Film Adaptations of Russian Classics in the 1990s–2000s* panel, conducted at the ASEEES Convention, 2020. This panel laid a foundation for this volume, and we are grateful for the opportunity we had to discuss our ideas with this group of enthusiastic and knowledgeable scholars. Our special thanks go to Professor Julian Graffy for his inspiring discussions and the most useful suggestions he made with regard to this project. We are also grateful to Dr Angus Wrenn and Andrew Smith for taking the time to read the drafts and for their continuous and selfless support, and to a large number of colleagues and friends with whom we have had the chance to discuss informally the themes and ideas of this volume.

INTRODUCTION: ON THE TEXT–FILM RELATIONSHIP – THE QUESTION OF APT AND INAPT ADAPTATIONS

Alexandra Smith and Olga Sobolev

The Drama of Authorship

For many years adaptation theory largely revolved around the question of fidelity to the original source. It relied on the notion of the author's intention as a benchmark for the success of the literary text and its adaptation.[1] In the last thirty years, scholars such as Sarah Cardwell, Deborah Cartmell and Imelda Whelehan have criticised the dominant view about the primacy of the literary source for the evaluation of film adaptations.[2] In her survey of the more recurrent theoretical approaches to film adaptations, Cardwell mentions medium-specific theories which see each separate medium as unique. She refers to George Bluestone's book *Novels into Film* 'as an archetypal example of a strong medium-specific approach'.[3] Bluestone thinks that each medium is autonomous and has its unique properties. He suggests that 'differences in form and theme are inseparable from differences in media'.[4] According to Bluestone, while time

---

[1] Thomas Leitch, *Film Adaptation and Its Discontents: From Gone with the Wind to the Passion of the Christ, Johns* (Baltimore, MD: Johns Hopkins University Press, 2007), p. 2.
[2] Sarah Cardwell, *Adaptation Revisited: Television and the Classic Novel* (Manchester: Manchester University Press, 2002); Deborah Cartmell and Imelda Whelehan, *Adaptations: From Text to Screen, Screen to Text* (Oxford: Oxford University Press, 1999).
[3] Cardwell, p. 45.
[4] George Bluestone, *Novels into Film: The Metamorphosis of Fiction into Cinema* (London: Cambridge University Press, 1957), p. 2.

serves as the formative principle in the novel, 'the formative principle in the film is space'. He goes on to say that: 'While the novel takes its space for granted and forms its narrative in a complex of time values, the film takes its time for granted and forms its narrative in arrangements of space.'[5]

Cardwell recognises the limitations of such an approach, highlighting advantages of the comparative approach which originated in the 1970s and was based on the narrative deconstruction of both film and book. As Cardwell notes, the comparative approach 'can explain instances of fidelity' and 'allows for the possibility of "faithful adaptation"', while recognising fundamental differences between the two media.[6] In contrast to specialists interested in the medium-specific approach, many film critics use the comparative approach together with semiotics in order to establish how 'the same narrative is told using different conventions'.[7] Michael Klein and Gillian Parker, prominent representatives of the comparative approach, justify their use of semiotics as follows:

> In addition to its distinct formal and expressive aspects, film also conveys a range of cultural signs – the facial expressions, gestures, dialects, dress, and style of its characters; the architecture, advertising, landscape, and common artifacts of its setting; the semiotic expression of a culture in a particular historical period.[8]

In Cardwell's opinion, such a structuralist-based conception of narrative enables directors to understand better which elements of a literary text 'can readily be transposed to film and which elements cannot'.[9] In her view, such an understanding of the creation and recreation of discourse helps to explain 'the success of some "faithful" adaptations'.[10]

In sum, the comparative approach enables interpreters to examine each adaptation's relationship with a source text effectively. Cardwell calls for the creators of those film adaptations which create a different discourse, altering considerably the transferrable elements of the literary text, to be judged on their own terms and 'not in terms of fidelity' to the source novel or the source story.[11] Broadly speaking, the approaches found in the present study exemplify

---

[5] Bluestone, p. 61.
[6] Cardwell, p. 52.
[7] Ibid., p. 56.
[8] Michael Klein and Gillian Parker, 'Introduction: Film and Literature', in *The English Novel and the Movies*, eds Michael Klein and Gillian Parker (New York: Frederick Ungar Publishing Company, 1981), pp. 1–13 (p. 3).
[9] Cardwell, p. 59.
[10] Ibid.
[11] Ibid., p. 60.

the comparative approach, and they also consider the existence of different types of adaptation such as transposition, commentary and analogy. Geoffrey Wagner describes transposition as faithful (*illustrative*) adaptation; he defines commentary as 'an infringement on the work of another' and he presents analogy as a separate 'work of art' which does not violate a literary original but intends either to reproduce the original minimally or not to reproduce it altogether.[12]

Robert Geal, in his 2019 book on film adaptations of William Shakespeare's works (and Shakespeare is the most frequently adapted author in the world's cinema), emphasises the importance of cultural studies to the development of adaptation theory. He favours dialogic criticism as part of film adaptation theory, a preference also exemplified by Thomas Leitch's pronouncement that all texts should be seen as intertexts, all reading should be viewed as re-reading, and all writing should be understood as re-writing. As Geal puts it, all texts 'are in some kind of complex dialogue with other texts and forms of discourse'.[13] For Geal, the process of adaptation pivots around the notion of the drama of authorship. Geal writes:

> The drama of authorship is an inevitable element of any film which foregrounds the fact that it is adapted from a canonical source, and which narrates according to the conventions of cinematic realism. Canonical realist adaptations reveal their constructed authorship and then subsume and obfuscate that revelation. The oscillation between these two enunciative registers is an anamorphic process.[14]

According to Geal, realist film adaptation masquerades itself as constructed discourse and 'transforms itself into an anamorphic hybrid of authored discourse'. He states that 'realist adaptation [. . .] does not just entail the shift of a text from one medium to another, and from one time period/culture to another'.[15] Rather, it implies a shift from discourse to anamorphic discourse.

'The word "adaptation"', writes Geal, 'has two interrelated meanings—adaptation is not just the replication of one fictional text by another fictional text; adaptation is also the process of changing a text in which authorial artifice is retroactively foregrounded into a text that announces, subsumes and obfuscates that artifice'.[16] Geal suggests viewing a Shakespearean film adaptation as

---

[12] Geoffrey Wagner, *The Novel and the Cinema* (Vancouver, BC: Fairleigh Dickinson University Press, 1975), pp. 223, 227.
[13] Robert Geal, *Anamorphic Authorship in Canonical Film: A Case Study of Shakespearean Film* (Cham: Palgrave Macmillan, 2019), p. 13.
[14] Ibid., p. 221.
[15] Ibid.
[16] Ibid.

'self-evidently a re-performance, and self-evidently something that a spectator knows is a fiction, rather than something spontaneously somewhat "real"'.[17] Similarly, we have chosen as our case studies several adaptations that examine various texts written by Russian nineteenth-century canonical authors. They explore the relationship between canonical texts and their re-performance in different contextual settings. While Geal's study claims that transposition elides 'the complex ways that Shakespearean film both re-performs artifice and simultaneously functions as realist cinema',[18] our book shows how dialogism illuminates the potential benefits of displacing the author. Geal's observation that dialogical criticism enables interpreters to understand clearly how 'a canonical voice historically used to assert a particular exclusionary hierarchy of identities can be reworked into a multiplicity of voices celebrating diverse inclusionary identities'[19] is fully applicable to our collection of essays which incorporates Russian, Francophone and Anglophone adaptations that reimagine the past through re-reading Russian classics either nostalgically or critically.

Geal's statement accords well with Robert Stam's call to move away from the examination of fidelity and transnational approaches to the source text by focusing on dialogic imagination and the notion of authorship. This approach enables the contributors to reveal the various strategies of filmmakers who use canonical texts to adapt the chosen source to new contexts in a way that enlivens an important text from the past by making it relevant to the present audience's experiences and aesthetic values. Following Stam's assertion that adaptations must adapt 'to changing environments and changing taste' and conform to new 'aesthetic norms', the chapters will discuss the role of filmmakers as co-authors and editors of the original texts, highlighting the dialogic strategies of their embedded adaptation.

Promoting Russian Literature through Film: Shifting Paradigms and Challenges

Film adaptations have played an important role in promoting Russian literature in the last hundred years, both in Russia and abroad. They continue to provide fertile ground for analysing the changing dynamics between literature, film and politics. The influence of historical factors on literary and filmic works also leaves a subject open to reinterpretation over time. Our changing perception of history often results in the desire not only to re-evaluate earlier literary texts from the aesthetic viewpoint but also to re-assess the ideas embedded in them. This trend can be well exemplified in the context of the collapse of the Soviet Union in 1991, which gave rise to a critical re-examination of Socialist

---

[17] Ibid., p. 222.
[18] Ibid., p. 223.
[19] Ibid., p. 226.

Realism, and its impact on the Russian educational canon and popular interpretations of Russian nineteenth-century literature that are found in contemporary culture and media. Such a re-examination enables filmmakers to engage in a dialogue between the past and the present that leads to the overcoming of a sense of alienation. Re-examination of the past through literature also often results in renewing the perception of the present.

By adapting classics as lenses for examining post-Soviet reality and for reviving the core tenets of the intellectual tradition, many Russian filmmakers have contributed to the ongoing debate about Russia's heritage and its cultural prestige abroad. In the last thirty years, many canonical interpretations of Russian classics promoted by Soviet institutions have withered away. In their place has come a more creative attitude towards canonical works, be they Russian or foreign. In their seminal study of film adaptations of Russian literature, Stephen Hutchings and Anat Vernitski view these developments positively. They think that 'reports of the death of Russian literary culture are premature' and state: 'This is thanks in no small part to the vitality of the *ekranizatsiia*.'[20] Tom Roberts adds another angle to the discussion of adaptations. He suggests that the post-Soviet representational crisis inspired many prominent post-Soviet film directors, including Kira Muratova, to turn to canonical authors to enrich their repertoire of communicative strategies. He describes Muratova's film *Chekhovian Motifs* (2002) as 'beautifully expressive' despite some 'semiotic and hermeneutic uncertainty' embedded in the film.[21]

During the late Soviet and post-Soviet periods, many more talented theatrical and film directors started exploring the infinite possibilities of reading literary masterpieces produced by Alexander Pushkin, Nikolai Gogol, Lev Tolstoy, Ivan Turgenev, and Anton Chekhov. While their adaptations have intrinsic value, they could also be seen as insightful comments on the era in which they were produced. Many of the innovative interpretations of familiar narratives that emerged in the period from 1970 to 2010 echo Mikhail Bakhtin's belief that, due to their open-ended nature, novels yield themselves to be re-read and re-interpreted in different contexts. Bakhtin affirms that the novel encounters the 'spontaneity of the inconclusive present' and that the novelist 'is drawn toward everything that is not yet completed'.[22] Bakhtin's interest in the open-ended

---

[20] Stephen Hutchings and Anat Vernitski, 'Introduction', in *Russian and Soviet Film Adaptations of Literature, 1900–2001: Screening the Word*, eds Stephen Hutchings and Anat Vernitski (London and New York: Routledge Curzon, 2005), pp. 1–24 (p. 22).

[21] Tom Roberts, '"Simply an anachronism": repetition and meaning in Kira Muratova's *Chekhovian Motifs*', *Studies in Russian & Soviet Cinema*, 7 (2013), 39–59 (p. 56). On this film see also Julian Graffy, 'Difficult people: Kira Muratova's Cinematic Encounter with Chekhov', *Essays in Poetics*, 31 (2006), 180–212.

[22] Mikhail Bakhtin, 'Epic and Novel', in *The Dialogic Imagination. Four Essays by M. M. Bakhtin*, ed. Michael Holquist (Austin: University of Texas Press, 1981), pp. 3–40 (p. 27).

nature of the novel inspired other scholars to look at literature as a cultural phenomenon inseparable from other contemporaneous developments. Julie Kristeva, for example, promotes the notion of intertextuality based on interaction between different texts. In Kristeva's opinion, all texts interact with each other in an intertextual way 'in the space of a given text'. Kristeva suggests that 'several utterances, taken from other texts, intersect and neutralize each other'.[23]

Kristeva presupposes that intertextual links between texts are multiple and are part of textual synchronicity. Yet Linda Hutcheon warns about the mechanical application of such a vision of intertextual interaction to adaptation. In her view, a true adaptation cannot be reduced to an intertextual reference: it should comprise a conscious and continuous engagement with the source material. Hutcheon's model of textual interaction envisages the open-ended nature of all texts. The novel, argues Hutcheon, 'immerses us through imagination in a fictional world'. In contrast, the showing mode of engagement used in plays and films 'immerses us through the perception of the aural and the visual'.[24] Hutcheon finds Darwin's theory of evolution helpful. In her view, it can be used for understanding narrative adaptation as 'a process of mutation and adjustment'. It makes stories both adaptable and adapted. 'Sometimes, like biological adaptation', affirms Hutcheon, 'cultural adaptation involves migration to favourable conditions: stories travel to different cultures and different media'.[25] Her view will be illustrated by the examples discussed in this volume. Several chapters will demonstrate how adaptations challenge the notions of priority and authority. It is not unusual for contemporary audiences to experience the literary text after seeing its well-executed cinematic adaptation. It will also be shown that adaptations transmit popular stories as 'timeless cognitive models' that 'make sense of our world and of human action in it'.[26]

Robert Stam, another prominent theoretician of adaptation, has a different approach to Hutcheon. He proposes to view film adaptation as an act of translation and a special kind of 'inter-semiotic transposition'.[27] Stam's approach is focused on intercultural communication. It is developed effectively in the collection of essays edited by Alexander Burry and Frederick H. White, *Border Crossing: Russian Literature into Film*, which examines 'how political and economic circumstances play a crucial role in dictating how filmmakers

---

[23] Julia Kristeva, *Desire in Language: A Semiotic Approach to Literature and Art* (New York: Columbia University Press, 1980), p. 36.

[24] Linda Hutcheon, *A Theory of Adaptation* (London: Routledge, 2006), p. 22.

[25] Ibid., p. 31.

[26] Ibid., p. 175.

[27] Robert Stam, 'The Dialogics of Adaptation', in *Film Adaptation*, ed. James Naremore (New Brunswick, NJ: Rutgers University Press, 2000), pp. 54–76 (p. 62).

transport their cinematic hypertext into this new cultural environment'.[28] Commenting on the appeal of Russian novels to filmmakers both in and outside Russia, Burry states that such writers as Tolstoy, Dostoevsky, and Turgenev established the international dominance of the Russian novel 'through compulsively readable narratives [. . .] and a nearly obsessive focus on what the critic Mikhail Mikhailov called the '"accursed questions"' pertaining to the existence of God and the 'revolutionary transformation of society'.[29]

The present volume will reassess Mikhailov's notion of accursed questions as a simplified branding of the Russian novel and will focus instead on the definition produced by the Russian and Soviet critic Lidiia Ginzburg: she labelled Russian fiction of the second half of the nineteenth century as 'psychological realism'. Ginzburg advocated self-reflection as an ethical activity, valuing thereby responsibility as an essential theme of psychological prose. In her seminal article 'On the Literary Hero', she maintains that 'literature always deals with values and evaluations'. In Ginzburg's view, 'the ethical principle for literature is an inner structural principle' and 'the traits of the literary hero are always evaluated through the ethical prism'.[30] As the chapters that follow will demonstrate, Ginzburg's assessment of literature is especially fitting for evaluating film adaptations produced between 1970 and 2020. This period is known for its wide use of neo-modernist and post-modernist techniques. As Jean-François Lyotard observes, in post-modernity there can be no single principle for making knowledge acceptable by everyone due to 'the decline of the legitimating power of grand narratives of speculation and emancipation'.[31]

In her essays, Ginzburg moulds Tolstoy as a precursor of many contemporary trends, including the examination of subjectivity and the rejection of established beliefs. Ginzburg's book *On Psychological Prose* highlights the relevance of Tolstoy's psychological analysis to contemporary scientific developments pertaining to the psychology of the individual, physiology, and psychoanalysis.[32] In Ginzburg's view, Tolstoy laid the foundation for Russian twentieth-century fiction:

> What for him had been merely a feature of the personality regarded dynamically, subsequently grew in importance, on occasion acquiring exceptional significance for the depiction of the twentieth-century human

---

[28] Alexander Burry, 'Introduction: Filming Russian Classics – Challenges and Opportunities', in *Border Crossing: Russian Literature into Film*, eds Alexander Burry and Frederick H. White (Edinburgh: Edinburgh University Press, 2016), pp. 1–16 (p. 16).
[29] Burry, 'Introduction: Filming Russian Classics', p. 1.
[30] Lidiia Ginzburg, *O literaturnom geroe* (Leningrad: Sovetskii pisatel', 1979), p. 131.
[31] Jean-François Lyotard, *The Postmodern Condition: A Report on Knowledge* (Manchester: Manchester University Press, 1984), p. 35.
[32] Lidia Ginzburg, *On Psychological Prose*, trans. by Judson Rosengrant (Princeton: Princeton University Press, 1991), p. 266.

being with his fragmented consciousness, but especially of the 'turn-of-the-century' Russian intellectual in the grip of decadent trends.[33]

Similarly, Virginia Woolf discovered in Tolstoy's fiction several new modes of perception of reality that are usually found in modernist art, including the principle of defamiliarisation. In her article, 'The Russian Point of View', Woolf asserts that Tolstoy's use of optics is comparable to viewing the world from a mountaintop with a telescope in our hands: a clear and sharp vision of the landscape is often interrupted in his works by a detail. She also sees Tolstoy and Turgenev as products of a Russian literary culture that favours open-ended narratives and a melancholic outlook. Woolf defines the Russian soul 'as the chief character of Russian literature'.[34] Woolf's desire to influence the readership and distribution of Russian literary works abroad by labelling them as something different from British literature and exotic is comparable to the process of branding that relies 'on quality control', 'the web of agencies' and 'brand myths'.[35] Furthermore, Woolf saw Russian realism as an antidote to Victorian literature.

In her analysis of Tolstoy's novel *War and Peace*, Laura Olson identifies several utopian aspects of the novel linked to Tolstoy's vision of Russianness: he sees Russian identity as being constantly shaped by its interaction with the West. Olson links Tolstoy's myth of national glory, national cohesiveness and family unity to his understanding of Russianness as the living embodiment of 'the spontaneous national spirit which stubbornly remains even after exposure to foreign influence, that which Kutuzov, Karataev, Pierre, and Natasha all possess'.[36] In Olson's view, Tolstoy's ideal of domesticity – as expressed in *War and Peace* – departs from the traditional vision of the aristocratic family driven by economic concerns. Olson claims that Tolstoy urges his readers to 'create a private life for themselves' and to 'devote themselves to raising children'.[37] Yet she finds such a view of personal happiness that reduces the individual spiritual quest of the novel to organising a self-contained utopian social unit, especially because 'in this utopia, both on the individual and national level, "the self" no longer needs to be defined for it exists in perfect harmony with its neighbours'.[38] Nevertheless, Tolstoy's engagement with the debates about

---

[33] Ibid.
[34] Virginia Woolf, 'The Russian Point of View', in *The Essays of Virginia Woolf*, ed. Andrew McNeillie (London: The Hogarth Press, 1994), IV, pp. 181–9 (p. 185–6).
[35] David Wengrow, 'Introduction. Commodity Branding in Archaeological and Anthropological Perspectives', in *Cultures of Commodity Branding*, eds Andrew Bevan and David Wengrow (London: Routledge, 2010), pp. 13–33 (p. 30).
[36] Laura Olson, 'Russianness, Femininity, and Romantic Aesthetics in *War and Peace*', *The Russian Review*, 56 (1997), 515–31 (p. 530).
[37] Ibid., p. 528.
[38] Ibid, p. 529.

the modern family and the woman question, as voiced in Russia and Europe in the 1860s, provides an opportunity for today's readers to reassess the utopian vision of modernity embedded in *War and Peace*.

Commenting on Tolstoy and film, Michael Denner concludes that 'the wavering between perceiving Tolstoy as a storyteller and moral thinker has greatly influenced cinematic adaptations of Tolstoy's works'.[39] Denner's statement accords well with Denise Youngblood's analysis of film adaptations of Russian classics in the pre-revolutionary period, in which she highlights their educational value, stating that their purpose was to improve cultural literacy by introducing less cultured audiences to the importance of Russian realist literature. In Youngblood's opinion, some adaptations 'made a genuine contribution to the evolution of Russian film art'.[40] According to Otto Boele's article on Evgenii Bauer's 1915 film adaptation of Ivan Turgenev's *After Death*, Turgenev was a less popular author among pre-revolutionary filmmakers:

> Between 1907 and 1918 Pushkin provided the inspiration for no less than 47 films. Gogol and Chekhov come in second and third place with 44 and 25 adaptations respectively. Turgenev was adapted 12 times during this period, still two times more than Dostoevsky. Although we cannot know for sure why pre-revolutionary film directors so rarely turned to Turgenev's work, we may conjecture that it was generally deemed unrewarding to adapt it for the screen.[41]

In contrast to pre-revolutionary filmmakers, Turgenev's novel *Fathers and Sons* appears to be important as a source work for adaptation for Soviet and post-Soviet directors.

While pre-revolutionary film adaptations sought to enrich their language and shift away from the dominance of a logocentric cultural landscape, Soviet film adaptors of Russian classics tended to infuse their versions with a socio-political slant. David Gillespie provides these examples:

> Alexander Ivanovsky's 1935 film of Pushkin's (unfinished) novella *Dubrovsky* shows the peasant masses joining Dubrovsky's revolt against the tyrannical landowner Troekurov, and even after the death of the hero

---

[39] Michael A. Denner, 'Introduction', in *Tolstoy on Screen*, eds Lorna Fitzsimmons and Michael A. Denner (Evanston: Northwestern University Press, 2015), pp. 3–20; kindle edition: loc.197.

[40] Denise J. Youngblood, *The Magic Mirror: Moviemaking in Russia, 1908–1918* (Madison and London: University of Wisconsin Press, 1999), p. 127.

[41] Otto Boele. 'After Death, the Movie (1915) – Ivan Turgenev, Evgenii Bauer and the Aesthetics of Morbidity', in *Turgenev: Art, Ideology and Legacy*, eds Robert Reid and Joe Andrew (Amsterdam and New York: Rodopi, 2010), pp. 253–68 (p. 253).

they continue their revolt and right social wrongs. [. . .] *The Lady with the Lapdog* [sic] (1960) 'transfers' Chekhov's 1899 drama with great fidelity and is distinguished by the excellent playing of the two leads (Iia Savvina and Alexei Batalov). [. . .] In certain background scenes the film serves up a depressing picture of the social ills (poverty, despair, moral corruption of the upper classes) of fin-de-siècle Russia. Kheifits's film, despite its closeness to Chekhov's text (right down to the dialogue), adds its own critical gloss to its depiction of Tsarist society, so that the old world is portrayed as morally redundant.[42]

Yet, as Gillespie points out, 'even in the Soviet years adaptations could be used to explore shifting priorities and to express ideas of nationhood'.[43]

Beyond discussing the ideological concerns of Soviet filmmakers who used adaptations as a prism through which Soviet reality could be evaluated, Gillespie provides a useful survey of auteur-like Soviet directors whose film adaptations were well-received in the Soviet Union and abroad. Commenting on Andrei Mikhalkov-Konchalovsky's version of Turgenev's novel *A Nest of Gentlefolk* (*Dvorianskoe gnezdo*, 1969), Gillespie notes that:

While sticking close to Turgenev's story of doomed love between Lavretsky, the Russian literary 'superfluous man' of wit and talent who can find no real fulfilment in society, and the moral and incorruptible young girl Liza, Konchalovsky allows his camera to sweep across great vistas and panoramas of an unspoilt Russian countryside, and his depiction of male-female relationships has a palpable and quite daring eroticism. His *Uncle Vania* [. . .] featured some of the great actors of the day, including Innokenty Smoktunovsky. [. . .] It concentrates on the interaction of various characters and is predominantly shot indoors, with brooding passions and unresolved personal dilemmas (as ever with Chekhov).[44]

According to Gillespie, in contrast to the nationalistic and ideological overtones found in Soviet film adaptations of Russian Golden Age literature, the audience for foreign films is exposed to certain traits of the 'Hollywoodisation' of Russian classics. Gillespie's examples of the latter include King Vidor's *War and Peace* and Richard Brooks's *The Brothers Karamazov*. In the same vein, he discusses the four English-language versions *of Anna Karenina* and defines them as 'showcases

---

[42] David Gillespie, 'The Art of Literary Adaptation and English-Language Film Interpretations of Russian Literature ("Anna Karenina")', *Procedia – Social and Behavioral Sciences*, 154 (2014), pp. 30–5 (p. 32).
[43] Ibid., p. 35.
[44] Ibid., p. 33.

for the female stars representing values of glamour, independence and vulnerability: Greta Garbo, Vivien Leigh, Sophie Marceau and Keira Knightley'.[45] He thinks that foreign adaptations of *Anna Karenina* have a strong focus on the central drama of Anna's role as a 'fallen woman'; and the female stars are usually 'encouraged to demonstrate the full range of their acting talents'.[46]

Clearly, Gillespie's historical analysis of film adaptations of Russian classics is informed by the Cold War binary division between Russia and the West. He has a firm belief in the role of film adaptations as a useful tool used by Russian intellectuals for fixing 'national identity in a time of flux' and exploring 'new realities from set positions.'[47] While being in agreement with Gillespie's assessment of general trends in the film adaptation of Russian classics, we would like to shift away from the use of binary oppositions towards the recognition that each adaptation of a canonical literary text is a re-performance of the original text in a different contextual setting. By adopting Geal's belief that 'dialogism has some distinct advantages over poststructuralism', we examine how 'film texts demonstrate evidence of various competing interpretations of how films operate'.[48] For Geal, adaptations of canonical original authors offer privileged conditions to film scholars to test how various strategies of interpretation function. He thinks that adaptations 'feature numerous diachronic interpretations of the same sources', making thereby 'the analysis of how these filmmaking strategies develop historically' more effective.[49] Similarly, the case studies included in our book demonstrate how the process of reworking elements of the original source serves as part of authorial anamorphism. Embracing Geal's call for 'the pluralistic approach to adaptational filmmaking and adaptational spectatorship',[50] we bring to the attention of our readers the exploration of authorship, dialogic imagination, and the manipulated pleasures of the re-performance of familiar literary sources.

It should be also mentioned that, unlike previous collections of essays on the film adaptation of Russian literature, our volume focuses exclusively on the second half of the nineteenth century. Such a focus enables the contributors to test Cartmell's thesis that the modernist novel 'does not translate so well to cinema as do its predecessors of the nineteenth century, as in the case of Dickens.'[51]

---

[45] Ibid.
[46] Ibid.
[47] Ibid., p. 35.
[48] Geal, p. 250.
[49] Ibid., p. 233.
[50] Ibid., p. 232.
[51] Deborah Cartmell, '100+Years of Adaptations, or, Adaptation as the Art Form of Democracy', in *A Companion to Literature, Film, and Adaptation*, ed. Deborah Cartmell (Oxford: Wiley-Blackwell, 2012), pp. 1–15 (p. 4).

Arguably, the visual tropes and cinematic quality of Russian nineteenth-century novels and stories played a significant role in the growing popularity of film adaptations at the beginning of the twentieth century. At the same time, many filmmakers in Russia saw the visualisation of literature as an opportunity to enhance the cultural value of film. Thus, commenting on the early adaptations of Dostoevsky's works, Nikita Lary maintains that 'the big pre-revolutionary film merchants were greedy for plots and eager to capitalize on the big literary names'.[52] Yet Lary also notes that not until after Stalin's death did Socialist Realist artists have a chance to continue the rich cinematic engagement with Dostoevsky that had started in the pre-revolutionary period. Given Dostoevsky's strong interest in spirituality and in the negative aspects of modern life, it is not surprising that foreign adaptations of his works were not always accessible to Russian audiences.

While Lary describes Soviet adaptations of Dostoevsky's works as oversimplified and ideologically-driven, he singles out Grigorii Kozintsev as a highly talented director who could 'finally rise to the demonic and tragic vision of Dostoevsky and make of it a space in which his imagination could move'.[53] Lary also mentions Viktor Shklovsky's brave 1930 attempt to produce a film adaptation of Dostoevsky's autobiographical work *The House of the Dead* (*Zapiski iz mertvogo doma*) amidst growing attacks on Dostoevsky in the Soviet Union. The film *Dead House* (*Mertvyi dom*) was directed by Vasilii Fedorov. Upon its release in April 1932, the film was severely criticised for failing to show antipathy toward Dostoevsky and for promoting his sentimentality as a positive character trait. Yet, as Lary points out, Shklovsky's idea to showcase the ability of Soviet filmmakers to produce a sound film in the style of the montage-oriented silent films was highly suitable for his Dostoevsky project. Unfortunately, Shklovsky's interpretation of Dostoevsky was overshadowed by ideologically driven adaptations of Russian classics. 'What makes Shklovsky's aesthetic approach suitable for Dostoevsky', writes Lary, 'is his concern with something akin to "idea-feelings"'.[54]

In contrast to Shklovsky, in 1934 Grigorii Roshal and Vera Stroeva produced the successful film *A Petersburg Night* based on Dostoevsky's story 'White Nights' and the unfinished novel *Netochka Nezvanova*. The film was praised as an expression of the Socialist Realist aesthetic. It was well received at the Second International Film Exhibition in Venice. Lary thinks that this film is worth remembering today because 'it shows the freedom of Roshal and Stroeva to find and make the norms of Socialist Realism at a time when these norms

---

[52] Nikita M. Lary, *Dostoevsky and Soviet Film: Visions of Demonic Realism* (Ithaca and London: Cornell University Press, 1986), p. 18.
[53] Ibid., p. 21.
[54] Ibid., p. 28.

were not fully laid down'. Lary also states that the film revises Dostoevsky in such a way as to present him as a precursor of Socialist Realism who was 'the visionary creator of the *Demons*'.⁵⁵ Lary's book convincingly argues that the use of Dostoevsky's works for film adaptations enabled Soviet filmmakers to compensate for Socialist Realism's inability to engage with the spiritual and artistic needs of Soviet audiences. It can be added to this observation that the film *A Petersburg Night* was used by the state as a part of cultural diplomacy and as a showcase for Soviet aesthetic experiments.

The chapters included in this volume aim to explore the dialogic imagination incorporated into film adaptations of the Russian classics with a view to understanding better the creation of polyphonic spaces through film, by assessing the impact of the heteroglossia of Russian novels on the domestic and international movie scene. Some chapters will also pay special attention to the ongoing creation of a branding strategy that adds value to the Russian contemporary cultural landscape and its engagement with the Russian literary heritage inside and outside Russia.

Cultural Diplomacy and National Branding

In 1785, one of the founding fathers of the United States, Thomas Jefferson, as ambassador to Paris, wrote to James Madison: 'you see I am an enthusiast on the subject of the arts [. . .] as its object is to improve the taste of my countrymen, to increase their reputation, to reconcile to them the respect of the world & procure them its praise.'⁵⁶ Over two hundred years later, culture's role in international relations has become still more important. With the advent of Joseph Nye's concept of 'soft power',⁵⁷ culture, and especially screen culture (dominant among the younger generation), has become a valuable resource for improving mutual understanding between countries and peoples, and for shaping the international image of the state, which nowadays is largely associated with the idea of 'branding'.

In similar fashion to Joseph Nye's concept of 'soft power', a country's brand is determined by diverse components such as culture, the education system, foreign policy, outstanding personalities, travel experience, exported goods and achievements that work as so-called 'communicators' and define the way in which a country is perceived by its own residents, citizens of other states, local and foreign firms, investors, governments, media and others. From the point of

---

⁵⁵ Ibid., pp. 47–8.
⁵⁶ Thomas Jefferson, Letter to James Madison. 20 September 1785, *Jefferson-Monticello* <http://tjrs.monticello.org/letter/1282> [accessed 14 August 2021].
⁵⁷ Joseph S. Nye Jr, *Soft Power: The Means to Success in World Politics* (New York: Public Affairs, 2004), p. ix.

view of political science, one of the main questions here is how successfully the country's branding strategy works in terms of configuring a positive perception of its national identity inside the country (associated with self-identity) and abroad, for in the era of mass communication the former and the latter can hardly be considered separately. In this sense, the notion of branding provides a broader conceptual framework than that of cultural diplomacy (essentially restricted to the idea of the exported image), and therefore offers a better fit for or reflection of the realities of the globalised modern world.

The image of Russia as a bearer of high culture is long-standing. Suffice it to refer to the Russomania of the early twentieth century and the unparalleled popularity of the Diaghilev seasons in Western countries. In the Soviet era, the notion of cultural politics and national branding was firmly associated with Communist Party policy and used as a major vehicle of propaganda and ideological control. The cultural proclivities of the Soviet audience were almost entirely shaped and defined by the Party's directives, but the situation turned out to be considerably more complex with regard to Soviet cultural diplomacy and the issues of branding. In this area, the Soviet authorities had to contend with a number of controversial problems. On the one hand, the ideologically loaded Soviet art had to become a new face and a new image of the country; on the other, it was necessary to take into account the demands and preferences of the receiving side.

Despite all the efforts of Soviet cultural institutions, contemporary Soviet art arguably made a negligible contribution to national branding, presenting poor competition for the so-called Russian classics, which throughout the Soviet decades constituted a major selling point in the West.[58] The problem concerned both the repertoire of the companies touring abroad and the export and distribution of Soviet cultural production. Both were mediated by private agencies, such as Columbia and Celebrity in the US, The Rank Organisation in the UK, or the Japanese New Artists Association, which were driven by the

---

[58] The Soviet cultural authorities were well aware of the issue, highlighted, for instance, in the Soviet Minister of Culture Ekaterina Furtseva's 1969 report on the 'unsatisfactory' prevalence of the classical repertoire in all areas of Soviet cultural export: 'Yet again they will tour with all things classic. [. . .] Considering the Soviet repertoire, there is at most Prokofiev, Shostakovich, Khachaturian, rarely Weinberg, and nothing else. [. . .] I have already drawn attention to this oversight in my conversation with Tovstonogov [the artistic director of the Leningrad Big Drama Theatre]. "You can't tour with Gorky's *Philistines* all the time," I claimed, "In Gorky's plays, they do nothing but dreaming; while we need to present the works that show our current achievements"' (TsAOPIM, Fond 957, Op. 1, D. 226, L. 193, quoted in Natal'ia Beloshapka, *Gosudarstvo i kul'tura v SSSR: ot Khrushcheva do Gorbacheva* [Izhevsk: Udmurdskii Universitet, 2021], p. 258).

pressures of marketing and preoccupied with their returns. Thus, in February 1973, for instance, Columbia Artists Management rejected the Soviet proposal to include contemporary Soviet ballets in the US tour of the Leningrad Kirov Ballet, urging the authorities to replace them with the classic productions of *Swan Lake*, *The Sleeping Beauty,* and *Giselle*. The latter were characteristically considered to be an established hallmark of the country and were likely to attract Western theatregoers.[59]

A similar trend was prevalent in the export of Soviet cinematic production. Western companies notoriously preferred to buy films based on adaptations of the Russian classics, rather than those concerning the realities of Soviet life. This was explained by the lack of demand for and interest in these subjects, typically dubbed anodyne and insipid by the Western public.[60] To deal with the issue, Sovexportfilm even developed a certain strategy of selling rental and distribution rights in the form of a package, in which the sought-after adaptations of the Russian classics were paired with the 'representative' contemporary dramas specially selected for these purposes by the Film Agency of the USSR. This, for instance, was how in 1968 the Soviet screen-versions of *Anna Karenina* and *The Brothers Karamazov* were sold to and distributed in the UK.[61]

According to research conducted by the Anholt-GfK Nation Brands Index (2017), the principal pillar of the national brand of Russia is its classical culture (mainly literature, music, and ballet): in this category, Russia occupies ninth place in the world rankings (with France, USA, Italy, Germany, and the UK being in the lead[62]). Given that Russia came in twenty-third in the overall ranking of the strongest national brands, one can easily project how much the country's position had been 'pushed forward' by its cultural indicators. And indeed, while the succession of political regimes tends to sink into oblivion with the flow of time, the emotional memory transmitted through generations seems to be remarkably long-lived; and for the Western audience, the image of Russia is still largely associated with Pasternak's *Doctor Zhivago* (the film version), Dostoevsky's *Crime and Punishment* and Tolstoy's *War and Peace*.

In this light, special attention should be given to small screen literary adaptations. TV adaptations of novels have grown more popular in recent years, supported by such major broadcast companies as the BBC and by the

---

[59] 'Dokumenty o sotrudnichestve s amerikanskoi firmoi "Kolumbiia"', 1973–8, RGALI, Fond 2329, Op. 35, Ed. khr. 61, L. 2.

[60] Beloshapka, p. 253.

[61] 'Spravka po fil'mam i kinorynku strany', 1970, RGALI, Fond 2918, Op. 4, Ed. khr. 318, L. 2.

[62] GfK, Press release, November 2017 <https://www.gfk.com/fileadmin/user_upload/2017-11-16_Anholt-GfK_NBI_2017_press_release_global_vfinal.pdf> [accessed 14 August 2021].

streaming services of Netflix and Hulu. The latter have accounted for the rise in the number of TV viewers,[63] and have also been the force behind some of the most successful book-to-screen adaptations, including, for instance, the 2016 BBC series of Tolstoy's *War and Peace* or the 2002 version of *Doctor Zhivago*. In this context, one can also mention the Russian 2014 mini-series of Dostoevsky's *Demons* and the 2017 *Anna Karenina*, available for the English-speaking audience on Amazon-Prime.

Books adapted to the small screen have been an undoubted success, which may be seen as challenging for the traditional art of cinematic translation, as well as ominous for the prospects of the written word, especially when projected upon the general tendency of a decline in reading. With regard to the former, there are indeed a number of undeniable parallels between TV serials and some structural and generic features of classical novels. To name but a few, one can say that both are essentially episodic (consisting of chapters), a TV series allows a much fuller coverage of the story given the characteristically lengthy format of classical works, and the format can also include a wider spectrum of secondary lines and figures that would otherwise have to be 'filtered out' by cuts. In this sense, TV adaptations may present certain advantages over the corresponding film versions; and according to many,[64] it seems likely that book-to-TV adaptations will only continue to increase in the near future.

Considering the world of letters, on the one hand, experts tend to see the relationship between literary works and their screen-versions as complementary rather than mutually exclusive. According to *Publisher's Weekly*,[65] the annual bestseller book lists tend to be dominated by novels that had their screen versions released earlier in the same year (this was certainly the case for Tolstoy's *War and Peace* after the BBC released its TV series in 2016). It, therefore, seems that TV may draw people back to reading: the target audience consisting of those whose interest in the text was kindled by the screen, as well as a number of so to speak connoisseurs, who in the words of Thomas Leitch, an expert in film studies, enjoy feeling at once inside the story, at the mercy of the whims of a storyteller who could take the story in an unexpected direction at any time,

---

[63] Netflix alone accounted for 10% of all time spent in front of the TV in the United States, as reported by CNBC in 2019 (Lauren Feiner, 'Netflix says it has 10% of all TV time in the US and discloses some colossal numbers for its shows', *CNBC*, 17 January 2019 <https://www.cnbc.com/2019/01/17/netflix-how-many-people-watch-bird-box.html> [accessed 14 August 2020]).

[64] 'The best book-to-TV adaptations', *Pan Macmillan*, 16 December 2021 <https://www.panmacmillan.com/blogs/fiction/book-tv-film-new-series-miniaturist> [accessed 14 August 2021].

[65] Clare Swanson, 'Bestselling Books of 2014', *Publisher's Weekly*, 2 January 2015 <https://www.publishersweekly.com/pw/by-topic/industry-news/bookselling/article/65171-the-fault-in-our-stars-tops-print-and-digital.html> [accessed 14 August 2021].

and outside the story, coolly comparing it to its source as better, worse, or different or, more precisely, the same but different.[66]

At the same time, there is a lot of controversy surrounding the overwhelming dominance of the visual in today's culture. The debate is at least two hundred years old: surprising as it may seem, Goethe's letter to Schiller (December 1797) offers an uncanny anticipation of the modern-day *status quo*:

> You will have heard a hundred times, that people, after reading a good novel, have wished to see the subject on the stage, and how many bad plays have thence arisen! Just so they wish to see every interesting situation in a novel at once engraved, in order that, to their imagination, no kind of activity be left [. . .] Now, these thoroughly childish, barbaric, tasteless tendencies the artist should oppose with all his might [. . .] But who can separate his ship from the waves on which it swims? Against wind and current one makes little head-way.[67]

Goethe's pessimistic guess regarding the decline of literary communication, developed in the twentieth century by Marshall McLuhan,[68] acquires a degree of sober foresight and frightening reality in today's world. The extinction of one of the existing modes of communication undoubtedly cannot be but detrimental to cultural capital (understood in Bourdieu's sense of the term) circulated and transmitted through generations. The process, regrettably, cannot be reversed: as Goethe put it 'against wind and current one makes little head-way'; though gaining some further insights into and understanding of the interaction between the visual and the verbal may help to develop a constructive approach to the problem.

The role of screen adaptations of Russian classics as a bearer of cultural capital within modern-day national branding is difficult to overestimate. This provides the rationale and the context for the discussion pursued in this volume, focusing on the analysis of the intercultural dialogue (understood in a broad sense of being carried out across temporal, national or aesthetic spaces) conducted through a series of foreign and Russian screen adaptations of canonical

---

[66] Quoted in Valerie Jones, 'TV Series Just May Be the New Books', *Deseret News*, 19 October 2019 <https://www.deseret.com/entertainment/2019/10/21/20897751/netflix-hulu-hbo-tv-goldfinch-lemony-snicket-handmaids-tale-game-of-thrones> [accessed 14 August 2021].

[67] Johann Wolfgang von Goethe, Letter to Schiller, December 1797, *Full correspondence between Schiller and Goethe, between 1794 and 1805* (New York, London: Wiley, and Putnam, 1845), p. 383.

[68] This idea was first outlined in McLuhan's pioneering work of 1951 '*The Mechanical Bride: Folklore of Industrial Man*' and developed further in his subsequent publications *The Gutenberg Galaxy: The Making of Typographic Man* (1962) and *Understanding Media: The Extensions of Man* (1964).

texts. It will be argued that this long-term dialogue has facilitated the configuration of the so-called literary-cinematic semantic space – a new synthetic artistic platform, characterised by the synergetic relations of its constituents and certain specific structural features, as well as by newly developed forms of artistic discourse. The objective is therefore twofold and concerns both the socio-cultural aspect of the phenomenon and its aesthetic paradigm drawn from the domain of the hermeneutic analysis of screen and literary texts.

This book builds on a rich field of previous research, exploring a series of compelling case studies (Stephen Hutchings and Anat Vernitski, *Russian and Soviet Film Adaptations of Literature, 1900–2001*, Routledge, 2004[69]), as well as the distinctive body of relatively recent scholarship which has expanded the study of screen adaptations of specific canonical authors (Lorna Fitzsimmons, Michael A. Denner, *Tolstoy on Screen*, Northwestern University Press, 2014; Philip French, 'Chekhov on Screen' in *The Cambridge Companion to Chekhov*, Cambridge University Press, 2000; Nikita M. Lary, *Dostoevsky and Soviet Film: Visions of Demonic Realism*. Cornell University Press, 1986; Catharine Nepomnyashchy, 'Re-Visioning the Past: Russian Literary Classics in Film', *World Literature Today*, 85, 2011).

It also draws on three recently published studies consolidating the scholarship of Russian and Western researchers, that laid the foundation for the debate conducted in this volume. Proceeding in chronological order, one should mention an insightful monograph by Valerii Mil'don, *Another Laocoon, or on the Boundaries of Cinema and Literature* (Rosspen 2007), which revives the discussion of the translatability of a literary work into the language of cinema and explores the aesthetic boundaries of the former and the latter. Secondly, an interdisciplinary volume edited by Alexander Burry and Frederick White, *Border Crossing: Russian Literature into Film* (Edinburgh University Press, 2016), which underscores the transcultural nature of any modern-day screen adaptation of a classical text, the meaning of which 'must be redefined to correspond with the new spatial and temporal territories'.[70] Finally Liudmila Fedorova's comprehensive monograph *Adaptation as a Symptom. Russian Classics on the Post-Soviet Screen* (NLO, 2021), which reflects on the cinematogenic nature (attracting multiple screen adaptations) of certain classical texts.

From the World of Letters to a Literary-Cinematic Space

Some attempt should be made to specify our approach to defining and exploring the idea of the literary-cinematic space and interpreting its semantic function. The proliferation of screen culture, as well as the general tendency towards

---

[69] See also a series of articles 'Russian Literature on the Silver Screen', *Russian Studies in Literature*, 40 (2004).
[70] Burry, 'Introduction: Filming Russian Classics', p. 7.

visualisation and symbolisation of information, has resulted in some deep changes concerning the hierarchical relations between a cinematic adaptation and its literary source. To a certain extent, one can talk about re-formatting the mindset of the mass viewer, as for the majority their knowledge of the classics is restricted to a TV serial or a film version, which, in the case of a successful adaptation, stimulates the viewer's inquiry into the original work. Following the trend, one can assume that in the near future the function of the literary-cinematic space will be considerably expanded, and apart from being a platform for the dialogue between the literary and cinematic forms of expression, it will turn into the main repository (in its active form) of the literary heritage and the main platform for its circulation and transmission.

On the one hand, this lends special significance to the so to speak cinematisation of the classics. On the other – the proliferation and circulation of unsuccessful screen copies of literary works shape a deformed image of the latter in the mindset of the viewer. This image is then multiplied and transmitted, in time resulting in the deformation of cultural capital in the process of its intergenerational reproduction. Such a phenomenon brings to the fore, or more precisely reactivates, the debate concerning the notion of a 'successful adaptation'. It is difficult to deny that the art of text-to-screen transposition is undoubtedly the art of 'losses', which occur not only because of the necessity to compress the content of a capacious novel into a less than three-hour-long film (to a certain extent this issue can be overcome in lengthy TV serial adaptations) but because the language and the aesthetic boundaries of cinema are different from those of a literary work. Considering that, modern critics tend to foreground this latter aspect of the text-to-screen transposition and elaborate the principles of a successful adaptation, remaining within the frame of a purely aesthetic perspective. According to Valerii Mil'don, one of the staunch supporters of this viewpoint, the dialogue between literature and cinema should be considered primarily as a 'specific case of the general aesthetic problem of the translatability of one artistic language into another'.[71]

Such an approach is not unjustified, for today one has to consider not only the losses that occur in the act of cinematic translation, but also such sociocultural and economic factors as the subordination of aesthetics to the pressure

---

[71] Valerii Mil'don, *Drugoi Laokoon, ili o granitsakh kino i literatury: estetika ekranizatsii* (Moscow: Rosspen, 2007), p. 12; Valerii Mil'don, 'Chto zhe takoe ekranizatsiia?', *Mir russkogo slova*, 3 (2011), 9–14 (p. 11).

Such an approach is not new: triggered by the advance of the 'talkies', the issue of translatability or the interaction between the literary and the cinematic aesthetic systems was raised by Rudolf Arnheim in his 1938 essay 'A New Laocoon: Artistic Composites and the Talking Film'. To highlight the continuity of the debate, the titles of Mil'don's and Arnheim's works refer to Gotthold E. Lessing's essay of 1766, 'Laocoon: An Essay upon the Limits of Painting and Poetry'.

of commercial goals, or the use of game technologies (typical in postmodernist culture) in the film-world, rendering the language of cinema even less compatible with that of the original work. Without denigrating the prominence of the question of aesthetic boundaries in the art of screen adaptation, we nonetheless set to challenge attempts to reduce this question to a purely aesthetic perspective. Any act of creative adaptation is a social act, which is not neutral in relation to aesthetics. We intend to demonstrate that social and aesthetic aspects are inseparable for the critical analysis of the underlying principles of text-to-screen transposition; and that it is this social or pragmatic (contextual) element that plays a crucial role in the dialogical interaction of literature and cinema within the literary-cinematic space of screen adaptations.

Two further points should be made in support of this claim. Firstly, with the advance of cinema, the readership – or the viewership – of the nineteenth-century novel was considerably expanded. This meant that a series of purely aesthetic issues inherent to the art of text-to-screen transposition acquired yet another layer of complexity associated with the social aspects of viewers' reception: there appeared an issue of transmitting the semantic spectrum of the novel to a mass audience far remote from the aesthetic and contextual frame of the original work.

Secondly, any given stage of cultural development thus shapes its specific mode of rendering and interacting with the real. This mode is mediated by the artistic output of the given time, setting the canons and principles of the author's creative viewpoint and expression. This canonical (for the given time) way of seeing works like a pair of 'glasses', imposing a filter or a certain socially constructed perspective on all aspects of artistic imagination. Characteristically, these 'glasses' remain unnoticed within the framework of their contemporary context. It is only due to the appearance of new ways of seeing (in the course of temporal or cultural displacement) that this 'optical filter' can be critically acknowledged and 'removed', thereby not only revealing previously hidden layers of meaning but also distinguishing them from the particularities of the author's personal views.

Such an interpretation, which is produced through the prism of the new optics, and which stands outside the text's hermeneutic original context is, according to the contemporary philosopher Slavoj Žižek, conceived as an act of 'violent disfiguring'[72] of the original source. Paradoxically, he claims, this disfiguration, 'irrespective of philological rules, sometimes anachronistic, often "factually incorrect", displaying the work from its proper hermeneutic context', brings about a 'shattering new insight' that comes much closer 'to the "truth" of the interpreted text than its historicist contextualisation'.[73] This point will be

---

[72] Slavoj Žižek, *The Plague of Fantasies* (London and New York: Verso Books, 1997), p. 95.
[73] Ibid., pp. 95–6.

discussed and elaborated on in this volume. In a series of case studies of Russian and Western adaptations of the canonical works of Russian classics, we examine the role and function of contextual 'disfiguration' (to use Žižek's wording) as a medium for and the active agent of the productive dialogue between the literary and cinematic forms of expression, as well as for the development of their synergetic relation within the frame of the literary cinematic cultural space.

The volume features a selection of screen adaptations of works by mid- and late nineteenth-century authors, who constitute the hallmark of the Russian cultural brand, finding favour with audiences in Russia and in the West and coming top of a recent list with the highest number of screen adaptations: Chekhov – 427 adaptations (including 300 by foreign directors); Dostoevsky – 201 adaptations (160 of them foreign); Tolstoy – 180 adaptations (120 of them foreign); and Turgenev – 90 adaptations (59 of them foreign).[74]

In Dialogue with the Classics

The volume consists of four parts. The first part, 'Goncharov and Turgenev: Adaptation as Nostalgia' discusses Nikita Mikhalkov's 1980 film *A Few Days from the Life of I. I. Oblomov* (a landmark screen work that first brought Goncharov's writings to the attention of Western viewers[75]) and Avdotya Smirnova's 2008 TV adaptation of Turgenev's novel *Fathers and Sons*. Both works are exemplary in showing how the ideological spirit of the day serves as a lens for a specific reading of the novel, highlighting some new layers of meaning that do not readily come across in the traditional hermeneutic interpretation of the works. While Mikhalkov's film is often seen as a critical comment on the stagnation of the Brezhnev period, Henrietta Mondry identifies it 'as a nationalistic narrative', especially because of its allegorical dichotomy that shows the eternal conflict between Russia and the West. Alexandra Smith's chapter discusses a more recent use of nostalgic overtones in Avdotya Smirnova's version of Turgenev's *Fathers and Sons*. The film engages with the post-Soviet nostalgic discourse and reimagines the pre-revolutionary past as a lost idyllic space. According to Smith, 'Smirnova's potential audience would be used to seeing cinematic representations of nostalgia in the 1990s and 2000s and would be expecting to see a path to national unity through the revival of Russian traditional values'.

---

[74] The list is provided by the popular site *Cinema-search* (*Kinopoisk*), 2016), quoted in *Kino i literatura*, *God Literatury*, 20 January 2016 < https://godliteratury.ru/articles/2016/01/19/kino-i-literatura> [accessed 29 December 2021].

[75] Mikhalkov's film was the second post-War Soviet screen adaptation (after Sergei Bondarchuk's *War and Peace*) to be shown and acclaimed in the West ('"Oblomov" – Russia's story of a fabulous idler', *The Christian Science Monitor*, 9 April 1981 <https://www.csmonitor.com/1981/0409/040902.html> [accessed 15 March 2021]).

The second part 'Reimagining Dostoevsky' explores the cases of creative 'disfiguration' produced by refracting his works through the lens of different aesthetic perspectives: Olga Hasty's analysis of a typically modernist reading of 'A Meek Creature' by Robert Bresson (*Une femme douce*, 1969) is juxtaposed to Tine Roesen's discussion of Richard Ayoade's postmodernist interpretation of *The Double* (2013). Hasty focuses on the deep psychological insights of Bresson's work as an example of reflective art, in which the pull towards emotional involvement is mediated and counterbalanced by the intellectual engagement of the viewer. Roesen, on the other hand, draws attention to the comic aspects of Ayoade's interpretation. The film transposes the original's gloomy landscapes of St Petersburg of the 1840s into the urban space of contemporary Britain, so that the retro-futuristic setting – within the logic of postmodernist aesthetics – enables the director to explore 'the cinematic slapstick potential of Dostoevsky's work.'

The third part 'Collaborating with Chekhov' features the author whose works have attracted the longest trail of screen adaptations. The question of the cinematogenic characteristics of a literary work continues to engage film scholars.[76] As a contribution to the debate, we argue that the screen popularity of Chekhov's works can be attributed to the 'writerly' (in Roland Barthes' sense of the term) qualities of his texts, which are poly-interpretative and do not impose their certain particular discourse on the recipient.[77] This section features examples of the poststructuralist approach to Chekhov, showing (in line with Barthes' views) how the reading of a text becomes as much an act of its creation as it is an attempt to understand what has already been created. Radislav Lapushin discusses three productions of Russian and American adaptations of Chekhov stories, all from the 2000s, drawing attention to the

---

[76] Alexander Burry offers a notion of a 'transpositional opening', associated with the amount of intertextual connection in the text, which, arguably, is 'especially inviting of further transpositions' (Alexander Burry, *Multi-Mediated Dostoevsky* [Evanston: Northwestern University Press, 2011], pp. 10, 34). Liudmila Fedorova, on the other hand, does not find this argument sufficiently convincing, claiming that any classical novel is 'transpositionally open', but certain texts attract more attention from filmmakers than others (Liudmila Fedorova, *Adaptatsiia kak symptom: Russkaia klassika na postsovetskom ekrane* [Moscow: NLO, 2021], p. 74).

[77] In his 1973 essay *S/Z*, Barthes distinguishes between a readerly text ('texte lisible'), which does not challenge the reader's position as a subject, and a writerly text ('text scriptible'), which allows the reader to break out of his/her subject position. While engaging with a 'writerly' text, the reader has to make an active effort and to re-enact the actions of the writer himself; this is an open text because it can always be written anew (Roland Barthes, *S/Z*, trans. by Richard Miller [New York: Hill and Wang, 1974], pp. 3–4).

structure of these works where the filmmaker becomes both interpreter and primarily co-author of the original source. The issue of co-authorship is central in the discussion of Louis Malle's film *Vanya on 42nd Street* (1994) conducted by Angus Wrenn. 'Less is more' is a quintessential leitmotif of Wrenn's examination, offering a nuanced analysis of Malle's minimalist aesthetics and his unique ability to project Chekhovian atmosphere and style through the most radical decontextualisation of the original play. Olga Partan also sees the effectiveness of Malle's dramatic approach in his rejection of everything related to the mimetic. This comes across clearly when juxtaposed with what Partan asserts is Michael Mayer's largely illustrative (based on the power of the visual) adaptation of *The Seagull* (2018).

The fourth part 'Engaging with Tolstoy' illustrates three ways of effective contextual 'disfiguration' most widely used nowadays in the process of text-to-screen transposition. The first is based on the idea of placing the adapted work within the content discourse shaped within the author's compositional oeuvre (including his reflections extracted from texts, diaries, letters, notebooks, etc.). Otto Boele's analysis of *A Simple Death* (1985), directed by Aleksandr Kaidanovsky as an adaptation of Tolstoy's story *The Death of Ivan Il'ich*, foregrounds the theme of death anxiety explored as a manifestation of a new existentialist trend in late Soviet cinema (represented by the works of Tarkovsky and Sokurov). Rather than focusing on one specific text under discussion, the film draws from the whole spectrum of Tolstoy's works, allowing the director to introduce and reinterpret highly sensitive, taboo topics in Soviet culture such as fear of death (thanatophobia).

The second approach draws upon the idea of the semantic and figurative modernisation of the context, which apart from exposing new layers of meaning, facilitates (by way of visualisation) the mass viewer's understanding of the original's inner logic. This approach is illustrated in Greg Dolgopolov's chapter, which examines a network of cinematic narratives engendered by Tolstoy's novella *The Forged Coupon*. Set in the modern-day, these narratives effectively convey all the complexity of Tolstoy's spiritual and moral concerns, exploring his key themes of fate, choice, contingency, redemption and forgiveness.

The third approach consists in contextualising the modern image (expected by the viewer) of a specific historical era. It is representative of present-day show-business performance (an all-star-cast, spectacular visual effects, etc.) and is characteristic of TV serials based on classical works. It is also targeted at the receptive potential of the viewer and enhances their susceptibility to the semantic sphere of the original text. Olga Sobolev's chapter discusses the recent BBC adaptation of Tolstoy's *War and Peace* (2016) in the framework of cultural branding. It examines how various adaptive strategies bring the novel closer to the British viewer while at the same time engaging critically with

Tolstoy's work. The debate also concerns the potential of an aesthetic (affective) rather than an efferent mode of text-to-screen transposition, which in the case of this adaptation made *War and Peace* one of the top fifty best-selling novels in the UK.

Some Concluding Remarks on the Implications of This Discussion

Communication between cultures can be made by way of direct and indirect dialogue conducted through several channels such as oral folk-culture, written records of the cultural legacy and electronic means of mass communication. In this context, literary classics, which cannot be seen other than as a manifestation of both the normative value-base of the country's cultural identity and the mindset of the bearers of this culture, are often regarded as an important contributor to the projection of the national image, circulated in the area of cultural diplomacy or for the purposes of international branding. The rapidly proliferating screen culture undoubtedly plays a significant role in the processes of such circulation and projection. It offers an important multi-dimensional platform for the popularisation of literary texts, as well as for actualising and contextualising various facets of their meanings. As argued in this volume, here we are not talking about the effect of cross-media convergence when a media product is promoted across other media platforms, but about a synergetic literary-cinematic space, defined as the interaction between two components with a combined effect greater than the sum of their separate impacts. This space, which implies some active and mutually enriching interaction between literary and cinematic forms of expression, is characterised by its broad range of repertoire, and by its capacity for consolidating and promulgating a considerable volume of information. The new type of artistic discourse which arises draws upon such structural features as collation of textual and multi-media material, symbolisation and visualisation of information, and extensive abbreviation of the source text without narrowing down the range of its metatextual meanings.

This new form of discourse also gives an extra dimension to the debate concerning the defining principles of cinematic adaptations, bringing to the forefront the notion of an interdisciplinary and intercultural co-authorship constructed on the basis of the given literary platform. As a creative interpreter, the director becomes a mediator between his audiences and the author, offering new ways of reading the work rooted in his own cultural canon, contemporary epistemological imperatives, and the particularities of the viewers' reception. This contextual (or pragmatic) element becomes of particular (but not quite prime) importance, as it defines the scale of the social impact of the thus co-authored screen-text. Operating as a lens for actualising the semantic spectrum of the work, resonating with and shedding new light on the fundamental social and existential concerns of the viewers, it underpins the ideas of continuity, change, and progression, which, as far as an artwork is concerned, cannot be regarded as other than the quintessence of 'living'.

Bibliography

Bakhtin, Mikhail, 'Epic and Novel', in *The Dialogic Imagination. Four Essays by M.M. Bakhtin*, ed. Michael Holquist (Austin: University of Texas Press, 1981), pp. 3–40.

Barthes, Roland, *S/Z*, trans. by Richard Miller (New York: Hill and Wang, 1974).

Beloshapka, Natal′ia, *Gosudarstvo i kul'tura v SSSR: ot Khrushcheva do Gorbacheva* (Izhevsk: Udmurdskii Universitet, 2021).

Bluestone, George, *Novels into Film: The Metamorphosis of Fiction into Cinema* (London: Cambridge University Press, 1957).

Boele, Otto, 'After Death, the Movie (1915) – Ivan Turgenev, Evgenii Bauer and the Aesthetics of Morbidity', in *Turgenev: Art, Ideology and Legacy*, eds Robert Reid and Joe Andrew (Amsterdam and New York: Rodopi, 2010), pp. 253–68.

Burry, Alexander, 'Introduction: Filming Russian Classics – Challenges and Opportunities', in *Border Crossing: Russian Literature into Film*, eds Alexander Burry and Frederick H. White (Edinburgh: Edinburgh University Press, 2016), pp. 1–16.

——, *Multi-Mediated Dostoevsky* (Evanston: Northwestern University Press, 2011).

Cardwell, Sarah, *Adaptation Revisited: Television and the Classic Novel* (Manchester: Manchester University Press, 2002).

Cartmell, Deborah, '100+Years of Adaptations, or, Adaptation as the Art Form of Democracy', in *A Companion to Literature, Film, and Adaptation*, ed. Deborah Cartmell (Oxford: Wiley-Blackwell, 2012), pp. 1–15.

——, and Imelda Whelehan, *Adaptations: From Text to Screen, Screen to Text* (Oxford: Oxford University Press, 1999).

Denner, Michael A., 'Introduction', in *Tolstoy on Screen*, eds Lorna Fitzsimmons and Michael A. Denner (Evanston: Northwestern University Press, 2015), pp. 3–20; kindle edition: loc.197.

'Dokumenty o sotrudnichestve s amerikanskoi firmoi "Kolumbiia"', 1973–8, RGALI, Fond 2329, Op. 35, Ed. khr. 61, L. 2.

Fedorova, Liudmila, *Adaptatsiia kak symptom: Russkaia klassika na postsovetskom ekrane* (Moscow: NLO, 2021).

Feiner, Lauren, 'Netflix says it has 10% of all TV time in the US and discloses some colossal numbers for its shows', *CNBC*, 17 January 2019 <https://www.cnbc.com/2019/01/17/netflix-how-many-people-watch-bird-box.html> [accessed 14 August 2020].

Geal, Robert, *Anamorphic Authorship in Canonical Film: A Case Study of Shakespearean Film* (Cham: Palgrave Macmillan, 2019).

GfK, Press release, November 2017 <https://www.gfk.com/fileadmin/user_upload/2017-11-16_Anholt-GfK_NBI_2017_press_release_global_vfinal.pdf> [accessed 14 August 2021].

Gillespie, David, 'The Art of Literary Adaptation and English-Language Film Interpretations of Russian Literature ("Anna Karenina")', *Procedia – Social and Behavioral Sciences*, 154 (2014), pp. 30–5.

Ginzburg, Lidia, *On Psychological Prose*, trans. Judson Rosengrant (Princeton: Princeton University Press, 1991).

Ginzburg, Lidiia, *O literaturnom geroe* (Leningrad: Sovetskii pisatel', 1979).

Goethe (von), Johann Wolfgang, Letter to Schiller, December 1797, *Full correspondence between Schiller and Goethe, between 1794 and 1805* (New York and London: Wiley, and Putnam, 1845).

Graffy, Julian, 'Difficult people: Kira Muratova's Cinematic Encounter with Chekhov', *Essays in Poetics*, 31 (2006), pp. 180–212.

Hutchings, Stephen and Anat Vernitski, 'Introduction: the *ekranizatsiia* in Russian culture', in *Russian and Soviet Film Adaptations of Literature, 1900–2001: Screening the Word*, eds Stephen Hutchings and Anat Vernitski (London and New York: Routledge Curzon, 2005), pp. 1–24.

Jefferson, Thomas, Letter to James Madison, 20 September 1785, *Jefferson-Monticello* <http://tjrs.monticello.org/letter/1282> [accessed 14 August 2021].

Jones, Valerie, 'TV Series Just May Be the New Books', *Deseret News*, 19 October 2019 <https://www.deseret.com/entertainment/2019/10/21/20897751/netflix-hulu-hbo-tv-goldfinch-lemony-snicket-handmaids-tale-game-of-thrones> [accessed 14 August 2021].

Kino i literatura, God Literatury, 20 January 2016 <https://godliteratury.ru/articles/2016/01/19/kino-i-literatura> [accessed 29 December 2021].

Klein, Michael and Gillian Parker, 'Introduction: Film and Literature', in *The English Novel and the Movies*, eds Michael Klein and Gillian Parker (New York: Frederick Ungar Publishing Company, 1981), pp. 1–13.

Kristeva, Julia, *Desire in Language: A Semiotic Approach to Literature and Art* (New York: Columbia University Press, 1980).

Lyotard, Jean-François, *The Postmodern Condition: A Report on Knowledge* (Manchester: Manchester University Press, 1984).

Lary, Nikita M., *Dostoevsky and Soviet Film: Visions of Demonic Realism* (Ithaca and London: Cornell University Press, 1986).

Leitch, Thomas, *Film Adaptation and Its Discontents: From Gone with the Wind to the Passion of the Christ* (Baltimore, MD: Johns Hopkins University Press, 2007).

Mil'don, Valerii, 'Chto zhe takoe ekranizatsiia?', *Mir russkogo slova*, 3 (2011), pp. 9–14.

——, *Drugoi Laokoon, ili o granitsakh kino i literatury: estetika ekranizatsii* (Moscow: Rosspen, 2007).

Nye, Joseph S. Jr, *Soft Power: The Means to Success in World Politics* (New York: Public Affairs, 2004).

'"Oblomov" – Russia's story of a fabulous idler', *The Cristian Science Monitor*, 9 April 1981 <https://www.csmonitor.com/1981/0409/040902.html> [accessed 15 March 2021].

Olson, Laura, 'Russianness, Femininity, and Romantic Aesthetics in *War and Peace*', *The Russian Review*, 56 (1997), pp. 515–31.

Roberts, Tom, '"Simply an anachronism": repetition and meaning in Kira Muratova's *Chekhovian Motifs*', *Studies in Russian & Soviet Cinema*, 7 (2013), pp. 39–59.

'Spravka po fil'mam i kinorynku strany', 1970, RGALI, Fond 2918, Op. 4, Ed. khr. 318, L. 2.

Stam, Robert, 'The Dialogics of Adaptation', in *Film Adaptation*, ed. James Naremore (New Brunswick, NJ: Rutgers University Press, 2000), pp. 54–76.

Swanson, Clare, 'Bestselling Books of 2014', *Publisher's Weekly*, 2 January 2015 <https://www.publishersweekly.com/pw/by-topic/industry-news/bookselling/article/65171-the-fault-in-our-stars-tops-print-and-digital.html> [accessed 14 August 2021].

'The best book-to-TV adaptations', *Pan Macmillan*, 16 December 2021 <https://www.panmacmillan.com/blogs/fiction/book-tv-film-new-series-miniaturist> [accessed 14 August 2021].

Woolf, Virginia, 'The Russian Point of View', in *The Essays of Virginia Woolf*, ed. Andrew McNeillie (London: The Hogarth Press, 1994), IV, pp. 181–9.

Wagner, Geoffrey Atheling, *The Novel and the Cinema* (Vancouver, BC: Fairleigh Dickinson University Press, 1975).

Wengrow, David, 'Introduction. Commodity Branding in Archaeological and Anthropological Perspectives', in *Cultures of Commodity Branding*, eds Andrew Bevan and David Wengrow (London: Routledge, 2010), pp. 13–33.

Youngblood, Denise J., *The Magic Mirror: Moviemaking in Russia, 1908-1918* (Madison and London: University of Denise J Wisconsin Press, 1999).

Žižek, Slavoj, *The Plague of Fantasies* (London and New York: Verso Books, 1997).

PART ONE

GONCHAROV AND TURGENEV: ADAPTATION AS NOSTALGIA

1. THE POLITICS OF NOSTALGIA: IVAN GONCHAROV'S *OBLOMOV* AND NIKITA MIKHALKOV'S FILM ADAPTATION

Henrietta Mondry

The title of the film adaptation – *A Few Days from the Life of I. I. Oblomov* (*Neskol'ko dnei iz zhizni I. I. Oblomova*, 1980) – suggests a selective approach to the text of one of the most famous Russian novels, Ivan Goncharov's *Oblomov*. Choices in selection are an integral part of the process of adaptation which, in this case, I argue, were motivated by dominant socio-political trends in the late 1970s. The film was directed by a celebrated Russian director of our times, Nikita Mikhalkov, and while it gained a number of international awards, it was received with a certain caution in the ideological atmosphere of its release in 1980. The history of its release first in Berlin and then in the Soviet Union reflects tensions around the subject matter of the novel and the film – a politicised trope of Oblomov and *oblomovshchina* in Russia and the Soviet Union. A film adaptation of this particular novel presents a case of interpretation of the text that exemplifies diverse evaluations of the text's messages. The history of the reception of the novel is an exemplary case of adaption, manipulation, and dialogue by the hesitant writer himself, critics belonging to various political affiliations and, as this chapter shows, the film director. These interpretations often form a dialogue with this novel's two main characters who, in turn, were originally conceived by Goncharov as embodiments of a dialogic relationship vis-à-vis each other.

The Oblomov–Stolz Dichotomy as a Socio-political Compass of the Age

Since the time of its publication in 1859, the novel has attracted controversial evaluations of its two main protagonists, the lazy and inert Oblomov and active half-Russian half-German Stolz.[1] The word *oblomovshchina* is Goncharov's own invention, and in the novel he makes Stolz coin the word to characterise the lifestyle led by Oblomov. The word became a Russian neologism and entered the vocabulary with astonishing speed. The second edition of Vladimir Dal''s *Dictionary of the Russian Language* (1881) already gives a definition of the word. In the dictionary underneath the entry 'oblamyvat'' – to break – Dal' gives the following definition of the word:

> *Oblomovshchina*, adopted from Goncharov's story: Russian apathy, laziness, inertness; indifference to the social question demanding group activities, vitality, decisiveness and resilience; a habit of expecting everything from somebody else, but not from oneself; refusing daily responsibilities, in line with the proverb: *To rely on others as on God, but to rely on oneself as on the Devil.*[2]

Of crucial importance for the ensuing interpretations of the novel as well as of the condition of *oblomovshchina* is the fact that the term was applied as a characteristic feature of the Russian national character: it is Russian apathy, laziness and inactivity that the term was supposed to define. As time progressed, in the 1880s the semantic field of the term *oblomovshchina* expanded and started to include an individualised *modus vivendi* made by choice. The neologism described the phenomenon identified and typified in realist literature and came to characterise human traits of character and patterns of behaviour in real life.

In spite of its literary origins, the term *oblomovshchina* entered Russian political discourse and was evoked both by literary critics and leading political personalities in debates around reforms and the role of progress in the improvement of Russian society. Disseminated by Nikolai Dobroliubov's article 'What is *oblomovshchina*?' (1859) – the work of a literary critic from the radical left – the term became a polarising notion between the camps of diverse political spectra. This divisive attitude to *oblomovshchina* has been a stable feature of Russian and Soviet social and political rhetoric. Great political leaders starting from Lenin used the term and the name of the book's eponymous character Oblomov to embody the obstacles facing society on its way to a better future. Every mention of Oblomov and *oblomovshchina* in Russian political discourse was a form of interpretation and adaptation of Goncharov's original creation.

---

[1] The novel existed in two parallel versions, the 1859 edition and the 1862 edition with later changes made by Goncharov. The first full academic edition of *Oblomov* with all variants came out in 1987. I use this edition, I. A. Goncharov, *Oblomov*, ed. L. S. Geiro (Leningrad: Nauka, 1987).

[2] Vladimir Dal', *Tolkovyi slovar' zhivogo velikorusskogo iazyka* (St Petersburg, Moscow: izdatel'stvo M.A. Vol'f, 1881), II, p. 593.

While in Goncharov's time the hero and his way of life were perceived in the context of the opposition between democratic Westernisers and Slavophiles, for Lenin (1922) it was all the classes of Russian society that needed to overcome the vice of this syndrome.[3] At the time of Mikhalkov's work on the film in the late 1970s, the reinterpretation of Oblomov and his friend Stolz as ideological opponents was gaining momentum in intellectual spheres, mainly represented by the officially-approved but loosely defined movement of Russophile *derevenshchiki*, or Village Prose writers, and their supporters among nationalistically inclined groups.

The film closes the 1970s and opens the 1980s, a period which ushered Perestroika and Glasnost reforms, and as such shares features which align it with both the conservative late 1970s and the trends which were formulated in the mid-1980s. In fact, the first signs of the conservative re-evaluation of the novel occurred with the publication of Goncharov's biography in the prestigious series 'The life of remarkable people', published by 'Molodaia gvardiia' in 1977, a year before Mikhalkov began work on the film adaptation of the novel. Authored by Iurii Loshchits (b. 1938),[4] a writer of conservative Russo-centric orientation, the book contained a new interpretation of Oblomov and the Oblomov-Stolz dichotomy, which departed markedly from previously accepted views on these characters and *oblomovshchina*. One of the earlier commentators on Mikhalkov's film, Alexander Batchan (1984), noted that Loshchits's interpretation of Goncharov's novel had had an impact on Mikhalkov's adaptation.[5] Loshchits rehabilitated Oblomov and aggressively defended him against previous leftist evaluations. He overturned former critical interpretations of what constituted the typically Russian traits of Oblomov, and claimed that the character had a philosophical depth and inner harmony which supported the continuity of the Russian state and the Russian way of life. Moreover, Loshchits gave a damning evaluation of Stolz and made overt allusions to the contemporary socio-political situation in the Soviet Union. While in Goncharov's novel Stolz was not constructed as Oblomov's enemy but shares with him many positive features of the Russian character, in Loshchits's book Stolz becomes a Mephistophelian character and an embodiment of Oblomov's personal and Russia's collective misfortunes. In Loshchits's opinion, 'Oblomov's Kingdom of dreams collapses not because he is too lazy, but because his friend is too active'.[6]

---

[3] V. I. Lenin, 'O mezhdunarodnom i vnutrennem polozhenii Sovetskoi Respubliki', in *Polnoe sobranie sochinenii* (Moscow: Politizdat, 1970), XLV, pp. 1–13.

[4] Iurii Loshchits, *Oblomov* (Moscow: Molodaia gvardiia, 1977).

[5] Alexander Batchan, 'Oblomovka – Love It or Leave It: A Commentary on Nikita Mikhalkov's Nostalgic Vision of Russia', *Russian History*, 11 (1984), pp. 327–42.

[6] Loshchits, p. 190.

As noted by Vladimir Kantor in a polemical 1989 article,[7] Loshchits's re-evaluation of Goncharov's *Oblomov* in a patriotic and markedly xenophobic tone is simultaneously a reflection of the main trends of the dominant cultural discourse of the late 1970s and an influential contribution to this discourse. I suggest that in the atmosphere of the late 1970s, Mikhalkov's film adaptation had to respond not only to the original text itself but to Loshchits's most recent and highly ideologised interpretation of the novel. It was clear that Loshchits's slimly concealed attack on aliens within and foreigners at large, personified by the figure of Stolz, was an indication that this rhetoric had official support. Mikhalkov had to consider issues of censorship, and to navigate between historical and current contrasting interpretations of the novel's protagonists, Oblomov and Stolz, as well as *oblomovshchina* as a social phenomenon. Loshchits's book, albeit in a biased way, made the novel topical and relevant for the decade of the 1970s.

In the 1970s and 1980s, censorship constraints were applied less stringently to film adaptations of nineteenth century classics. Elena Prokhorova notes that

> Film adaptations of approved works (those that were previously published in the USSR) meant looser script supervision and carried special prestige in a logocentric Russo-Soviet culture. At the same time, directors had more freedom to produce genre films under the label of 'adaptation' [. . .] and to infuse the plot with contemporary allusions. Mikhalkov's adaptation of Goncharov, for example, can be read both as a commentary on Stagnation [. . .], as well as a loving tribute to nineteenth century Russian culture [. . .]. Mikhalkov's adaptations, [. . .] precipitated the return of pre-revolutionary Russian culture to Soviet screens. Immaculately stylized as genre vehicles, these films claimed continuity between the Russian and the Soviet cultures and empires.[8]

I suggest that reading the film as a commentary on Stagnation relates more to the vantage point of the mid 1980s when this term entered political discourse during Perestroika reforms. In my view Mikhalkov's adaptation of *Oblomov* glorified a more reflexive lifestyle based on individual leanings and predispositions rather than forced collective activities set by the Party and the Soviet State. It is for this reason that Mikhalkov's interpretations of Oblomov and Stolz are closer to the discourse of the *derevenshchiki* and the new interpretation encapsulated in Loshchits's book. It has been stressed that the *derevenshchiki* occupied a secure and privileged position in domestic Soviet cultural politics

---

[7] V. K. Kantor, 'Dolgii navyk k snu (razmyshlenie o romane I. A. Goncharova *Oblomov*), *Voprosy literatury*, 1 (1989), pp. 149–85.

[8] Elena Prokhorova, 'Cinema of Stagnation Late 1960s–1985', in *The Russian Cinema Reader. Volume II, the Thaw to the Present*, ed. Rimgaila Salys (Boston: Academic Studies Press, 2013), pp. 104–14 (p. 108).

in the late 1970s. Kathleen Parthe has noted that this kind of production 'got easily past the censors before Gorbachev. [. . .] Village Prose writers exploited a residual nationalism of Party and government leadership and the reading public.'[9] The movements' critics noted that lamenting for the Russian village 'became the official line, and *derevenshchiki* were able to establish for themselves a secure and eventually powerful position in the literary establishment'.[10] It is obvious that by aligning his aesthetic and intellectual discourse to this group of Russian patriots, Mikhalkov secured a relatively safe position for himself in the ideological and cultural scene of the end of the decade. Notably, Joseph Brodsky characterised 'peasant prose' and its adherents as having 'a strong tendency towards nationalistic self-appreciation'.[11] Moreover, Brodsky claimed that this writing marks a stylistic and aesthetic retreat. My discussion takes into account these characterisations of the prevailing features of the dominant cultural productions of the epoch.

Loshchits's book laid bare some prevailing trends of the late 1970s in relation to nationalism and views on Russia's past and present. Politically, the decade of the 1970s was characterised by the phenomenon of the so called Third Wave of emigration from the Soviet Union mainly by Soviet Jews and dissidents. The decade was marked by the sharp political divide in international politics between the West and the Soviet Union, following the Arab–Israeli War of 1967 with the Soviet Union supporting Arab countries under the pretext of helping the developing world. Soviet mass media started a prolonged anti-Zionist campaign which resulted in antisemitism in various institutions, including in higher education and in the workplace. Following the signing of the Helsinki accords in 1973 and 1975 guaranteeing human rights, the Soviet Union allowed the first mass emigration of Jewish people to Israel. Strikingly, the character of Stolz from Goncharov's novel provided commentators like Loshchits with an opportunity to treat him as a crypto-Jew. In spite of the clarity of his half-German half-Russian parental roots in the novel, Loshchits finds a way to typify him as an alien on Russian soil. Moreover, Loshchits uses characterisations and imagery which create associations with the Jewish Other. This association is masterfully achieved by taking quotes out of context, or by deconstruction. The first strategy is evident in this narrative:

> What does it mean, in reality: 'he lived for the second time, walked through familiar places'?! It seems that in a moment the writer will reveal the secret of the creature who already lives for the second time,

[9] Kathleen Parthe, *Russian Village Prose: The Radiant Past* (Princeton: Princeton University Press, 1992), p. 91.
[10] Ibid.
[11] Joseph Brodsky, *Less Than One: Selected Essays* (New York: Farrar, Straus, Giroux, 1986), pp. 294–5.

or, perhaps, who has lived already many times, wandering through centuries and countries?[12]

This commentary skilfully introduced the theme of the Wandering Jew, suggesting that Oblomov conceived Stolz as a crypto-Jew. In order to make a transition to the conspiracy master plot of Jewish influence in finances and business transactions, Loshchits comes up with the passage in which he ironically describes what would happen without Stolz's business activities:

> Why shouldn't there be a new project?! Then people will stop being hectic and will have a chance to rest. By getting rid of the ships and the trains the slaves will escape from the underground mines; they will abandon their huts in dirty towns; trade will stop, money wallets of the Rothschilds will get thinner, the vodka monopolies will be closed down.[13]

The passage contains the repertory of traditional anti-Jewish propaganda, dating back to the 19th century. It includes references to Jewish bankers, such as the Rothschilds used by Dostoevsky in his novel *The Adolescent* (1875) as well as in his infamous articles on 'The Jewish question' in *the Diary of the Writer* (1878).[14] Needless to say, these topics are not to be found in Goncharov's text.

While Loshchits skilfully alludes to the main features of conspiracy narratives originating in the nineteenth century, he introduces topics which are relevant to contemporary Soviet discourse of the 1970s. In line with the Village Prose conservative values concealed under ecological awareness themes, he blames the Stolzes for their corrupting influence of the Russian landscape and its people. His list of undesirables and their activities includes 'tourists who travel to look at foreign wonders,' and suggests that putting a stop to this would lead to the restoration of fields and forests.[15] The attack on international tourism is supposed to justify Oblomov's aversion to travel abroad, but it goes beyond the relevance to the novel and its time. The choice of the word 'foreign' in 'foreign wonders' ('*zamorskie diva*'),[16] suggests crossing the sea and the word 'foreign' here relates to distant travel overseas, rather than abroad. This choice hints at geographical locales that are situated beyond European borders and are in line with the destinations of the 'tourists' who leave for the United States or Israel – the two main destinations of the emigration out of the Soviet Union in the 1970s.

---

[12] Loshchits, p. 188.
[13] Ibid., p. 201.
[14] Mark Ural'sky and Genrietta Mondri, *Dostoevsky i evrei* (St Petersburg: Aleteiia, 2021), pp. 513–626.
[15] Loshchits, p. 201.
[16] Ibid.

The second important theme linked to travel and tourism relates to ecology and preservation of nature. It has been noted that Mikhalkov's film adaptation capitalises on the representation of the Russian landscape and the film sharply contrasts cityscapes with rural landscapes.[17] In doing this Mikhalkov follows the trends of the 1970s in creating complex hierarchies between the foreignness of the architectural constructions in St Petersburg and the unspoiled natural landscapes of the idealised countryside. While Mikhalkov does not pick up Loshchits's theme of the crypto-Jew as the agent of modernity,[18] he nevertheless follows Loshchits's hostile evaluation of Stolz. In his interview (1980) he stated that 'the vice of Oblomovism has been replaced by the vice of Stolzism'.[19]

Film adaptation theorists suggest that, when analysing adaptations of classical texts, it is equally important to examine the meaning not only of those episodes that are included or changed, but also of the omitted material.[20] I will proceed by taking this approach into account, and will demonstrate the meaning of omitted, selectively included, and synthesised episodes as a form of dialogue conducted by Mikhalkov with the source texts: the novel, Loshchits's monograph and the discourse of the Village Prose.

Meaningful Omission: Removing Tarant'ev and his Xenophobic Diatribes

In Part 1 of the novel in the midst of Oblomov's inability to move out of the apartment to which he is comfortably accustomed, and while anxiously expecting the arrival of his friend Stolz, a conversation between Oblomov and his acquaintance Tarant'ev takes place. At this time of crisis Oblomov needs help from Stolz, who on numerous occasions has helped him out of the trouble caused by Oblomov's inability to organise his own affairs. Tarant'ev comes from the same area as Oblomov and Stolz (the Volga region) but is presented by Goncharov as a crude and exploitative manipulator of Oblomov's meek nature. Goncharov presents Tarant'ev in an overtly negative light as instrumental in the gradual

---

[17] Birgit Beumers, 'The Mikhalkov brothers' view of Russia', in *Russian and Soviet Film Adaptations of Literature, 1900–2001: Screening the Word*, eds Stephen Hutchings and Anat Vernitski (London: Routledge, 2005), pp. 135–52; see also Russell Scott Valentino, 'Adapting the Landscape: Oblomov's Vision in Film'. Ibid. pp. 153–63.

[18] On anti-Semitic views of Jews as the agents of modernity see Steven Marks, *How Russia Shaped the Modern World* (Princeton: Princeton University Press, 2003), pp. 140–76.

[19] Cited in Andrei Plakhov, 'Postizhenie ili adaptatsiia?', *Iskusstvo kino*, 6 (1980), pp. 49–68 (p. 50).

[20] Colin MacCabe, 'Introduction', in *True to the Spirit: Film Adaptation and the Question of Fidelity*, eds Colin MacCabe, Cathleen Murray and Rick Warren (Oxford: Oxford University Press, 2011), pp. 3–25.

demise of Oblomov. It is Tarant'ev who arranges Oblomov's relocation to the house in the Vyborgskaia part of St Petersburg – the low-class suburb which becomes a parody of Oblomovka. It is in this house that Oblomov is exploited by Tarant'ev's friends, who almost ruin his fortune. It takes Stolz to undo the unscrupulous dealing of Tarant'ev and his friends and to save Oblomov and his estate from bankruptcy.

Mikhalkov omits the scene in which Tarant'ev vilifies Stolz. In the novel, the scene aims to expose the employment of xenophobic rhetoric as a calculated strategy to achieve self-serving goals. Goncharov makes Tarant'ev use the most grotesque set of accusations against Stolz as a foreigner, proving that the writer attributed special importance to Tarant'ev's hate speech:

> What kind of a benefactor have you found? – Tarant'ev interrupted Oblomov. A cursed German, a scheming rogue! Tarant'ev had some kind of instinctive aversion to foreigners. For him Frenchman, German, or Englishman were synonymous with scoundrel, swindler, trickster, or bandit. He did not differentiate between these nations: they were all the same in his eyes.[21]

Oblomov defends Stolz as the most helpful and honest person and demands from Tarant'ev respect for his friend. Goncharov devotes two pages to Tarant'ev's hateful and absurd accusations against Stolz and other foreigners who allegedly exploit Russia and Russians. His speech is an example of defensive xenophobia and obscurantism. As a result of Mikhalkov's omission of Tarant'ev from the film adaptation, the balance of positive and negative characters is shifted. Stolz emerges as the only strong opponent of Oblomov, and this makes him bear an additional load of negativity associated with cynicism and business acumen. In the novel Tarant'ev represents shady and dishonest practices, while Stolz is shown as a straight and honest businessman. More importantly, by omitting xenophobic attacks the film loses the authorial irony which exposes the mixture of envy and self-interest underpinning the vilification of the foreign/ethnic Other. The fact that Tarant'ev is Oblomov and Stolz's '*zemliak*' ('fellow countryman'), who comes from the same part of Russia as the two main protagonists, gives this character an additional significance. Tarant'ev's is a third possible attitude towards life which shifts the dichotomy embodied by the Oblomov-Stolz dynamics. In the novel Tarant'ev stands for the most cynical and immoral way to live and conduct business. Additionally, he stands for another way of treating friendship as a form of exploitation and betrayal – something that is absent in the Oblomov-Stolz relationship. Goncharov introduces this episode early in the

[21] Goncharov, *Oblomov*, p. 43.

novel, in Chapters 3 and 4 of Part 1, before the arrival of Stolz. He prepares the readers for understanding Stolz not only as a successful individual but also as a person who is not fully accepted in Russian society by xenophobic and obscurantist men like Tarant'ev. To include the grotesque diatribes of Tarant'ev in the adaptation would have meant showing political leanings which were out of favour by the conservative nationalistic officialdom of the late 1970s.

Adding and Adjusting: the Bathhouse Episode

Of special relevance to the question of fitting an adaptation into the political atmosphere is the scene in which Oblomov and Stolz have an intense conversation that identifies their core difference. The dialogue allows the participants to express their views, with Oblomov showing a hitherto unexpected depth of thinking and existential sensibilities. Stolz comes out in this dialogue as existing in a different sphere from that of Oblomov. His views are perfectly rational and relate to the practical side of human existence as a participant in a society who contributes to 'progress' and is ethically concerned also with the improvement of the lives of the lower classes. While Stolz functions in the sphere of practicality and active life, Oblomov with his lack of productivity belongs to the past. His inner leanings and ideals are regressive.

The most striking addition to the scene in the film is its choice of location in the bathhouse. In the novel the conversation takes place in Oblomov's apartment after an exhausting day which he spent unwillingly socialising with business people. In the novel Oblomov sits on the sofa in the cocooning atmosphere of his apartment (which he finds traumatic to move out of). In the film the location for this important dialogue is transposed to the rural bathhouse with its multifunctional resting room (*predbannik*). The winter landscape complements the atmosphere of rural Russia. As noted by Ethan Pollock, the rural bathhouse 'could work as a symbol of unadulterated Russianness to writers of the 1960s and 1970s, [. . .] concerned with the erosion of traditions in general,' and this setting was used for the same purpose in the films of the period.[22] Mikhalkov's choice of the bathhouse fits the trends of the glorification of Russianness in vogue with the Village Prose topos. Oblomov draws his strength in this essentialised atmosphere of snow-covered land in order to confront Stolz and express his most sacred thoughts. In this scene Oblomov emerges for the first time in the film as an internally complex individual with intense workings of the mind.

---

[22] Pollock notes that scenes in the bathhouse often were settings to express masculinity for disenfranchised Soviet men. He writes that for Mikhalkov the rural *bania* 'encapsulates Russian authenticity' (Ethan Pollock, 'Real Men Go to the Bania: Postwar Soviet Masculinities and the Bathhouse', *Kritika*, 11 (2010), pp. 47–76 [p. 61]).

In the scene, Mikhalkov uses the representation of corporeality to create a binarism between Oblomov and Stolz. With the bathhouse's presupposed exposure of the undressed bodies, the camera focuses on Stolz's naked and athletic torso. Oblomov's body is not exposed as he is covered by a gown. The camera exhibits Stolz's muscular body while he is engaged in the all-Russian bath-ritual of flogging himself with dry birch tree branches for some time while he concurrently exchanges opinions with Oblomov. Yet the conversation, while formally dialogic, only shows the width of the gap between the opinions of the two interlocutors. The difference in their behaviour in the bathhouse is meant to stress this difference: while Stolz is physically active by doing various sporty exercises, Oblomov sits on the bench pouring out his thoughts. Strikingly, the scene ends in Oblomov's rare but angry outburst in response to Stolz's forceful attempt to pull him into bathhouse sporty games.

The scene is provocatively ambivalent, as it shows not only Stolz's normative behaviour for the Russian bathhouse in winter, but also his aggressive insistence on Oblomov's participation in physical activities. The scene reveals Stolz's aggressive and overpowering nature. Oblomov's dramatised reaction is meant to bring ambiguity to this cinematic moment. His cry, 'I do not like

Figure 1.1   Oblomov (Oleg Tabakov) tells Stolz (Iurii Bogatyrev) that he refuses to go (away). Oblomov turning his back and not showing his face invests his answer with suggestive anonymity. *A Few Days from the Life of I. I. Oblomov*, directed by Nikita Mikhalkov, 1980.

this sort of thing!' in a tearful voice, sounds like a protest against the application of physical strength. The cry, uttered twice, and the prolonged posture of Stolz's forcefully locking his arm around Oblomov's shoulders, is semiotically complex. In it the material and the semiotic intersect in order to form a site of power struggle. Oblomov's tearful cry in a high-pitched voice introduces an aspect of gender, contrasting the effeminised, flabby Oblomov draped in the loose gown with the manly and sporty Stolz. Yet representing Stolz through the emphasis of his physical strength contrasts him unfavourably with the mild and reflexive Oblomov. This calculated strategy puts Stolz hierarchically at a lower level in terms of the cultural values of the intelligentsia. Moreover, an inbuilt ambiguity around Oblomov not wanting to fool around with a man in the bathhouse is meant to compromise Stolz. The viewer is invited to decipher Oblomov's cry 'I do not like this' since it is intentionally vague. This male to male encounter in the bathhouse gives the scene risqué sexual connotations, as the line between homosocial and homosexual contact can be seen as porous. Oblomov comes out 'straight' and simple by constructing an invisible physical boundary between himself and Stolz.

The scene in the bathhouse, while entailing a meaningful dialogue involving a clash of opinions, impacts the viewer not only by the verbal formulations but also by the complex referential set of symbols. Verbally, the duel between Oblomov and Stolz does not allow the viewer to choose the winner because both men give intelligent arguments *pro et contra*. In this verbal exchange there are no victors. The visual helps the viewer to choose the winner, and it is Oblomov who is intended to win the sympathy of the audience. Thus during a touching revelation of Oblomov's profound inner thoughts the camera focuses on a decorative arrangement on the windowsill in the bathhouse front room. The objects form a *nature morte* and they consist of branches of dried red berries and a cup with a yellow butterfly in it. The detail is shown during Oblomov's retelling his thoughts at the sight of a tree that he imagines to be five hundred years old and its leaves that perish every year in autumn and appear anew in spring.

Oblomov is clearly concerned with the question 'Why and for what do we live?' rather than 'How to live?' – what for him is the shallower question. He expresses himself as an intuitive thinker and admits that he is not able to formulate his thoughts in a logocentric discourse, but this revelation does not make his preoccupation with ontological questions any less profound. The butterfly in the cup as well as the dried red berries still contain life and symbolically represent the state of Oblomov's life as a form of still-life. The visual ensemble suggests that he leads his life in the modus of self-preservation, choosing to be cocooned in order to survive the beatings of the surrounding environment. Like the butterfly, Oblomov is both dead and alive. His refusal to live life actively is a form of fear of death as much as fear of life. Oblomov's story ends with the admission that no tree lives for 500 years, and since it is told with tears streaming down his face it reveals the source and reason for his inertia. It is a fear of death which has a paralysing effect on his life, and the still-life framed by the camera helps the viewer to perceive Oblomov as a tragic figure.

Mikhalkov's representation of the dialogue between Oblomov and Stolz allows him to enter into an authorial dialogue with Goncharov. Mikhalkov changes the setting of the scene that, in the novel, consists of the clearest formulations of the two characters' views on life. Mikhalkov exposes the corporeal and inner differences between the two protagonists. By inventing a scene of Stolz's pressurising Oblomov into physical activity albeit in a playful manner, Mikhalkov hints that he has noticed a certain harshness in Stolz which Goncharov did not make overt. It is clear that Mikhalkov aims to compromise Stolz and by doing this he follows the discourse of the 'apologetics of Oblomov' present in Loshchits's book, the discourse that was identified by Vladimir Kantor in 1989 as dominant for the 1970s.[23]

In Kantor's interpretation, given at the time when pluralism of opinion became a new feature of the Glasnost public discourse, Goncharov intended Stolz to represent the synthesis of two cultures. In order to avoid interpretation of Stolz as a German, Goncharov intentionally stressed in the novel that Stolz's native language was Russian, and that he was baptised into the Russian Orthodox faith. Polemicising with the kind of interpretation of Stolz that is given by Loshchits, Kantor states that in the character of Stolz Goncharov suggests that possession of two cultures enriches human development and, by implication, has the potential to enrich the culture of the country in which a bicultural person lives. Of relevance is Kantor's reminder of Bakhtin's notion of dialogism in culture, according to which any culture is situated at the borders and is actualised in a form of a dialogue. By representing Stolz as an alien figure, Kantor maintains, Loshchits undermines the dialogic nature of culture. Moreover, Kantor argues that in the figure of Stolz Goncharov promotes biculturalism as a productive state of being. Returning to Mikhalkov's adaptation, I suggest that by following Loshchits's narrative and portraying Stolz as inflexible and set in his opinions, Mikhalkov impairs the constructive aspect of the dialogue between Oblomov and Stolz, ignores the role of Stolz's biculturalism and undermines his active contribution to Russian society.

To Invent the Bicycle, to Re-write the Ending

In the novel Stolz stays outside of the romantic relationship that develops between Oblomov and Olga. While he has introduced Oblomov to Olga as part of the plan to keep Oblomov alert under the patronage of this charming

---

[23] Kantor, p. 150.

young woman, the relationship between the two reached breaking point while Stolz was abroad. In the film Stolz is shown as a manipulative and treacherous actant at the end of Oblomov's courtship of Olga. In the novel Oblomov withdraws from the relationship out of fear of its pace and Olga's forceful nature. Withdrawal is crucial in the novel, as it leads to Oblomov's nervous breakdown and Olga's trauma. Olga and her aunt seek a cure from this unhappy experience in the trip to Europe where they meet Stolz quite by chance. It is in this setting that a new and mature relationship develops between Stolz and Olga. Goncharov spends the whole of Chapter 4 in Part 4 of the novel demonstrating Stolz's moral and emotional support of Olga, his wisdom and psychological insight into the heart of the young woman. In this chapter Stolz is shown as not only a deeply thinking but also a deeply feeling person.

The film rushes toward the end from the first part of the novel to the last one and re-writes the denouement in the Oblomov-Olga romance, by assigning a formative role to Stolz. It has been noted that in the novel Stolz often appears as a *deus ex machina* to solve the periodic crises in which Oblomov finds himself. In Mikhalkov's adaptation, a Mephistophelean Stolz appears as a controlling manipulator in the midst of the blossoming romance. This is in sharp contrast to the narrative in the novel that shows Oblomov's willing withdrawal and gradual regression into the world of pseudo-Oblomovka with the earthly Pshenitsyna.

Mikhalkov's adaptation not only adds the scene of Stolz's direct presence during Oblomov's cathartic moment of breaking off his romance with Olga, but also finds an ingenious way to widen the interpretative possibilities of the rift between the main protagonists. The scene acquires a highly symbolic character due to the introduction of a three-wheeled bicycle, a nineteenth century symbol of modernity and mobility. It is only appropriate to the main narrative of the dichotomy between the old ways of life and the new, alien ways that it is Stolz who brings Olga an English bicycle as a present. In the second half of the nineteenth century this machine epitomised freedom of movement and stood for the modernisation of life.

Additionally, it promoted exercise across genders and allowed women to become engaged in a more athletic lifestyle. Strikingly, the film chooses this cinematic moment for a concurrent cathartic conversation between Stolz and Oblomov while Olga is riding the bicycle. The scene ends in Oblomov's refusal to try to ride the bicycle, but his refusal encodes something more important than fear of the new machine. Rather, in a determined and emotionally-charged tone, Oblomov utters the same phrase: 'I will not go!' four times punctuated by significant pauses. Oblomov's categorical refusal 'to go' grows in tonality from quiet to more affirmative and strongly assertive. The scene becomes the last dialogue with undertones of an ideological duel between the two protagonists. Oblomov's categorical refusal and Stolz's aggressive insistence on Oblomov's taking a ride suggest that a principle underpins this stand-off.

The scene's use of defamiliarisation makes Oblomov's statement strange and therefore endows it with a special hidden meaning.[24] Notably, Stolz uses the word 'poidem' ('let us go by foot') rather than 'poedem' ('let us take a ride') when he invites Oblomov to join in riding the bicycle for fun. Oblomov's use of 'I will not go!' encodes, I propose, an allusion to the concurrent discourse around those who 'go away' as opposed to 'staying put' – the public discourse that acquired ideological connotations in the 1970s.[25] This narrative was most overtly applied in the interpretation of Stolz in Iurii Loshchits's book, where, as stated earlier, Stolz is presented as an 'international tourist' on the go, a veiled counterpart to those Soviet citizens who emigrated from the Soviet Union in the 1970s. By making Oblomov formulate his categorical refusal 'I will not go [away],' or leave, Mikhalkov identifies not only Oblomov's but his own position, which was politically topical in the last years of the 1970s when the film was made. Theorists of the process of interpretation suggest that the meaning of the sign is affected by the background, education, culture and other experiences of the reader or viewer.[26] Of special relevance to understanding Mikhalkov's scene is the opinion that 'understanding of the meaning of a text involves taking on an appropriate ideological identity'.[27] This leads to the 'obligation to adopt a "subject-position"' in relation to the cinematic text.[28] Mikhalkov manipulates the viewer to adopt an 'ideological identity' informed and formed by the dominant political discourse.

Fittingly, in 1979, the year of the film's completion, Mikhalkov's elder brother, the talented film director Andrei Konchalovsky, left Russia for the US to advance his career in Hollywood.[29] In this daring filmic scene, I propose, Mikhalkov enters into a dialogic relationship not only with the new interpretation of the novel but also with his brother and his divergent political leanings. Under the political and personal circumstances, 'I will not go!' in the film becomes a vehicle for Mikhalkov to publicly declare his loyalty to the native country.

Of special relevance to the adaptation's decision to depict Stolz as an alien figure are explanations given by the actor Oleg Tabakov who plays Oblomov.

---

[24] Defamiliarisation is a technique used in art to make the ordinary look strange and endow it with new meaning.

[25] Batchan is right to explain this statement as 'the director's attitude to the recent emigration movement from the USSR' (Batchan, p. 337).

[26] David Crow, *Visible Signs: An Introduction to Semiotics in the Visual Arts* (Lausanne: AVA Publishing, 2010), p. 180.

[27] Daniel Chandler, *Semiotics* (London: Routledge, 2007), p. 187.

[28] Ibid.

[29] On the brothers' different ideological views see Denise Youngblood, 'The Cosmopolitan and the Patriot: the Brothers Mikhalkov-Konchalovsky and Russian Cinema', *Historical Journal of Film, Radio and Television*, 23 (2003), pp. 27–41.

In his interview for the journal *Iskusstvo kino* in 1979 Tabakov gives a clear message that Stolz is an outsider to 'this land': 'For us it is a matter of principle that the values of this land ['*etoi zemli*'] differ sharply from the values of a different land ['*inoi zemli*'], on which Stolz grew.'[30]

This choice of words to formulate the differences between Stolz and Oblomov is highly indicative of the general ideological position invested in the Oblomov-Stolz dynamics in the film.[31] By stressing the notion of *this* and the *other* land the actor adheres to the dominant nationalist narrative of the 1970s as espoused by the Village Prose followers, as well as by literary critics such as Loshchits. Tabakov's blatant error in stating that Stolz grew up in a different land only further amplifies the ideological tenets under which the film was directed. Tabakov forgets that Goncharov's Stolz and Oblomov grew up side by side in the same part of Russia, and that Stolz was educated in Russia, and not abroad.

The Grand Finale: The Mother Syndrome – Conflating Biological Mothers and the Motherland

Through the film there are constant flashbacks to Oblomovka with the recurring theme of the love of Oblomov's pious mother for her son. This longing for mother is conflated with the longing for Oblomovka and its Arcadian delights. Nostalgia for the lost past is linked with the trauma of the missed love of a caring mother. These flashbacks, I suggest, give a psychological nuance to Oblomov's condition and offer a more sophisticated view of *oblomovshchina* as a phenomenon that goes beyond the social side of this condition. Such psychological depth is implicitly present in the novel with all three main protagonists, Oblomov, Stolz and Olga, being shown as affected by present or absent mothers. In Oblomov's case, Mikhalkov's adaptation succeeds in conveying the role of Oblomov's attachment to his mother by using flashbacks to his childhood. In the case of Stolz the film also includes an episode related to Stolz's trauma with his absent Russian mother, who died early and left him to be shaped by his German father. In a flashback episode it is simple Russian peasant women on the estate who kiss and bless the young Stolz as his father sends him away into the big world to fend for himself. However, in the novel Goncharov makes it quite clear that Stolz's Russian mother managed to leave her imprint on the boy's character with 'her songs and tender whisper'.[32]

---

[30] Oleg Tabakov, 'Trudnoe znakomstvo s Oblomovym', *Iskusstvo kino*, 4 (1979), pp. 80–2.
[31] On Mikhalkov's nationalist nostalgia see Birgit Beumers, *Nikita Mikhalkov: Between Nostalgia and Nationalism. The Filmmakers Companion 1* (London: I. B. Tauris, 2005).
[32] Goncharov, *Oblomov*, p. 348.

The film adaptation does not evoke Stolz's memories of his mother, but rather repeats the same flashback of the little Oblomov and his mother in Oblomovka at the end of the film to parallel the concurrent arrival of Pshenitsyna, mother of little Andrei. In this final episode the boy's cheerful cry 'Mummy has come back!' replicates little Oblomov's cry in the flashback. During this concluding cinematic moment both Stolz and Olga experience emotions, manifested by Olga's tears and Stolz's pensive withdrawal into the inner world. The scene expresses Mikhalkov's understanding that all three main protagonists have been psychologically shaped by their personal past and that, to a degree, their destinies were determined by their present or absent mothers. It is not in vain that Olga is an orphan in the novel, which explains her emotional and psychological immaturity and need for a mentor.

Strikingly, in the novel when Olga recovers from the breakup with Oblomov, she tells Stolz that she trusts him 'without limits, as my own mother'.[33] Moreover, during her confession and decisive conversation with Stolz she intuitively admits that her confusion relates to the absence of a mother: 'perhaps the heart will understand that I do not have a mother, that I was lost in the forest.'[34] Symptomatically, in the novel Olga starts her psychological recovery after the healing conversation with Stolz, who responded to her confession by helping her to analyse her inner feelings and emotions. This medicalised vocabulary – '*vyzdorovet'*' ('to get healthy') – is indicative of Stolz's positive effect on her. The film re-writes Stolz's role in this medicalisation motif from positive to negative.

In the final scenes of the film this aspect of the Stolz-Olga relationship is turned upside down. Olga is shown in a melancholic state and her condition is medicalised: she asks her friend to fetch her medicine. The last shot of Olga shows her in a lachrymose state taking her medicine at the arrival of Pshenitsyna to visit Oblomov's little son. In this emotive scene Olga's personal loss is paralleled by the loss of the past world represented by the flashback of the recurring scene of the little Oblomov joyfully crying 'Mummy has arrived!' This conflation of Olga's implied personal loss and the loss of an idealised historical past, emblematised by the figure of the absent Oblomov, corresponds to the metanarrative of nostalgia for the lost world promoted by the Village Prose of the 1970s. Oblomov becomes synonymous with the lost world in which men like him were nurtured by their loving mothers in harmonious rural settings.

Oblomov's concealed mother syndrome is covertly present in the novel and underpins his need of cocooning and protection from life's turbulences. In the final stage of his life this trauma of separation finds compensation in his marriage to the caregiving Pshenitsyna. Pshenitsyna's surname (derived from the word 'wheat') is symbolic of the traditional Russian cultural notion of mother

---

[33] Goncharov, *Oblomov*, p. 323.
[34] Ibid., p. 325.

earth. The film omits the long descriptions of *byt* which are scrupulously crafted by Goncharov, occupying most of Part 3 of the novel. The voice-over of the narrator in the film fills the gap with a short summary stating that Oblomov married Pshenitsyna and died seven years later entrusting his son from this marriage to the care of Stolz. By omitting Oblomov's regression into the world of inactivity and Pshenitsyna's inability to shield him from the dangerous intrigues of her exploitative brother and Tarant'ev, the film cuts out Goncharov's exposure of the dangers of escapism.[35] In the novel, both Oblomov and Pshenitsyna become victims of fraud and would have lost Oblomovka with all their livelihood had it not been for Stolz's interference. It is thanks to Stolz that the last years of Oblomov were comfortable and the financial security of his widow became guaranteed. By cutting out this negative reliance on the protective power of nanny-like Pshenitsyna the film adds to a biased interpretation of the Oblomov-Stolz dynamic.

The film ends with the scene of Pshenitsyna's visit by her and Oblomov's son to Stolz's country estate. The scene shows a cheerfully running little Andrei, who was named by Oblomov in honour of Andrei Stolz, as a tribute to their friendship. Mikhalkov's adaptation amplifies the parallelism between the role of motherly love and the role of native space where nature and nurture coexist in effortless harmony. In line with the Russocentric narratives of the 1970s, the film blurs the line between birth mother and Mother as native land. The adaptation imposes a symbolic understanding of Mother as situated at the intersection of biological mother, pagan Mother soil and Christian Mother of God. The final scene makes this intersection visually and audially clear: the little boy Andrei runs along the green fields, shouting the word 'Mummy!' under the musical background of Rachmaninov's 'Vespers'. This Eastern Orthodox chant with the Church Slavonic prayer affirming the existence of God accompanies the view of the idyllic pastoral landscape with the flowing river – the symbol of eternal movement – and the little boy gradually disappearing into the distance. The flowing river symbolically connects past and future to emphasise the power of cultural continuity in line with the tenets of the Village Prose movement. The landscape is both real and symbolic, and the technical act of freezing the frame instils in the space a sense of timelessness. Mikhalkov artistically creates a meaning for this space that promotes the notion of nature as Russia's spiritual cradle. This employment of the symbolic aspect of the sceneries of central Russia typologically and ideologically departs from the visual typology of representing Russia's spaces as vast and fitting for a multinational state.[36] In line with the ideals of the

---

[35] On the role of Tarant'ev in the novel see Kantor, p. 153.

[36] On this visual tradition in Soviet films of the Stalin era see Emma Widdis, 'Russia as Space', in *National Identity in Russian Culture: An Introduction*, eds Simon Franklin and Emma Widdis (Cambridge: Cambridge University Press, 2004), pp. 30–49.

Village Prose, the idyllic Russian landscape unifies individuals and families with the native land. The scene uses all the components of the Russocentric discourse which was canonised (and even parodied by its opponents) by the end of the 1970s: rural landscape, river, forest and peasants.[37]

In this final scene the chronotopic unification of space and time brings Russia's past, present and future together.[38] It guarantees a future for Russia as the ultimate Mother/land and for its people, sanctified by the Eastern Orthodox faith. The scene promotes an organicist and essentialist connection between the people and the land. Significantly for the ideological message of the adaptation, the camera shot uses contrast between light and darkness: it first shows the sunny landscape with little Andrei and Pshenitsyna, while capturing the darker atmosphere of the house with Olga and Stolz sitting in it. This semiotic division of space delineates the confined atmosphere of the interior and the expanding space of the Russian land. The use of contrasting colour helps to achieve the desired effect, allegorically presenting the divide between dark and bright spaces. The adaptation manipulates the novel's presentation of Stolz and Olga's country estate which is situated in the Crimea and further promotes a positive role of cultural diversity by detailed descriptions of foreign and antique artefacts collected by Stolz. By changing the geographical location

Figure 1.2   Freezing the frame blurs the line between past and present. Little Andrei Oblomov (Fedor Stukov) amidst the rural scenery. *A Few Days from the Life of I. I. Oblomov*, directed by Nikita Mikhalkov, 1980.

---

[37] Among the parodies on *derevenshchiki* is Voinovich's play *The Tribunal* (1980) which exposes the hypocrisy of these Soviet writers. See a discussion in Parthe, pp. 90–1.

[38] See Beumers, 'The Mikhalkov brothers' view of Russia'.

of Stolz's estate from the multi-ethnic and multi-cultural Crimea to central Russia, the adaptation markedly changes Goncharov's ideological stance.[39] The final scene in Mikhalkov's adaptation manages simultaneously to align itself both with the Village Prose writers' views on Russia's past as a regrettable loss and with the optimism of Socialist Realism in presenting a bright future for the new generation.

The inclusion of a religious thematic is Mikhalkov's addition to the novel, which, as noted by its commentators, does not raise issues of religion and faith.[40] *Oblomov* is a metaphysical novel with existential insights, but its three main protagonists do not have religious leanings. By introducing motifs of Eastern Orthodox faith Mikhalkov demonstrates his affiliation with the prevailing trends of the decade.[41] His ability to make these additions shows that it was possible to introduce aestheticised religious themes because they were compatible with the nationalist pathos of Russian self-assertiveness at the turn of the 1970s and 1980s. This form of Russian self-assertiveness grew in the 1980s and acquired unparalleled proportion after the collapse of the Soviet Union. It is for this reason that Mikhalkov's political importance also grew in the Russian film industry in post-Soviet Russia.[42]

From the vantage point of 1989, completing the decade of reforms ushered in by Perestroika, supporters of change saw Mikhalkov's adaptation as representative of the 1970s and belonging to the past. The film was judged as a 'sentimental interpretation of the novel's central character, Oblomov' and was put side by side with Loshchits's 'open apologetics' of Oblomov.[43] At the closure of the 1980s, the new discourse of Glasnost promoted pluralism and dialogic thinking, as was exemplified by the programmatic multidisciplinary volume *Inogo ne dano* (1988). Notably, in this volume *oblomovshchina* was recalled by sociologists as a syndrome that hinders the success of perestroika.[44]

---

[39] Notably, Loshchits uses Stolz's decision to buy a house in Crimea as a proof of his crypto-Jewishness as he trades with the Odessa merchants (Loshchits, p. 158).
[40] Setchkarev maintains that 'Oblomovism can claim a certain kinship with Buddhism', and its inertia is a brand of Nirvana (Vsevolod Setchkarev, *Ivan Goncharov: His Life and His Work* [Wurzburg: Jal-verlag, 1974] p. 153).
[41] Frederick H. White includes Mikhalkov's *Oblomov* among the films which provide safe cultural anchor at the time of political uncertainty (Frederick H White, 'Conclusion. Passport Control – Departing on a Cinematic Journey', in *Border Crossing: Russian Literature into Film*, eds Alexander Burry and Frederick H. White [Edinburgh: Edinburgh University Press, 2016], pp. 239–64 (p. 244).
[42] Mikhalkov has been the Chairperson of the Union of Filmmakers since 1997.
[43] Kantor, p. 150.
[44] Tat'iana Zaslavskaia, 'O strategii sotsial'nogo upravleniia perestroikoi', in *Inogo ne dano*, ed. Iurii Afanas'ev (Moscow: Progress, 1988), pp. 9–50.

Film adaptation as a form of interpretation of the novel stimulated heated debates between critics of diverse spectra well into the post-Soviet 1990s. Mikhalkov's adaptation became both hypotext and hypertext in these historical dialogues. In films made in the post-Soviet period Mikhalkov continued to glorify a conservative Russian past and in *The Barber of Siberia* (*Sibirskii tsiriul'nik*) (1999) even sentimentalised the Romanov dynasty. He employed the same idyllic rural landscape with the river that he used in the adaptation of *Oblomov* in *Burnt by the Sun* (*Utomlennye solntsem*) (1994). His most recent film adaptation of Ivan Bunin's work, *Sunstroke* (*Solnechnyi udar*) (2014), continues the idealisation of Russia's past and the Russian national character. In it an idyllic Russian town on the Volga with its lush green landscape is emblematic of Russia's sentimentalised past supposedly devoid of social conflict.

In his autobiographical documentary *Anna from 6 to 18*, made with French co-producers and released in 1993, when Mikhalkov himself became an enterprising 'international tourist', he included scenes from *A Few Days from the Life of Oblomov*. The scenes were those of little Oblomov in the Arcadian Oblomovka estate, and they were supposed to parallel and contrast the childhood experience of his daughter Anna (b.1974), brought up in the last decades of the Soviet Union and during its collapse. By transposing the scenes from his film adaptation into a family documentary, Mikhalkov asserts his place in the country's history not only as a transmitter of its culture but also genealogically. He positions himself among multiple generations of Russians, including those who, while resembling Stolz more than Oblomov, ostensibly are proud to have Russia as their Motherland.

Bibliography

Batchan, Alexander, 'Oblomovka – Love It or Leave It: A Commentary on Nikita Mikhalkov's Nostalgic Vision of Russia', *Russian History*, 11 (1984), pp. 327–42.

Beumers, Birgit, 'The Mikhalkov brothers' view of Russia', in *Russian and Soviet Film Adaptations of Literature, 1900–2001: Screening the Word*, eds Stephen Hutchings and Anat Vernitski (London: Routledge, 2005), pp. 135–52.

———, *Nikita Mikhalkov: Between Nostalgia and Nationalism. The Filmmakers Companion 1* (London: I. B. Tauris, 2005).

Brodsky, Joseph, *Less Than One: Selected Essays* (New York: Farrar, Straus, Giroux, 1986).

Chandler, Daniel, *Semiotics* (London: Routledge, 2007).

Crow, David, *Visible Signs: An Introduction to Semiotics in the Visual Arts* (Lausanne: AVA Publishing, 2010).

Goncharov, I. A., *Oblomov*, ed. L. S. Geiro (Leningrad: Nauka, 1987).

Dal', Vladimir, *Tolkovyi slovar' zhivogo velikorusskogo iazyka* (St Petersburg, Moscow: izdatel'stvo M.A. Vol'f, 1881).

Lenin, V. I., 'O mezhdunarodnom i vnutrennem polozhenii Sovetskoi Respubliki', in *Polnoe sobranie sochinenii* (Moscow: Politizdat, 1970), XLV, pp. 1–13.

Kantor, V. K., 'Dolgii navyk k snu (Razmyshlenie o romane I. A. Goncharova "Oblomov"', *Voprosy literatury*, 1 (1989), 149–85.

Loshchits, Iurii, *Oblomov* (Moscow: Molodaia gvardiia, 1977).

MacCabe, Colin, 'Introduction', in *True to the Spirit: Film Adaptation and the Question of Fidelity*, eds Colin MacCabe, Cathleen Murray and Rick Warren. (Oxford: Oxford University Press, 2011), pp. 3–25.

Marks, Steven, *How Russia Shaped the Modern World: from Art to Anti-Semitism, Ballet to Bolshevism* (Princeton: Princeton University Press, 2003).

Parthe, Kathleen, *Russian Village Prose: The Radiant Past* (Princeton: Princeton University Press, 1992).

Plakhov, Andrei, 'Postizhenie ili adaptatsiia', *Iskusstvo kino*, 6 (1980), pp. 49–68.

Pollock, Ethan, 'Real Men Go to the Bania: Postwar Soviet Masculinities and the Bathhouse', *Kritika,* 11 (2010), pp. 47–76.

———, *Without the Bania We Would Perish: A History of the Russian Bathhouse* (New York: Oxford University Press, 2019).

Prokhorova, Elena, 'Cinema of Stagnation Late 1960s–1985', in *The Russian Cinema Reader. Volume II, the Thaw to the Present*, ed. Rimgaila Salys (Boston: Academic Studies Press, 2013), pp. 104–14.

Setchkarev, Vsevolod, *Ivan Goncharov: His Life and His Work* (Wurzburg: Jal-verlag, 1974).

Tabakov, Oleg, 'Trudnoe znakomstvo s Oblomovym', *Iskusstvo kino*, 4 (1979), pp. 80–2.

Ural'sky, Mark and Genrietta Mondri [Henrietta Mondry], *Dostoevsky i evrei* (St. Petersburg: Aleteiia, 2021).

Valentino, Russell Scott, 'Adapting the Landscape: Oblomov's Vision in Film', in *Russian and Soviet Film Adaptations of Literature, 1900–2001: Screening the Word*, eds Stephen Hutchings and Anat Vernitski (London: Routledge, 2005), pp. 153–63.

White, Frederick H., 'Conclusion. Passport Control – Departing on a Cinematic Journey', in *Border Crossing: Russian Literature into Film*, eds Alexander Burry and Frederick H. White (Edinburgh: Edinburgh University Press, 2016), pp. 239–64.

Widdis, Emma, 'Russia as Space', in *National Identity in Russian Culture: An Introduction*, eds Simon Franklin and Emma Widdis (Cambridge: Cambridge University Press, 2004), pp. 30–49.

Youngblood, Denise, 'The Cosmopolitan and the Patriot: the Brothers Mikhalkov-Konchalovsky and Russian Cinema', *Historical Journal of Film, Radio and Television*, 23 (2003), pp. 27–41.

Zaslavskaia, Tat'iana, 'O strategii sotsial'nogo upravleniia perestroikoi', in *Inogo ne dano*, ed. Iurii Afanas'ev (Moscow: Progress, 1988), pp. 9–50.

Filmography

A Few Days from the Life of I. I. Oblomov (Neskol'ko dnei iz zhizni I. I. Oblomova) directed by Nikita Mikhalkov (USSR, Mosfilm, 1979).

Anna from 6 do 18 (Anna ot 6 do 18), directed by Nikita Mikhalkov (Russia, France, Camera One. Trite Productions, 1993).

2. ADAPTING TURGENEV'S NOVEL AS A PASTORALE: AVDOTYA SMIRNOVA'S *FATHERS AND SONS*

Alexandra Smith

Ivan Sergeevich Turgenev, one of the most celebrated Russian nineteenth-century writers, was often criticised by his contemporaries for having a westernising outlook. Yet, as Frank Seeley suggests, Turgenev's works tend to reveal his preference for home-grown Russian settings, showing a 'countryman's precise and detailed knowledge of vegetable and animal life and atmospheric conditions'.[1] While some of Turgenev's works were influenced by romanticism, most of them incorporate symbolism, mysticism, and the supernatural. In general, his mode of writing can be described as philosophical. According to James B. Woodward, 'in each of the novels there is a significant substratum of philosophical ideas'.[2] Woodward affirms that Turgenev presents himself as an impassionate observer of reality.[3] Turgenev's striving for objectivity and his self-presentation as a writer-observer who studies human behaviour make him unique among Russian writers. In Woodward's opinion, Turgenev's novels and essays 'are the creations of a writer who is concerned [. . .] with the tragedy of the human condition'.[4] Likewise, Maria Ledkovsky points to Turgenev's ability

---

[1] Frank Seeley, *Turgenev: A Reading of His Fiction* (Cambridge: Cambridge University Press, 1991), p. 36.
[2] James B. Woodward, *Metaphysical Conflict: A Study of the Major Novels of Ivan Turgenev* (Munich: Verlag Otto Sagner, 1990), p. v.
[3] Woodward, p. 1.
[4] Woodward, p. 2.

to reveal 'the significance of the irrational in human life'.[5] It would be wrong therefore to interpret his works as being preoccupied solely with social issues.

According to Robert Reid, many readers think that art, not ideology was Turgenev's major concern.[6] Additionally, Turgenev's unique position as a cosmopolitan writer with close ties to France, Germany and Britain enabled him to popularise Russian literature abroad. Turgenev's international reputation, as Reid asserts, 'provided a cultural benchmark for successive generations of Russian émigrés'.[7] Reid thinks that Turgenev's influence was felt also by post-Soviet practitioners of the new Russian novel and by filmmakers.[8] In the present chapter I will discuss Avdotya Smirnova's 2008 television series based on Turgenev's *Fathers and Sons* with a view to highlighting the democratising effect of her adaptation and her role as a co-author of the text participating in a dialogue with previous adaptors of his novel. Smirnova's version of Turgenev's novel illustrates well Deborah Cartmell's statement that 'the adaptor need not be a servant of the adapted author'.[9] As Cartmell puts it, the adaptor should feel 'free to change the text to appeal to a mass contemporary rather than elite audience'.[10] As will be demonstrated below, Smirnova's version of *Fathers and Sons* shifts the stance of Turgenev's novel in some subtle ways to a more feminist position. By portraying Odintsova positively, Smirnova celebrates the independent mind of the modern woman. She abandons the concept of fidelity to the source text and reproduces the essence of Turgenev's writing in a cinematic idiom.

Turgenev's *Fathers and Sons* on the Silver Screen in the 1910s and 1920s

In the period of the early development of Russian cinema between 1907 and 1918 there were twelve film adaptations of Turgenev's works, which may be regarded as a surprisingly low number given the author's ability to create visually striking landscapes and characters. This might be explained by the lack

---

[5] Marina Ledkovsky, *The Other Turgenev: From Realism to Symbolism* (Wurzburg: Jal-Verlag, 1973), p. 15.

[6] Robert Reid, 'Introduction. Turgenev: Art, Ideology, and Legacy', in *Turgenev: Art, Ideology, and Legacy*, eds Robert Reid and Joe Andrew (Amsterdam and New York: Rodopi, 2010), pp. 1–22 (p. 1).

[7] Ibid.

[8] Ibid.

[9] Deborah Cartmell, '100+ Years of Adaptations, or, Adaptation as the Art Form of Democracy', in *A Companion to Literature, Film, and Adaptation*, ed. Deborah Cartmell (Chichester: Blackwell Publishing Ltd, 2012), pp. 1–13 (p. 8).

[10] Ibid.

of cinematographic techniques capable of transforming Turgenev's narratives into cinematic language. Evgenii Bauer, a prominent pre-revolutionary director, admitted that the cinema 'still has not found the movements and the pace that epitomise Turgenev's delicate poetry'.[11] Yet Bauer's adaptation of Turgenev's 1883 story *Klara Milich*, titled *After Death* (Posle smerti, 1915), can be seen as an imaginative dialogue with Turgenev's text. As Rachel Morley notes, 'Bauer modernises his screen version of the literary text' by 'setting it in the early twentieth-century present in which it was shot'.[12]

In 1915, Russian director Viacheslav Viskovsky produced the first film adaptation of *Fathers and Sons* which focused on Bazarov's tragic love and death. His film may have been inspired by public debates about anarchy and nihilism in Russia in the 1900s and 1910s. In 1907 Blok defined Mikhail Bakunin as a passionate nihilist.[13] Yet the pre-revolutionary image of Turgenev was more associated with melancholy than with radical thinking, as captured in the *Brockhaus and Efron Encyclopaedic Dictionary*:

> A meek soul, a melancholic, a herald of unrequited love [. . .]; a Westerner and a liberal, convinced that only the assimilation of the basic principles of universal human culture could lead Russia from the darkness [. . .] and that the revolutionary movement had no soil in Russia.[14]

This entry points to the complexity and contradictory nature of Turgenev's personality as reflected in his works.

Following the implementation of the first five-year plan for the socialist restructuring of the Soviet Union, some cultural figures started forging a new image of Turgenev as a precursor of revolutionary change. In 1929 Vsevolod Meyerhold planned a film adaptation of *Fathers and Sons*. Vladimir Maiakovsky was eager to play Bazarov but was rejected by Meyerhold. Yet Victor Erlich asserts that a close look at Maiakovsky's early poetry 'reveals the presence of what might be

---

[11] Quoted in O. F. Boele, 'After Death, the Movie (1915) – Ivan Turgenev, Evgenii Bauer and the Aesthetics of Morbidity' in *Turgenev: Art, Ideology and Legacy*, eds Robert Reid and Joe Andrew (Amsterdam and New York: Rodopi, 2010), pp. 253–68 (p. 254).

[12] Rachel Morley. 'Performing femininity in an Age of Change: Evgenii Bauer, Ivan Turgenev and the Legend of Evlaliia Kadmina', in *Turgenev: Art, Ideology, and Legacy*, eds Robert Reid and Joe Andrew (Amsterdam and New York, Rodopi, 2010), pp. 269–316 (p. 271). See also: Rachel Morley. *Performing Femininity. Woman as Performer in Early Russian Cinema* (London and New York: I. B. Tauris, 2017), pp. 171–203.

[13] A. Blok, 'Mikhail Aleksandrovich Bakunin', *Sobranie sochinenii*, 6 vols (Leningrad: Khudozhestvennaia literatura, 1982), IV, pp. 31–5.

[14] S. A. Vengerov, 'Turgenev', in *Entsiklopedicheskii slovar'* (St Petersburg: Izdatel'stvo F. A. Brockhaus and I. A. Efron, 1902), XXXIV, pp. 96–106.

called the Bazarov syndrome'.[15] Erlich thinks that Maiakovsky's nihilism is akin to Bazarov's outlook based on the rejection of traditions.

According to Meyerhold's assistant director Porfirii Podobed, their ideal actor for the role of Bazarov role should look like a real man; he needed to have a charming smile; he should look intelligent and have an unusual appearance in the style of Leonid Leonidov, or young Maiakovsky.[16] According to Alexander Gladkov, Meyerhold liked Turgenev's *Fathers and Sons* all through his life and he recognised himself in Bazarov.[17]

Despite Anatoly Lunacharsky's rejection of Meyerhold's film script, in 1936 Lunacharsky delivered a lecture about Russian literature of the 1860s in which he defined *Fathers and Sons* as the most important phenomenon of Russian life in the 1860s. Lunacharsky described it as a lively novel that triggered many debates which were still relevant to Soviet readers in the 1930s.[18] Irina Koznova describes one attempt to create a new image of Turgenev suitable for Soviet education thus: 'In the first Soviet years, critics of the pre-revolutionary school noted that Turgenev, 'like us', existed 'on the threshold of two cultures'. An important attribute was his duality, which reflected the Janus-faced nature of Russia'.[19] Soviet critics felt that the dynamics of Turgenev's works mirrored the dynamics of Russian life. For Lunacharsky, Turgenev was a real humanist and a role model for Soviet intellectuals. In his essay on Turgenev, Lunacharsky claimed that Turgenev's optimism regarding social changes inspired many adherents who became the best Marxists.[20] According to Koznova, in the 1930s Turgenev became re-invented as a writer whose emphasis on the positive role of literature in society was relevant to Soviet literary culture. She writes:

> As a historical novelist, Turgenev studied life broadly and therefore his work was proclaimed to be relevant to Soviet culture. Turgenev was recognized not only as an artist of the word but also as an innovator who possessed a new way of observing life and its tendencies.[21]

---

[15] Victor Erlich, 'The Dead Hand of the Future: The Predicament of Vladimir Maiakovsky', *Slavic Review*, 21(1962), pp. 433–40 (p. 433).

[16] Vladimir Zabrodin, 'Evgenii Bazarov V. E. Meierkhol'da. Novye materialy', *Kinovedcheskie zapiski*, 76 (2005), pp. 70–111.

[17] A. K. Gladkov, *Meyerhold. V dvukh tomakh* (Moscow: Soiuz teatral'nykh deiatelei RSFSR, 1990), I, p. 22.

[18] A. V. Lunacharsky, 'Literatura shestidesiatykh godov', *Klassiki russkoi literatury* (Moscow: Goslitizdat, 1937), pp. 197–233 (p. 219).

[19] Irina E. Koznova, 'The Figure of Ivan Turgenev in Soviet Culture', *Russian Studies in Philosophy*, 56 (2018), pp. 416–24 (p. 418).

[20] A. Lunacharsky, 'Lektsiia o Turgeneve', *Russkaia literature,* 4 (1961), pp. 134–8.

[21] Koznova, p. 421.

Paradoxically, the Soviet vision of Turgenev as an optimistic humanist stands in contrast to the pre-revolutionary image of Turgenev as a melancholic writer lamenting the disappearance of Russian idyllic life.

Soviet Adaptations of *Fathers and Sons* from the 1950s to 1980s

With the emergence of new hopes for cultural experimentation associated with the Thaw period, some Soviet intellectuals wanted to utilise Turgenev's novels for the education of young people. In 1958 Adolf Bergunker and Natal'ia Rashevskaia produced their film version of *Fathers and Sons* for Lenfilm, the second largest film studio in the Soviet Union. Its emphasis on the new ideological trends advocated by young people in the novel reflects the mood of the Thaw period well. This production coincided with the revival of Soviet internationalism in the post-Stalin era and engages with the topical issues of the day, including the role of technological progress in the post-war restructuring of society. It alludes to the growing role of young people in new cultural developments. According to Katerina Clark, several young writers and poets of the late 1930s and early 1940s, including Olga Berggolts, became instrumental in promoting concepts such as sincerity, genuineness and the lyric, all of which became crucial for the formation of a new cultural and literary discourse during the Thaw.[22] Clark writes:

> Central to self-expression in her account is expression of one's own inner emotions and intimate feelings [. . .]. What she and others who took similar positions at this time objected to was the overly schematic accounts of love relations presented in socialist realist texts.[23]

In the context of the growing rejection by younger writers and filmmakers of politicised love plots in Soviet literature and films, Bergunker's and Rashevskaia's adaptation of *Fathers and Sons* resonated well with the concerns of a younger generation interested in the complexity of human psychology.

In her article 'A Conversation about the Lyric' published in *Literaturnaia gazeta* (Literary Newspaper) on 16 April 1953, Berggolts suggests that Soviet literature is 'in crying need of true lyric poetry'.[24] Likewise, calls for a different attitude to private life in Soviet culture were also manifested in late 1950s cinema.

---

[22] Katerina Clark, '"Wait for Me and I Shall Return": The Early Thaw as a Reprise of Late Thirties Culture?', in *The Thaw: Soviet Society and Culture During the 1950s and 1960s*, eds Denis Kozlov and Eleonory Gilburd (Toronto: University of Toronto Press, 2013), pp. 85–108.
[23] Clark, p. 89.
[24] Clark, p. 88.

As Clark puts it, 'the war fiction and films that began appearing around 1957 were written as conscious re-evaluations of the standard heroic war fiction of late Stalinism'.[25] The demands for greater realism were entwined with criticism of the standard expressions of heroism and triumphalism. As Oksana Bulgakova notes, many films continued to promote the preservation of the communal world with its hierarchy of values which precluded full realisation of the individual personality. 'Only in screen adaptation policy,' writes Bulgakova, 'do we observe a break'.[26] Yet the ideological shift in Soviet neo-realist cinema films resulted in a different vision of the enemy: many films started featuring, in addition to foreign spies and western capitalists, 'a conservative, a bureaucrat, or an individualist'.[27] Viewed in this context, the 100-minute film version of *Fathers and Sons* by Bergunker and Rashevskaia might be seen as an embodiment of the eagerness of Soviet cultural figures to break the mould of the socialist realist canon.

According to Liudmila Saraskina, the main emphasis of the film is on the desire of young people like Bazarov to fight for their beliefs. Viktor Avdiushko, the actor who plays Bazarov, resembles the young Maiakovsky: tall, serious, strong and passionately desiring to change the world. While Bazarov's love for Odintsova is subdued in the film, his ideologically-driven personality and his desire to fight for his beliefs are foregrounded. Saraskina writes: 'The film is based on the schematic rendering of the plot of Turgenev's novel revolving around the main ideological debates.'[28]

The film features Bazarov's intellectual superiority towards his friend Arkadii Kirsanov (Eduard Martsevich). The phrase 'we want to fight' reinforces Bazarov's vision of himself as a leader of the new movement. Bazarov's infatuation with Odintsova is presented as a temporary distraction from his scientific work. The image of Bazarov as a gifted scientist in the adaptation by Bergunker and Rashevskaia exemplifies well the preoccupation of Nikita Khrushchev's government with technical modernisation policies. Given that the relation between science and creative imagination was a major concern for Russian intellectuals of the 1950s and 60s, the film by Bergunker and Rashevskaia can be seen as an extension of the contemporary debates between the so-called lyricists and physicists.[29] James Andrews writes: 'This debate appeared in the

---

[25] Clark, p. 101.
[26] Oksana Bulgakova, 'Cine-Weathers: Soviet Thaw Cinema in the International Context', in *The Thaw: Soviet Society and Culture During the 1950s and 1960s*, eds Denis Kozlov and Eleonory Gilburd (Toronto: University of Toronto Press, 2013), pp. 436–81 (p. 447).
[27] Bulgakova, p. 448.
[28] L. I. Saraskina, 'Bal'nye kollizii russkikh romanov v ekrannykh proektsiiakh', *Khudozhestvennaia kul'tura*, 1 (2018), pp. 132–65 (p. 160).
[29] These terms appear in Boris Slutsky's 1959 poem 'Physicists and Lyricists' (Fiziki i liriki).

Young Communist League (*Komsomol*) press in the late 1950s and early 1960s pitting nineteenth-century realists against creative physical scientists who had abandoned the constraints of positivism.'[30] This debate was especially evident in Soviet public discourse following the launch of the first sputnik in 1957.

In 1983 the Russian film director Viacheslav Nikiforov created a four-episode television series based on Turgenev's novel for the Belarus'film studio. In his hands, Bazarov (Vladimir Bogin) appears to be a person with a complex personality full of contradictions. Odintsova (Natalia Danilova) is also portrayed as a multi-faceted person who experiences an emotional inner struggle. As Saraskina points out, the ball scenes included in the film suggest that Bazarov is affected by the beauty and elegance of Odintsova and struggles to suppress his human emotions. As she puts it, this film version highlights a strong trait of the romantic mindset in Bazarov's behaviour.[31] Leonid Pavliuchik states that all the characters in this version look human and open-minded. He asserts that Bazarov stands out as visionary, strong-willed and courageous. Pavliuchik welcomes Nikiforov's attempt to free the image of Bazarov from the Soviet pedagogical canon and suggests that people like Bazarov are badly needed in Russia in the 1980s, just as they were needed in the 1860s.[32] The film reflects the growing concern among Soviet intellectuals about the stagnation of the Brezhnev period: they felt a strong need for reforms in social and economic life.

Nikifirov's film was produced two years before Mikhail Gorbachev's period of openness and social restructuring began. It creates an atmosphere of the anticipation of change in Russia. One of the unusual features of the film is the highly positive image of Katia, Odintsova's sister, who is portrayed in Nikiforov's adaptation as a gifted pianist. Her performances of Mozart and Schubert inspire Arkadii Kirsanov. They also affect one of the boy servants from Odintsova's household who is featured playing the piano on his own in the episode showing Bazarov and Arkadii's stay in Odintsova's house. It implies that Turgenev foresaw some of the major democratic developments of the twentieth century that enabled people from all backgrounds to be united as a nation around shared cultural values. The film also incorporated music composed by the popular Soviet composer Valery Zubkov who wrote a song based on the words of Boris Kulikov for Arkadii Kirsanov (Vladimir Konkin) 'I had a dream. . .' ('*I snilos' mne . . .*'). According to Konkin, the words of the song were not included in the film because Soviet censors thought that the image of Kirsanov should not

---

[30] James T. Andrews. 'An Evolving Scientific Public Sphere: State Science Enlightenment, Communicative Discourse, and Public Culture from Imperial Russia to Khrushchev's Soviet Times', *Science in Context*, 26 (3), 2013, pp. 509–26 (p. 522).

[31] Saraskina, p. 162.

[32] L. Pavliuchik, 'I vnov' –"Ottsy i deti"', *Sovetskaia kul'tura*, 46 (1983), 4.

overshadow that of Bazarov.³³ Clearly, the censors wanted to make sure that the prevalent Soviet canonical interpretation of Bazarov as a positive hero and a revolutionary should be observed in this adaptation. It is worth noting, though, that the song Zubkov composed for this film features a lyric hero who dreamed about wealth and happiness, implying thereby the presence of nostalgic longing for the pre-revolutionary past. The song track without words included in the film also invokes a nostalgic feeling towards the past.

Avdotya Smirnova's Version of *Fathers and Sons*

The 2008 four-episode television adaptation of *Fathers and Sons* has several similarities with the 1983 adaptation: both aspire to subvert the Soviet pedagogical canon which presents Bazarov as a man of action. Most importantly, Smirnova's version contains nostalgic overtones and idyllic images of the pre-communist past. It contributes to the post-Soviet trend of using film as a nation builder. In their analysis of Russian television culture in the 2000s, Stephen Hutchings and Natalya Rulyova highlight the importance of film adaptations to nation building as follows: 'Foreign classics featured alongside resurrected native classics as part of a policy of bolstering pride in the Russian contribution to world culture.'³⁴ They also suggest that film adaptations of the 2000s benefitted from the demise of socialist realism. Hutchings and Rulyova write:

> However, there were good ideological reasons why Dostoevskii's works had lain dormant during the Stalin period, and why, with some exceptions, even Turgenev [. . .] had not featured prominently in the Soviet literary canon. [. . .] [T]he spate of Chekhov and Turgenev serialisations raised questions about the exclusion of texts whose luxuriant television production [. . .] encouraged nostalgia for pre-revolutionary values and lifestyles.³⁵

While Smirnova's interpretation of *Fathers and Sons* exemplifies the post-Soviet nostalgia for pre-revolutionary values, it also alludes to the vision of glamorous lifestyles promoted by Russian contemporary culture.

---

[33] The song and Konkin's commentary are available here: <https://www.youtube.com/watch?v=CwUaRDTWoLo> [accessed 1 July 2021]. Another quote from Konkin's story about this song is available here: <https://frolovchik.livejournal.com/187552.html> [accessed 1 July 2021].

[34] Stephen Hutchings and Natalya Rulyova. 'Introduction', jn *Television and Culture in Putin's Russia: Remote Control*, eds Stephen Hutchings and Natalya Rulyova (London and New York: Routledge, 2010), pp. 1–28 (p. 6).

[35] Ibid.

In a 2007 interview, Smirnova admits that she likes Nikiforov's 1983 adaptation, but she considers it affected by the Soviet pedagogical canon which presents Bazarov as a precursor of communism. Unlike her predecessors, Smirnova interprets the novel as a novel about love. Smirnova thinks that it was wrongly interpreted as an ideological narrative. She states: 'it tells us that any ideology, be it aristocratic or nihilistic, has a corrosive effect upon human relationships and makes life bleaker.'[36]

The Russian actor Andrei Ustiugov who plays Bazarov in Smirnova's film, also emphasises his desire to free Bazarov from Soviet interpretations. He admits that playing Turgenev in Aleksei Borodin's production of Tom Stoppard's trilogy of plays *The Coast of Utopia* at the Russian Academic Youth Theatre in Moscow had helped him to understand Turgenev better.[37] By wearing the same wig in Borodin's production of *The Coast of Utopia* and in Smirnova's television series, the actor brings together the images of Turgenev and Bazarov, suggesting thereby that Turgenev in *Fathers and Sons* bid farewell to his temporary infatuation with scientific materialism.

Figure 2.1 Andrei Ustiugov as Bazarov in *Fathers and Sons*, directed by Avdotya Smirnova, 2008.

---

[36] Irina Azarova, '*Otsy i deti* v Ovstuge', *Brianskaia tema*, 5 (2007) <https://tema32.ru/articles/2007/05/1031/> [accessed 2 July 2021].
[37] Ibid.

In her blurb on the website of the TV channel *Kul'tura*, Smirnova states that she considers *Fathers and Sons* to be one of the best Russian novels of all time. She praises it for its psychological insights. In her opinion, Turgenev's psychological realism should appeal to contemporary readers. Smirnova defines Evgenii Bazarov as both an attractive and an unpleasant character. According to Smirnova, the Soviet pedagogical canon was wrong to single out Bazarov as a positive hero by downplaying his psychological complexity. Smirnova sees her film as a homage to the Russian aristocracy and to Russian nineteenth-century literature.[38]

Smirnova admits that she and Aleksandr Adabashian, the film script's co-writer and costume designer, did not observe the principle of fidelity to the novel but imaginatively used some of the devices embedded in the novel. For example, they took the idea suggested in the novel of the doubling of Pavel Petrovich Kirsanov and Bazarov and created a scene in which Odintsova presents Bazarov with a beautiful sapphire ring when seeing him on his deathbed. This scene echoes Pavel Kirsanov's love story featuring a ring given to him by the object of his love.

Furthermore, while visiting Bazarov on his deathbed, Odintsova wears a dark blue dress that boasts a large brooch with blue stones. Together with the episode of the sapphire ring given to Bazarov before his death, the appearance of Odintsova as a lady in blue enhances the impression she makes on Bazarov: she presents herself as a sphynx-like visual spectacle. At the same time, this scene invokes the use of jewellery in Victorian culture as class markers, in the style of Charles Dickens's novel *Little Dorrit*,[39] where the jewellery of Mrs Merdle represents high society and its values. Given that Odintsova is a rich widow, it is not far-fetched to suggest that her gesture of presenting Bazarov with an expensive ring alludes to the importance of gender roles in marriage located within a capitalist system of values and consumerist culture. In her eyes, such a gift should make Bazarov realise that the romantic power of seduction continues to bind people together, despite the popularity of radical beliefs. It also reinforces the power of the image of the bejewelled female in the socio-economic hierarchy and exemplifies the role of jewellery in the identity formation of many characters in 19th-century novels.[40]

---

[38] 'Avdotya Smirnova', *Radio Maiak* <https://radiomayak.ru/persons/person/id/882/> [accessed 24 October 2021].

[39] *Little Dorrit* was filmed as a series for the BBC in 2008. The script was produced by Andrew Davies, who would later adapt *War and Peace* (see Olga Sobolev's contribution to this volume, Chapter 10).

[40] Jean Arnold, *Victorian Jewellery, Identity and the Novel: Prisms of Culture* (London and New York: Routledge, 2011), p. 2.

Odintsova's fashionable appearance towards the end of Smirnova's film as a lady in blue wearing a stunning black hat, and as a Parisian-like beauty in the second episode that takes place on her estate (for which the estate of poet Fedor Tiutchev was used), resembles French impressionist paintings. For example, in episode two Odintsova goes for a walk with Bazarov in her park: wearing a light dress and holding a parasol, she resembles many women featured in the paintings of Monet and Renoir.[41] Ruth Iskin writes: 'Monet's early paintings of the second half of the 1860s [. . .] demonstrate that the representations of the modern woman as a chic Parisienne in a fashionable toilette played a prominent role in the Impressionist painting.'[42] According to Iskin, for most Impressionists the chic Parisienne had become a replacement for rural working women who attracted them earlier as objects of their paintings. 'She also played a central role,' asserts Iskin, 'in the shift from academic to modern painting led by Manet and the Impressionists'.[43] By bringing some visual analogies between Odintsova and the chic Parisienne in her adaptation of *Fathers and Sons*, Smirnova moulds the image of Turgenev into the painter of modern life as discussed in Charles Baudelaire's essay 'The Painter of Modern Life' (1863). Baudelaire writes: 'Observer, philosopher, *flaneur* – call him what you will [. . .]; he is the painter of the passing moment and of all the suggestions of eternity that it contains.'[44]

In the style of the Impressionists who painted their Parisian contemporary women with their fashionable clothes and accessories in the countryside as well as in the city, Smirnova reimagines Turgenev as a contemporary of the Impressionists and of Baudelaire who depicts the imprint of urban consumer culture on nature. In the hands of Smirnova, Odintsova becomes obsessed with fashion and orders new fashionable boots for her sister Katia. Smirnova goes as far as making both sisters sing a French version of her song about the passing moments of happiness. Smirnova and Adabashian wrote the song for the series. Such a gesture enables Smirnova to bring Russian consumer culture of the late imperial period closer to post-Soviet consumerism. Her gesture can be compared to the desire of the curators of the Valentin Serov exhibition in Moscow in 2015 to feature mostly Serov's portraits of prominent Russian aristocrats alongside idyllic spaces. As Tatiana Efremova puts it, the Serov exhibition 'had transgressed the confines of an artistic event and transformed into a site of contestation about patriotism, national pride, Russian

---

[41] *Ottsy i deti*, directed by Avdotya Smirnova (Mosfilm, 2008), part 2.
[42] Ruth E. Iskin, *Modern Women and Parisienne Consumer Culture in Impressionist Painting* (Cambridge: Cambridge University Press, 2007), p. 198.
[43] Ibid.
[44] Charles Baudelaire, 'The Painter of Modern Life', *The Painter of Modern Life and Other Essays*, trans. and ed. Jonathan Mayne (London: Phaidon Press, 1964), pp. 4–5.

history and culture'.⁴⁵ Efremova appreciates Serov's lyrical realism, his effective use of tradition and innovation, his simplicity, and his 'artistic universality'.⁴⁶ The same characteristics can be applied to Turgenev's *Fathers and Sons*. Likewise, the concluding passages of *Fathers and Sons* convey the signs of artistic universality and lyrical realism. Joseph L. Conrad finds Turgenev's juxtaposition of natural and artificial worlds and use of the pastoral in his novels are unusually striking.⁴⁷ Conrad thinks that the flowers on Bazarov's grave depicted in the final passage of the novel 'symbolise all that is good and permanent in life on earth'.⁴⁸

By featuring idyllic images of the Russian countryside and aristocratic lifestyle, Smirnova's adaptation implies that the world created in Turgenev's novels would be more attractive to post-Soviet readers than the gruesome reality found in contemporary Russian fiction. Smirnova's adaptation does not show any flowers on Bazarov's grave, and it features a wintry landscape at the end of the series. Yet Smirnova has appropriated the image of flowers as a symbol of beauty and eternity for the opening scene of each episode. The image of freshly cut flowers is accompanied by a beautiful contemporary song. Such a scene repeated in every episode signifies the presence of a pastoral space which is much removed from contemporary urban life. Smirnova's poeticised depiction of rural Russian life is justified by the novel's use of pastoral resources and its lyrical realism.

According to Russell Valentino, while Bazarov's nature is essentially antipastoral, Arkadii embodies the pastoral qualities of Russia's life that could ensure an evolutionary model of modern developments. As Valentino contends, Arkadii's 'natural closeness to the land and its inhabitants' is 'foregrounded in the novel as a positive trait'.⁴⁹ He elucidates: 'Arkadii's love for nature is portrayed as an inherent quality'.⁵⁰ While ignoring the fact that *Fathers and Sons* contains a generic hybridisation comprising pastoral, picaresque and medieval resources that 'coalesce or conflict',⁵¹ Smirnova has chosen to focus

---

⁴⁵ Tatyana Efremova. '"It was Totally Worth It . . .": Patriotic Consumption in the Queue to Serov's Exhibit', *Studies in Russian, Eurasian and Central European New Media (digitalicons.org)*, 16 (2016), pp. 31–50 (p. 32).
⁴⁶ Ibid., p. 33.
⁴⁷ Joseph L. Conrad, 'Turgenev's Landscapes', *Russian Language Journal*, 41 (1987), pp. 119–34 (p. 130).
⁴⁸ Ibid.
⁴⁹ Russell S. Valentino, 'A Wolf in Arkadia: Generic Fields, Generic Counterstatement and the Resources of Pastoral in *Fathers and Sons*', *The Russian Review*, 55 (1996), pp. 475–93 (p. 479). The attention of Valentino to the role of Arkadii motivates his spelling 'Arkadia' in the title of his article.
⁵⁰ Ibid.
⁵¹ Ibid., p. 492.

on the pastoral qualities of the novel. Her adaptation exposes Bazarov's ideas as radically subversive and dangerous for Russia: that is why the initial title of the adaptation was *Bazarov's Error* (*Oshibka Bazarova*).

In addition to writing the script, Smirnova directed the four-episode mini-TV series single-handedly. She added her own touches to the plot, including a few scenes that were inspired either by the novel or by some drafts of the novel. In her lecture on directing and screenwriting, Smirnova offers a more detailed vision of *Fathers and Sons*:

> Turgenev's novel is not political, as is commonly believed, but antipolitical. This is a story about how only those who embrace life can attain happiness [. . .] and those who follow any rigid ideological scheme [. . .] face human bankruptcy.[52]

Smirnova also talks about an invented scene in which Bazarov visits Odintsova and confesses his love for her. The scene takes place in a room with a large table holding crystal glasses and vases. While the light reflecting on these objects contributes to the creation of a poetic mood, Smirnova inscribes this episode with a symbolic meaning: she wanted to use the trembling glasses and vases as a symbol of the fragile nature of the Russian aristocracy threatened by people like Bazarov. The idyllic representation of the Russian countryside and family life in the 19th century is given more prominence in Smirnova's film than the ideological arguments between Pavel Kirsanov and Bazarov.

Smirnova explains in one of her lectures on directing that she wanted to create her adaptation in the style of British TV adaptations of Jane Austen's works. She sees Turgenev as the most British-like Russian writer.[53] Indeed, in Smirnova's hands Turgenev's characters of aristocratic background become visualised as characters from British costume dramas. Her adaptation offers a partially idealised image of nineteenth-century life in Russia and in Europe shaped by the popular imagination of the post-Soviet period. It is largely characterised by the de-ideologisation of culture, post-Soviet nostalgia and the critique of the Soviet past.

Arguably, Smirnova forges her image of Turgenev's novel not as an interpreter but as an author of her own text imbued with her own personal worldview. Smirnova's film can be seen as a communicative space which is organised as 'a set of verbalised film dialogues as well as different montage

---

[52] A. Smirnova, 'Rezhisser protiv stsenarista', *Seans*, 25 August 2011 <http://snimifilm.com/post/zhurnal-seans-avdotya-smirnova-rezhisser-protiv-stsenarista-video> [accessed 2 November 2020].

[53] Ibid.

techniques'.⁵⁴ Smirnova's intention to have a single clearly expressed authorial position is subordinated to her desire to demonstrate to the post-Soviet audience the importance of anti-political messages embedded in Turgenev's novel. It echoes Dmitrii Bykov's observation about the suggestiveness of Turgenev's mode of writing that combines contradictory interpretations. As Bykov points out, 'Turgenev weaves a fine-meshed network, reproducing not a single layer of reality, but two or three underlying themes'.⁵⁵ O.V. Cherkezova identifies the lyrical theme as a striking feature of Smirnova's adaptation.⁵⁶ She fails to mention, however, that the reception of Turgenev as poet-philosopher had been discussed widely in literary scholarship prior to Smirnova's adaptation. Dale Peterson, for example, identifies Turgenev's mode of writing as 'poetic realism'.⁵⁷ Likewise, Smirnova interprets Turgenev as an observer of Russian life who views reality through the lenses of poetry.

Figure 2.2 Natal'ia Rogozhkina as Odintsova in *Fathers and Sons*, directed by Avdotya Smirnova, 2008.

⁵⁴ Nadezhda F. Kolganova, 'The Communicative Space of Film Adaptation: Avdotya Smirnova's Adaptation of Turgenev's *Fathers and* Sons', *Russian Studies in Philosophy*, 56 (2018), pp. 425–33 (p. 428).
⁵⁵ Dmitrii Bykov, 'Nashe kino segodnia absoliutno mertvo', *Kinopoisk,* 4 September 2017 <https://www.kinopoisk.ru/media/article/3026203/> [accessed 3 November 2020].
⁵⁶ O.V. Cherkezova, '*Ottsy i deti* I. S.Turgeneva v kinoretseptsii Smirnovoi', *Vestnik TGPU,* 139 (2013), pp. 63–8 (p. 64).
⁵⁷ Dale E. Peterson, *The Clement Vision: Poetic Realism in Turgenev and James* (Port Washington, NY: Kennikat Press, 1975), pp. 4–5.

Adabashian, the co-author of the film's script and its costume designer, emphasises the role of the costumes in making the film more attractive. Having previously worked with Nikita Mikhalkov on the film *Oblomov*,[58] he says that in contrast to Mikhalkov's film, which features opera-like costume designs, he wanted to modernise the style of clothes featured in *Fathers and Sons*, so that the audience could be better engaged with the characters.[59] The audience is exposed therefore to an imagined vision of the past communicated through the appearance of the main characters as people who partly resemble contemporary Russians.

By likening Turgenev's novel to an English novel and by depicting the Russian aristocracy as an extension of European aristocracy, Smirnova invokes in her audience a nostalgic longing for the idyllic past destroyed by the 1917 Bolshevik revolution. As has been mentioned earlier, the post-Soviet composer Steblev's romance 'When the soul . . .' is used to open every episode together with the visual image of flowers. As a framing device, it reinforces the point about the importance of family happiness and bonding with nature for the construction of Russian identity in modern times. Instead of using a nineteenth-century romance, Smirnova inserts a romance created by Steblev. It is composed in the style of nineteenth-century songs and it celebrates love as a sacred 'dream of soul' ('*son dushi*').

By presenting the notion of the soul and the idea of the spiritual connection with the natural environment as the most important of human values, Smirnova recycles the myth of Russia found in Russian classical novels – as discussed in Virginia Woolf's essay 'The Russian Point of View'. Woolf locates the open-ended quality of Turgenev's works and his melancholic outlook in most works of Russian literature. She sees the image of the Russian soul 'as the chief character of Russian literature'.[60] Woolf was especially attracted to Russian writers' ability to capture 'universal emotions'.[61] Woolf's vision of Russian literature remains topical in today's Anglophone world and, as Darya Protopopova notes, it inspires Russian intellectuals to explore western stereotypes of Russians for their own self-definition and for cultural diplomacy.[62]

Smirnova's adaptation of Turgenev's novel brings the Tolstoyan idyllic image of a happy family and transplants it into the space of Turgenev's novel.

---

[58] See Henrietta Mondry's discussion of this film in Chapter 1 of this volume.

[59] Aleksandr Adabashian, 'Rezhissura – eto sklad kharaktera', *Iskusstvo kino*, 5 (2010). <http://old.kinoart.ru/archive/2007/05/n5-article19> [accessed 6 November 2020].

[60] Virginia Woolf, 'The Russian Point of View', in *The Essays of Virginia Woolf*, ed. Andrew McNeillie (London: The Hogarth Press, 1994), IV, pp. 181–9 (pp. 185–6).

[61] Ibid.

[62] Darya Protopopova. 'Preface', *Virginia Woolf's Portraits of Russian Writers: Creating the Literary Other* (Newcastle upon Tyne: Cambridge Scholars Publishing, 2019), pp. vii–xv (p. xiv).

Smirnova's cinematographic version of Turgenev's novel downplays the clash of ideological beliefs between Pavel Petrovich and Bazarov, and focuses on the theme of love. According to Cherkezova, Smirnova's adaptation foregrounds family life in an idyllic way, suggesting thereby that Bazarov's arrival at the estate did not affect the core beliefs and way of life of progressive Russian aristocrats such as Nikolai Kirsanov.[63]

Smirnova presents *Fathers and Sons* as a quintessentially Russian novel that connects Turgenev both to his literary predecessors and to his followers. Her use of landscape in the film also has a unifying function by bringing together literary landscapes and contemporary historic places. Thus the filming of Nikolai Kirsanov's estate took place on Turgenev's own estate in the Orel region known as Spasskoe-Lutovinovo; Odintsova's estate was filmed in Tiutchev's estate Ovstug located in the Briansk region; and Bazarov's parents' house and its surroundings were created out of various old houses found in contemporary Russian villages.[64] The adaptation also alludes to other works of Russian literature featuring failed heroes. The images of flowers and female singing, for example, invokes Goncharov's novel *Oblomov* which features Olga as an accomplished singer. David Allan Lowe sums up the role of *Fathers and Sons* in Russian literary history as follows: 'Not only does it reflect what has gone before in the works of Pushkin, Lermontov, and Gogol, but it introduces themes and methods [. . .] that predict the future development of the Russian novel down to the present day.'[65] It can be added to this observation that the novel explores the prevalent themes in European literature pertaining to the myths of the Golden Age and Paradise.

In Alexander Fischler's opinion, while Nikolai Kirsanov's view of nature 'as a source of permanence and source of beauty' prevails in the novel, Bazarov's view of nature as a ground for testing and a scientific workshop is rejected.[66] Being profoundly influenced by Goethe, Turgenev developed a strong belief in the importance of the human bond with nature long before writing *Fathers and Sons*. In a letter to Bettina von Arnim, Turgenev describes his vision thus: 'To achieve the ultimate bond between the human soul and nature [. . .] is the most perfect, the most profound event of our life.'[67] By downplaying

---

[63] Cherkezova, p. 65.
[64] 'Ottsy i deti (film 2008)', *Wikipedia* <https://ru.wikipedia.org/wiki/Отцы_и_дети_(фильм,_2008)> [accessed 6 November 2020].
[65] David Allan Lowe, 'Turgenev's *Fathers and Sons*' (unpublished PhD thesis, Indiana University, 1977), p. 207.
[66] Alexander Fischler, 'The Garden Motif and the Structure of Turgenev's *Fathers and Sons*', *Novel: A Forum on Fiction*, 9 (1976), pp. 243–55 (p. 248).
[67] Quoted in Eva Kagan-Kans, 'Turgenev, the Metaphysics of an Artist, 1818–1883', *Cahiers du monde russe et soviétique*, 13 (1972), pp. 382–405 (p. 392).

ideological references to scientific ideas and utilitarian beliefs of the 1860s, Smirnova's adaptation reveals an important philosophical substructure of the novel. Yet she has misunderstood Turgenev's paradoxical thinking that is well captured in Eva Kagan-Kans's observation: 'While he is opposed to analysis and reflection, and advocated spontaneity, this spontaneity motivates his heroines and manifests itself as a [. . .] destructive force synonymous with the power of fate. His men are victims of both intellect and instinct.'[68]

In her analysis of Turgenev's metaphysics, Kagan-Kans asserts that the domestic happiness enjoyed at the novel's end by Arkadii and Katia would be unacceptable to Turgenev as an alternative path of self-development. In her view, for Turgenev the idea of constant strife and responsiveness to beauty and life were preferable to the comfort of domestic happiness as exemplified by the marriage of Katia and Arkadii based on bourgeois complacency.[69] She refers to Turgenev's words about the spleen of life being analogous with death, and his understanding of life as a constant struggle against adversaries of life and difficulties. As Kagan-Kans puts it, Turgenev ascribes human dignity with moral value by defining it 'as the main purpose of life'.[70]

Smirnova's adaptation uses the scene of Bazarov's death as a powerful example of the importance of human dignity in one's life. In the novel Bazarov talks on his deathbed about the importance of dying decently without giving up his struggle against fate, and in the film his inner struggle is shown with sympathy. In Smirnova's hands, Bazarov becomes a better human being by addressing his anxiety about death openly in front of Odintsova and without reference to his plans to change Russia. Bazarov's final monologue depicts him as a fearless scientist. He says: 'After all, I am a giant. Now I have only one task left: to die more decently' ('Ведь я гигант. Теперь одна задача – умереть поприличнее'[71]). The difference between the two sentences is significant. In the original, by using the word 'decently' Bazarov acknowledges that the final moment of his life inscribes his life with true meaning. He is elevated to heroic status because he is given a chance to behave in a stoic way by accepting his own mistakes. In Smirnova's version, Bazarov's life preceding his death has already been portrayed as a meaningful life because his nihilism is shown as an extension of scientific activities.

Such an ending implies compassion towards his life and death. His death is interpreted as the fatal mistake of a scientist. Smirnova displaces Bazarov's

[68] Ibid., p. 404.
[69] Ibid.
[70] Ibid., p. 405.
[71] I. S. Turgenev, *Ottsy i deti*, in *Sobranie sochinenii*, 30 vols (Moscow: Nauka, 1981), VII, pp. 7–188 (p.182).

anxiety for death and presents his last monologue as an expression of the passive acceptance of his fate. She sets aside Dmitrii Pisarev's opinion about Bazarov's death as the 'great deed' of a stoic who does not behave submissively and who continues to rebel against natural laws on his deathbed.[72] Irene Masing-Delic identifies some autobiographical features in Bazarov's death, seeing it as a celebration of such values as beauty, culture and the aesthetic appreciation of life. 'The ideological defeat and Bazarov's death', maintains Masing-Delic, 'symbolise Turgenev's rejection of his own rationalism [. . .]. The unexplained aesthetic system prevails.'[73]

Taking a cue from Masing-Delic, we can interpret Bazarov's statement that he must die in a way more decently than he lived as Smirnova's desire to explore the healing power of the Russian nineteenth-century novel. Smirnova uses her television series as a nation-building narrative to unite a post-Soviet audience in the process of critical re-evaluation of Bazarov's worldview and its treatment in Soviet textbooks. The scenes depicting Bazarov's death can be also seen as a symbolic collective burial of those Russian and Soviet intelligentsia beliefs pertaining to the power of progress and the utilitarian treatment of culture.

Jasmijn Van Gorp lists the adaptation of Russian classics as a third important national genre, together with the historical film and war film – all of them are widely supported by the government as nation building tools subordinated to the preservation of cultural memory and the natural heritage. As Van Gorp points out, 'the heritage film is the reproduction of literary texts, artefacts, and landscapes which already have privileged status within the accepted definition of the national heritage'.[74] In Smirnova's version, the celebration of Russian national unity and spiritual values is especially evident in the final episodes that take place after Bazarov's death. These episodes present a group scene featuring Katia playing at the piano, Nikolai Kirsanov playing the cello, and Arkadii with Pavel Kirsanov, Fenechka and her son and his nurse sitting together in the same room listening to the music. Smirnova's adaptation highlights the importance of the Russian countryside and folk culture to Russian identity. It exemplifies Van Gorp's observation that 'the significance of folk culture to the nation ties in with the wider tendency to consider peasants as guardians of ancient

---

[72] D. I. Pisarev, 'Bazarov. *Ottsy i deti*. Roman I. S. Turgeneva', in *Literaturnaia kritika*, 3 vols (Leningrad: Khudozhestvennaia literatura, 1981), I, pp. 230–81.

[73] Irene Masing-Delic, 'Bazarov pered sfinksom: nauchnoe anatomirovanie I esteticheskaia forma v romane Turgeneva *Ottsy i deti*', *Revue des études slaves*, 57 (1985), pp. 369–83 (p. 383).

[74] Jasmijn Van Gorp, 'Inverting film policy: film as nation builder in post-Soviet Russia, 1991–2005', *Media, Culture, and Society*, 33 (2011), pp. 243–58 (p. 247).

national habits, and the countryside the true heart of the nation'.[75] In contrast to Smirnova, the concluding scene of Berkunger and Rashevskaia's 1958 version celebrates Bazarov's parents as truly religious people who tend Bazarov's grave: they are depicted before the grave in winter with a Russian Orthodox church in the background.[76] The harsh wintry image of the countryside and the commemoration of the dead at the end of the 1958 adaptation can be seen as a symbolic allusion to the revival of spiritual values in the post-Stalin period and the necessity of preserving commemorative religious rituals.

Nikiforov's 1983 adaptation includes a summary of the fates of various characters following Bazarov's death, enabling it to maintain some fidelity to Turgenev's novel. Yet the 1983 version's final scenes focus not on Bazarov's parents standing at their son's grave in winter but on the nearby river and the trees. In a symbolic way, such an extensive portrayal of the thawed river can be interpreted as a celebration of the Russian landscape and Russian identity. The solemn music which accompanies this imagery of nature in anticipation of spring creates an optimistic mood. The film concludes with a scene featuring Bazarov's parents walking home along the river. They are presented from an aerial perspective as small figures slowly walking across a snow-covered meadow. These images invoke Isaak Levitan's paintings of Russian rural life in winter, and many landscapes created by the Peredvizhnik Association artists in the 1860s. As Rosalind Sartorti asserts, landscape paintings created by Russian realists associated with the Peredvizhnik group were the most popular at their exhibitions and they remain highly popular among contemporary viewers.[77]

Commenting on the reproduction of the Peredvizhnik landscapes in Russian popular culture and in twentieth-century textbooks, Sartorti affirms that they continue to play an important part in the construction of collective memory and sites of memory. She suggests that Shishkin and Levitan 'became part of the collective memory in the sense of Pierre Nora's *lieux de mémoire*' and were turned into 'icons of Russianness' by the Russian popular imagination.[78] Sartorti's observations on the immersion of Soviet consumers into an imagined universe with unchanging scenery through reproductions of famous paintings on chocolate wrappers, postcards and framed copies of individual paintings can be easily extended to post-Soviet consumers and art lovers, including Smirnova, who utilises them in her adaptation.

---

[75] Van Gorp, p. 247.

[76] *Ottsy i deti* (film), directed by Adol'f Bergunker and Natal'ia Rashevskaia (Lenfilm, 1958) <https://www.youtube.com/watch?v=-AuON8bjYF4> [accessed 22 July 2021].

[77] Rosalinde Sartorti, 'Pictures at an exhibition: Russian land in a global world', *Studies in East European Thought*, 62 (2010), pp. 377–99 (p. 379).

[78] Ibid., p. 387.

Unlike Nikiforov's 1983 adaptation, which has a utopian vision of the Russian nation united by shared values and shaped by European and Russian canonical cultural heritage, Smirnova's version promotes contemporary music composed in the style of nineteenth-century music, including romances by the composer and cello player Aleksey Steblev. She also uses her own father, Andrei Smirnov, for the role of Pavel Kirsanov. According to Lidiia Maslova, by removing ironic touches from how Turgenev portrays Pavel Kirsanov in the novel, Smirnova has created a noble image of the aristocrat who epitomises Russian cultural values. He is portrayed as a tragic and superfluous individual forced into exile by socio-political circumstance. At the end of episode four of Smirnova's version, the carriage taking Pavel Kirsanov abroad at one point runs alongside the carriage with Bazarov's coffin that is being followed by his parents, and eventually it overtakes it. Symbolically, this episode alludes to the fate of many Russian aristocrats who fled Russia after the 1917 October revolution. The nostalgic overtones in Smirnova's film reveal her desire to lament the pre-revolutionary past.[79] The lamenting mood invokes Russian lamenting folk poetry performed by women. The Russian critic Lidiia Maslova goes as far as to suggest that Smirnova's adaptation of *Fathers and Sons* resembles 'a sentimental woman's novel'.[80]

Maslova's opinion notwithstanding, it is important to bear in mind that the film script was written by two people: Smirnova and Adabashian. Their textual transposition of Turgenev's *Fathers and Sons* espouses the scenic structure and dramatic codes of the medium of film. According to Jack Boozer, 'the composition of the screenplay illuminates the evolution of ideas' and determines 'the film production's relationship to its source text'.[81] It is central to the collaborative authorship that lies at the heart of film adaptation.

The prominent image of Pavel Kirsanov's carriage heading for Europe in the concluding scenes of the film overshadows the image of Bazarov's parents at the grave of their son. The close-up of Pavel Kirsanov, who resembles a displaced noble hero, articulates the theme of the Russian journey and national identity. The final scenes depict the vastness of Russian space, conforming thereby to the prevalent trope in Russian literature and film that links the

---

[79] Similarly, Smirnova's 2021 TV eight-part drama *Vertinsky* is imbued with nostalgic overtones in the episodes featuring the pre-revolutionary past.

[80] Lidiia Maslova, 'Semeinyi podriad v inter'ere. Problemy ottsov i detei na telekanale *Rossiia*', *Kommersant*, 11 October 2008 <https://www.kommersant.ru/doc/1038933> [accessed 5 July 2021].

[81] Jack Boozer, 'Introduction: The Screenplay and Authorship in Adaptation', in *Authorship in Film Adaptation*, ed. Jack Boozer (Austin: University of Texas Press, 2008), pp. 1–30 (p. 1).

concept of boundless territory to the notion of national identity. According to Emma Widdis, the emphasis on travel as conveyed in Russian literature and visual arts often signifies the historical path of the nation and symbolises endless potential. She writes: 'The *"put"*, or journey, of Russia's history, is as chaotic, adventurous, and fraught with challenges as the real *"put"* through her landscape.'[82]

In Smirnova's adaptation, the motif of the journey incorporates important elements of the pastoral as a narrative mode comprising contrast, nostalgia and return. It implies a perspective of temporal distance between present and past events aiming to revive the notions of boundaries and boundary-crossing as fundamental for understanding the Russian Arcadia's pastoral space which, in Rachel Polonsky's view, is vast and free from restraint.[83]

As has been demonstrated above, Smirnova's interpretation of Turgenev's *Fathers and Sons* implies a certain analogy between the 1860s and the 2000s, suggesting thereby that these two historical periods are transitional and are marked by intellectual debates about the future of Russia. Her television series was produced in 2008: by this time only 40% of the film market was comprised of Russian films. As Stephen Norris puts it, 'success [. . .] came by merging the past with contemporary patriotism'.[84] According to Norris, in the beginning of the 2000s there was a widely felt desire for patriotism. He writes: 'Homegrown products increasingly were sold by appealing to patriotism as a brand. [. . .] New 'national' advertising found that patriotism sold best when packaged as part of Russian history.'[85]

By offering a new interpretation of Turgenev's *Fathers and Sons*, Smirnova contributes to the growing trend of promoting patriotism as an emotional brand that invokes idyllic images of Russian life and the values of the pre-revolutionary period. It engages with widespread contemporary discussions about patriotism and belonging in contemporary Russia. Smirnova's adaptation laments the loss of Russia's late imperial glory (in the style of Stanislav Govorukhin's 1992 documentary *The Russia That We Lost*) and celebrates a new sense of Russianness that stretches beyond the Soviet period. It promotes Russian classical literature as an active site of memory which enables the audience to replace previous historical memories with new ones.

---

[82] Emma Widdis, 'Russia as Space', in *National Identity in Russian Culture: An Introduction*, eds Simon Franklin and Emma Widdis (Cambridge: Cambridge University Press, 2004), pp. 30–50 (p. 42).

[83] Rachel Platonov, 'Remapping Arcadia: Pastoral Space in Nineteenth-Century Russian Prose', *The Modern Language Review*, 102 (2007), pp. 1105–21 (p. 1121).

[84] Stephen M. Norris, *Blockbuster History in the New Russia: Movies, Memory, and Patriotism* (Bloomington, IN: Indiana University Press, 2012), p. 4.

[85] Ibid., p. 12.

Bibliography

Adabash'ian, Aleksandr, 'Rezhissura –eto sklad kharaktera', *Iskusstvo kino*, 5 (2010) <https://old.kinoart.ru/archive/2007/05/n5-article19> [accessed 6 November 2020].

Arnold, Jean, *Victorian Jewellery, Identity and the Novel: Prisms of Culture* (London and New York: Routledge, 2011).

'Avdotya Smirnova', *Radio Maiak* <https://radiomayak.ru/persons/person/id/882/> [accessed 24 October 2021].

Azarova, Irina, '*Ottsy i deti* v Ovstuge', *Brianskaia tema*, 5 (2007) <https://tema32.ru/articles/2007/05/1031/> [accessed 2 July 2021].

Baudelaire, Charles, *The Painter of Modern Life and Other Essays,* trans. and ed. Jonathan Mayne (London: Phaidon Press, 1964).

Blok, Aleksandr, 'Mikhail Aleksandrovich Bakunin', *Sobranie sochinenii*, 6 vols (Leningrad: Khudozhestvennaia literatura, 1982), IV, pp. 31–5.

Boele, Otto F., 'After Death, the Movie (1915) – Ivan Turgenev, Evgenii Bauer and the Aesthetics of Morbidity' in *Turgenev: Art, Ideology and Legacy*, eds Robert Reid and Joe Andrew (Amsterdam and New York: Rodopi, 2010), pp. 253–68.

Boozer, Jack, 'Introduction: The Screenplay and Authorship in Adaptation', in *Authorship in Film Adaptation*, ed. Jack Boozer (Austin: University of Texas Press, 2008), pp. 1–30.

Bulgakova, Oksana, 'Cine-Weathers: Soviet Thaw Cinema in the International Context', in *The Thaw: Soviet Society and Culture During the 1950s and 1960s*, eds Denis Kozlov and Eleonory Gilburd (Toronto: University of Toronto Press, 2013), pp. 436–81.

Bykov, Dmitrii, 'Nashe kino segodnia absoliutno mertvo', *Kinopoisk,* 4 September 2017 <https://www.kinopoisk.ru/media/article/3026203/> [accessed 3 November 2020].

Cartmell, Deborah (editor), *A Companion to Literature, Film, and Adaptation* (Chichester: Blackwell Publishing Ltd, 2012).

Cherkezova, O. V., '*Ottsy i deti* I.S. Turgeneva v kinoretseptsii Smirnovoi', *Vestnik TGPU*, 139 (2013), pp. 63–8.

Clark, Katerina, '"Wait for Me and I Shall Return": The Early Thaw as a Reprise of Late Thirties Culture?', in *The Thaw: Soviet Society and Culture During the 1950s and 1960s*, eds Denis Kozlov and Eleonory Gilburd (Toronto: University of Toronto Press, 2013), pp. 85–108.

Conrad, Joseph L, 'Turgenev's Landscapes', *Russian Language Journal*, 41 (1987), pp. 119–34.

Efremova, Tatyana, '"It was Totally Worth It . . .": Patriotic Consumption in the Queue to Serov's Exhibit', *Studies in Russian, Eurasian and Central European New Media (digitalicons.org)*, 16 (2016), pp. 31–50.

Erlich, Victor, 'The Dead Hand of the Future: The Predicament of Vladimir Maiakovsky', *Slavic Review*, 21(1962), pp. 433–40.

Fischler, Alexander, 'The Garden Motif and the Structure of Turgenev's *Fathers and Sons*', *Novel: A Forum on Fiction*, 9 (1976), pp. 243–55.

Gladkov, A. K., *Meierkhol'd. V dvukh tomakh* (Moscow: Soiuz teatral'nykh deiatelei RSFSR, 1990).

Gorp (Van), Jasmijn, 'Inverting film policy: film as nation builder in post-Soviet Russia, 1991–2005', *Media, Culture, and Society,* 33 (2011), pp. 243–58.

Hutchings, Stephen and Natalya Rulyova, 'Introduction', in *Television and Culture in Putin's Russia: Remote Control*, eds Stephen Hutchings and Natalya Rulyova (London and New York: Routledge, 2010), pp. 1–28.

Iskin, Ruth E., *Modern Women and Parisienne Consumer Culture in Impressionist Painting* (Cambridge: Cambridge University Press, 2007).

Kagan-Kans, Eva, 'Turgenev, the Metaphysics of an Artist, 1818–1883', *Cahiers du monde russe et soviétique*, 13 (1972), pp. 382–405.

Kolganova, Nadezhda F., 'The Communicative Space of Film Adaptation: Avdotya Smirnova's Adaptation of Turgenev's *Fathers and Sons*', *Russian Studies in Philosophy*, 56 (2018), pp. 425–33.

Koznova, Irina E., 'The Figure of Ivan Turgenev in Soviet Culture', *Russian Studies in Philosophy*, 56 (2018), pp. 416–24.

Ledkovsky, Marina, *The Other Turgenev: From Realism to Symbolism* (Wurzburg: Jal-Verlag, 1973).

Lowe, David Allan, 'Turgenev's *Fathers and Sons*' (unpublished PhD thesis, Indiana University, 1970).

Lunacharsky, A.V., 'Lektsiia o Turgeneve', *Russkaia literatura*, 4 (1961), pp. 134–8.

———, 'Literatura shestidesiatykh godov', *Klassiki russkoi literatury* (Moscow: Goslitizdat, 1937), pp. 197–233.

Masing-Delic, Irene, 'Bazarov pered sfinksom: nauchnoe anatomirovanie i esteticheskaia forma v romane Turgeneva *Ottsy i deti*', *Revue des études slaves*, 57 (1985), pp. 369–83.

Maslova, Lidiia, 'Semeinyi podriad v inter'ere. Problemy ottsov i detei na telekanale *Rossiia*', *Kommersant*, 11 October 2008 <https://www.kommersant.ru/doc/1038933> [accessed 5 July 2021].

Norris, Stephen M., *Blockbuster History in the New Russia: Movies, Memory, and Patriotism* (Bloomington, IN: Indiana University Press, 2012).

'Ottsy i deti (fil'm 2008)', *Wikipedia* <https://ru.wikipedia.org/wiki/Отцы_и_дети_(фильм,_2008)> [accessed 6 November 2020].

Pavliuchik, L., 'I vnov' –" Ottsy i deti"', *Sovetskaia kul'tura*, 46 (1983), 4.

Peterson, Dale E., *The Clement Vision: Poetic Realism in Turgenev and James* (Port Washington, NY: Kennikat Press, 1975).

Pisarev, D. I., 'Bazarov. *Ottsy i deti*. Roman I. S. Turgeneva', in *Literaturnaia kritika*, 3 vols (Leningrad: Khudozhestvennaia literatura, 1981), 1, pp. 230–81.

Platonov, Rachel, 'Remapping Arcadia: Pastoral Space in Nineteenth-Century Russian Prose', *The Modern Language Review*, 102 (2007), pp. 1105–21.

Protopopova, Darya, *Virginia Woolf's Portraits of Russian Writers: Creating the Literary Other* (Newcastle upon Tyne: Cambridge Scholars Publishing, 2019).

Robert Reid, 'Introduction. Turgenev: Art, Ideology, and Legacy', in *Turgenev: Art, Ideology, and Legacy*, eds Robert Reid and Joe Andrew (Amsterdam and New York: Rodopi, 2010), pp. 1–22.

Saraskina, L. I., 'Bal'nye kollizii russkikh romanov v ekrannykh proektsiiakh', *Khudozhestvennaia kul'tura*, 1 (2018), pp. 132–65.

Sartorti, Rosalinde, 'Pictures at an exhibition: Russian land in a global world', *Studies in East European Thought*, 62 (2010), pp. 377–99.

Seeley, Frank *Turgenev: A Reading of His Fiction* (Cambridge: Cambridge University Press, 1991).

Smirnova, Avdotya, 'Rezhisser protiv stsenarista', *Seans*, 25 August 2011 <https://snimifilm.com/post/zhurnal-seans-avdotya-smirnova-rezhisser-protiv-stsenarista-video> [accessed 2 November 2020].

Turgenev, I. S., *Ottsy i deti,* in *Sobranie sochinenii*, 30 vols (Moscow: Nauka, 1981), VII, pp. 7–188.

Valentino, Russell S., 'A Wolf in Arkadia: Generic Fields, Generic Counterstatement and the Resources of Pastoral in *Fathers and Sons*', *The Russian Review*, 55 (1996), pp. 475–93.

Vengerov, S. A., 'Turgenev', in *Entsiklopedicheskii slovar'* (St. Petersburg: Izdatel'stvo F. A. Brockhaus and I. A. Efron, 1902), XXXIV, pp. 96–106.

Zabrodin, Vladimir, 'Evgenii Bazarov V. E. Meierkhol'da. Novye materialy', *Kinovedcheskie zapiski,* 76 (2005), pp. 70–111.

Widdis, Emma, 'Russia as Space', in *National Identity in Russian Culture: An Introduction*, eds Simon Franklin and Emma Widdis (Cambridge: Cambridge University Press, 2004), pp. 30–50.

Woodward, James B., *Metaphysical Conflict: A Study of the Major Novels of Ivan Turgenev* (Munich: Verlag Otto Sagner, 1990).

Woolf, Virginia, 'The Russian Point of View', in *The Essays of Virginia Woolf*, ed. Andrew McNeillie (London: The Hogarth Press, 1994), IV, pp. 181–9.

Filmography

Fathers and Sons (*Ottsy i deti*), directed by Adol'f Bergunker and Natal'ia Rashevskaia (USSR, Lenfilm, 1958).

Fathers and Sons (*Ottsy i deti*), directed by Viacheslav Nikiforov (USSR, Telefil'm, 1983).

Fathers and Sons (*Ottsy i deti*), directed by Avdotya Smirnova (Russia, Mosfilm, 2008).

PART TWO

REIMAGINING DOSTOEVSKY

3. DOSTOEVSKY AND BRESSON: FROM 'A MEEK CREATURE' TO *UNE FEMME DOUCE*

Olga Peters Hasty

> He [Bresson] is the French cinema, as Dostoevsky is the Russian novel and Mozart is German music.
>
> ~ Jean-Luc Godard

> The unknown is what I wish to capture.
>
> ~ Robert Bresson

> Love of power and love of liberty are in eternal antagonism.
>
> ~ John Stuart Mill

Dostoevsky's works have inspired a vast range of literary, staged and cinematic responses. The plenitude of dramatic story lines, striking characters and vivid settings opens a vast perspective on the human condition and offers bounteous material with which artists working in other media can connect. Continuous creative engagements with Dostoevsky's writings at different times, in diverse cultures and in various media attest to the universality of the existential themes the author explores and open ever new perspectives on the concerns themselves and on the works that grow out of them. As the author himself insists and Alexander Burry examines in his far-reaching study, *Multi-Mediated Dostoevsky,* transmediation cannot – nor is it intended to – coincide fully with the Russian author's vision or capture any given work in its entirety. The very richness of design that draws creative artists to engage with Dostoevsky's writings makes this as impossible as it is undesirable.[1] As various artists respond to Dostoevsky in their own media, they tease out individual strands of his densely woven, multi-layered works, charting their own course through his fictional worlds and moving beyond them.

Hailed as 'one of the early directors of *cinéma d'auteur* – most often quoted by the following generation of directors for his originality',[2] the French filmmaker Robert Bresson (1901–1999) is known for the distinctive approach to film adaptation that grew out of his cinematographic principles. In an interview with Paul Schrader, Bresson provides a succinct description of how he relates to literature in his films:

> I want to be as far from literature as possible, as far from every existing art. Until now, I have found only two writers with whom I could agree: George Bernanos, a little, not too much, and, of course, Dostoevsky. I would like the source of my films to be in me, apart from literature. Even if I make a film from Dostoevsky, I try always to take out all the literary parts. I try to go directly to the sentiments of the author and only what can pass through me. I don't want to make a film showing the work of Dostoevsky.[3]

Using this statement as a point of departure, the present article will focus on Bresson's ninth feature film *Une femme douce* (1969), which, as its title indicates and its opening credits confirm, engages Dostoevsky's story 'A Meek Creature' (1876).[4] The film offers ideal ground for studying how Bresson creates a profound connection with the Russian writer, defying conventional notions about adaptation and engaging not with the plot, but with the ideational domain and formal properties of the story. Joining Dostoevsky in his existential quest, Bresson interacts with the deeper philosophical and spiritual underpinning of his work. In doing so, he puts hypotext and hypertext on equal footing, thus bringing his film and Dostoevsky's story into mutually enriching interanimation.

I will outline first the basic precepts of Bresson's cinematography and then the idiosyncratic filmic ties with Dostoevsky that they inform. This will launch

---

[1] Alexander Burry, *Multi-Mediated Dostoevsky* (Evanston: Northwestern University Press, 2011), p. 3. Burry offers a comprehensive discussion of Dostoevsky's own views on transmediation and the type of transpositions for which his works are particularly well-suited. Burry's is the most extensive study devoted to transmediations of Dostoevsky's work to date.

[2] Frederick H. White, 'Conclusion: Passport Control – Departing on a Cinematic Journey', in *Border Crossing: Russian Literature into Film*, eds Alexander Burry and Frederick H. White (Edinburgh: Edinburgh University Press, 2016), pp. 239–64 (p. 253).

[3] Paul Schrader, 'Robert Bresson, Possibly: Interview by Paul Schrader', in *Robert Bresson, Revised*, ed. James Quandt (Toronto: TIFF, 2011), pp. 693–705 (p. 696).

[4] I thank Katherine A. Hasty, whose valuable insights I have folded into this article.

my study of how Bresson relates to 'A Meek Creature' in *Une femme douce* without 'showing the work of Dostoevsky' and yet enlarging on it. With no pretensions to exhausting this vast topic, I consider three different levels at which Bresson interacts with Dostoevsky – ideational, structural and intertextual. Here, I first note existential concerns Bresson shared with Dostoevsky and the question of women's place in society that figured prominently in the creative artists' respective worlds as they worked on the story and the film. I then discuss the singular appropriateness of 'A Meek Creature's' form to Bresson's cinematography. Finally, I devote serious attention to the ramifications of what is widely seen as Bresson's perplexing interpolation into the film of a poorly acted scene from Shakespeare's *Hamlet*. As we shall see, it is just when *Une femme douce* seems furthest from 'A Meek Creature' that Bresson is closest to Dostoevsky.

Breaching the Surface – Bresson's Cinematography and his Ties with Dostoevsky

Pulling away from conventions and working against the grain of his medium, Bresson developed a profound cinematographic vision which he conceived as a means to penetrate appearances and to draw viewers beyond the surface of the screen. This idiosyncratic use of the visual to privilege interiority is vital to Bresson's efforts to realise his dictum that film does not replicate existing worlds – actual or fictional – but creates anew. As Bresson describes it,

> Cinema must be something different—not controlled. It must be the equivalent of life, like any art, but certainly not copied or simulated. There must be elements of life, of reality, captured separately, little by little with the extraordinary machine which is the camera. Then when you put them together in a certain way, a sudden life comes out of it – cinematic life, which is not at all like everyday life. Nor is it like the life of the theatre.[5]

Dedicated to the uniqueness of his medium, Bresson resists its degeneration into a story-telling venue that offers visual replicas of literary works and surrenders its distinctive features to theatricality. As one of his cinematographic precepts proclaims, there are 'two types of film': 'those that employ the resources of the theatre (actors, direction, etc.) and use the camera in order *to reproduce*' and 'those that employ the resources of cinematography and use to camera *to create*'.[6]

---

[5] Robert Bresson and Ronald Hayman, 'Robert Bresson: In conversation with Ronald Hayman', *The Transatlantic Review*, 46/47 (1973), pp. 16–23 (p. 16).
[6] Robert Bresson, *Notes on Cinematography*, trans. Jonathan Griffin (New York: Urizen Books, 1977), p. 2. Original emphasis.

In his determination to banish theatricality – that domain of simulation – from his films, Bresson steers clear of casting experienced actors in his works, suppresses affect, and admonishes his cast members not to act, but to simply *be* in front of the camera. He explains, 'It is not a matter of acting "simple" or of acting "inward" but of not acting at all.'[7] This radical reduction of communicative means is evident at every level of Bresson's work. 'I want to express things with a minimum of means, showing nothing that is not absolutely essential.'[8] How Bresson achieves this goal is cogently described by Colin Burnett:

> Like his verbal theorising, Bresson's craft practice promoted the virtues of creation by negation. He adopted an artistic process of *dépouillement* (paring away), eliminating from his style those techniques that encouraged the viewer to interpret the image as a text (a direct stimulation of verbal associative thought) or a tableau (a direct display of beauty that rewarded aesthetic contemplation).[9]

Burnett notes also the consistency with which Bresson employs *dépouillement*, including the filmmaker's replacement of the professional actor with 'a new cinematic body – the *modèle* – whose minimally communicative gestures and movements were matched with an opaque, "detached" lighting style and, later, uniform polychromatic color schemes'.[10] The Russian filmmaker Andrei Tarkovsky comments appreciatively on this economy of means, 'I have always been amazed by Bresson: his concentration is extraordinary. Nothing incidental could ever creep into his rigidly ascetic selection of means of expression.'[11]

Essential to revitalising his medium and to achieving the interiority he strives for in his films, Bresson's meticulously crafted minimalism is also crucial to weaning viewers from the passive consumption of his work to which conventional cinema had accustomed them. Even before reader response theory flourished as it did just when Bresson was making *Une femme douce*, his cinematography anticipated its basic premises: 'A book, a painting, or a piece of music – none of these things has an absolute value. The value is what the viewer, the reader, or the listener brings to it.'[12] Bresson's sparse, elliptical films

---

[7] Ibid., p. 49.
[8] Charles Thomas Samuels, 'Encountering Robert Bresson', in *Robert Bresson, Revised*, ed. James Quandt (Toronto: TIFF, 2011), pp. 667–91 (p. 669).
[9] Colin Burnett, *The Invention of Robert Bresson: The Auteur and His Market* (Bloomington: The University of Indiana Press, 2017), p. 152.
[10] Ibid., p. 170.
[11] Andrey Tarkovsky, *Sculpting in Time: Reflections on the Cinema*, trans. Kitty Hunter-Blair (Austin: University of Texas Press, 1987), p. 189.
[12] Samuels, p. 677.

lead viewers past the surface of the screen to a newly made world in whose constitution they are enjoined to participate.

Bresson's distinct cinematography also challenged conventional notions about film adaptation. Putting his films on equal, independent footing with source texts that he draws into his creative orbit, Bresson eschews what most easily transfers into film. He refuses to replicate verbal material with visual images and avoids using plot as a primary structuring device. Providing only vestiges of narrative, Bresson interacts with his source text at its ideational level, entering into an intermedial exchange – not with the work itself, but with what it conveys about its author's thinking and, in *Une femme douce*, also with the form in which Dostoevsky couches his story. Using parametric narration, which privileges style over plot, Bresson takes his film and its viewers into a space of creative interaction with the source text that enriches and is itself enriched by his transmediation. Crucially, Bresson's method is consistent with Dostoevsky's own preference for the 'maximally free transposition methodology' that Burry examines in his study.[13]

Bresson readily acknowledges Dostoevsky's importance to his creative work, but his ties with the Russian writer are not always apparent. Certainly, Bresson's minimalism does not call Dostoevsky's poetics of excess to mind, while the filmmaker's suppression of plot makes the connections less evident. This leads to different assessments as to which of Bresson's films are connected with Dostoevsky's writings. Thus, for example, Sergei Iutkevich sees Dostoevsky only in the two films that make the ties overt: *Une femme douce* (1969), the focus of this article, and Bresson's following film *Quatre nuits d'un rêveur* (1972), that interacts with 'White Nights'.[14] Others recognise Dostoevsky's *Crime and Punishment* and 'The Gambler' in Bresson's *Pickpocket* or note films inspired by isolated scenes from Dostoevsky's novels.[15] Taking a broader approach, Mireille Latil le Dantec observes insightfully that nearly all twelve feature films that Bresson made over his thirty-five-year career are 'informed by Dostoevskian elements'.[16]

In Dostoevsky Bresson recognises a kindred spirit. Contrasting him to Tolstoy, who 'works much more from the outside than from the inside', Bresson explains, 'With Dostoevsky you feel "I'm sure you don't make mistakes about human

---

[13] Burry, p. 2.
[14] Sergei Iutkevich, '"Sinematograf" Robera Bressona', *Iskusstvo kino*, 2 (1979), pp. 145–58 (p. 151) and 3 (1979) pp. 145–59 (p. 152).
[15] See essays devoted to Bresson and Dostoevsky in the collections edited by Alexander Burry and Frederick H. White, *Border Crossing: Russian Literature into Film* (Edinburgh: Edinburgh University Press, 2016) and by James Quandt, *Robert Bresson, Revised* (Toronto: TIFF, 2011).
[16] Mireille Latil Le Dantec, 'Bresson, Dostoevsky', in *Robert Bresson, Revised*, ed. James Quandt (Toronto: TIFF, 2011), pp. 413–25 (p. 414).

beings." That's what I'm looking for – to remain on the inside.'[17] Bresson taps into this interiority as he pushes past story lines to participate in explorations of the human condition and the search 'for the soul' that he discerns in Dostoevsky's works.[18] The affinity between them runs deep. Allen Thiher's observation that in most of Bresson's films, 'the narrative turns in one way or another on isolation and humiliation, on estrangement and the impossibility of a desired community',[19] applies equally to Dostoevsky's works. Brian Price's description that 'Bresson's treatment of space throughout his career has been largely restrictive. His characters are always isolated and subject to confinement', holds for Dostoevsky's art as well.[20] This is also true of what Le Dantec describes as 'signs of the mystery of a being seeking the Other and the Self' in Bresson's films.[21] Bresson finds this shared ground conducive to creative self-realisation: 'even in an adaptation you can put a lot of yourself, especially with Dostoevsky who goes so deeply into emotions.'[22]

Prominent among the human concerns that preoccupy both artists is the deleterious exercise of power and its corrosive effects on the selfhood both of those subjected to it and those who wield it. This theme, which courses through much of Dostoevsky's and Bresson's creative work, is concentrated in 'A Meek Creature', which implicates power in alienation and oppressive confinement in the material world. In this story, Dostoevsky explores the causes and consequences of the narrating pawnbroker's destructive need to dominate others, together with the perils and limits of his domination. The power the pawnbroker claims springs from the material world with its offers of privilege deriving from social standing (reputation, rank, ancestry, gender) and especially money, which plays a negative role throughout Dostoevsky's writings and Bresson's films.[23] Reacting to humiliation that he seeks to displace onto others, the pawnbroker is trapped in a vicious circle of alienation that he perpetuates with his own behaviour. In the misguided supposition that he can regain his selfhood by exercising power over others, he revels in the ascendency he claims over the young woman whom he induces to marry him and whom he drives to take her own life.

---

[17] Bresson and Hayman, p. 22.
[18] Bresson explains that he connects with Bernanos and Dostoevsky because 'Both writers are searching for the soul' (Samuels, p. 672).
[19] Allen Thiher, 'Bresson's *Un condamné à mort*: The Semiotics of Grace', in *Robert Bresson, Revised*, ed. James Quandt (Toronto: TIFF, 2011), pp. 287–97 (p. 292).
[20] Brian Price, *Neither God nor Master: Robert Bresson and Radical Politics* (Minneapolis: University of Minnesota Press, 2011), p. 108.
[21] Le Dantec, p. 418.
[22] Bresson and Hayman, p. 22.
[23] For an outstanding study of money in Dostoevsky's works, see Boris Christa, 'Dostoevskii and money', in *The Cambridge Companion to Dostoevskii*, ed. W. J. Leatherbarrow (Cambridge: Cambridge University Press, 2002), pp. 93–110.

Beyond the obvious changes that accompany Bresson's transmediation of story to film, and the indigenisation that takes it from St Petersburg of 1876 to Paris of 1969, are the shared ideational concerns that easily traverse this spatio-temporal and cultural divide and bridge Bresson's stylistic differences with the author of 'A Meek Creature'.[24] As one critic observes, 'what Bresson has made of it is a study of emotions, reduced to their pristine essentials, while suppressing any theatrical exhibition of these feelings and states of being'.[25] In the filmscript for *Une femme douce*, which he wrote himself, Bresson pares down the loquacious pawnbroker's narrative to a minimum, sketching it with sparse, impassively delivered lines. Price notes that 'As the pawnbroker, Guy Fangin resists the hysterical inflections of Dostoevsky's protagonist. Long passages – entire sections of thought – are reduced to simple statements delivered in monotone.'[26] Thus, for example, the Meek Creature's family situation, which Dostoevsky's pawnbroker describes at length, is conveyed in the film with swift, economic strokes: the narrator states simply that her parents are dead, her relatives use her as a servant, and she spends what little money they give her on books. Douce herself says only that her home and the people in it are sinister. The downfall from military officer to pawnbroker in the aftermath of refusing to fight a duel that Dostoevsky's pawnbroker relates is similarly condensed in Bresson's film, where the modernised narrator is a former bank manager who summarises his downfall in a single sentence.

Drawing on his own medium, Bresson uses camera work and editing to convey the pervasive sense of entrapment, disjunction and alienation of Dostoevsky's story. Narrow camera angles, medium shots and close-ups of characters, constricted framing and an avoidance of panoramic views limit what appears on the screen. Detached gestures, fragmented images, long silences and an intrusive soundtrack of urban traffic contribute to a sense of isolation and unease, while the repeated traversals of liminal spaces – hallways, stairwells, entryways – create an unsettled mood. The impassive non-professional actors, whom Bresson trains to minimise affect, create an atmosphere bereft of human relations.

The Woman's Plight – on Matrimony as Captivity

Dostoevsky and Bresson accord considerable prominence to oppressed and victimised women in their works. Notably, 'A Meek Creature' and *Une femme douce* were created in periods when women's traditional roles in society were

---

[24] To distinguish between Dostoevsky's and Bresson's nameless titular characters, I will refer to them as the Meek Creature and Douce, respectively.
[25] Lee Atwell, '*Une femme douce*', *Film Quarterly*, 23 (1970), pp. 54–6 (p. 54).
[26] Price, p. 114.

challenged in their creators' respective cultures. Nina Pelikan Straus describes the 'growing anxiety concerning the treatment of women under the law' that Dostoevsky records in 'A Meek Creature'[27] and sees the story as 'the repository in fiction for Dostoevsky's most intense inscription of gender differences'.[28] Triggered by a series of women's suicides that he notes in *The Diary of a Writer*, this concern developed in tandem with ongoing debates in Russia relating to women's issues. Dostoevsky was a great admirer of George Sand, whose popularity in Russia and influence on the 'woman question' cannot be exaggerated. Animated by ideas promulgated in her novels, he folded her thinking into his own writings. Pelikan Straus notes his 'incorporation of Sandean elements into heroines on one hand, and compulsion to fictionalise darkest male sexual fantasies on the other'.[29] Sand, who died on 8 June 1876, just as Dostoevsky was finishing 'A Meek Creature' was clearly on his mind as he wrote.[30]

Another influential champion of the woman's cause whose work affected Dostoevsky is John Stuart Mill. Pelikan Straus notes that 'Like other novelists who wrote after 1869 when Mill's *On the Subjection of Women* was published, Dostoevsky dramatised the effects of liberal and socialist ideas on male-female relations'.[31] This important, widely debated work, which came out in two Russian translations, is referenced in 'A Meek Creature', which testifies to the ills of a woman in matrimonial captivity that Mill decried.

A full century after *On the Subjection of Women* appeared, Bresson was making *Une femme douce* in the immediate aftermath of May '68, a social rebellion in France that, among other things, 'entailed a radical questioning of domesticity, and a liberation of female sexuality from essentially patriarchal conditions of motherhood and monogamy', together with 'a liberation of sexual desire from domestic servitude'.[32] Working, as he did, in a 'system that makes it difficult for women to sustain themselves outside the institution of marriage, which trades economic solvency for sex',[33] Bresson recognised in 'A Meek Creature' problems beleaguering women in Dostoevsky's time that

---

[27] Nina Pelikan Straus, *Dostoevsky and the Woman Question: Rereadings at the End of a Century* (New York: St Martin's Press, 1994), p. 5.
[28] Ibid., p. 16.
[29] Ibid., p. 14.
[30] Dostoevsky's essays 'George Sand's Death' (*Smert' Zhorzh Zanda*) and 'A Few Words about George Sand' (*Neskol'ko slov o Zhorzh Zande*) appeared in *The Diary of a Writer* in June of 1876. 'A Meek Creature' came out in *The Diary of a Writer* in November of that year.
[31] Pelikan Straus, p. 120.
[32] Price, p. 101, p. 113.
[33] Ibid., p. 101.

persisted in his own.[34] This similarity reflects the tenacity of power structures that continually reassert themselves in the aftermath of drives for social justice. Indeed, 1969, the year Bresson finished *Une femme douce,* was marked by just such a return to the status quo in the wake of the social unrest of May '68. As Price summarises, 'The young woman's frustrated attempts to live that liberation in *Une femme douce* and to support herself financially suggest the extent to which a patriarchal ideology and a normative conception of female sexuality were reasserting themselves in 1969.'[35]

'A Meek Creature' and *Une femme douce* show women struggling against societal strictures that stand in the way of their self-realisation and leave them vulnerable to ill treatment. In Bresson's indigenisation, Douce has more agency than her Russian counterpart, and the inequality between her and the pawnbroker is mitigated. The difference in their ages is not as pronounced, she offers more resistance to her husband and she is characterised by an irrepressible love of learning. 'She is much cleverer than he', Bresson explains in an interview, 'which is the opposite of Dostoyevsky, in which the girl is an innocent, stupid waif'.[36] With this difference, Bresson intensifies the injustice of matrimony, which remains the primary source of support and subjection of women. Resisting the pawnbroker's insistence that she marry him, Douce explains that marriage bores her and that she wants something more. The scene is set in the Jardin des Plantes, where they are seen through the fencing of an animal cage in a shot indicative of confinement. When the pawnbroker replies that millions of women hope for marriage, Douce, who has no desire to ape those 'millions', replies only, 'Sure. And there are monkeys too', while the camera follows a captive monkey in the cage. Following her against her wishes into her apartment house after this outing, the pawnbroker stands in the stairwell insisting, '*Dites oui, dites oui*', as she enters what she calls her 'sinister' home with its 'sinister' inhabitants without responding. In the next shot, an official pronounces them man and wife and they sign the marriage registry. The inescapability of matrimony is driven home. What marriage bodes for Douce is intimated already by the books she flings into the back of his car when they set off for the park – a sign of the schooling she abandons to assist in the pawnshop upon marrying him.

Douce's entry into socially prescribed captivity is celebrated in a fine restaurant, her husband slips a ring onto her finger, they sip wine. Back at their apartment she playfully initiates sexual activity with him, laughs, bounces on the bed,

---

[34] In November 1968 there was a theatrical production of *La Douce,* adapted from Dostoevsky by Gabriel Blonde for the Théâtre Studio. This suggests that Bresson was not alone in recognising the story's relevance in France at the time. It is not known whether or not Bresson saw this staged version. I thank Jake Robertson for this information.

[35] Price, p. 101.

[36] Samuels, p. 689.

Figure 3.1 Pawnbroker (Guy Frangin) and Douce (Dominique Sanda) in front of the monkey cage at the Jardin des Plantes, *Une femme douce*, directed by Robert Bresson, 1969.

and emits squeals of pleasure under the covers, but her pleasure is short lived. As Douce frolics on their wedding night the pawnbroker announces in voice-off commentary, '*j'ai jeté de l'eau froide sur cet enivrement*'. The next shot shows his wife assisting him in the pawnshop, as he takes charge and sets down rules, emphasising her financial dependence on him. As in Dostoevsky's story, matrimony and money are the primary sources of the pawnbroker's control over his wife. Douce, however, is more resistant and persists in her determination to learn and to experience life. She reads avidly, studies, listens to music, and visits art and natural history museums. Bresson explains, 'I only wanted to show that marriage wasn't enough to her, that it disappointed her. As Goethe says, marriage has something awkward about it. [. . .] I only made her say that she wants marriage to be more than marriage.'[37] The phrase 'more than marriage' indicates not a restrictive, legally binding contract that puts the wife into a subservient position, but a human relationship between equals who respect one another's selfhood.

Time and Memory – Beyond Representation

Invested in the human concerns expressed in 'A Meek Creature', Bresson also realised that its form was ideally suited to his cinematography. What Dostoevsky

[37] Ibid., p. 689.

describes as the 'fantastic' form of his story insists on the immediacy of his narrator's ongoing recollections.[38] This shifts the focus from events that occurred in the past to the narrator's memories of them unfolding in the present. Rather than give readers a first-person account of what transpired, Dostoevsky shows his narrator in the very act of assembling – literally re-collecting – episodes and images of previously experienced events. Conditioned by his psychological trauma, the narrator's subjective recollections of the past run up against the objective reality of an immutable present that holds the corpse of the woman he drove to suicide.

By situating the eventfulness of the story in the mind's eye of the remembering narrator, Dostoevsky expands its potential for signification. In the nineteenth century, memory was increasingly regarded as a primary individuating characteristic, and the reminiscences through which the story emerges serve to characterise the narrator. Couched in the pawnbroker's self-revelatory retrospective is Dostoevsky's oblique portrayal of his character – the forces that shaped him, the public humiliation that compromised his selfhood and the consequences of that damage to himself and those around him. Moreover, as the remembering narrator confronts his remembered self he becomes both subject and object of his ruminations and, seeing self as other, marks the tension between inner and outer selves that bedevils so many of Dostoevsky's characters. The unreliable narrator of this story thus serves Dostoevsky as a reliable means to convey more than what the pawnbroker recounts. The pawnbroker's divided self, the discontinuity of his recollections, and his self-contradictions create apertures that allow the reader to see beyond his narrative to apprehend what his author invests in the story.

With this 'fantastic form', Dostoevsky pushes against conventional literariness, much as Bresson subsequently pushed against conventional film practice. The degree to which the form of 'A Meek Creature' corresponds with Bresson's cinematographic precepts significantly deepens the ties between the story and his film, exemplifying le Dantec's incisive observation, 'What is remarkable in Bresson's later films is the extent to which the filmmaker's compositional demands not only outstrip traditional concerns of literary adaptation to the screen [. . .] but, more importantly, are also in line with the Russian writer's preoccupations.'[39] Like Dostoevsky, Bresson insists on the immediacy of the pawnbroker's process of recollection. As he situates his film in the present to show not actual events, but how the pawnbroker remembers them, 'The camera becomes the "invisible stenographer" Dostoevsky once imagined to explain how his pawnbroker's thoughts made it to the page.'[40] *Une femme*

---

[38] F. M. Dostoevsky, 'Krotkaia', in *Polnoe sobranie sochinenii*, 30 vols (Leningrad: Nauka, 1972–90), XXIV (1982), p. 5.

[39] Le Dantec, p. 423.

[40] Price, p. 115

douce thus achieves the immediacy and penetration of the surface in terms of which Bresson defines cinematography.

The importance Bresson ascribed to the dual temporality of Dostoevsky's story is evident from his insistence that he uses no flashbacks:

> I hate flashbacks. There are no flashbacks in the film: it is all a matter of the live husband now confronting his dead wife. Walking around the corpse, he says, 'I had only desired her body,' and there it is: dead. People saw the film as a series of flashbacks, but it is all life in the face of death.[41]

This distinction is as vital to Bresson's film as it is to Dostoevsky's story, both of which centre on memory in action to show the past inhering in the present. Countering commentators who erroneously speak of flashbacks in Bresson's film, Manohla Dargis cogently summarises:

> the entire film remains in the present tense; the images spring not from some objective past ('what really happened'), but from the husband's own insistent present; the scenes that take place before the woman's death are not instances of mercurial movie magic, of cinematic time-travel, but are instead the husband's sense of that past as it exists in his here and now. For him, the past is ever-present.[42]

At pains to prevent the pawnbroker's recollections from being taken for flashbacks, Bresson avoids dissolves – those conventional markers of temporal shifts – and smooths over the transitions between the pawnbroker's recollections and the room he paces for the duration of the film. Sounds and events from the pawnbroker's memories and from his actual surroundings repeatedly merge into one another.[43] The primary marker of transitions between the places he remembers and the space in which he recalls them is the body of his wife, shot from various angles and only infrequently shown in its entirety. Like Dostoevsky, Bresson highlights the pawnbroker's negotiations between his inward self – the locus of memory and imagination – and the outward self that confronts the actual world and his situation in it.

Composed of episodes the pawnbroker retrieves from his memory, 'A Meek Creature' is ideally suited for Bresson's cinematography in two important ways: it accomplishes the interiority he seeks and frees the on-screen action of his film from reproducing either a storyline or an existing world, allowing him to newly show the recollected scenes and images that flash on the narrator's

---

[41] Samuels, p. 688.
[42] Manohla Dargis, '*Une femme douce*', *Film Comment*, 35 (1999), pp. 41–3 (p. 42).
[43] Price, p. 113.

inward eye. Moreover, the ellipses, fragmentation and discontinuity – those distinctive features of Bresson's cinematography that he developed to avoid representation – are characteristic of a remembering mind, which calls up not smoothly flowing storylines in fully staged settings, but disjointed scenes in lightly sketched terrain. Additionally, showing memory in action offers a way to resolve the awkward incongruity of conveying first person narration through the third person perspective of the camera, a solution Bresson uses to advantage also in other films.[44] Dostoevsky's pen and Bresson's camera are aimed not at what happened, but at how it appears in the mind's eye of the remembering pawnbroker.

The Hamlet Scene – Being in Life and Art and the Perils of Seeming

Like Dostoevsky, Bresson recognises the potential vested in intertextual references and uses them to deepen his works and to generate interconnections that expand beyond them.[45] The far-reaching ramifications of Bresson's reference to Shakespeare's *Hamlet* that I next explore demonstrate the profundity of Bresson's creative vision in its connection with Dostoevsky's. In keeping with 'A Meek Creature', Bresson's pawnbroker takes his wife to the theatre, but while the story simply mentions two of the three plays they attend, Bresson has the couple watch a performance of *Hamlet*, which is not referenced in the story. Why he chooses to do so is not immediately apparent, but exploration of this question meets with rich reward.

Near the middle of the film, when Douce has refused to submit to her husband's will and the pawnbroker – mad with jealousy – suspects her of infidelity, Bresson shows them at a production of Shakespeare's tragedy. In a scene that commentators find baffling and overly long,[46] Bresson devotes a full five minutes

---

[44] Notable examples include *Journal d'un curé de campagne* (1951) and *Pickpocket* (1959).

[45] It is beyond the scope of this article to consider the rich variety of interpolations in Bresson's film, including an excerpt from a movie that the pawnbroker and Douce go out to see, various television offerings, passages from books that she reads out loud to him, and both classical and popular records that she listens to.

[46] Gaëlle Ginestet, '*Une femme douce* by Robert Bresson: *Hamlet* or Anti-Cinematography', in *Shakespeare on Screen: Hamlet*, eds Sarah Hatchuel & Nathalie Vienne-Guerrin (Rouen, Havre: Publications des Universités de Rouen et du Havre, 2011), pp. 291–308 (p. 299). In 'Robert Bresson: A Symposium', James Quandt says, 'My question is: why does he bother to insert this critique (emphasised when Dominique Sanda checks the text of the play when they return home from the theatre)?' (Nicole Brenez et al., 'Robert Bresson: A Symposium', in *Robert Bresson, Revised*, ed. James Quandt [Toronto: TIFF, 2011], pp. 595–627 [p. 609]). In his interview with Bresson, Samuels observes, 'It's not that it's boring, but I begin to be puzzled about its function' (Samuels, p. 690).

to the overacted, poorly staged events portrayed on the stage. With characteristic reticence, Bresson says little about why he includes this scene in his film. Pressed in an interview to comment on this perplexing interpolation, he says only, 'Hamlet I included because I hate such theatrical shouting. I have myself seen it performed by a French company that omitted Hamlet's advice to the players because it contradicted their style.' Adding only that it sets up the scene that follows, Bresson muses, 'Perhaps it is too long, but I simply couldn't cut it.'[47] It is clear that the excerpt from *Hamlet* is of consequence for Bresson, who directed it himself, instructed his players in how to act badly,[48] and shot the scene differently from the rest of the film.[49]

In an incisive article devoted to this interpolation, Gaëlle Ginestet discusses various levels at which Shakespeare's tragedy signifies in Bresson's film: 'Different kinds of echoes are to be found in *Une femme douce*, visual, diegetic, textual or in terms of characterisation.'[50] Of particular interest to us here is her observation, 'The excerpt from *Hamlet* has a didactic purpose for Bresson: it functions as a lesson of cinematography and as a condemnation both of cinema as it was practiced by other filmmakers and theatre when it is poorly directed.'[51] With this 'lesson' Bresson foregrounds his banishment of theatricality from his films. He underscores it in the immediately following scene, when upon returning home, Douce reads aloud the passage from *Hamlet* which, as she notices, is omitted from the production: Hamlet's advice to the players who are to perform his play.[52]

Bresson's conviction 'that costume drama violates the essence of cinema which is immediacy',[53] is front and centre in the insert from *Hamlet*. At the same time, the scene launches an expansive network of interconnections that enlarge on Dostoevsky's story and his film. To begin with, the theatricality Bresson banishes from his films figures in Dostoevsky's writings among the symptoms of dysregulated characters. Recognising the deleterious causes and consequences of performative behaviour, Dostoevsky creates characters whose exaggerated enactments of assumed roles exacerbate their condition. As shame, guilt and the avoidance of responsibility trigger a need to deflect attention from the discredited self, theatricality offers a means of concealment,

---

[47] Samuels, p. 690.
[48] This is apparently why they were spared having their names appear in the film credits.
[49] Ginestet, p. 302.
[50] Ibid., p. 292.
[51] Ibid., p. 292.
[52] Samuels, pp. 689-90. William Shakespeare, *Hamlet*, III. 2 <https://www.gutenberg.org/files/1524/1524-h/1524-h.htm> [accessed 19 October 2021].
[53] Ibid., p. 674.

but one that comes with perils of its own. Recourse to projecting a contrived identity marks the degradation of salubrious self-awareness into excruciating self-consciousness that erodes selfhood and promotes untoward behaviour. Born of a preoccupation with how the counterfeit self is perceived in the surrounding world, this self-consciousness feeds the very quandaries that give rise to it, intensifying the mutually reinforcing failures to connect with the self and with others. Vivid examples of Dostoevskian characters mired in such predicaments range from the Underground Man to Fyodor Karamazov, and include the narrating pawnbroker of 'A Meek Creature' who has much in common with his early predecessor.

The importance Bresson assigns the *Hamlet* scene reflects, among other things, his recognition of the close ties between his own cinematographic objections to theatricality and the dangers it holds for human interaction that Dostoevsky projects through various characters. The reference to *Hamlet* also elaborates on connections between Shakespeare's tragedy and 'A Meek Creature' that are relevant to other works by both artists. Whether or not Bresson knew of the prominent role that Hamlet and 'Hamletism' played in the discourse of the nineteenth-century Russian intelligentsia, as an incisive reader well-versed in *Hamlet* and thoroughly familiar with Dostoevsky's writings, he could recognise resonances of Shakespeare's tragedy and the existential questions concentrated in it throughout the Russian author's works. Inasmuch as echoes of *Hamlet* are distinguishable in Bresson's articulation of his cinematographic principles, this further deepens his ties with Dostoevsky.

Of particular significance to the present study is that Shakespeare's Hamlet ultimately succumbs to the very failing against which he warns his players. Early in the tragedy the Danish prince insists on 'being' rather than 'seeming' ('Seems, madam! Nay it is; I know not "seems"'[54] in terms that Bresson draws on to describe his own move away from theatricality in *Notes on Cinematography*: 'BEING (models) instead of SEEMING (actors).'[55] Yet as Hamlet feels increasingly marginalised at court and incapable of decisive action, he disremembers his disdain for 'actions that a man might play' and, betraying 'that within which passeth show',[56] lapses into an increasingly theatrical madness to elude reckoning with himself and those around him. Among the tragic consequences of Hamlet's feigned derangement are Ophelia's genuine madness and suicide, the deaths of Polonius, Rosenkranz, Guildenstern and finally his own death amidst the bodies of the queen, the king and Laertes strewn on the stage in the closing scene of *Hamlet* that Bresson shows in his film. The end of Shakespeare's

---

[54] Shakespeare, *Hamlet*, I. 2.
[55] Bresson, *Notes on Cinematography*, p. 1. (Emphasis in original).
[56] Shakespeare, *Hamlet*, I. 2.

tragedy displays the tragic consequences of muddying the essential binary 'to be or not to be', first with the theatrical 'seeming' that brought the yet living Hamlet into a state of 'not being', and then with the death-dealing 'seeming' of the fraudulent duel designed to murder the Danish prince.

Increasingly absorbed in projecting contrived self-images and devising mental scripts for the benefit of illusory spectators, Dostoevsky's pawnbroker follows a similarly destructive trajectory. Indeed, the very role of pawnbroker he takes on purportedly to avenge himself on society smacks of unwholesome theatricality. Though they assume different guises, the affectations of Dostoevsky's pawnbroker and Shakespeare's Hamlet convey the degree to which 'seeming' alienates them from self and others and the tragic consequences of such alienation. As for Dostoevsky, so too for Bresson, the resulting desolation is neither life nor death but a form of death in life. This is where both artists leave the pawnbroker at the end of their works.

The interpolated scene of Hamlet's swordfight with Laertes is important also because it introduces into Bresson's film the indispensable theme of the duel that his indigenisation of Dostoevsky's story does not accommodate. As the narrator of 'A Meek Creature' recounts, the breaking point in his life comes when he refuses to engage in a duel as demanded by the honour code of his regiment from which he resigns just ahead of being expelled from it. This disgrace precipitates his subsequent self-abasement, which he frames as his revenge on society. This putative revenge takes the form of exercising control over others, a drive to dominate that leads him to construe all human relations as power struggles. Not content with his dominant position over his desperate customers, the pawnbroker marries, having first ensured his position of dominance over the woman he makes his wife. His sense of power derives from the sizeable list of advantages he claims over her, including age, gender, money and matrimony. Even as he revels in this marked inequality, the pawnbroker refers to their relationship as a 'duel' with obsessive frequency. This reflects his inability to free himself from the trauma that leaves him mired in shame and the adversarial stance he assumes vis-à-vis the surrounding world. Engaging in a 'duel' in which he is sure to win, he plans to score a victory to compensate for the duel he did not fight.

In *Une femme douce*, the duel that precipitated the pawnbroker's downfall is replaced with a financial infelicity that cost him his position of bank manager. This replacement captures the loss of social standing suffered by Dostoevsky's pawnbroker and the importance he ascribes to money but loses the duel and its ramifications that are essential to the story. With his interpolation of the duelling scene from *Hamlet*, Bresson recuperates this loss, and does so, moreover, by invoking a work whose probing existential questions overarch those of Dostoevsky's story and his own film.

The duel from Shakespeare's tragedy that Bresson shows in his film marks Hamlet's transition from the private contemplation of his own life or death to the public arena of a duel, a contest that degrades the question 'to be, or not to be' to the choice of overpowering or being overpowered. Bresson's exaggeration of the theatricality intrinsic to duelling with the poor acting and bad costuming he imparts to the scene underscores the debasement of the essential question 'to be, or not to be' first to the narrowed choice of 'to kill or not to kill' of duelling, and finally to the poisoned cup and envenomed rapier of murder masquerading as a duel.

Notably, it is the choice 'to kill or not to kill' that the Meek Creature considers when, believing her husband to be asleep, she points a gun at his head and stands poised to free herself from his tyranny. With her decision to refrain from discharging the gun, she pulls back from committing murder but also from the contest of wills into which her husband drew her. Her refusal to pull the trigger is a moral victory that reaffirms her selfhood and marks her withdrawal into an inner world over which he has no dominion.

In the pawnbroker's distorted vision, his wife's decision marks his victory in his 'duel' with her. The speciousness of this claim is signalled by the misnomer he applies to the episode, every detail of which is retrograde to basic duelling practices.[57] The single weapon stands out in particular. This is the gun the pawnbroker puts in his pocket when he sets off to eavesdrop on his wife's tryst with Efimovich and then, after interrupting the meeting and bringing her home, leaves prominently displayed on the table. Here the question arises as to what the self-styled Mephistopheles of a pawnbroker intends with this suggestive, ominously ambiguous gesture.

Recognising its disturbing indeterminacy, Bresson attends to it in his film. He gives Douce time to look at the gun, pick it up and hold it, capturing a profound moment of uncertainty as she stands in silence before advancing toward her husband. In Dostoevsky's story, the pawnbroker describes his wife deciding whether or not to kill him. Bresson expands his narration to include also the choice of whether she should kill herself. At this point in the film, the gun has already figured as an instrument of murder in the pawnbroker's imagination. Seized by jealous rage when he sees Douce talking to a man who is visiting the

---

[57] Commentators treat the term 'duel' as a metaphor for the contest of wills between the pawnbroker and his wife in the first half of the story. While this is certainly apt, I suggest that in the context of this story the literal meaning also plays an important function and must be considered. Dostoevsky has his dysregulated narrator trying to compensate for a duel he did not fight with a 'duel' in which he heavily stacks the odds against his 'opponent' to guarantee his own victory. This treacherous departure from duelling etiquette is an important component of the story to which Dostoevsky's repeated iterations of the word 'duel' draw the reader's attention. Note that Dostoevsky has Efimovich refer to duelling norms when the pawnbroker bursts in on his tryst with the Meek Creature.

pawnshop for the third time, the pawnbroker expresses a desire to shoot him. Like Dostoevsky's character, he takes the gun along when he goes to spy on his wife's assignation. Earlier in his film, Bresson suggests another way the gun might be used when the pawnbroker, agitated by his wife's prolonged absence after a quarrel, expresses apprehension that she might take her own life. By leaving the gun on the table he provides her with an opportunity to do so.

Because *Une femme douce* opens with Douce's suicide, viewers know already that she will not use the gun against herself. For Bresson, the point is to have them experience not suspense, but the gravity of the decision she considers and the choice she makes. Contemplating the murder and the suicide that the gun offers, Bresson's Douce resists both temptations that her husband put in her way. This throws the spuriousness of the pawnbroker's claim to victory into high relief and suggests that his designation of the episode as a duel is not simply an inaccuracy, but an effort to mask the deadly intent behind his gesture. As in his entire relationship with his wife, he stacks the odds so heavily against her that what he insists on calling a duel is in fact a scheme devised to secure victory over her that ultimately fails. Although it bears no outward resemblance to the contrived murder of Hamlet masquerading as a fair contest, the pawnbroker's rigged 'duel' with his wife replicates its falsehood and its perversion of the essential question 'to be, or not to be'. The deceitful theatricality that Bresson accentuates in his filmed scene from *Hamlet* is replicated by the pawnbroker, whose faithless 'seeming' similarly stifles genuine 'being'.

Bresson opens *Une femme douce* with a sequence of three shots: a table tipping over and a rocking chair set in motion on a balcony, then a white shawl floating slowly and gracefully downward, followed by cars screeching to a halt and the legs of onlookers surrounding the prone body of a woman next to whose face is the small pool of blood noted by the narrator in Dostoevsky's story. The advantage of beginning with the end is something Bresson learned from the Russian author: 'As Dostoevsky frequently does, I present the effect before the cause. I think this is a good idea because it increases the mystery; to witness events without knowing why they are occurring makes you desire to find out the reason.'[58] Intensifying viewers' desire to learn what leads up to this ending, Bresson's beginning provides a lens through which to assess the pawnbroker's account and, crucially, heightens awareness of Douce's story, enhancing the significance of her suicide.

As noted above, the power that the pawnbroker claims over his wife is rooted in the material world. That it dissipates in the domain of the ineffable is thrown into high relief by her trajectory, which is glimpsed beyond the pawnbroker's controlling narrative. The restrictions the pawnbroker imposes on his wife's freedom of movement and his claim to her body are offset by the series of

---

[58] Samuels, p. 681.

Figure 3.2 Douce (Dominique Sanda) shown dead on the pavement after her leap from the balcony, *Une femme douce*, directed by Robert Bresson, 1969.

her escalating departures over the course of 'A Meek Creature'. She first departs from the pawnshop as a slighted customer, then from their apartment which he forbids her to leave, from her marriage vows (the assignation with Efimovich) and from the matrimonial bed.[59] This succession of physical leave-takings is followed by a series of departures of a different order. Upon falling ill, she loses consciousness, leaving her insensate body behind. She next withdraws from the contest of wills into which her husband drew her, then departs into her second illness and, upon recovering, retreats into an inner world of her own. This marks the recuperation of her selfhood, which she reclaims by assuming responsibility for her actions, nurtures with her reading, and marks with the singing that alerts the pawnbroker that she has eluded his control. When he resorts to hyperbolised self-deprecation in an effort to reclaim control over her, she responds with compassion. She also understands that his theatrical outburst of love harbours a claim on her body and signals not a change of heart, but his attempt to reassert control over her. Choosing not to sacrifice herself to his needs as others of Dostoevsky's women characters do, nor to succumb to the power he holds over her, she abandons her body – the single vestige of her selfhood over which he can assert control – and effects the ultimate departure into death. The pawnbroker remains alone, captive to the confines of the material world that delimit his

[59] It is only after the Meek Creature does not spend the night in their matrimonial bed that her pawnbroker purchases the cot and screen.

power. Contemplating his wife's lifeless body, he expresses dread at its removal for burial which, as he says, will leave him completely alone. This patent failure to see past the physical body to what enlivened it emblematises the lifelessness of his own existence – his death in life.

Recognising the importance of the Meek Creature's departures, Bresson trains his camera on her recurrent comings and goings and on the doors and stairways she repeatedly traverses. He ends *Une femme douce* with the first two shots of the opening suicide sequence – the disturbed chair and table on the balcony and the beautifully floating white shawl – but replaces the third shot of cars screeching to a halt and spectators gathering around the body with a shot of Douce lying in her coffin, her final departure now complete. Rather than contemplate her life or her death, the pawnbroker fixes only on the body over which he sought control for the duration of Dostoevsky's story and Bresson's film. He holds her for a moment, asking that she open her eyes one last time, and the scene closes with the lid of the coffin being slowly, methodically screwed down. The pawnbroker's desolation is complete.

Douce's death that opens and closes Bresson's film could not be more different from the staged 'deaths' in the *Hamlet* production he includes in it. As Ginestet describes, Bresson opposes the theatrical deaths acted for all to see in the *Hamlet* scene to the private, unseen moment of Douce's death. The floating white scarf that replaces the plummeting body reflects Bresson's conviction that 'one must not show a person dying because it is impossible to do so'.[60] Rather than show the impossible moment of death, Bresson uses the contrast between the histrionic on-stage deaths in the scene from *Hamlet* and the exquisite delicacy of Douce's suicide sequence to capture the difference between the falsehood of the theatrical murder-cum-duel and the integrity of the private choice Douce makes to pull back from the damnable 'to kill, or not to kill' to confront for herself alone the unmuddied choice 'to be, or not to be'.

In *Une femme douce*, Bresson shows not Dostoevsky's work, but the 'being' that is essential to the Russian writer's quest, to his own cinematography and to genuine communion with the self and others – in life and in the creative domain. Ultimately the profound ties between 'A Meek Creature' and *Une femme douce* spring from their creators' all-embracing vision of art, life and death untainted by seeming.

BIBLIOGRAPHY

Atwell, Lee, '*Une femme douce*', *Film Quarterly*, 23 (1970), pp. 54–6.
Brenez, Nicole, Kent Jones, Daniel Morgan, Brian Price, James Quandt and Jonathan Rosenblum, 'Robert Bresson: A Symposium', in *Robert Bresson, Revised*, ed. James Quandt (Toronto: TIFF, 2011), pp. 595–627.

---

[60] Ginestet, p. 305.

Bresson, Robert, *Notes on Cinematography*, trans. Jonathan Griffin (New York: Urizen Books, 1977).
Bresson, Robert and Ronald Hayman, 'Robert Bresson: In conversation with Ronald Hayman', *The Transatlantic Review*, 46/47 (1973), pp. 16–23.
Burnett, Colin, *The Invention of Robert Bresson: The Auteur and His Market* (Bloomington: The University of Indiana Press, 2017).
Burry, Alexander, *Multi-Mediated Dostoevsky: Transposing Novels into Opera, Film, and Drama* (Evanston: Northwestern University Press, 2011).
Christa, Boris, 'Dostoevskii and money', in *The Cambridge Companion to Dostoevskii*, ed. W. J. Leatherbarrow (Cambridge: Cambridge University Press, 2002), pp. 93–110.
Dargis, Manohla, '*Une femme douce*', *Film Comment*, 35 (1999), pp. 41–3.
Dostoevsky, F.M., 'Krotkaia', in *Polnoe sobranie sochinenii*, 30 vols (Leningrad: Nauka, 1972–90), XXIV (1982), pp. 5–35.
Ginestet, Gaëlle, '*Une femme douce* by Robert Bresson: *Hamlet* or Anti-Cinematography', in *Shakespeare on Screen: Hamlet*, eds Sarah Hatchuel & Nathalie Vienne-Guerrin (Rouen, Havre: Publications des Universités de Rouen et du Havre, 2011), pp. 291–308.
Iutkevich, Sergei, '"Sinematograf" Robera Bressona', *Iskusstvo kino*, 2 (1979), pp. 145–58 and 3 (1979), pp. 145–59.
Le Dantec, Mireille Latil, 'Bresson, Dostoevsky', in *Robert Bresson, Revised*, ed. James Quandt (Toronto: TIFF, 2011), pp. 413–25.
Pelikan Straus, Nina, *Dostoevsky and the Woman Question: Rereadings at the End of a Century* (New York: St Martin's Press, 1994).
Price, Brian, *Neither God nor Master: Robert Bresson and Radical Politics* (Minneapolis: University of Minnesota Press, 2011).
Samuels, Charles Thomas, 'Encountering Robert Bresson', in *Robert Bresson, Revised*, ed. James Quandt (Toronto: TIFF, 2011), pp. 667–91.
Shakespeare, William, *Hamlet* <https://www.gutenberg.org/files/1524/1524-h/1524-h.htm> [accessed 19 October 2021].
Schrader, Paul, 'Robert Bresson, Possibly: Interview by Paul Schrader', in *Robert Bresson, Revised*, ed. James Quandt (Toronto: TIFF, 2011), pp. 693–705.
Tarkovsky, Andrey, *Sculpting in Time: Reflections on the Cinema*, trans. Kitty Hunter-Blair (Austin: University of Texas Press, 1987).
Thiher, Allen, 'Bresson's *Un condamné à mort*: The Semiotics of Grace', in *Robert Bresson, Revised*, ed. James Quandt (Toronto: TIFF, 2011), pp. 287–97.
White, Frederick H., 'Conclusion: Passport Control – Departing on a Cinematic Journey', in *Border Crossing: Russian Literature into Film*, eds Alexander Burry and Frederick H. White (Edinburgh: Edinburgh University Press, 2016), pp. 239–64.

Filmography

Une femme douce, directed by Robert Bresson (France, Marianne Productions, Parc Film, 1969).

4. FUNNY AND FRIGHTENING: DOSTOEVSKY'S *THE DOUBLE* IN RICHARD AYOADE'S INTERPRETATION

Tine Roesen

At first glance it seems surprising that the celebrity comedian and actor Richard Ayoade (b. 1977), perhaps best known from the Channel 4 sitcom *The IT Crowd* (2006–2013), should take on the project of adapting a Dostoevsky novella for a contemporary audience. A notoriously dark and complicated Russian classic in the hands of a British comedian? However, Ayoade's film *The Double* (2013) had a generally positive reception, and a Guardian reviewer even praised Ayoade for turning 'an unpromising Dostoevsky story into a quick-witted, elegant and genuinely unsettling film.'[1] Other reviewers have been more appreciative of the qualities of the source text, Dostoevsky's *The Double* (*Dvoinik*, 1846/1866), as a ground-breaking identity drama, and of the way Ayoade and co-scriptwriter Avi Korine transposed the qualities of the literary work into a completely different setting. In the present chapter, I follow this line of thinking while analysing Ayoade's adaptation in further depth than has yet been attempted. I do so after a presentation of Dostoevsky's source text in quite some detail. I shall highlight those particulars of Ayoade's interpretation that I regard as congenial, specifically: its chronotope; its dark, primarily linguistic humour; and its elaboration of the hero's quest for manhood. In doing so, I shall consider the effect of apparent deviations from the Russian original and discuss Ayoade's authorship in terms

[1] Peter Bradshaw, 'The Double review – A brilliantly realised nightmare universe', *The Guardian*, 3 April 2014 <https://www.theguardian.com/film/2014/apr/03/the-double-review-richard-ayoade> [accessed 1 September 2021].

of a benevolent manipulation through which he creatively widens Dostoevsky's images and vocabulary while remaining true to the already modern spirit of his novella. In my analysis, Ayoade's ambition is not so much to translate a Russian literary classic into a modern British or Anglophone film version, as it is to bring out the novella's transcultural, world literature qualities in a screening true to contemporary globalised culture.

Dostoevsky's Double

Dostoevsky's *The Double* appeared in 1846 as the young writer's second published work after the novel of letters *Poor Folk*. Compared to his later novels, it is a small work, a novella comprising only 120 pages in the academic edition of his collected works, where *Crime and Punishment* comprises 420 pages. Whereas the early works in general have often been disregarded as minor sketches and mere preparations for the writer's later major novels – with the curious exception of *Poor Folk*, which was the absolute favourite of the Soviet school system – *The Double* has been acclaimed and is well-known worldwide for its psychologically gripping plot. I shall now briefly recapitulate this plot and highlight the characteristics of the novella as a basis for analysing Ayoade's interpretation.

Dostoevsky's hero, Iakov Petrovich Goliadkin, is a titular councillor, working in the St Petersburg bureaucracy of the 1840s. He has ambitions of climbing the career ladder but is also afraid of transgressing proper behaviour and is hampered by a timid personality. A perpetual inner dialogue or dispute goes on in his head, and his frequent change of mind is accompanied by a change of direction as he roams about the city. He obviously has no stable sense of self, and during the story's four days we watch his identity crisis culminate in the appearance of an identical double, evidently bent on taking his place in the office and in life.

On day one, Goliadkin wakes up to an exciting adventure. He has rented a carriage, as well as an outfit for his man servant, Petrushka, and dresses up to go to Nevskii Prospekt – the place to be seen for someone going to a party, as he allegedly is. However, when he is in fact spotted, first by two co-workers, and then by his boss, he shrinks back: 'It's quite all right; this is not me at all, Andrey Philippovich, it's not me at all, not me, and that's all about it.'[2] He is prompted to make a detour to see his doctor, Christian Rutenspitz, who is puzzled by Goliadkin's alternations between silent pain and ramblings about his own honesty and the lies and conspiracies of his 'enemies'. The doctor recommends that Goliadkin go out more and enjoy himself. Back on Nevskii

---

[2] Fyodor Dostoyevsky, *Notes from Underground. The Double*, trans. Jessie Coulson (London: Penguin Books, 1972), p. 132.

Prospekt, Goliadkin goes on a shopping spree, browsing and bargaining for hours, but buying very little. Finally, he heads to the party, which turns out to be a birthday celebration for his former benefactor, Olsufii Ivanovich's young daughter, Klara Olsufievna. To his shock and detriment, he is refused entry at the front door, but sneaks up the back stairs where he spends several hours contemplating whether to enter the house. He finally crashes the party and manages to have a (disastrously clumsy) dance with Klara before being kicked out. Walking home through the cold and dark Petersburg night he feels finished as a human being, annihilated, and suddenly senses another presence nearby. He spots a man looking suspiciously like himself, follows him through the streets to his own flat, where to his horror he recognises him as 'himself, none other than himself, Mr Golyadkin himself, another Mr Golyadkin, but exactly the same as himself – in short, in every respect what is called his double'.[3]

On the morning of the second day, Goliadkin wonders whether the double had been a feverish dream or maybe a new attack from his enemies. He picks up the courage to go to work, where the double now also appears and is introduced as Iakov Petrovich Goliadkin, a new employee. Goliadkin is shocked, and without any luck tries to convince his immediate superior that their likeness is uncanny and that it is a scandal. After work, Goliadkin junior (the double) pays a humble visit to Goliadkin senior and spends the night after a jolly evening with drinks, mutual confidences and sworn friendship.

The following morning, Goliadkin junior has left without a sign, but turns up at work where he now acts with confidence and slyness, stealing assignments from Goliadkin senior, while mocking and harassing him. This continues after work, and Goliadkin senior finally writes a letter to his namesake demanding an explanation and appealing to his honour and friendship. However, the teasing continues, and after wild dreams, including images of innumerable doubles springing up from the ground around him, Goliadkin decides, on the morning of the fourth day, to act decisively against his enemies. He writes to Goliadkin junior: 'Either you or I, one or the other, but both of us together is impossible!', adding that if necessary, he is ready to fight a duel.[4] When he finally catches up with his double, however, he still tries to make peace with him and implores him to tear up the letter or at least 'read it in the opposite sense'.[5] But Goliadkin junior mockingly flees him again, and there is no way of denying that Goliadkin senior has been replaced at work by his double. Goliadkin senior is crushed and confused when he suddenly finds a letter in his pocket written by Klara, who declares her love for him and begs him to save her from her home prison

---

[3] Ibid., p. 173.
[4] Ibid., p. 232.
[5] Ibid., p. 253.

by secretly eloping with her the following night. He sets out to do so and seems already far away in his preoccupations when he is given notice of redundancy. He also finds a message that Petrushka has left for a better master. Stripped of everything, reduced to a freezing man with a hired coach, he is back in the courtyard in front of Olsufii Ivanovich's house, where a party is again being held. He is still waiting for Klara, whom he sees as a spoiled, silly girl but nevertheless feels obliged to save, when he is spotted from the house and brought inside. He is met with compassion for his poorly state, but there is no sign that Klara recognises him, and Goliadkin identifies several doubles and tries to explain himself. Finally his doctor arrives and escorts him to a place outside the city. Goliadkin junior is hanging on to their carriage for quite a while. It is clear to the reader that Goliadkin is being taken to a mental asylum, but in Goliadkin's eyes the doctor is the devil who brings doom.

INTERPRETATIONS OF *THE DOUBLE*

The young Dostoevsky had high hopes for his *Double*. Having been initially praised for *Poor Folk*, but also criticised for its wordiness and, not least, mocked for his vanity and lack of self-control in handling his fame, he was confident that his second work would once and for all establish him as a great writer. But *The Double* was almost uniformly so heavily disparaged that he himself began to see it as a failure, although still insisting that it had some points of genius.[6] For Breger and other psychologically focused scholars, these clear signs of Dostoevsky's own conflicted self reinforce the interpretation of the novella as, not least, motivated by self-scrutiny.[7] Dostoevsky planned for the novella's revision, which happened only after his arrest and Siberian exile (1849–59),[8] and the revised 1865 edition is the one that has been published and read since, both in Russian and in translation. The revision deleted some repetitions and minor motifs while elaborating the main motifs; it removed the original mock-heroic chapter titles ('Chapter one, in which our hero wakes up' etc.); and it changed the subtitle of the novella from 'The adventures of Mr Goliadkin' to 'A Petersburg poem', which emphasised both the role of St Petersburg in the novella and the affinity to Nikolai Gogol's works – his poem *Dead Souls* and his cycle of *Petersburg Tales* (1835–42).[9]

---

[6] Fedor Dostoevsky, *Polnoe sobranie sochinenii*, 30 vols (Leningrad: Nauka, 1972–90), I (1972), pp. 483–4.
[7] Louis Breger, *Dostoevsky. The Author as Psychoanalyst* (London and New York: Routledge, 1989), pp. 107–26.
[8] Dostoevsky, pp. 484–5.
[9] Ibid. p. 486.

The revisions did not, however, remove the negative criticism. Despite Belinsky's benevolent attempts to modify and excuse, the reception in 1846 had been harsh, one critic even calling the work 'a sin against artistic conscience' and contributed to establishing a well-known commonplace in Dostoevsky reception ever since: he seemed to write in haste and by commission, and 'this will never lead to poetic creations, but only to nightmares'.[10]

By the 1880s, developments within modern psychology led to a renewed interest in Dostoevsky's works in general, and in *The Double* in particular. This interest was based on a general agreement that Dostoevsky developed the demonic/gothic motif of the double familiar from E. T. A. Hoffmann's stories into a psychologically realistic mode, inspired by, but also going beyond Gogol. In 1885 Vladimir Chizh published 'Dostoevsky as psychopathologist',[11] and some years later Otto Rank's analysis of *The Double* from a psychopathological point of view insisted on its accurate portrayal of a paranoid state.[12] Kohlberg, analysing Goliadkin as he would analyse patients, has since refuted the diagnosis of paranoia and of split personality, talking about an 'obsessive-compulsive neurosis' and 'a conflict between autonomy and shame or doubt'.[13] Louis Breger, whose monograph on Dostoevsky draws parallels between the process of writing and psychoanalysis, has defined the novella as 'an experiment with projection, splitting and dissociation'.[14] Several Freudian interpretations exist,[15] but in addition to purely psychological analyses, researchers also eventually took an interest in the literary structure of the novella and the structural role of the double.

Viktor Vinogradov in his 1922 ground-breaking study of Gogol and Dostoevsky as fathers of Russian naturalism showed how Dostoevsky's *Double* not only was inspired by Gogol's fantastic plot and narration, particularly in *The Nose* and *Diary of a Madman*, but also transposed the events to a tragicofantastic level through bringing the perspective of the narrator closer to the hero's perspective and his feverish imagination.[16]

Mikhail Bakhtin in his famous book on Dostoevsky's poetics (1929/1963) saw this as no less than a small-scale Copernican revolution: 'Not only the

---

[10] Ibid., pp. 490–1.
[11] V. F. Chizh, *Dostoevsky kak psikhopatolog* (Moscow: Universitetskaia tipografiia, 1885).
[12] Otto Rank, *Der Doppelgänger* (Vienna: Internationale Psychoanalytische Verlag, 1925).
[13] Lawrence Kohlberg, 'Psychological Analysis and Literary Form: A Study of the Doubles in Dostoevsky', *Daedalus*, 92 (1963), pp. 345–62 (pp. 352–3).
[14] Breger, p. 124.
[15] See Natalie Reber, *Studien zum Motiv des Doppelgängers bei Dostojevskij und E. T. A. Hoffmann* (Giessen: Marburger Abhandlungen zur Geschichte und Kultur Osteuropas, 1964) for a 1964 overview.
[16] V. V. Vinogradov, *Evoliutsiia russkogo naturalizma. Gogol i Dostoevsky* (Leningrad: Izd. Akademiia, 1929), pp. 279–90.

reality of the hero himself, but even the external world and the everyday life surrounding him are drawn into the process of self-awareness, are transferred from the author's to the hero's field of vision.'[17] Bakhtin also defined the position of the author with regard to the hero in Dostoevsky's polyphonic novel as a 'dialogic position, one that affirms the independence, internal freedom, unfinalizability and indeterminacy of the hero'.[18] For Bakhtin, Dostoevsky's dialogic imagination manifests itself in the ideas in his works. They are inseparable from persons and their voices and ever developing live dialogic interactions[19] as well as in double-voiced, internally dialogised discourses.[20] Already from his first works, Dostoevsky develops the characteristic speech style of his whole oeuvre, a style defined by 'the intense anticipation of another's words'[21] and what Bakhtin elsewhere calls the super addressee, the indirectly addressed third, representing an 'absolutely just responsive understanding'.[22] Goliadkin's discourse in *The Double* is a particularly clear example of this style: his speech partly simulates total independence, partly tries to avert the attention of others, and partly expresses his subordination to others and his hope of being understood on a higher level – his entire inner life develops dialogically.[23] In Bakhtin's analysis, Goliadkin junior springs from one of Goliadkin's own voices, his self-sufficient, confident voice, and the narration itself is also a continuation and development of this voice – thus not only telling us about Goliadkin but also shouting mockingly into his ear.[24]

Albeit Bakhtin's definition of polyphony, in general, and his analysis of *The Double*, in particular, have been criticised and modified by Wolf Schmid,[25] Bakhtin's main observations on *The Double* are generally accepted. Moreover, Bakhtin's points combine well with psychological analyses of the novella while not letting us forget the particular characteristics of voice, perspective and narration of this work of literature. The mocking narration enhances the tragicomedy of the novella's plot, and we shall see how this narration is transferred into Ayoade's visual version.

---

[17] Mikhail Bakhtin, *Problems of Dostoevsky's Poetics*, trans. Caryl Emerson (Minneapolis and London: University of Minnesota Press, 1984), p. 49.
[18] Ibid., p. 63.
[19] Ibid., pp. 85–8.
[20] Ibid., pp. 203–4.
[21] Ibid., p. 205.
[22] Mikhail Bakhtin, 'The Problem of the Text in Linguistics, Philology, and the Human Sciences', in *Speech Genres and other Late Essays*, trans. Vern W. McGee (Austin: University of Texas Press, 1986), pp. 103–31 (p. 126).
[23] Bakhtin, 'The Problem of the Text', pp. 211–12.
[24] Ibid., pp. 215, 220–1.
[25] Wolf Schmid, *Der Textaufbau in den Erzählungen Dostoevskijs* (Amsterdam: Verlag B. R. Grüner, 1986).

In addition to his influential analysis of the dialogic poetics of *The Double*, Bakhtin has also contributed to our understanding of this work with his concept of the 'chronotope' to distinguish dominant combinations of time and space through European literary history. He singles out the chronotope of the *threshold* and related chronotopes (staircase, front hall, corridor, street, square) as always metaphorical and symbolic. He discusses the main places of action in Dostoevsky's works as places where crisis-like events occur, including 'the falls, resurrections, renewals, epiphanies, decisions that determine the whole life of a man'. Bakhtin suggests that in this chronotope 'time is essentially instantaneous': it gives an impression that 'it has no duration and falls out of the normal course of biographical time'.[26] In no other work by Dostoevsky, I would claim, is the threshold as dominant as in *The Double*: Goliadkin waits either on staircases or in front halls or on literal thresholds; he also runs back and forth in the streets, along the embankments or across the bridges of St Petersburg. And the city itself, 'the most abstract and intentional city in the whole round world' according to Dostoevsky's Underground Man,[27] plays a part in this abundance of crises. True to the Petersburg myth – as conveyed and developed in Pushkin's *Bronze Horseman* (1837) and Gogol's *Petersburg Tales* – any person who lives in St Petersburg is bound to experience both ontological and epistemological uncertainty. In his philosophical interpretation of *The Double*, Seitz aptly concludes on the conundrum of Goliadkin's double, that is, the way the novella evades or attempts to decide to what extent the double is a figment of Goliadkin's mad imagination: 'What this is all supposed to "mean" would be up for grabs were we not to acknowledge that meaning is overrated. What we witness in this story is not meaning but deadly shadows.'[28]

Of all the many interpretations of *The Double*, John Jones's reading remains the richest, in that it appreciates both the genius and the humour of Dostoevsky's linguistic art. He has aptly described Goliadkin's frightening identity problem as 'nobody to be and nowhere to go', and his identity loss as being completed in an eternal present without any real context: he is 'naked will facing contextless choice, an abstract and banal figurine positioned in a nightmare existential present'.[29] There are many signs in the text that time and place have no solidity for Goliadkin. On top of all the thresholds, he is constantly surprised by the passing of time, always focusing on a new 'tomorrow', and in a remarkable passage

---

[26] Mikhail Bakhtin, 'Forms of Time and of the Chronotope in the Novel', in *The Dialogic Imagination*, ed. Michael Holquist, trans Caryl Emerson and Michael Holquist (Austin: University of Texas Press, 1981), pp. 84–258 (p. 248).

[27] Dostoyevsky, p. 17.

[28] Brian Seitz, *Intersubjectivity and the Double. Troubled Matters* (New York: Palgrave Macmillan, 2016), p. 65.

[29] John Jones, *Dostoevsky* (Oxford and New York: Oxford University Press, 1985), p. 94.

towards the end, he reflects that maybe the love letter he has just received was written tomorrow rather than yesterday. Similarly, his office, flat and possessions lack solidity. We are not sure whether they all exist, since they seem to be constituted solely by their place in Goliadkin's meandering reflections – his busy but futile shopping spree at the beginning of the story being a case in point. In Jones's words, Goliadkin is Mr Naked, Mr Stripped, a linguistic ectoplasm.[30]

This linguistic ectoplasm comprises, as we have seen, some aspects of dialogism. And here yet another dualism deserves to be mentioned. Goliadkin's vocabulary is not only characterised by ethical dichotomies such as timid versus egoistic, good versus bad, friends versus enemies, but also by words that have double meanings, that is homonyms of metaphorical and literal meanings, respectively. Dostoevsky lets Goliadkin linger somewhere in between the meanings of expressions such as: 'going one's own way', 'standing firm', 'falling', and 'taking a courageous step', among others. Representing absurd constellations within Goliadkin's mind of, on the one hand, moral and existential questions and, on the other, banal observations and activities, this homonymic confusion secures a profoundly tragic but also hilarious humour. One of the best examples occurs during Goliadkin's initial visit to his doctor, who asks:

> 'Tell me, please, where are you living now? Yes . . . I should like . . . I think you were formerly living.'
>
> 'I was living, Christian Ivanovich, I was living even formerly. I must have been, mustn't I?' answered Mr Golyadkin, accompanying his words with a little laugh, and slightly disconcerting Christian Ivanovich with his reply.[31]

Ayoade picks up on this homonymic humour right in the opening line of his film.

Ayoade's Interpretation of Dostoevsky's Double

The 1 hour 29 minute-film opens in the early hours on a subway train. Half-asleep, a young man (Jesse Eisenberg), whose name is Simon James as we will later learn, is on his way to work. The very first piece of dialogue in the film signals both its central, absurd drama and its humorous gist. A man who suddenly appears in front of Simon says: 'You're in my place.' 'I'm sorry?' Simon replies. 'You are in my place,' the man repeats. Simon looks around and the camera follows his gaze on the otherwise empty train and its empty seats. Simon stands and gives his seat to the unknown man. And thus, his loss of foothold in the world has begun.

Simon does not work behind a desk in nineteenth-century Russian state administration, but behind a computer in a fictitious company providing

---

[30] Ibid., p. 59.
[31] Dostoyevsky, p. 143.

Figure 4.1 Simon and James (Jesse Eisenberg), *The Double*, directed by Richard Ayoade, 2013.

'data-processing solutions', the equipment signalling sometime in the 1980s. Having lost his identity card on the first morning – timidly letting other people into the train before barely succeeding to get out, his suitcase stuck in the door – he relies on his colleagues' recognition of him to be allowed into work, but even after seven years he is not recognised by anyone. To the security guard, the equivalent of Dostoevsky's doormen, identity does not exist separately from identity card, so he repeatedly considers him a visitor and issues him only one-day passes. On the first of these passes he even misspells his name as Simon Ames. It is one of many linguistic identity jokes: the surname Ames serves as anagram of the word 'same'. Likewise, when Simon's double appears, his name is not identical to his, but mirrors it: Simon James is doubled by James Simon, who is also played by Jesse Eisenberg (in technically impressive co-acting scenes). This is in the spirit of Dostoevsky who used this kind of joke in his early works such as *Poor People* and *A Novel in Nine Letters*.

Other plays on the notions of sameness, difference and doubling reappear throughout the film. The film showcases the intricate interplay with the double embedded in Dostoevsky's novel. In a cruder fashion the idea of copying is related to technical problems, including several instances when Simon wants two copies of a sheet, but the printer always produces one copy, and he must go to a central (monstrous) copy machine to get another copy. Not only is he mocked that he only wants one copy, he also – quite funnily as the plot develops – must beg for this copy. A benefit associated with this tedious repetition is the beautiful young woman, Hannah (Mia Wasikowska), who works in the copy room – Klara Olsufievna's realistic new position in a mixed-gender work environment. The highest authority in the workplace, who in Dostoevsky's work is His Excellency, is here the Colonel, a sea captain-like figure absurdly dressed all in white and featured in numerous pictures hanging in the rooms and corridors of the workplace as well as in video commercials.

The main events follow Dostoevsky's original storyline, with the same growing mental confusion and thus dissociation from a concrete time and place. Day one is an ordinary workday, except for Simon's loss of his identity card. In the evening, the company throws a mandatory party where Simon looks forward to seeing Hannah, but he is refused access because he cannot prove his identity and, after sneaking in, is thrown out in disgrace. 'This is not me', he yells to the Colonel as he is being forced to leave, directly quoting Goliadkin's ominous self-denial to his superior on Nevskii Prospekt. Walking home alone through the dark evening, Simon is upset by seeing a glimpse of someone looking like himself. He relaxes by watching a hard-boiled action series called *The Replicator* on a small TV, but also by spying on his neighbours opposite through a telescope. A man standing on a ledge waves at him and then jumps to his death. Simon is questioned by the police.

Day two is yet another working day where a new employee is introduced: James Simon. Nobody recognises Simon's anguish at their similarity, but they welcome the brash James with a warmth they have obviously never shown to the timid Simon. The two doubles have a night out, James going after girls but also defending Simon from being beaten up, and they flee in common youthful joy. James spends the night at Simon's place. On day three, James enjoys popularity and success at work and lets Simon do his entrance test as well as all the hard work, while he seduces their superior's punk-style teenage daughter Melanie, for whom Simon had just been appointed a mentor. James helps Simon invite Hannah on a date, but during the disastrous rendezvous, where Simon as usual fails to make conversation or to convince the waitress to serve him, Hannah is only interested in Simon insofar as he can help her get in touch with James.

On what may be day four, James helps Simon on his next date with Hannah, having persuaded Simon to go as 'James'. 'Isn't that unethical?', asks Simon, to which James mockingly replies: 'How sweet.' James helps Simon through a radio connection, but then, when Simon fails to follow his instructions, steps in to take his own place on the date and disappears with Hannah after a deep kiss and the applause of the restaurant's staff and guests. Next day, James steals Simon's work on rationalisation processes and is invited to join the Colonel in the 'Honor Lounge', Ayoade's American version of His Excellency's office in the Petersburg bureaucracy. Simon confronts James, asking him to stop taking advantage of Melanie and Hannah, but James threatens to set up Simon as the seducer of the teenager. He also forces Simon to swap apartments and uses Simon's words about Hannah to seduce her.

Finally, the combination of Simon's lack of company ID and James having taken his place causes Simon's total annihilation. He has a last meeting with the HR department and is told: 'You don't exist anymore. According to the system you have never existed.' Simon replies in almost the exact same words used by Goliadkin in his dialogue with doctor Rutenspitz: 'But I used to exist.' After this, Simon explodes in front of everybody at the workplace, insisting on his own identity: 'I am a person! I exist! I am a human being!' He calls out James as a dangerous fraud, using uncharacteristically vulgar words: 'You fuckers don't know what you're up against!'

The ending after this climax diverges from Dostoevsky's *Double* in several ways. Whereas Goliadkin is taken away by his doctor to a mental asylum, Simon is thrown out of the workplace. Back home, he writes two suicide notes. Both are addressed 'To Whom It May Concern.' The first, left on his table, says: 'I have decided to end my life because I no longer exist. A person shall amount to something and not float around this earth like a ghost.' Once again, the audience encounters linguistic humour as well as Ayoade's matching Seitz's image of 'deadly shadows' (mentioned above), and a nod at Gogol's Petersburg tale *The Overcoat*, whose protagonist becomes a ghost. Simon's second suicide note, put in the pocket of his jacket, simply says: 'I am a ghost.' Having written the notes, he suddenly becomes aware of Hannah lying unconscious in the apartment opposite him, and he takes her to hospital, where he is assumed to

Figure 4.2 Simon (Jesse Eisenberg) and Hannah (Mia Wasikowska), *The Double*, directed by Richard Ayoade, 2013.

be her husband and the father of the child she is expecting. Hannah hates him for rescuing her from her suicide attempt and tells him to kill himself. After he has left, however, we see her digging into the pockets of his jacket, which she is wearing. She finds the scraps of her own discarded drawings, which he has retrieved from the garbage container and put back together. The scene ends with Hannah smiling softly.

Meanwhile, Simon gets a phone call that his mother is dead and is to be buried by midnight. He rushes off, and of course James is already at the (macabre, almost Von Trier-like) funeral. Simon attacks him but is himself attacked by a devilish-looking and sounding priest who literally shoves him into the open grave. He wakes up in the early morning, visits Hannah and asks her: 'Do you know who I am, do you recognise me?', which her eyes confirm. He then goes to his own flat, ties an unconscious James to the bed, and we begin to suspect his intricate plans and the circular composition of the film. Simon jumps to his death from the ledge outside James' flat, but while this causes James' death, Simon miraculously survives and is accompanied in the rescue ambulance by Hannah.

Apart from this happy ending, where the beloved woman replaces the devil-like figure of Goliadkin's doctor, and the future seems to spell recovery, other alterations have appeared during the film. Most remarkably, Simon has a mother, whom he visits regularly in a creepy nursing home. Sadly, even his own mother does not recognise him. 'Which one was you?' she asks after seeing a video commercial from his company. In the plot, she and the nursing home seem to replace Goliadkin's former landlady Karolina Ivanovna and her boarding house. Simon's obligations to visit his quite hateful and raving mother and her greedy caretakers elaborate the issue of Goliadkin's guilt, having paid for his one-time lodgings by promising marriage to the landlady, a promise never kept. He fled from it and now he is haunted by his guilty conscience, as we learn from several Freudian slips in Goliadkin's ramblings.

Another remarkable difference is in the character of the two heroes: Simon does not seem quite as ambitious as Goliadkin, who from the beginning is bent on proving his (higher) worth and place in society. Simon has ideas on how to 'rationalise processes' to the benefit of his company, but they do not seem to be crucial to him. Simon also generally seems timid. These differences may be caused by the differences between literature and film, for while we have access to Goliadkin's ambition through his inner dialogue or stream-of-consciousness, we only know Simon from his visual appearance and actual utterances. However, one hint that Simon may be more ambitious and aggressive than he seems, is his apparent addiction to the series *The Replicator*, featuring a gunslinging hero and scenes reminiscent of *The Terminator* (1984). And of course, the vile actions of his double may spring from his own secret desires. But in Ayoade's version, the double actually seems to be identified less with the hero's own ambitious side than with the expectations of those who surround him, i.e., that he make himself noticed and distinguish himself. I would see this shift as a comment by Ayoade on the development of modern capitalist society and on its work culture. His film suggests that nowadays, whether you want to or not, you are expected to be and act like an ambitious individual. This is not so much a deviation from Dostoevsky's work as it is an update of his acute sense of the influence of modernity on human society and the individual. In the following sections, I shall highlight those aspects of Dostoevsky's novella which Ayoade picks up with similar genius.

Adaptation of a Chronotope

Ayoade does not let his version of *The Double* take place in St Petersburg of the 1840s, but transposes the gist of this myth-ridden city into an urban wasteland in the form of an abandoned factory building that he and his crew happened to find. It is situated in the UK, we are told by Ayoade, but geographically and temporally it looks anonymous in its monstrosity.[32] While hardware, software and video games featured in the film signal the 1980s, other interiors seem to point further back, and the prison-like apartment buildings as well as soft drinks of peculiar, synthetic colours have a futuristic, dystopian aura. Characters speak English, but their accents differ considerably, and the setting is demonstratively multicultural: most of the music in the soundtrack is Japanese or South Korean pop music, and costumes are stylistically all over the place. The ominous, sonorous pulse of the basic soundtrack, moreover, adds to the dystopian feel. This whole 'retro-futuristic' setting, as Ayoade himself called it,[33] is his way of bringing the story up to date without designating a specific time or place. As I see it, he thereby manages to highlight the novella's transcultural qualities through a distorted view of contemporary globalised culture. Ironically, this apparent deviation from historical Dostoevsky may be seen as congenial to the authorial intention. Simon is, just like Goliadkin, 'an abstract and banal figurine positioned in a nightmare existential present'.[34]

As Connor Doak has pointed out, the film's dim light and yellow-green colours are true to Goliadkin's experience of the Petersburg morning light coming through his windows on the very first page of the novella.[35] Moreover, the

---

[32] 'Filmmaker Richard Ayoade discussed his new film "The Double" starring Jesse Eisenberg and Mia Wasikowska during a Q&A following a screening at New Directors/New Films 2014', *Film at Lincoln Center* <https://www.youtube.com/watch?v=KgLGR8nQyaU> [accessed 1 September 2021].

[33] Ibid.

[34] Jones, p. 94.

[35] Connor Doak, 'Gender Trouble in The Double: Masculinity in Dostoevsky's Novella and Ayoade's Film', in *The Bloggers Karamazov*, 2015 <https://jordanrussiacenter.org/news/gender-trouble-double-masculinity-dostoevskys-novella-ayoades-film/#.YTCsLNMzbq0> [accessed 1 September 2021].

life-threatening conditions of St Petersburg for a lonely clerk – wind, rain, snow, cold, floods, but also hyper reflexivity, confusion and madness – seem to converge in the high frequency of suicides mentioned by police officers, and to be symbolised in a pigeon crashing against the company building early in the film, its mutilated body landing right in front of Simon. To Simon, minding his work but also trying to find a way out of his loneliness, suicide clearly presents itself as an option. Moreover, Ayoade intensifies the identity theme by confronting his hero with a workplace dominated by inhuman computers and machines and immersing him in a labyrinthic culture dominated by TVs, videos and video games. It is an early version of virtual reality, but it is already ominous for solid human existence.[36]

Ayoade's sense of Dostoevsky is mirrored by Dostoevsky's sense of modernity, his prefiguring of the existential nightmares in the works of Franz Kafka, Albert Camus and Jean-Paul Sartre. According to Jones, *The Double* is even closer to Kafka than to Gogol: Goliadkin's nobody to be and nowhere to go resembles 'the Kafkaesque mouse caught between the trap of self and the cat of other people, institutions, the open world'; and, like his modernist successors, Dostoevsky presents his hero as contextless choice facing naked will.[37] Goliadkin thus prefigures the plight of twentieth-century urban man and his self-alienation, with Ayoade meeting him halfway and taking him to a suitably monstrous factory.

The temporal and spatial contextlessness of Dostoevsky's *Double* is also, I believe, represented by Ayoade in the film's many abrupt cuts and in the anonymous and sparse interiors of Simon James' work cubicle and flat, and also, incidentally, his private desk drawer. When the single man is placed within such barren frames, we are close to the dark humour of modernist absurd drama a la Beckett.

Dostoevsky's Humour Transposed

Although the atmosphere is generally more ominous in Ayoade's version, he follows the Russian original insofar as Goliadkin's story goes from mostly comic, via tragicomic to tragic and dark, without, however, leaving its dark humour behind.

When asked in 2014 how, adapting a book about madness, he succeeded in making it funny, Ayoade immediately countered: 'The book is funny!', later adding: 'I like films that are both funny and frightening.'[38] Dostoevsky's novella

---

[36] See also Seitz, pp. 150–1.
[37] Jones, pp. 72–3.
[38] 'CBC: Richard Ayoade & Jesse Eisenberg on *The Double*', 2014 <https://www.youtube.com/watch?v=Wm_E8bQ2wwg> [accessed 1 September 2021].

is, indeed, already both funny and frightening. There is slapstick humour when Goliadkin – not unlike Rowan Atkinson's Mr Bean in the British sitcom – dresses up and travels around town, as well as when he attempts to dance with Klara at her birthday ball. And there are plenty of practical jokes featuring the double as stand-in or usurper. More profound, however, is the already mentioned humour emanating from Goliadkin's homonymic confusion, which goes all the way to confusing living somewhere with living at all, being alive.

The humorous aspects of *The Double* have not always been appreciated. Many analyses ignore them, others typically deem them ill-placed and excessive, in the vein of Donald Fanger:

> The story of Mr. Golyadkin is told from a Golyadkin-like point of view. This conveys an element of realistic strangeness admirably at times, but it wears badly and eventually muddles the perspective to produce a kind of unintentional grotesquerie, like that of a joke in bad taste that goes on and on.[39]

Breger is more appreciative, calling the novella 'a brilliant and darkly humorous study, far ahead of its time'.[40] And Morson is in my view close to incorporating Dostoevsky's model reader, when he defines the novella as metaphysical comedy: 'Dostoevsky creates humor from metaphysical quandary. Whenever the novella suggests that subjectivity is bifurcated or duplicated, we laugh at the absurdity.' Morson sums up: 'The story's deep humor derives, in short, from Goliadkin's recognition, and simultaneous refusal to recognise, that the double is not just like him but is him, and that he is his own impersonator.'[41]

As is already clear from the above summary, Ayoade has an eye for the cinematic slapstick potential of Dostoevsky's work, but also shows a keen awareness of its both practical and metaphysical identity jokes as well as its homonymic tragicomedy. His transposition of the literary text into film includes a translation of textual features into body language and mimicry, placing them into the storyline itself. Here we also see how Ayoade develops and expands humorous features already present in the novella. I shall discuss a few significant examples.

---

[39] Donald Fanger, *Dostoevsky and Romantic Realism: A Study of Dostoevsky in Relation to Balzac, Dickens, and Gogol* (Evanston: Northwestern University Press, 1965), p. 160.
[40] Breger, p. 112.
[41] Gary Saul Morson, 'Me and My Double: Selfhood, Consciousness, and Empathy in The Double', in *Before They Were Titans: Essays on the Early Works of Dostoevsky and Tolstoy*, ed. Elizabeth Cheresh Allen (Boston: Academic Studies Press, 2015), pp. 43–60 (pp. 47, 49).

After the initially witnessed suicide, when Simon is questioned by the police, he wonders why the man did it. One police officer says: 'He left a note saying he was lonely.' And the other officer adds: 'More exercise, that's important.' This absurd comment is, of course, an echo of Dostoevsky's Dr Rutenspitz advising Goliadkin to get over his problems by getting out among people and having a drink or two. In Dostoevsky's version, it is a piece of advice testifying to the doctor's understanding of Goliadkin's social anxiety but also to his complete lack of Fingerspitzengefühl – which is tragic for the suffering Goliadkin, but also an absurdly funny situation. Ayoade certainly proves his Fingerspitzengefühl when transposing this into another absurdity, namely into what is in our day considered the rational solution to any human problem: physical exercise. Moreover, when Simon asks his superior whom the new employee resembles, Harris replies: 'Who did you have in mind?' Simon answers: 'Me, for instance.' Here, Ayoade is true to Goliadkin's personality-undermining tendency to think of himself in statistical terms. In Russian 'for instance' is '*naprimer*', one of Goliadkin's favourite expressions also about himself.

The film's visual identity jokes are also directly inspired by Dostoevsky, who on the first morning makes Goliadkin check the mirror to confirm his identity, and later lets him mistake the image of the double for his mirror image twice. Ayoade expands Dostoevsky's use of mirrors and mirroring by juxtaposing lonely characters in the lit-up windows of, firstly, dark subway trains, then dark houses. And when James shows up as the new employee we see the two doubles side by side, each augmented by a mirror image.

Goliadkin's alienated presence in relation to other people, whom he studies at a distance, is picked up by Ayoade not only when he lets Simon spy on the opposite block of flats, particularly Hannah's flat, through a telescope, but also when people around Simon display uncanny, inhuman features. Examples are colleagues dancing in robot-like fashion at the work party and the inhabitants of the old people's home sitting in stiff postures to the background music of a merry-go-round. Moreover, both Hannah and Simon themselves admit to feeling like Pinocchio, the wooden boy. This Gogolian theme in Dostoevsky is realised most conspicuously by Ayoade when Simon yells at the 'fuckers' at work while waving an artificial arm that has come off one of his older co-workers.

Goliadkin's alienated relation to objects, which seem also to look at and communicate with him, another feature borrowed from Gogol, is picked up by Ayoade, who not only lets the workplace printer ignore Simon's orders and gives the elevator a mind of its own whenever Simon enters it, but also, absurdly, has a large volume knob come off like a bogus knob when Simon tries to silence the background music, so he can hear better what James is saying to Hannah in the café. Indeed, both the café and Simon's workplace appear thoroughly bogus: they represent a mixture of historic Russian Potemkin villages and contemporary plastic showrooms.

As for the metaphysical humour and homonymic tragicomedy of Dostoevsky's *Double*, Ayoade brilliantly exploits the transferal of his hero's workplace to a private company prone to (ab)using advertisement language. This language is ripe with the doubleness of, on the one hand, an alleged higher purpose and true care for the well-being of its customers, and, on the other, its brazen willingness to say and pretend anything to sell its products. Thus, in video commercials the colonel is presented in voice-over as follows: 'The colonel knows people. There is no such thing as special people. [. . .] The colonel makes your business his business.' In this way Goliadkin's homonymic confusion is exposed through commercialist hypocrisy, and the fake paternal guardianship of His Excellency in Russian bureaucracy of the 1840s is transposed to contemporary capitalist consumer blandishment.

The dark humour of Dostoevsky's story is preserved also in Ayoade's happy ending, where we detect a bittersweet tone and a sense of metaphysical humour in Simon's last words. The rescuing policeman comments on Simon's survival: 'There aren't too many like you, are there, Simon?', and Simon answers, half-smiling and indirectly addressing both Hannah and us as his super addressees: 'I'd like to think I'm pretty unique.' Simon, of course, has good reason to smile, having killed off his double, survived, and won the heart of the woman he loves. My final point will be how this apparently blatant deviation from the source text may also be interpreted as a benevolent manipulation on Ayoade's part through which he ascertains his own authorship while also being true to Dostoevsky's authorship.

What Does it Take to Be(come) a Man? Ayoade's Co-authoring

Apart from adding a happy ending to Dostoevsky's original, Ayoade has greatly expanded the role of the love story, with Hannah at the centre of Simon's attention as much more of a main character than Klara Olsufievna. Moreover, the physical aspect of love, which is only hinted at very discreetly in the novella, is elaborated extensively in the film and acted out by James and others. In this expansion and elaboration I see less a simple modernisation and more Ayoade's appreciation of the crucial role which the love story in fact plays for Goliadkin. This happens reluctantly to Goliadkin, it seems as if he must play this role although he really does not want to – yet, in the end, he focuses his identity project on the romantic dream of saving a damsel in distress, finding true love and leaving the city for an imaginary (and clichéd) little hut on the seashore. Throughout most of Dostoevsky's novella, this role of romantic hero is primarily hinted at in the subtext, in half-spoken words and unclear allusions, but the mysterious letter summoning Goliadkin to come to young Klara's rescue discloses what is at stake and leads directly to the story's climax and Goliadkin's final downfall. In other words, the solution to his problem of 'nobody to be and nowhere to go' is inevitably related to a *male* identity project.

Goliadkin continues the quest of titular councillor Makar Devushkin in Dostoevsky's first novel, *Poor Folk*. Devushkin's ambition to be someone, to develop his own style instead of just copying, is inextricably bound to his romantic ambitions in relation to his young pen friend, Varvara. However hopeless this quest may seem, he apparently strives for artistic manhood. In this novel, as everywhere in Dostoevsky's later works, the question of romantic love is connected to a concern for the possibility of Christian brotherhood, of love or friendship, or even just honest human relationships in a society dominated by short-sighted self-interest, cynicism and exploitation. This concern is also Goliadkin's. Albeit Goliadkin's double seems to incarnate and thus confirm the ambitious part of his character, he protests against his immoral and inappropriate actions and appeals to him for friendship. However, Goliadkin apparently cannot escape grasping at the only socially defined role available for him: the proud and courageous man ready with the pistols, if necessary, and willing to save any young lady, no matter how he feels about it.

In addition to elaborating on this masculine quest, Ayoade introduces conspicuous examples of dominant, destructive masculinity into his film: Simon enjoys a hard-boiled TV series, clearly admiring its macho hero, and James seems to be a serial seducer and even seduces the boss's very young daughter. Ayoade also introduces the theme of homosexuality: James repeatedly calls out Simon's timidity among women as suspicious and asks him whether he is a homosexual. He also tells Simon how unacceptable this would be.[42]

The boldest move, however, is Ayoade's introduction of a happy ending, which is nowhere to be found in the whole of Dostoevsky's oeuvre, except perhaps in the epilogue of *Crime and Punishment* (1866). Since the ending follows Simon's resurrection from the grave, into which he was pushed by the devil/priest, it is possible to interpret it as the dream that never happened, and thus Ayoade's explication of Goliadkin's imagined future on the seashore. We may also, however, regard it as the denouement of the film's plot, and thus Ayoade's bold assertion of his authorship, a signature move emphasising the status of the film as more than a simple adaptation. The details of the ending cause me to prefer the latter interpretation, for rather than resembling Goliadkin's/Simon's romantic dream, which would make for a clichéd, contradictory addition, a 'Hollywoodisation', the last scene plays out in the spirit of the metaphysical irony of both heroes' quests. It is likely inspired by the glimpse of a new life experienced by the murderer Raskolnikov in a Siberian prison camp, where he is accompanied by the faithful prostitute Sonia. Ayoade gives us the only possible happy ending to Dostoevsky's *The Double*: humiliated, broken and scarcely united, two lonely people appreciate the rescuing hands of uncomprehending

---

[42] See Doak's ('Gender Trouble in The Double') analysis of this theme in terms of performative gender identity and homosocial desire.

authorities, while at the same time clearly also appreciating the absurdity of their own situation and of the human condition as such.

Bibliography

Bakhtin, Mikhail, 'Forms of Time and of the Chronotope in the Novel', in *The Dialogic Imagination*, ed. Michael Holquist, trans Caryl Emerson and Michael Holquist (Austin: University of Texas Press, 1981), pp. 84–258.

———, *Problems of Dostoevsky's Poetics*, trans. Caryl Emerson (Minneapolis and London: University of Minnesota Press, 1984).

———, 'The Problem of the Text in Linguistics, Philology, and the Human Sciences', in *Speech Genres and other Late Essays*, trans. Vern W. McGee (Austin: University of Texas Press, 1986), pp. 103–31.

Bradshaw, Peter, 'The Double review – A brilliantly realised nightmare universe', *The Guardian*, 3 April 2014 <https://www.theguardian.com/film/2014/apr/03/the-double-review-richard-ayoade> [accessed 1 September 2021].

Breger, Louis, *Dostoevsky, The Author as Psychoanalyst* (London and New York: Routledge, 1989).

'CBC: Richard Ayoade & Jesse Eisenberg on *The Double*', 2014 <https://www.youtube.com/watch?v=Wm_E8bQ2wwg> [accessed 1 September 2021].

Chizh, V.F., *Dostoevsky kak psikhopatolog* (Moscow, 1885).

Doak, Connor, 'Richard Ayoade: The Double (2013)', *Kinokultura* 45 (2014) <http://www.kinokultura.com/2014/45r-double.shtml> '[accessed 1 September 2021].

Doak, Connor, 'Gender Trouble in The Double: Masculinity in Dostoevsky's Novella and Ayoade's Film', in *The Bloggers Karamazov*, 2015 <https://jordanrussiacenter.org/news/gender-trouble-double-masculinity-dostoevskys-novella-ayoades-film/#.YTCsLNMzbq0> [accessed 1 September 2021].

Dostoevsky, Fedor, *Polnoe sobranie sochinenii*, 30 vols (Leningrad: Nauka, 1972–90).

Dostoyevsky, Fyodor, *Notes from Underground. The Double*, trans. by Jessie Coulson (London: Penguin Books, 1972).

Fanger, Donald, *Dostoevsky and Romantic Realism: A Study of Dostoevsky in Relation to Balzac, Dickens, and Gogol* (Evanston: Northwestern University Press, 1965).

'Filmmaker Richard Ayoade discussed his new film "The Double" starring Jesse Eisenberg and Mia Wasikowska during a Q&A following a screening at New Directors/New Films 2014', *Film at Lincoln Center* <https://www.youtube.com/watch?v=KgLGR8nQyaU> [accessed 1 September 2021].

Jones, John, *Dostoevsky* (Oxford and New York: Oxford University Press, 1985).

Kohlberg, Lawrence, 'Psychological Analysis and Literary Form: A Study of the Doubles in Dostoevsky', *Daedalus*, 92 (1963), pp. 345–62.

Morson, Gary Saul, 'Me and My Double: Selfhood, Consciousness, and Empathy in *The Double*', in *Before They Were Titans: Essays on the Early Works of Dostoevsky and Tolstoy*, ed. Elizabeth Cheresh Allen (Boston: Academic Studies Press, 2015), pp. 43–60.

Rank, Otto, *Der Doppelgänger* (Vienna: Internationale Psychoanalytische Verlag, 1925).

Reber, Natalie, *Studien zum Motiv des Doppelgängers bei Dostojevskij und E. T. A. Hoffmann.* (Giessen: Marburger Abhandlungen zur Geschichte und Kultur Osteuropas, 1964).

Schmid, Wolf, *Der Textaufbau in den Erzählungen Dostoevskijs* (Amsterdam: Verlag B. R. Grüner, 1986).
Seitz, Brian, *Intersubjectivity and the Double. Troubled Matters* (New York: Palgrave Macmillan, 2016).
Vinogradov, V. V., *Evoliutsiia russkogo naturalizma. Gogol i Dostoevsky* (Leningrad: Izd. Akademiia, 1929).

FILMOGRAPHY

The Double, directed by Richard Ayoade (UK, Alcove Entertainment, British Film Institute, Film 4, 2014).

PART THREE

COLLABORATING WITH CHEKHOV

5. 'THE PATHS I HAVE ESTABLISHED ...': CHEKHOV ON THE RUSSIAN AND AMERICAN SCREEN

Radislav Lapushin

Chekhov noted in a letter of 20 October 1888, shortly after he received the prestigious Pushkin Prize: 'Everything I have written will be forgotten in 5–10 years, but the paths I have established will remain intact and secure, and this is my only merit.'[1] By the 'paths' he had 'established' Chekhov meant something very specific, namely his contribution to the genre of the short story and its reputation in the literary world and among readers. Yet over time, these words have acquired a much broader meaning, signifying the extent of Chekhov's explicit and, most provocatively, implicit presence in the arts today, be it literature, theatre or cinema. This chapter offers three cases of contemporary American and Russian films – Michael Meredith's *Three Days of Rain* (2002), Arthur Allan Seidelman's *The Sisters* (2005), and Karen Shakhnazarov's *Ward No. 6* (*Palata № 6*, 2009) – which represent different models of adaptation and the transformation of Chekhov's works on screen in the twenty-first century. Taken together, these diverse films demonstrate not only Chekhov's pervasive presence in today's cinema but also the complexity of cinematic adaptation where the filmmaker becomes both coauthor and interpreter of the original source.

---

[1] Anton Chekhov, *Polnoe sobranie sochinenii i pisem*, 30 vols (Moscow: Nauka, 1974–83), *Pis'ma*, III, p. 39.

Chekhov in the Rhythm of Jazz

'I love all films that start with rain.'[2] The poet Don Paterson, who wrote this line, would definitely admire Michael Meredith's *Three Days of Rain*. This 97-minute film has few minutes free of rain. The rain's transparent yet impenetrable walls separate characters from each other and the world around them. Different and yet somewhat similar in their misery, rich and poor, old and young, all of these characters are residents of Cleveland at the beginning of the twenty-first century. There is another feature that they have in common: almost all owe their existence to Chekhov, whose stories serve as the blueprint for the movie's script. Some of these characters on screen are recognised immediately, others deviate more substantially from their literary antecedents.

The aged taxi driver John has just learnt that his son is dead (the director assigned this role to his own father, the former football star quarterback, Don Meredith). As anyone familiar with Chekhov's 'Grief' can guess, John is trying to share his 'grief' with his passengers. Absorbed in their own misery, happiness or loss, they are unwilling to listen to someone else's story. 'I'm here to suffer pain. These things – I'm destined to hear them!' exclaims a passenger played by Blythe Danner in a cameo appearance. This emotional outburst does not come directly out of Chekhov's work; it does seem Chekhovian, however, in its hidden irony toward the self-obsessed character. Who is she? The princess from Chekhov's story of the same name? Arkadina from *The Seagull*? John himself does not seem to rely on his passengers' attention and sympathy. Toward the end of the movie, he has coffee at an empty night cafeteria and finally tells the story of his loss to a tired waitress, a much more casual ending compared to Chekhov's cabby talking to his horse. At least she lets him speak, and this is perhaps the highest level of communication available in the modern world.

Another aged father, Waldo by name, is a loyal customer of the bar 'The Blue Bird'. Following in the footsteps of Musatov, his counterpart from Chekhov's short story 'The Father', he inventively wheedles cash from his son (Bill Stockton) while, in his own words, 'assuming the part of an abused father' in the senior centre where he lives. An inspired and virtuosic liar who is disarmingly sincere even in his lies, a skilful manipulator who is vulnerable and incurably lonely, he is a natural charmer, unlike his enormously patient but somewhat colourless son. Played by John Cassavetes' alumnus Peter Falk (known to the wider audience as Inspector Columbo), this role is arguably the most expressive and memorable performance in the movie.

One more variation on the theme of fathers (in this case, mothers) and children is provided by the young Tess (Merle Kennedy), an emotionally unstable

---

[2] Don Paterson, 'Rain' <https://www.newyorker.com/magazine/2008/05/26/rain-poems-don-paterson> [accessed 31 July 2021].

and childishly fragile drug addict who comes to the family of a judge and his wife to babysit their foster child. The child appears to be Tess's own daughter, of whom she has lost custody. Having realised that a literary inspiration for this subplot is the tragic 'Sleepy', a Chekhov reader is left in suspense: is Tess finally going to kill the baby in her care as did Chekhov's protagonist, a nursemaid 'about thirteen', when in a state of severe sleep deprivation?

Unlike Tess, we soon recognise the prototype of yet another cinematic protagonist, railway janitor Dennis (Joey Bilow). A rail nut is found in his locker. Did he unscrew it because of his ignorance, as the protagonist of Chekhov's 'The Malefactor' did? Or is he rather a victim of the intrigues of his supervisor, who wants to push Dennis out of his job to make room for a relative? Dennis looks innocent, harmless and meek. The finale adds an anecdotal twist to this variation on Chekhov's story. Walking down the railways with a blissful smile on his face, Dennis unscrews one nut after another and neatly collects them in a cardboard box. However, as we learned before, the trains bypass these railways anyway. If they did not, Dennis would have left Cleveland long ago for some 'better place'. While Dennis's story deviates from that of Chekhov's 'malefactor', it is still essentially a Chekhovian story.

'I am just a goddamn tilemaker,' another protagonist challenges the heavens (Michael Santoro). The rain has destroyed his work. His girlfriend has just left him. He has no money to pay his rent. In despair, he is rushing to the widow of the man who has not paid for his work (Penny Allen). She is his last hope. The widow, however, is focused on her grief. She refuses to be distracted and write a cheque. The tilemaker, in turn, refuses to leave her apartment (now it is clear that we are dealing with a paraphrasing of Chekhov's vaudeville 'The Bear'). Both are equally stubborn and self-absorbed. Finally, the morning finds them in the same bed, sleeping next to each other.

In contrast to the tilemaker, the last of the movie's protagonists, Alex (Eric Avari), is a well-off man with an apparently perfect family life. At night he goes with his wife (Maggie Walker) to a restaurant for dinner with lively conversation, friendly jokes and an atmosphere of mutual understanding. There is a small incident on their way home: a homeless man asking for some change or, at least, a doggie bag with the take-home dessert. Jen, Alex's wife, refuses: the dessert is for her sister. This incident, as Jeannette Catsoulis writes in *The New York Times*, 'opens a wound in the marriage that neither knew was there [. . .] It's the film's most Chekhovian moment: a marriage torn apart by chocolate mousse.'[3] As in Chekhov's short story 'The Cossack', Alex tries without success to find the

---

[3] Jeannette Catsoulis, 'Tales of Isolation and Urban Desperation', *The New York Times*, 30 September 2005 <http://movies.nytimes.com/2005/09/30/movies/30rain.html> [accessed 31 July 2021].

beggar in order to help him. Most importantly, he comes to see his wife of many years in a new light: 'You're not a kind person,' he says bitterly to Jen, as his counterpart does in the story. Due to its apparent moral lesson, this story is commonly defined in Chekhov criticism as one of his 'Tolstoyan' works. The movie takes the story out of the Easter context (hence a replacement of a 'holy Easter cake' with chocolate mousse) and substitutes a recently married couple for a couple that has been married for a long time. Most importantly, it leaves the ending more ambiguous and more 'Chekhovian' than it appears to be in the original.

The movie thus unites six of Chekhov's short works – five stories and a one-act play – written in his 'middle' period and representative of the multifariousness of Chekhov's art. Speaking of artistic results, it is unsurprising that the more successful adaptations are those based on less masterful stories ('The Father' and 'The Cossack'). Indeed, it is difficult to imagine an adaptation of 'Grief' that would do justice to this story's poetic richness and ambiguity. For any director, it would be challenging to match a finale like this one:

> Iona is silent for a while and then continues:
>
> 'That's how it is, old girl . . . Kuzma Ionych is no more [. . .] Now let's say you had a little foal, and you were its mother . . . And what if your little foal were to depart his life . . . You'd be sad, wouldn't you?'
>
> The little horse, chews, listens and breathes on the hands of her master . . . Iona gets carried away and tells her everything.[4]

A critical discussion about the 'true' meaning of this finale has been going on for a long time.[5] In the space of his four-page story, Chekhov has brought together the ostensibly incompatible features of anecdote, parable and tragedy, naturalistic sketch and biblical poetry so that the very borderline between literary discourses has become blurred. No matter how convincing Don Meredith is in his role, his final talking to a deaf ear leaves no doubt about the nature of this miscommunication.

Even more damaging is the movie's treatment of 'Sleepy'. Attached to the perspective of its young protagonist, the story depicts her gradual descent into madness through incomparable visual imagery and permanent fluctuation between

---

[4] Anton Chekhov, 'Grief', trans. Rosamund Bartlett, in *Anton Chekhov's Selected Stories*, ed. Cathy Popkin (New York and London: W. W. Norton & Company, 2014), pp. 42–7 (p. 47).

[5] Consider the telling title of Robert Louis Jackson's article 'Kontsovka "Toski": ironiia ili pafos?' ['The Ending of "Grief": Irony or Pathos?'], *Russian Literature*, 40 (1996), pp. 355–62. See also A. D. Stepanov, *Problemy kommunikatsii u Chekhova* (Moscow: Iazyki slavianskoi kul'tury, 2005), pp. 261–5.

dream and reality. These 'proto-cinematic' qualities are sacrificed in the movie for the sake of a straightforward criminal plot: the judge is a sexual molester who mercilessly exploits Tess. In the end, she chooses to kill her own infant child – who, as I have mentioned before, is also the judge's stepdaughter – to prevent the girl from reliving and suffering her mother's fate.

It would be unjust, however, to state that the poetic qualities of Chekhov's prose and drama are not taken into account by the creators of *Three Days of Rain*. The action switches from story to story but the movie is not disjointed. In addition to a thematic unity, there is also a poetic unity achieved through the use of cinematic devices.

Consider the rain, which acquires a symbolic quality. Chekhov says of his cab driver's misery: 'His grief is immense and boundless. If you were to open up Iona's chest and pour all the grief out of it, you would probably flood the entire planet, yet it is not visible.'[6] No one says these words in the movie, but Iona's misery and that of the other protagonists *are* 'visible' and embodied in the image of the never-stopping rain that literally 'floods' the 'whole world', or at least, the whole of Cleveland. Like any symbol, the rain cannot be reduced to a single definition. Standing for the characters' inescapable misery, it also speaks of their isolation and disconnection. It symbolises something that exceeds human power and is beyond human control. Not accidentally, commenting on the weather, a mysterious jazz radio DJ mentions the inability of human beings 'to escape the occasional act of God'. The rain in the movie is anything but just a background. It should be treated as the key character, and the noun 'rain' in the title *Three Days of Rain* almost takes on the quality of a proper name.

Another important factor that accounts for the unity of the film is its original soundtrack created by jazz composer and arranger Bob Belden. The very first words we hear in the movie come from the voice of the invisible radio DJ (only at the very end do we see him and realise that the voice belongs to the singer-songwriter Lyle Lovett) who provides a live report from a jazz festival taking place in Cleveland. The festival accounts for an almost uninterrupted stream of music accompanying the action. No character goes to a concert or pays any serious attention to this music. Yet unnoticed by them, the music played by the greatest representatives of modern jazz intertwines with their lives. It says in its subtle language what they are unable to say. It bridges their disparate fates and makes them echo one another, no matter that they are not even aware of each other's existence. The voice of their suppressed humanity, the music gives their sufferings substance and depth. It refuses to judge. It does not interfere with events but rather glimmers through them. In short, the music's role in the movie is analogous to that of the author/narrator's word

---

[6] Chekhov, 'Grief', p. 46.

in Chekhov's stories. Consider along these lines the description of the parents who have just lost their only child from the short story 'Enemies': 'There was something in the overall insensibility, in the mother's pose, in the equanimity on the doctor's face that appealed to and touched the heart—it was the subtle, nearly imperceptible beauty of human sorrow [. . .] which only music, it seems, can convey.'[7] This is what the jazzy soundtrack does in *Three Days of Rain*: it conveys this 'beauty of human sorrow' in the language of music. The poetic qualities of the original texts – in particular, their artistic richness and ambiguity – have not always found their way into the movie's script. This deficiency is, to a certain degree, redeemed by the persistent presence of the music.

So far, we have discussed the literary source of *Three Days of Rain*. Yet the movie also has a cinematic one apparently not related to Chekhov. To recall the aforementioned review in *The New York Times*: '*Three Days of Rain* belongs to the now-familiar genre of overlapping tales of urban desperation staked out by Robert Altman in *Short Cuts*.'[8] Indeed, Altman is so pivotal to this genre that, as Maria del Mar Azcona points out, 'the adjective "Altmanesque" soon emerged as a shorthand term to almost any kind of multi-stranded parallel storytelling and was applied to movies as varied as *Boogie Nights* (1997), *Magnolia* (1999) [. . .] and *Happy Endings* (2005), among many others'.[9]

There are some obvious correspondences between *Short Cuts* and *Three Days of Rain* on the level of themes and characters. Compare, for instance, Peter Falk's character with Jack Lemmon's from *Short Cuts*: both of these fathers are equally talkative, self-absorbed, disconnected from their respective families, and hopelessly lonely. The kinship between the two movies can be traced on the musical level as well: the jazzy soundtrack, so crucial for *Three Days of Rain*, could have been suggested by *Short Cuts* (one of the characters here is a jazz singer, which allows for the pervasive presence of jazz on and 'behind' the screen[10]). Both movies share an appearance by Lyle Lovett. 'Inspired by the short stories of Anton Chekhov', as the credits of *Three Days of Rain* state, this movie can be seen as equally inspired by Robert Altman's groundbreaking film.

---

[7] Anton Chekhov, 'Enemies', trans. Constance Garnett, with revisions by Cathy Popkin, in *Anton Chekhov's Selected Stories*, pp. 87–98 (p. 89).

[8] Catsoulis, 'Tales of Isolation and Urban Desperation'. Roger Ebert compares *Three Days of Rain* to another film 'in the genre of interlocking stories about lonely lives', Rodrigo Garcia's *Nine Lives* (2005) (Roger Ebert, 'Chekhov in Cleveland' < https://www.rogerebert.com/reviews/three-days-of-rain-2005> [accessed 31 July 2021]).

[9] Maria del Mar Azcona, 'A Cinema of Plenty: Robert Altman and the Multi-Protagonist Film', in *Robert Altman: Critical Essays*, ed. Rick Armstrong (Jefferson, North Carolina, and London: McFarland & Company, 2011), pp. 139–55 (p. 141).

[10] On the importance of jazz for *Short Cuts*, see Krin Gabbard, 'The Hypertext of *Short Cuts*. The Jazz in Altman's Carver Soup', in *Robert Altman: Critical Essays*, pp. 20–37.

Yet stressing the importance of *Short Cuts* as a prototypical model for films like *Three Days of Rain*, one should not forget that the former has its own literary source, namely the short stories of Raymond Carver, who was dubbed 'America's Chekhov'.[11] Carver's indebtedness to Chekhov runs deep, both artistically and personally.[12] As he pointed out in an interview, Chekhov 'gave voice to people who were not so articulate. He found a means of letting those people have their say as well. So in writing about people who aren't so articulate and who are confused and scared, I'm not doing anything radically different.'[13] It would be difficult to argue with Ewing Campbell's point that 'the indirect, understated form [Chekhov], as much as anyone, helped develop was the prototype of the modern short story. American writers, in particular, have followed these paths, but none as consistently and successfully as Raymond Carver.'[14] Thus, the cinematic path from *Short Cuts* to *Three Days of Rain* was also, to some extent, 'established' by Chekhov.

Moreover, there seems to be a clear affinity between the episodic genre of films like *Short Cuts* or *Three Days of Rain* and the Chekhovian type of short story. First of all, the protagonists of these short stories are common people deeply embedded in the routine of their lives and unable to escape this routine even through dreaming. Neither heroes nor villains, they are disconnected from tradition and religion, from people close to them, and from their own better selves. But 'captives of their times', they are also, to use Boris Pasternak's line, 'hostages of eternity' whose misery possesses an existential dimension and redeeming qualities. Clearly, these characters belong to the world of short stories rather than to that of novels. We enter their lives momentarily, with no introduction. We leave them abruptly, with no sense of closure, and not fully aware of whether we are going to see them again. We have snapshots of their

---

[11] Quoted in James Plath, 'On Raymond Carver', in *Critical Insights: Raymond Carver*, ed. James Plath (Ipswich, MA: Salem Press, 2013), pp. 3–18 (p. 16).

[12] As his *New York Times* obituary put it: 'Hours before he died, Ms. Gallagher [Carver's widow and a poet – RL] said, he spoke of how much he liked the stories of Chekhov. The last story in Mr. Carver's last book of stories was about the death of Chekhov' (Stewart Kellerman, 'Raymond Carver. Writer and Poet of the Working Poor, Dies at 50', *The New York Times*, 3 August 1988 <https://www.nytimes.com/1988/08/03/obituaries/raymond-carver-writer-and-poet-of-the-working-poor-dies-at-50.html> [accessed 31 July 2021]). Fittingly, Françoise Sammarcelli calls this last story, 'Errand', 'a tribute to Chekhov's art of brevity and intensity' (Françoise Sammarcelli, 'What's Postmodern about Raymond Carver?', in *Critical Insights: Raymond Carver*, ed. James Plath [Ipswich, MA: Salem Press, 2013], pp. 226–43 [p. 236]).

[13] Quoted in Ewing Campbell, *Raymond Carver: A Study of the Short Fiction* (New York: Twayne Publishers, 1992), p. 111.

[14] Ibid., p. 3.

lives rather than developed biographies. Naturally, such fragmentation is almost an intrinsic feature of the genre of episodic, multi-protagonist films.

Consider also the principle of interlocking several stories that are connected by their common themes (leitmotifs) and subtle allusions to one another rather than by a definite plot. Each Chekhov story is a finished work and can be read independently of all others, yet all shed additional light on one another, commenting on each other's themes and characters. As has been noted in Chekhov scholarship, the parallels and interconnections between the writer's different works are so extensive that all of them can be viewed as an 'integral resonant space'.[15] For example, a character or motif that has been on the periphery of one work can naturally move to the foreground of some other. Correspondingly, a story developed in the major key can be rewritten in the minor one or vice versa. This explains why, even though Chekhov left behind only one cycle, his 'little trilogy' ('The Man in a Shell', 'Gooseberries', and 'About Love'), a number of cycles have been discovered in his oeuvre by generations of literary critics. This also explains why an apparently accidental selection of short stories can be reworked to become a basis for an episodic yet integral script, as has been the case with *Three Days of Rain* and numerous other – mostly Russian – film adaptations based on Chekhov's 'motley stories'.[16]

It is worth noting that *Motley Stories* is not simply the title of one of Chekhov's first collections (published in 1886).[17] It is also the principle on which he structures his collection, bringing together characters representative of diverse social groups, professions and backgrounds and mixing the elements of comedy and drama, tragedy and farce. The same principle frequently applies to movies that belong to the genre associated with *Short Cuts*. *Motley Stories* could be an alternative title for many of them.

Chekhov's presence in this cinematic genre is not confined to his work as a storyteller. Think of his major plays. Obviously, they have a linear development of plot and are not cut into separate independent subplots. Yet the term 'decentralisation' is aptly applied to Chekhov's innovative treatment of plot, meaning that instead of one central event, around which the whole

---

[15] On Chekhov's artistic world as an integral text, see I. N. Sukhikh, *Problemy poetiki Chekhova* (St Petersburg: Filologicheskii fakul'tet Sankt-Peterburgskogo gosudarstvennogo universiteta, 2007), pp. 103–20.

[16] Consider for example adaptations by prominent Russian directors such as Iakov Protazanov's *Chiny i liudi* (*People and Ranks*, 1929), Mikhail Shveitser's 'dilogy' *Karusel* (*The Carousel*, 1970; 1976) and *Smeshnye liudi!* (*Funny People!* 1977), Sergei Solov'ev's *Semeinoe schast'e* (*Family Happiness*, 1969) and *O liubvi* (*About Love*, 2003).

[17] Two of the stories adapted for *Three Days of Rain* ('Grief' and 'The Malefactor') were part of this collection.

action unfolds, the audience is faced with a number of intertwined micro-events and micro-plots.[18] 'Decentralisation' is equally evident on the level of characters: in place of several protagonists and the supporting cast, there is a well-elaborated network of characters, each of whom has the potential to become a protagonist. All characters are mutually reflective of one another. Thus, Chekhov's drama also paves the way to the genre of overlapping tales represented by movies like *Short Cuts* or *Three Days of Rain*.

One can speculate that while preserving its general mood, imagery, setting and a similar cast of characters, *Three Days of Rain* could be based on some other – and not necessarily Chekhovian – short stories or be an original script rather than an adaptation. My point is that in either case, giving credit to Chekhov as an 'inspiration' would be a proper and well-deserved acknowledgment.

Three Sisters from New York

According to Mikhail Iampolski, in film or texts, 'what is traditionally considered a quote may end up not being one, while what is not traditionally seen as a quote may well be one'.[19] The above analysis of *Three Days of Rain* has demonstrated this paradox vividly. Blythe Danner's character does not come directly from any Chekhov work. However, she is more 'Chekhovian' than, for example, the movie's version of the protagonist of 'Sleepy'. Similarly, a chocolate mousse, which, as Jeanette Catsoulis justly claims, is responsible for the 'movie's most Chekhovian moment' is also absent in the original. Our next adaptation is a case study of this tension between fidelity to the 'spirit' and fidelity to the 'letter'.[20]

For a Chekhov scholar, Arthur Allan Seidelman's movie *The Sisters* is instructive in two respects: how faithfully it follows and, simultaneously, how strikingly it departs from its original source, *Three Sisters*. Based on his stage play, Richard Alfieri's script transfers the action from provincial Russia to the spacious faculty lounge of a university in New York. The change in the setting, however, leaves Chekhov's protagonists instantly recognizable. Who is this professor of English with his tired, all-knowing eyes by the name of Dr Cherbin (Rip Torn)? Evidently, it is Chebutykin. Despite his academic status, he is never

---

[18] See, for example, Z. S. Papernyi, '*Vopreki vsem pravilam . . .*': *P'esy i vodevili Chekhova* (Moscow: Iskusstvo, 1982).

[19] Mikhail Iampolski, *The Memory of Tiresias: Intertextuality and Film* (Berkeley: University of California Press, 1998), p. 31.

[20] Fidelity, of course, is one of the most crucial terms in the debates on adaptation. See, for instance, Robert Stam, 'Beyond Fidelity: The Dialogics of Adaptation', in *Film Adaptation*, ed. James Naremore (New Brunswick, NJ: Rutgers University Press, 2000) pp. 54–76.

On fidelity to the 'spirit' see also Angus Wrenn's contribution to this volume 'Louis Malle and *Uncle Vanya*' (Chapter 6).

Figure 5.1 Marcia (Maria Bello) and Vincent (Tony Goldwyn), *The Sisters*, directed by Arthur Allan Seidelman, 2005.

without a newspaper, reading aloud items from the criminal beat to his younger colleagues. And who are these two men playing chess: one with a dreamy and romantic appearance (Chris O'Donnell), another unshaven and sardonic (Eric McCormack)? It does not take long to identify who of them is a reincarnation of Tuzenbakh (now he is David Turzin, a professor of philosophy, which is hardly surprising considering Tuzenbakh's penchant for philosophising) and who is the new Solionyi, whose name now is Gary Sokol, "promoted" from staff captain to professor of political science.

As in Chekhov's play, the action unfolds unhurriedly and is filled with apparently insignificant bits of conversation. The camera leaves the closed space only to introduce some new characters on their way to the lounge. Finally, the two older sisters come in: Olga, also a professor (Mary Stuart Masterson), and Marcia (Maria Bello), both of whom are loaded with gift-wrapped packages. As anyone familiar with Chekhov's play would immediately guess, these gifts are intended for the youngest sister, Irene (Erika Christensen), whose birthday is about to be celebrated in that very lounge.

But first, an unexpected visitor from the sisters' past comes to the club, the former TA of the late father, who was also a professor and chancellor, by the name Vincent Antonelli (Tony Goldwyn). Like his obvious model, Vershinin, Vincent is well mannered, sensitive and disappointed. He also has a hysterical wife and two daughters of whom he is very fond. But most importantly, he is a living reminder of the sisters' supposedly happy and harmonious past in their house in Charleston, SC, to which they are dreaming of returning sometime in the future.

Meanwhile, there is yet another guest at the party, the sisters' brother Andrew (Alessandro Nivola). Unlike his Russian counterpart, he has succeeded in becoming a professor, and his specialty is music, which is arguably a nod to Andrei's playing violin. His professorship, however, does not make him a happier man. As expected, he has already fallen under the spell of his own Natasha, renamed Nancy (Elizabeth Banks), the vulgar bird of prey who is going to take control of his life. Finally, the last guest, Marcia's husband, the psychologist Dr Harry Glass (Steven Culp), arrives. And the subject of his conversation with his wife is also of no surprise for those acquainted with *Three Sisters*: there is to be an important reception tonight, which Marcia, contrary to her wishes, has to attend along with her husband.

Thus, all the major characters in the movie have their counterparts in *Three Sisters*. Moreover, the dynamics of their relations and the general development of the events in *The Sisters* follow the pattern of Chekhov's play closely. Suffice it to recall the aborted love affair between Marcia and Vincent, or the dramatic triangle of Irene, David and Gary, or Nancy's taking from the sisters their dream house in Charleston. Even the inversion of the 'capital–province' opposition – living in New York, the American sisters are longing for their family home in Charleston – might be viewed as Chekhovian in its hidden irony.

However, in the course of the film, certain 'skeletons in the closet' are revealed that could hardly be imaginable in Chekhov's play. To begin with, the idealised and mythologised father, whose cult the two older sisters carefully preserve, is revealed to have been an ominous figure: he molested his daughter Marcia when she was a child. This could explain her excessive nervousness and agitation as well as account for her failed marriage. Meanwhile, Olga has her own secret: she is a closet lesbian who hides her sexual orientation even from those closest to her – the sisters. The youngest of them, Irene, a vulnerable and sensitive university student with childishly plump cheeks, who is overprotected by Olga and Marcia, appears to be a drug addict. Overdosing, she loses consciousness on her way home after the birthday party. Luckily, the devoted Turzin-Tuzenbakh happens to be there at this moment and takes her to hospital.

What can we make of these changes? Of course, any adaptation, no matter how reverential, inherently contains an element of rivalry and rebellion. I find it suggestive that in the course of the movie each of the older siblings (Olga, Marcia, Andrew) is trying to resist the late father's authority and, consequently, establish herself or himself as the head of the family. In line with the movie's psychoanalytical implications, this struggle can be viewed as a challenge issued by contemporary artists to a father-figure of the modern theatre – and, to a great extent, cinema as well – Anton Chekhov. It is as if they were saying: 'Now we know more about these issues than you did in your time; we know all too well, for instance, about the other – abusive – side of the father-figures or about repressed sexuality and the inevitable fallibility of memory as well as the danger of fictionalising the past. Thus, we are in a position to update the original source and fill its gaps with some definite and explanatory content.'

In doing this, however, the departure from Chekhov is not simply on the level of content but also on that of poetics. On this level, paradoxically, the new incarnations of Chekhov's characters look pre- rather than post-Chekhovian and more 'traditional' than their original counterparts. To elaborate on this point, it can be useful to recall the well-known criticism of the sound film from Horkheimer and Adorno's *Dialectic of Enlightenment*: 'The sound film [. . .] leaves no room for imagination or reflection on the part of the audience.'[21] The analogy between Chekhov's plays and silent films is perhaps not too preposterous if one brings to mind the signature pauses of this writer so indispensable to the verbal texture of his drama. In general, pauses, omissions, ellipses and gaps are the writer's innovative devices in the presentation of his characters. They are his way of generously leaving 'room for imagination or reflection on the part of the audience'.

Loaded with too much background, Chekhov's characters lose something crucial to their personalities: their elusiveness and resistance to any kind of pigeonholing. They become demystified. They cease to be evocative of one another. They can be rationalised and explained, which is arguably the worst-case scenario for a Chekhovian protagonist. Of course, to appreciate this elusiveness of the original characters one has to go beyond the characters and plot lines to the play's integral poetic texture with its elaborate network of leitmotivs and allusions, its subtle rhythmic design, and its organisation of space and time.[22]

A similar loss of subtlety is evident in the general representation of life in the movie. The Moscow of *Three Sisters*, as is well known, is far from being just a geographical point of destination. The true and full meaning of this poetic symbol escapes interpreters as easily as Moscow itself escapes the play's protagonists. It speaks of their lost past, their suppressed desires and unfulfilled wishes. It represents the very best in them that can be sacrificed under no conditions. Simultaneously, this Moscow stands for the vanity of their dreams, their state of denial, and their inability to cope with life as it is. While the Charleston of Seidelman's movie is also quite an ambivalent image – introduced as a lost

---

[21] Max Horkheimer and Theodor W. Adorno, *Dialectic of Enlightenment*, trans. John Cumming (New York: Herder and Herder, 1947/1972), p. 126.

[22] On the poetic side of Chekhov's prose and drama, see Radislav Lapushin, *'Dew on the Grass': The Poetics of Inbetweenness in Chekhov* (New York: Peter Lang, 2010).

paradise of childhood, it appears at the same time to be a place of abuse, a hell for at least one of the sisters – its ambivalence is of a different nature. It, too, can be rationalised and explained. This Charleston *is* the city one can find on the map, buy tickets for and go to. Had the greedy and insensitive Nancy not sold the house, the sisters (at least, Irene) would probably wind up there sooner or later.

Not only are subtlety and elusiveness central to Chekhov's characters and his play in general, they also account for the play's adaptability to various cultural environments. The gaps deliberately left by Chekhov in his characters' backgrounds and motivations seem constantly to provoke generations of artists, allowing them to bridge these gaps according to the spirit of their times as well as their own artistic personalities and inclinations. Ironically, these very qualities responsible for the play's adaptability are often the first to be sacrificed when Chekhovian characters and motifs are transplanted to a new setting.

The Eternal Ward No. 6

Any classical hypotext comes along with the history of its reception, that is, with the interpretative baggage that must necessarily be confronted by the director. Chekhov's 'Ward No. 6' (1892),[23] a story about a doctor who winds up a patient locked in his own hospital, is a paradigmatic example of a work with baggage. Some of the story's first readers immediately recognised the power of its symbolism and insight into Russian life at large. These readers were not fooled by the protagonist's conviction that Ward No. 6 is an ugly fixture of one provincial town and an exception rather than a rule.[24] Contrary to such thinking, the writer Nikolai Leskov characterised the story thus: 'Ward No. 6 is everywhere. It is Russia . . . Chekhov himself did not mean it in the way he wrote it (he told me this), and yet it is so. His Ward is Rus!'[25]

In hindsight, one can treat this remarkable statement as an artistic exaggeration concerning the Russia of the time. However, another sensitive reader, in this case, ten years younger than Chekhov, responded to the story in an

---

[23] I cite the film's title in italics and place the story's title between quotation marks. In all other cases the ward is considered a location and is treated as a proper noun.

[24] 'Andrei Yefimych knows that, given present-day views and tastes, such an abomination as Ward No. 6 is possible only two hundred miles from the railroad, in a town where the mayor and all the councilmen are semi-literate bourgeois [. . .] anywhere else the public and the newspapers would long ago have smashed this little Bastille to bits.' (Anton Chekhov, 'Ward No. 6', trans. Constance Garnett, with revisions by Cathy Popkin, in *Anton Chekhov's Selected Stories*, pp. 234–81 (p. 252).

[25] Quoted in *Primechaniia* to 'Ward No. 6' in Chekhov, *Polnoe sobranie sochinenii i pisem. Sochineniia*, VIII, p. 458.

Figure 5.2   Ragin (Vladimir Il'in), *Ward No. 6*, directed by Karen Shakhnazarov, 2009.

equally emotional way. According to his sister's memoirs, he said to her: 'When I finished reading this story yesterday evening, I became downright terrified. I couldn't remain in my room; I got up and left. I felt just as though I were locked up in Ward No 6.'[26] A quarter of a century later this hypothetic prisoner of Ward No. 6 would become the actual leader of the Bolshevik revolution and head of the first Soviet Government, which is, ironically, a reversed trajectory in relation to Chekhov's protagonist who moved from someone in charge of Ward No. 6 to this ward's patient deprived of any rights.

The undying relevance of 'Ward No. 6' in the context of Soviet life is proven by numerous accounts of how the text has been perceived over time. For the official Soviet discourse, 'Ward No. 6' served as an indictment of Tsarist Russia and a proto-revolutionary work.[27] Conversely, in her conversation with Isaiah Berlin in 1956, Anna Akhmatova, famously not a fan of Chekhov, used this story as a secret code allowing her to communicate her situation in the post-War decade to an outsider. As Berlin recalled, 'she told me something of her experience as a condemned writer: of the turning away of some whom she considered faithful friends, of the nobility and courage of others; she had reread Chekhov whom she had once condemned so severely and said that at least in

[26] V. I. Lenin, *O literature i iskusstve* (Moscow: Khudozhestvennaia literatura, 1976), p. 609.
[27] See, for example, V. V. Ermilov, *Chekhov* (Moscow: Molodaia gvardiia, 1946), p. 242.

"Ward No. 6" he had described her situation accurately, hers and many others'.²⁸ In a similar vein, Aleksandr Solzhenitsyn saw this story as a prophecy of 'the future Soviet psychiatric hospitals' (*psikhushki*),²⁹ meaning, of course, 'punitive psychiatry' practised to punish political opponents (dissidents) during the times of 'stagnation'.

Moving from the Soviet period to Putin's Russia, I will restrict myself to one relatively recent source, a blog post from 2011 by the political observer Leonid Radzikhovsky about Platon Lebedev, the closest associate of Mikhail Khodorkovsky, who had once again been denied a pardon. Proclaiming that the decision regarding the 'Lebedev case' was 'anticipated, hopeless, meaningless, petty, malicious, absurd and inevitable', Radzikhovsky cites a scene from Chekhov's story, in which, locked in the ward, Ragin is hopelessly trying to 'get out'. Then, after recounting Lenin's reaction to this story, Radzikhovsky concludes on a fatalistic note: 'Vladimir Il'ich was strong—not like Andrei Efimych or Ivan Dmitrich. He broke Ward No. 6, and built in its place Ward No. 666. Nothing else is built in this country, and if it is built, then it doesn't stand.'³⁰

Based on these representative examples, one can see how effortlessly Chekhov's text transcends a particular historical period, extending from the times of Imperial Russia to the Soviet (Stalinist, Brezhnevian) and post-Soviet periods. Moreover, it appears that this story and its title image of Ward No. 6 have long moved beyond the realm of literature and become a manifestation of the darkest, most unbearable aspects of Russian life itself, the ones that, regardless of any social changes and cultural developments, remain intact. I would argue that in his movie, Karen Shakhnazarov adapts for the screen not just Chekhov's text, but also the vision of Russian reality that it has generated from the time of its publication up to now— the vision of Ward No. 6 as a microcosm of Russia/Rus.

As a work of cinema, Shakhnazarov's *Ward No. 6* speaks in several languages simultaneously. In her extended analysis of the movie, Yana Meerzon calls it a 'cinematic paratext' (and 'cinematic potpourri') that 'employs a variety of today's cutting-edge cinematic devices' such as 'interviews with the patients of Nikolo-Poshekhonskii asylum, mockumentary footage of the fictional characters made with a handheld camera, and scenes a la silent movies'.³¹ An overlap of

---

²⁸ Isaiah Berlin, *Personal Impressions* (New York: Viking Press, 1981), p. 201.
²⁹ Aleksandr Solzhenitsyn, 'Okunaias' v Chekhova' <http://magazines.russ.ru:81/novyi_mi/1998/10/solg.html> [accessed 31 July 2021].
³⁰ Leonid Radzikhovsky, 'Ward No. 6' [Blog] <http://www.echo.msk.ru/blog/radzihovski/797254-echo/> [accessed 31 July 2021].
³¹ Yana Meerzon, 'Interrogating the Real: Chekhov's Cinema of Verbatim. "Ward Number Six" in Karen Shakhnazarov's 2009 Film Adaptation', in *Adapting Chekhov: The Text and its Mutations*, eds J. Douglas Clayton and Yana Meerzon (New York: Routledge, 2013), pp. 274–94 (p. 276).

these languages creates a very idiosyncratic world, which is both real and surreal, contemporary and timeless.

The movie opens with a series of interviews conducted at the mental asylum. The camera moves from one patient to another. Each of them responds to questions about their backgrounds, dreams, and so on. These interviews imbue the movie with a non-fictional, documentary air. Thus when the next 'hospital' sequence starts with a doctor speaking to the camera, it is not immediately clear that he is an actor (Evgenii Stychkin) playing the role of Dr Khobotov – a character created by Chekhov. Similarly, when the camera first lands on another Chekhov character, Ivan Dmitrich Gromov (Aleksei Vertkov), he is indistinguishable from other patients.

By reinforcing the non-fictional nature of his work, the director does not let us forget that we are dealing with a cultural artefact.[32] He does this through his use of the mockumentary form, the content of which is heavily reliant upon Chekhov's text, but sometimes offers small yet consequential alterations and manipulations. For example, the text provides some information on Ragin's predecessor, the nameless 'old' doctor 'of whom people declared that he secretly sold the hospital alcohol and kept a regular harem of nurses and female patients'.[33] In the movie, we see this character himself (Aleksei Zharkov) repeating these accusations in his real-time 'documentary' interview. He does it in a matter-of-fact and unforced manner, apparently without expressing any feelings of regret or shame. Similarly, the narrator's characterisation of Dr Khobotov ('He regards his colleague [Andrei Efimych] as a sly old rascal, suspects him of being a man of large means, and secretly envies him. He would be very glad to take his post'[34]) is also transferred to the screen almost verbatim. It is, however, presented to us as part of this character's 'interview', which is also uttered in an emotionless tone. Such examples add a surreal quality to the movie as a whole and to the documentary level.

Perhaps the director intended to create a cinematic world in which the very borderline between the real and the surreal/the absurd is blurred. Indeed, what from a common-sense perspective could be considered as surreal, grotesque or absurd (the monastery turned into a mental asylum, a doctor who shamelessly speaks to the camera of his excessive misdeeds, and so on) reveals itself in this movie as just the 'normal' reality of a Russian provincial town. In this context, one is tempted to add a metapoetic dimension to the brief verbal exchange between Dr Khobotov and one of his mental patients, a 'genius', Igor Iakovlevich,

---

[32] As Meerzon points out, 'By gradually increasing the surrealistic feel of his movie, Shakhnazarov forces his audience to constantly wonder whether what we see on-screen is real of fictional' (Ibid., p. 288).

[33] Chekhov, 'Ward No 6', p. 244.

[34] Ibid., p. 253.

whose paintings are hung on the asylum's walls: 'Are you an artist-avant-gardist?' he is asked. 'No, I'm a realist,' he responds.[35]

A similar interrelationship exists in the opposition between the timeless and the contemporary. 'We tried to immerse Chekhov's plot in today's reality', explains Shakhnazarov, regarding his decision to transfer the events of Chekhov's story from the end of the 19th century to the beginning of the 21st (the action takes place in 2007).[36] The signs of this reality are numerous, especially in the way the movie depicts Moscow. The visual image of this Moscow is defined by traffic jams, flashy storefront displays, strip clubs and casinos. Correspondingly, when Ragin (Vladimir Il'in) is 'interrogated' by his supervisors, one of them recalls his vacation in Antalya, a Turkish resort popular in post-Soviet Russia. Moreover, the overall characterisation of the protagonist is historically precise and particular: his misery is emblematic of that of the 'Thaw' intelligentsia that has been alienated and marginalised in a new Russia.

On the other hand, all signs of modernity notwithstanding, one can agree with Dmitrii Bykov's claim that rather than 'carrying the plot over into the present', Shakhnazarov 'smeared it over the last five centuries of Russian history'.[37] The very choice of the ancient monastery turned into a mental asylum as a movie's key setting produces an aura of timelessness and overt symbolism. The timeless and the timely meet each other in one of the movie's first scenes, which takes place in 1606 and depicts the founding of the Nikolo-Poshekhonskii monastery by the grey-haired monk Varlaam and two young nuns silently walking through a swampy wilderness.

From 1606 to modern-day Moscow, from the monastery founded on the swamp to a strip club – what dizzying and striking contrasts! However, the movie is rather preoccupied with continuity. Social changes are palpable, but the 'order' and the basics of life remain the same. A manifestation of this 'sameness' is Shakhnazarov's casting: the same actor plays the ancient monk Varlaam and the ward's current caretaker, Nikita. Such a choice can be easily justified: after all, the monastery *is* transformed into a mental asylum, so it is only logical that a modern reincarnation of the monk is attached to a modern reincarnation of the monastery. For a reader of Chekhov, however, this decision is rather shocking. It is not by chance that Nikita is the very first character introduced in the story: he is an embodiment of the cruelty and abuse constitutive of Ward No. 6.

---

[35] For a different interpretation of this dialogue, see Alexander Burry, '"A Vicious Circle": Karen Shakhnazarov's *Ward no. 6*', in *Border Crossing: Russian Literature into Film*, eds Alexander Burry and Frederick H. White (Edinburgh: Edinburgh University Press, 2017) pp. 121–39 (p. 133).

[36] Quoted in Meerzon, p. 286.

[37] Quoted in Marina Timasheva, 'Vse puti vedut v palatu', *Radio Svoboda*, 25 June 2009 <http://www.svoboda.org/content/article/1762281.html> [accessed 31 July 2021].

Compared to the Nikita of Chekhov's text, the image of Nikita in the movie is no less severe. Although his 'beatings' are not as graphic as in the story and happen off screen, there is little doubt that he is willing to do anything to preserve 'order' as he understands it.

Meanwhile, there is also another reincarnation of even greater importance. The movie's climactic scene is that of the New Year party in the mental asylum. Unlike his literary counterpart, Ragin survives his stroke and remains in the asylum. A young patient inviting him to dance is none other than one of the nuns we previously saw with Varlaam. Even more intriguingly, this nun is associated with Chekhov's story's most striking yet frequently neglected poetic image: that of a 'herd of deer, extraordinarily beautiful and graceful' that Ragin sees in a hallucination right before his death. In the movie, these deer appear as part of the tangible world in the scene with Varlaam and the two nuns. In a close-up, we see one of these nuns (the one who will later approach Ragin) stop and look at the deer. Thus, at the scene of the party, the reincarnation of the nun brings to Ward No. 6 the idea of an undying sanctity, spaciousness and beauty. As Shakhnazarov explains, 'the disbelieving Dr Ragin is granted mercy for his suffering.'[38] Along these lines, some critics see the movie's finale as illuminating and believe that it reinstates the necessity of faith, 'no matter how absurd it may be'.[39]

However, as Alexander Burry demonstrates in his perceptive analysis, the movie's apparent 'happy ending' is questionable. In particular, 'the image of Nikita leading a celebration, immediately following the scene of his brutal beating of Ragin and Gromov, seems incongruous and even grotesque'.[40] It is also indisputable that after the party is over, all the patients will be returned to their wards, with no opportunity to realise the dreams they revealed previously in the documentary footage. In the shot that immediately follows the New Year party, we see the panoramic view of the monastery surrounded by darkness. With the golden cupola reaching to the sky and an empty expanse of snowy space in front of the monastery, the view is beautiful and calm. On the other hand, the audible howling of the wind seems somewhat overbearing, especially if one recalls that behind the walls of the monastery there is Ward No. 6.

In my view, the final image of Ward No. 6 is left deliberately unsettling and ambiguous. An interesting question is whether this ambiguity is in accordance with Chekhov's own position and artistic style. After all, as Donald Rayfield aptly summarises, Chekhov is 'the most subtle of Russian writers and one who appears capable of holding two opposite views and having two opposite intentions

---

[38] Quoted in Timasheva, 'Vse puti vedut v palatu'.
[39] Quoted in Meerzon, p. 285.
[40] Burry, p. 134.

simultaneously'.[41] The 'subtle' and 'elusive' Chekhov, however, could also be clear and direct. The movie version of Nikita is likely influenced by another character besides his antecedent in Chekhov's story: the assistant doctor, Sergei Sergeich, who is characterised by the narrator as 'religious'. 'The icon was put up at his expense; at his instructions, a patient reads an akathist aloud in the consulting room on Sundays, and, after the reading, Sergei Sergeich himself goes through the wards with a censer and burns incense.'[42] Chekhov's attitude toward this character (and this kind of religiosity, which is capable of reconciling itself with Ward No. 6), is anything but ambiguous. For him, Ward No. 6 is an absolute and unredeemable evil. The moment of belated epiphany experienced by the literary Ragin is triggered not by mercy 'granted' to him, but by Ragin's realisation of his responsibility for this evil:

> He bit the pillow from pain and clenched his teeth, and all at once through the chaos in his brain there flashed the terrible unbearable thought that these people, who seemed now like black shadows in the moonlight, had to endure this same pain day after day for years. How could it have happened that for more than twenty years he had not known it and had refused to know it? He had known nothing of pain [...] but his conscience, as unyielding and as brutal as Nikita, made him turn cold from the crown of his head to his heels.[43]

In Chekhov's world, Ward No. 6 still can be challenged: it is symptomatic that the protagonist's conscience reveals itself as a real, physical force. The movie adds a fatalistic aura to the eternal image of Ward No. 6 by establishing it as an indispensable part of the Russian landscape.

Apart from having Chekhov as their literary source, the three movies I have discussed here share little in common. They also differ in their approach to their respective hypotexts. While Meredith's *Three Days of Rain* strives to render the poetic qualities of Chekhov's prose and drama through visual and audible devices, Seidelman's *The Sisters* overlooks it altogether. Shakhnazarov's *Ward No. 6* adapts for the screen not just Chekhov's story per se, but the vision of Russian reality it has generated from the time of its publication up to now. It is exactly Chekhov's flexibility, his openness to different kinds of approaches and manipulation that predetermine his everlasting, both explicit and implicit, presence in the arts today. In the end, there is no single image of Chekhov. There are only numerous 'paths' established by him that lead in different, sometimes opposite, directions.

---

[41] Donald Rayfield, *Understanding Chekhov: A Critical Study of Chekhov's Prose and Drama* (Madison: The University of Wisconsin Press, 1979), p. vii.
[42] Chekhov, 'Ward No. 6', p. 246.
[43] Ibid., p. 280.

Bibliography

Azcona, Maria del Mar, 'A Cinema of Plenty: Robert Altman and the Multi-Protagonist Film', in *Robert Altman: Critical Essays*, ed. Rick Armstrong (Jefferson, North Carolina, and London: McFarland & Company, 2011), pp. 139–55.

Berlin, Isaiah, *Personal Impressions* (New York: Viking Press, 1981).

Burry, Alexander, '"A Vicious Circle": Karen Shakhnazarov's *Ward no. 6*', in *Border Crossing: Russian Literature into Film*, eds Alexander Burry and Frederick H. White (Edinburgh: Edinburgh University Press, 2017), pp. 121–39.

Campbell, Ewing, *Raymond Carver: A Study of the Short Fiction* (New York: Twayne Publishers, 1992).

Catsoulis, Jeannette, 'Tales of Isolation and Urban Desperation.' *The New York Times*, 30 September 2005 <http://movies.nytimes.com/2005/09/30/movies/30rain.html> [accessed 31 July 2021].

Chekhov, Anton, *Anton Chekhov's Selected Stories*, ed. Cathy Popkin (New York, London: W. W. Norton & Company, 2014).

———, *Polnoe sobranie sochinenii i pisem*, 30 vols (Moscow: Nauka, 1974–83).

Ebert, Roger, 'Chekhov in Cleveland' < https://www.rogerebert.com/reviews/three-days-of-rain-2005> [accessed 31 July 2021].

Ermilov, V. V., *Chekhov* (Moscow: Molodaia gvardiia, 1946).

Gabbard, Krin, 'The Hypertext of Short Cuts: The Jazz in Altman's Carver Soup', in *Robert Altman: Critical Essays*, ed. Rick Armstrong (Jefferson, NC and London: McFarland & Company, 2011), pp. 20–37.

Horkheimer, Max and Theodor W. Adorno, *Dialectic of Enlightenment*, trans. John Cumming (New York: Herder and Herder, 1947/1972).

Iampolski, Mikhail, *The Memory of Tiresias: Intertextuality and Film* (Berkeley: University of California Press, 1998).

Jackson, Robert Louis, 'Kontsovka "Toski": ironiia ili pafos?', *Russian Literature*, 40 (1996), pp. 355–62.

Kellerman, Stewart, 'Raymond Carver, Writer and Poet of the Working Poor, Dies at 50', *The New York Times* (3 August 1988) <https://www.nytimes.com/1988/08/03/obituaries/raymond-carver-writer-and-poet-of-the-working-poor-dies-at-50.html> [accessed 31 July 2021].

Lapushin, Radislav, *'Dew on the Grass': The Poetics of Inbetweenness in Chekhov* (New York: Peter Lang, 2010).

Lenin. V. I., *O literature i iskusstve* (Moscow: Khudozhestvennaia literatura, 1976).

Meerzon, Yana, 'Interrogating the Real: Chekhov's Cinema of Verbatim. "Ward Number Six" in Karen Shakhnazarov's 2009 Film Adaptation', in *Adapting Chekhov: The Text and its Mutations*, eds J. Douglas Clayton and Yana Meerzon (New York: Routledge, 2013), pp. 274–94.

Papernyi, Z. S., '*Vopreki vsem pravilam . . .*': *P'esy i vodevili Chekhova* (Moscow: Iskusstvo, 1982).

Paterson, Don, 'Rain'. (26 May 2008) <https://www.newyorker.com/magazine/2008/05/26/rain-poems-don-paterson> [accessed 31 July 2021].

Plath, James, 'On Raymond Carver', in *Critical Insights: Raymond Carver*, ed. James Plath (Ipswich, MA: Salem Press, 2013), pp. 3–18.

Radzikhovsky, Leonid, 'Ward No. 6 [Blog]' <http://www.echo.msk.ru/blog/radzihovski/797254-echo/> [accessed 31 July 2021].
Rayfield, Donald, *Understanding Chekhov: A Critical Study of Chekhov's Prose and Drama* (Madison: The University of Wisconsin Press, 1979).
Sammarcelli, Françoise, 'What's Postmodern about Raymond Carver?', in *Critical Insights: Raymond Carver*, ed. James Plath (Ipswich, MA: Salem Press, 2013), pp. 226–43.
Solzhenitsyn, Aleksandr. 'Okunaias' v Chekhova' <http://magazines.russ.ru:81/novyi_mi/1998/10/solg.html> [accessed 31 July 2021].
Stam, Robert, 'Beyond Fidelity: The Dialogics of Adaptation', in *Film Adaptation*, ed. James Naremore (New Brunswick, NJ: Rutgers University Press, 2000), pp. 54–76.
Stepanov, A. D., *Problemy kommunikatsii u Chekhova* (Moscow: Iazyki slavianskoi kul'tury, 2005).
Sukhikh, I.N., *Problemy poetiki Chekhova* (St Petersburg: Filologicheskii fakul'tet Sankt-Peterburgskogo gosudarstvennogo universiteta, 2007).
Timasheva, Marina, 'Vse puti vedut v palatu', *Radio Svoboda*, 25 June 2009 <https://www.svoboda.org/a/1762281.html> [accessed 31 July 2021].

Filmography

The Sisters, directed by Arthur Allan Seidelman (USA, Persistent Entertainment, 2005).
Three Days of Rain, directed by Michael Meredith (USA, Shoreline Entertainment 2002).
Ward No. 6 (*Palata № 6*), directed by Karen Shakhnazarov (Russia, Mosfilm, Kur'er, 2009).

6. LOUIS MALLE AND *UNCLE VANYA*

Angus Wrenn

To a degree even greater than applies with, for example, opera, cinema is a quintessentially collaborative artform. Almost without exception, a film given a commercial release on any scale is not an expression of even the director's intentions in isolation, but the product of multiple authors, screenplay writers, camera operators, casting directors, producers and executive producers, post-production and film conglomerate magnates. At the most commercial end of the spectrum a major Hollywood production can even become an exercise in so-called 'product placement' and 'subliminal brand endorsement', in the shape of James Bond's Aston-Martin, or Michael J. Fox's Nike trainers in *Back to the Future* (1985). Does a film come into existence primarily as an act of artistic expression, or first and foremost to shift popcorn and soft drinks? Scarcely a big budget production by American standards ($1.75 million), Louis Malle's film *Vanya on 42nd Street* (1994) might seem a long way from Hollywood films of that sort, but even here, as will be seen, questions of something akin to brand promotion are not entirely irrelevant.

Nonetheless, it is hard to see how this film could be further from the expected Hollywood model, even though Malle filmed in the United States rather than his native France, and he uses an entirely American cast. In the first case, the film is a screen adaptation of a stage play, not a formula favoured by the Hollywood commercial 'blockbuster' system, rare exceptions being *12 Angry Men* (1957), *A Streetcar Named Desire* (1951),[1] or Mike Nichols's *Who's Afraid of Virginia*

---

[1] *12 Angry Men* (directed by Sidney Lumet) was adapted from a 1954 eponymous television play by Reginald Rose; *A Streetcar Named Desire* (directed by Elia Kazan) was an adaptation of Tennessee Williams's eponymous play of 1947.

Woolf? (1966), adapting Edward Albee's 1962 stage play. However, *Vanya on 42nd Street*, as an adaptation of a late nineteenth-century classic Russian stage play, involves still further layers in the process of collaboration. In another, political sense of the word, collaboration might be said to explain the fact that Malle spent the later 1970s making films in North America rather than in his native France, and in English. *Lacombe Lucien* (1974) is today highly regarded by film historians but at the time of its release its frank depiction of the realities of collaboration in the Vichy era proved divisive in France and spurred Malle's move to the USA for two of his greatest subsequent successes, *Pretty Baby* (1978) and *Atlantic City* (1980).

The analysis given here of Louis Malle's version of *Uncle Vanya* will set it in the context of other cinematic versions earlier and subsequent, with continued reference to elements both excluded and added, and attempt to assess the degree to which exclusion and addition are key to the success or otherwise of Malle's film.

In transferring a stage play to the cinema, as part of collaboration there will be contributions from multiple hands. There will also be a question of selection, regarding what must be left out from the original theatrical script and what, if anything, may be added. Brian McFarlane in *Novel To Film* (1996), admittedly looking at the process by which a novel (rather than a stage play) can be adapted into film, asks: 'in the transposition process, just what is it possible to transfer or adapt from novel to film; and (b) what key factors other than the source novel have exercised an influence on the film version of the novel?'[2] Geoffrey Wagner, again writing of the relationship between films and novels, distinguishes between films which amount to 'transpositions' of the original literary text, those which function as 'commentaries', and a third category, films which represent an analogy with the source work.[3]

McFarlane and Wagner establish a division of cinematic versions of written texts into those which exhibit 'fidelity' in the sense of sticking literally to the sequence of events, the precise roster of characters and the exact words used in the dialogue of the original literary work undergoing adaptation, and those which edit the published text with varying degrees of severity, as well as those which interpolate extra scenes no more than implied by the dialogue and action of the original. Still others introduce novel elements found nowhere in the original, or transpose the original play forward in historical period or to a quite different geographical and cultural context. Two of the films mentioned in passing here, Michael Blakemore's *Country Life* (1994) and Anthony Hopkins's *August* (1996) are very much in this category, using Chekhov's text as essentially a starting point for reworkings stripped of all Russian associations and

---

[2] Brian McFarlane, *Novel to Film* (New York: Oxford University Press, 1996), p. 22.
[3] Geoffrey Wagner, *The Novel and the Cinema* (Rutherford: Fairleigh Dickinson University Press, 1975), pp. 219–31.

relocated to Australia and North Wales respectively, although both are far closer to Chekhov's time (the play was published in 1898) than the New York of the 1990s which features in Malle's film. The theorist whose concepts can most definitively be said to lie behind Malle's film, in that they exerted a profound influence upon André Gregory, whose stage production Malle was filming is, however, surely the Polish stage director Jerzy Grotowski (1933–1999), founder of the so-called Theatre of Poverty. This chapter will endeavour to establish the degree to which Malle's film remains consistent with Grotowski's theories, and whether, when a version conceived for the stage is transferred to the screen, fundamental shifts occur.

In terms of McFarlane's 'key factors other than the source' Hopkins and Blakemore exploit the panoramic aspects allowed by cinema not merely to suggest but to show the surrounding landscape, which works well in many ways as a substitute for the Russian provinces, arguably striking more of a chord with a British, North American or Australian audience, but in another sense it amplifies what is no more than suggested and discussed in the original Chekhov stage play, where we do not see beyond the edge of the garden. The analogy with iconography in art history might be the depiction of the Virgin in the Annunciation. St Luke (like Chekhov, a doctor and writer) makes no mention of the Virgin being able to read, let alone possessing any books. St Ambrose, in the third century AD, merely says that Mary was 'studious', yet by the Middle Ages she is depicted reading in what resembles a monastic library when visited by the Archangel.[4] Chekhov, writing only for the stage, could not give us more than a little of the garden and a terrace in Act I, while the remaining three acts all take place indoors. Hopkins and Blakemore, reinterpreting *Uncle Vanya*, shoot on location and give us great sweeping North Welsh and New South Welsh landscapes, with scarcely more strictly literal Chekhovian authority than the Virgin's book and library. Malle's version, in distinction from these, confines itself, after the introductory scenes on the 42nd Street pavement (before rehearsal gets under way), to interior settings.

Surely the most prominent form of collaboration represented by the film *Vanya on 42nd Street* is that between Louis Malle and the director of the run of theatrical rehearsals he was filming, André Gregory. The latter was, at least at this time, known more for his work in the theatre than on screen, as a celebrated off-Broadway avant garde director, although he had in fact taken film roles for Scorsese (*The Last Temptation of Christ*, 1988) and even in the action film *Demolition Man* (1993). Gregory can surely make a claim, given that the Malle film is a record of his own personally selected troupe of actors' rehearsals of *Uncle Vanya*, to be thought of as a co-director of the film.

---

[4] Laura Saetveit Miles, 'The Origins and Development of the Virgin Mary's Book at the Annunciation', *Speculum* 89, 3 (2014), pp. 632–69 (p. 639).

While Malle accounts for the choice of camera angles, and for the supposedly 'real life' scenes which bookend the rehearsals, as well as the selection of soundtrack music, surely Gregory is responsible for the way scenes are delivered on the stage of the New Amsterdam Theater. This is not, however, the original venue where the majority of the four-year run of rehearsals were in fact held, because the Victory Theater became unavailable. Having suggested that Gregory, the stage director, had more say in the casting than Malle as director of the film subsequently shot, a further caveat must be entered, for the octogenarian Ruth Nelson, playing the Nanny, who constituted a link to the tradition of American performances of Chekhov going back to the era of Lee Strasberg (Gregory's own mentor), suffered a fatal stroke. Thus the cast seen in the film is not quite the same one which undertook the run of rehearsals, although Gregory was able to secure Phoebe Brand for the filming in Nelson's place, and she was of similar vintage (born in 1907) and could also claim credentials with the Group Theatre going back to the 1930s.

The cast reflects two aspects which arguably single it out from most filmed productions. Firstly, none of its members were – at the date of filming, and at least by Hollywood standards – headline stars. Julianne Moore (Elena) has since attained major fame but was in 1994 still at the beginning of her career. George Gaynes on the other hand enjoyed some fame in the *Police Academy* series of slapstick comedies, which could scarcely be further removed from his work here in Chekhov. Otherwise, none of the cast of Malle's film would normally head a bill. That distinguishes it markedly from either the 1963 Stuart Burge *Uncle Vanya* starring Laurence Olivier and Michael Redgrave, or the Anthony Hopkins and Michael Blakemore versions from the 1990s. A second important aspect of Gregory's cast is that they are just about uniformly American in background and accent.

Quite the opposite effect was sought in the Burge 1962 Chichester Festival production, where Fay Compton in the role of the mother definitely adopted an accent approximating to what might be termed 'English as spoken by a native Slav'. In Franchot Tone's 1957 film of a New York stage production, the title role was taken by George Voskovec, a migrant from Czechoslovakia rather than a native English speaker. In the television film made by the National Theatre and WNET in America, David Warner (as Astrov) has an English accent, Ian Bannen (Serebriakov) a Scottish brogue, Mary Mastrantonio (Yelena) her Canadian accent and Rebecca Pidgeon (Sonia) her American one. The two English language versions contemporary with Malle's film, *Country Life* (1994) and *August* (1996), with actor-directors taking major roles – Anthony Hopkins in the Vanya equivalent title part 'Ieuan Davies', and Michael Blakemore as the Serebriakov equivalent 'Voysey' – depend (perhaps especially in the case of *August*) upon a major headlining star.

Gregory's choice for Astrov in *Vanya on 42nd Street*, Larry Pine, was not actually much younger than Olivier was at the time of Burge's adaptation,

Figure 6.1   Julianne Moore (as Yelena), Larry Pine (as Dr Astrov) and Wallace Shawn (as Vanya) in *Vanya on 42nd Street*, directed by Louis Malle, 1994.

being 48 at the time of filming. (Sam Neill in the Blakemore film and Gawn Grainger in *August* are both 48.) But it was surely Olivier's star status which led to him appearing, in his mid-fifties, in this younger man's role in the Burge film. (Joan Plowright, then recently married to Olivier, played Sonia, suggesting that Olivier had control of casting at Chichester.) While Larry Pine is himself only a few years younger, the fact that he dresses casually (wearing jeans) contrasts acutely with Olivier's formal waistcoat. (David Warner is similarly formally attired in the television version shortly before that of Louis Malle.) The combination of old school stage declamation and formal period attire robs the earlier actor, for all his unsurpassed eminence, of the intimacy and casual aspect which Pine is able to achieve for Malle and makes it harder for Olivier especially to seem credibly the age Chekhov gives to Astrov.

Malle's English language film *My Dinner with André* (1981), following on from his 1970s successes *Pretty Baby* and *Atlantic City*, and like them made in North America, came as a surprise, given that it goes entirely against the premises of the big American studios, with its eschewal of plot as well as action, which indeed in this case consists entirely of a conversation between two New Yorkers over dinner. As will be seen, this film is, however, in its way considerably indebted to Chekhov.

My Dinner with André, quintessentially collaborative, is a rendering of a New York avant garde off-Broadway success which Gregory co-authored with Wallace Shawn, both actors playing themselves on stage and subsequently in

Malle's screen version. The film is thoroughly Chekhovian in conception, with conversation and musing speculation predominating entirely over action. Perhaps the most celebrated moment of the film is that where the utopian visionary Gregory declares that it is sheer boredom which is effectively making contemporary New Yorkers as susceptible of manipulation by a malign system as any dwellers in a futuristic dystopia, exclaiming: 'We're bored. We are all bored now.' On the surface, given that the line is delivered by a character called André Gregory who is being played by the real life André Gregory, that might seem to be the end of the matter. However, the stress upon boredom surely also harks back to the exclamation made in Chekhov's *Uncle Vanya* by Serebriakov in Act II: 'Because of me you're all ready to collapse, all of you. Everyone bored.'[5]

Malle, who had hitherto had no involvement with transforming stage plays into cinema, became intimately involved in the process of editing down the eight hours of taped conversations between Gregory and Wallace Shawn which the latter eventually turned into the version given on stage. Moreover, Malle became a theatre practitioner himself, actually directing Gregory and Shawn in the brief stage run of *My Dinner with André* given in London, in November 1980, by way of preparation for the filming which took place in the USA a few months later.

The route by which Malle came to Chekhov for what was to prove his final film is an unusual and multifaceted process. As indicated, *My Dinner with André* already embodies some key Chekhovian characteristics. However, at the end of the 1980s, after moving back from the USA to France, to make the highly autobiographical *Au Revoir Les Enfants* (1987), set during the Second World War, Malle produced the comedy *May Fools* (*Milou en mai.*) Outwardly, this appears to be a thoroughly Gallic film, given that it is set in the France of May 1968, brought to a standstill by student riots and a general strike, while President De Gaulle fled to temporary exile. A bourgeois Parisian family find themselves frustrated in holding a funeral for their freshly deceased matriarch, down at her country estate in the south-west of France. They are throughout at odds not only with the striking gravediggers and other members of the working-class, but also the mother's ageing stay-at-home son Milou, who has loyally devoted his life to her, and acted as guardian of the distinctly rundown family estate. He passionately and perhaps hopelessly fights against it being put

---

[5] *Vanya on 42nd Street*, screenplay by David Mamet <https://www.scripts.com/script.php?id=vanya_on_42nd_street_22745&p=11> [accessed 1 September 2021]; based on Anton Chekhov, *Uncle Vanya*, adapted by David Mamet, trans. by Vlada Chernomordik (New York: Grove Press, 1989).

Later in the play (Act III), Elena complains of being bored in the absence of her husband, and likewise Sonia says to Elena 'I know you're bored. It's so contagious. Uncle Vanya has it now.'(Ibid.)

up for sale. There are of course parallels with Jean Renoir's classic of French cinema *The Rules of the Game* (*La règle du jeu*, 1938), with its stinging satire at the expense of the Parisian rentier class, not to mention Luis Buñuel's *The Discreet Charm of the Bourgeoisie* (*Le Charme discret de la bourgeoisie*, 1972). But just as pronounced is the debt to Chekhov, with the idea of the selling up of a rural estate by bourgeois metropolitan relatives (*The Cherry Orchard*) and Milou, clinging onto the estate in opposition to them,[6] corresponding remarkably closely to *Uncle Vanya*. Malle was not alone among leading French directors in this period in the interest he displayed in Chekhov. Patrice Chéreau, much more a man of the theatre than Malle (as both actor and director), had made the film *Hôtel de France*, reworking Chekhov's early, rarely performed, and extremely lengthy play *Platonov*, located in a contemporary French provincial setting, as recently as 1987.

Having taken the subordinate role in *My Dinner with André*, Shawn returned thirteen years later in the title role for *Vanya on 42nd Street*. Whereas Shawn features both as himself (in the introductory footage outdoors on 42nd Street), and in the role of Vanya, though Gregory also appears in the Chekhov film he does so only as himself in real life (in his capacity as director). Playing oneself raises questions regarding 'emotional memory', the principle associated above all with Gregory's mentor Lee Strasberg (himself in turn crucially inspired by the great Russian director Konstantin Stanislavski, whom Gregory also revered, especially early in his career).[7] If an actor is calling upon his own actual memories in order to bring to life the lines ascribed to him in the play, this is surely a radically different undertaking from that envisaged by Strasberg, where the actor is being asked to match personal memory with the written text in order to amplify the character presented.

It is possible to see how pervasive the concept of collaboration may be said to become in this instance. In the film's 'real life' scenes, very much the work of Malle, which bookend those from *Uncle Vanya* performed in the New Amsterdam Theater, Gregory, the actor delivering the lines, would be (as in *My Dinner with André*) so to speak collaborating with himself, drawing, a la Strasberg, upon emotional memories of his own past personal experience, with the novel nuance of doing so in order to play himself. The dialogue which precedes the first rehearsed scene from Chekhov's play has Shawn (also at this

---

[6] Played by Michel Piccoli, later to star on stage in Peter Brook's Chekhov-inspired *Your Hand in Mine (Ta Main Dans La Mienne*, 2003).

[7] 'I was very driven when I was younger. I wanted to be Stanislavsky. I was filled with absurd goals like that' (Robert Weinert Kendt, 'André Gregory: "The Creative Process is Very Mysterious"', *American Theatre*, 3 April 2020 <https://www.americantheatre.org/2020/04/03/andre-gregory-the-creative-process-is-very-mysterious/> [accessed 1 September 2021].

point playing himself) explaining to a fictional guest 'Mrs Chao' (Madhur Jaffrey) that Gregory is not a member of the cast but the director. Given that the cast are wearing their ordinary everyday clothes, Mrs Chao's mistake is entirely pardonable, and reinforces the film's playful unannounced switching between 'reality' and 'make believe'.

To Chekhov by Way of New York: Malle's Route to *Vanya*

The earlier film *My Dinner with André*, with its cast of two most quintessentially American figures, indeed both of them emphatically New Yorkers, might seem to be remote from the world of the late nineteenth-century Russian provincial estate which is the setting for both *Uncle Vanya* and so many of Chekhov's other plays. Indeed, in numerous respects the play has a pronounced New York ambience. However, on closer inspection, the text penned by Shawn also contains a number of elements which combine to suggest that Chekhov's *Uncle Vanya* may well have been on Shawn, Gregory and Malle's minds even at that point, more than a dozen years before. Just as, in the Chekhov play, Vanya, fulminating about the life he thinks he has sacrificed to the end of promoting Serebriakov's career, exclaims 'I could've been a Schopenhauer. I could've been the new Dostoevsky! I could've designed a new philosophy!'[8] so too Schopenhauer comes up in the conversation between Gregory and Shawn in *My Dinner with André*: 'There are different questions. Does she enjoy the ears being nibbled? How intensely can you talk about Schopenhauer at some elegant French restaurant? Whatever nonsense it is. It's all, I think to give you the semblance that there's firm earth.'[9]

Furthermore, Astrov's early espousal of 'green utopianism' in the Chekhov: 'Our forests fall before the axe. Billions of trees, all perishing. The homes of birds and beasts being laid waste. The level of the rivers falls, and they dry up';[10] and his (for the 1890s) progressive vegetarianism ('And then let them find someone whom they can't pigeonhole . . . and that one's the most eccentric person. I love the forest. I don't eat meat . . . A most eccentric person'[11]) both foreshadow the enthusiastic references made by André Gregory (the character) to ecological utopianism, and to the importance of trees, in Shawn's play: 'you'd hear that someone had met him at a party and he'd been telling people that he talked with trees or something like that. Obviously something terrible had happened to André.'[12] And these are mentioned also in connection with

---

[8] *Vanya on 42nd Street*, screenplay.
[9] *My Dinner with André*, screenplay, scripts.com <https://www.scripts.com/script/my_dinner_with_andre_14321> [accessed 1 September 2021].
[10] *Vanya on 42nd Street*, screenplay.
[11] Ibid.
[12] *My Dinner with André*, screenplay.

Grotowski's experimental theatre group: 'So, I went to Poland, and it was this wonderful group of young men and women. And the forest he had found us was absolutely magical.'[13]

And finally, even the dynamic between the Gregory character and the Shawn character in *My Dinner with André* seems imbued with something of the uneasy relationship that persists between Serebriakov and Vanya – Shawn, like Vanya, is the stay-at-home figure, rarely leaving New York, complaining about his lack of success as a writer, while Gregory is the figure who has travelled elsewhere, and is highly, even alarmingly, articulate and intellectual. Moreover, just as Serebriakov holds the purse strings in the Chekhov play, so too Gregory has greater wealth than Shawn and seems to be able to assert himself and take the initiative (it is at his prompting that the dinner is taking place at all, whereas Shawn starts by expressing misgivings about their forthcoming encounter).

Saving Theatre from Cinema: Chekhov in the Wake of Theatre of Poverty

The roster of important (if possibly unwitting) collaborators at one remove associated with *Vanya on 42nd Street* must definitely be extended to include the controversial Polish avant garde director Jerzy Grotowski, founder of the so-called Theatre of Poverty movement, which developed in the 1960s then-communist Poland, before being exported further west when the Pole went into exile in the USA and Italy. Grotowksi's influence upon Gregory in *My Dinner with André* is acknowledged by the actor-director to have been profound. Interviewed by Todd London in *This Is Not My Memoir* he says: 'We were inspired by Grotowski's 'poor theater' principles. Since the theater cannot compete with the visual magic of film it must find what is unique to itself. To do so, we asked what the theater can do without.'[14]

The guiding principle of Grotowksi's radical approach to stage theatre is the eschewal, as far as possible, of all the traditional accoutrements of conventional theatre – costume, scenery and props – in order, relying on the fundamental, inherent qualities of a given actor's personality and performance, to get to the heart of a play's action and its significance. Traditional theatre, with its illusion of environment and setting would constitute 'rich' theatre, the term given a pejorative charge. 'This "synthetic theatre" is the contemporary theatre, which we readily call the "Rich Theatre" – rich in flaws.'[15] In his manifesto *Towards*

---

[13] Ibid.
[14] Todd London and André Gregory, *This Is Not My Memoir* (New York: Farrar, Straus and Drew, 2020) <https://books.google.co.uk/books?id=K_2wDwAAQBAJ&q=grotowski#v> [accessed 1 September 2021].
[15] Jerzy Grotowski, *Towards a Poor Theatre* (New York: Routledge, 2002), p. 19.

a Poor Theatre, Grotowski, growing up in Soviet-dominated Poland, stresses his debt to the original director of *Uncle Vanya*, and many other works of Chekhov's besides, at the Moscow Art Theatre, Konstantin Stanislavski: 'I was brought up on Stanislavski; his persistent study, his systematic renewal of the methods of observation [. . .] Stanislavski asked the key methodological questions. Our solutions, however, differ widely from his – sometimes we reach opposite conclusions.'[16]

Perhaps ironically, in the context of this discussion, Grotowksi stresses the stimulus towards a new conception of theatre by way of response to technological development:

> What is unique about it? What can it do that film and television cannot? Two concrete conceptions crystallized: the poor theatre, and performance as an act of transgression. By gradually eliminating whatever proved superfluous, we found that theatre can exist without make-up, without autonomic costume and scenography, without a separate performance area (stage), without lighting and sound effects, etc. It cannot exist without the actor-spectator relationship [. . .] No matter how much theatre expands and exploits its mechanical resources, it will remain technologically inferior to film and television. Consequently, I propose poverty in theatre.[17]

There is a striking irony here. Grotowski developed Theatre of Poverty, with its rejection of costume, make-up, scenery and more, on the assumption that cinema and television had definitively challenged traditional stage theatre's role. Yet Gregory's theatrical work first in *My Dinner with André* and subsequently in the version of *Uncle Vanya* rehearsed in New York and then filmed by Malle is paradoxically inspired by a thinker who deemed theatre 'technologically inferior to film'.

Rejecting costume, scenery and stage props so that the actor must rely upon personal acting powers to bring a character to life on stage (very often there is not even a stage as such), Grotowski places the actor at the heart of the process and sees the actor, without make-up, costume, props and scenery to fall back on, forced to exploit his own characteristics to convey a role persuasively. In this process Grotowski looks upon himself as director as far from an autocrat, and very much a collaborator, almost midwife in the rehearsal process:

> I am not simply the director or producer or 'spiritual instructor'. In the first place, my relation to the work is certainly not one-way or didactic.

---

[16] Ibid., pp. 15–16.
[17] Ibid., pp. 18–19.

> If my suggestions are reflected in the spatial compositions of our architect Gurawski, it must be understood that my vision has been formed by years of collaboration with him.[18]

A more readily grasped analogy for the general thrust of Grotowski's method might, aptly, be found in the principle known as 'Chekhov's gun': 'One must never place a loaded rifle on the stage if it isn't going to go off. It's wrong to make promises you don't mean to keep.'[19] Grotowski's stripping away of props, costume and scenery arguably has the effect of increasing the significance and relevance of the few features which are allowed to remain, rather than distracting the viewer with details of a now bygone world, such as samovars, bowties and crinolines, which could allow the later audience to lapse into thinking the disillusion demonstrated on stage is a phenomenon peculiar to that bygone age rather than timeless and universal.

There is surely a strong case for saying that, though it is cinema rather than live theatrical performance, *Vanya on 42nd Street*, with its two directors, Gregory and Malle, is in many ways, if not all, true to Grotowski's conception. The detailed implications of a production inspired by Grotowski's precepts may be seen in the following sections.

Escaping the Comfort Zone of the Past: Updating Chekhov

Grotowski prescribes the absence of stage and period costumes in his drama. There is a potential within Theatre of Poverty for an element of Brechtian *Verfremdungseffekt*, 'alienation or distancing effect', but arguably Grotowski's rejection of the traditional 'willing suspension of disbelief' dating back to Coleridge in *Biographia Literaria*[20] is still more extreme. Brecht wishes his audience to reflect on the stakes in the real world beyond the walls of the theatre in which they sit, and himself espouses a specific (socialist) politically engaged agenda. Grotowski is likewise certainly capable of being blatantly political. His 1962 production of Stanisław Wyspiański's *Akropolis* (1904), which would make Grotowski's name, updated the action of the classic Polish writer's play so that cast and audience appeared to be sitting inside the

---

[18] Ibid., pp. 24–5.
[19] Anton Chekhov, letter to Aleksandr Semenovich Lazarev (pseudonym of A. S. Gruzinsky), 1 November 1889, in Leah Goldberg, *Russian Literature in the Nineteenth Century: Essays* (Jerusalem: Hebrew University, Magnes Press, 1976), p. 163.
[20] Coleridge speaks of 'a semblance of truth sufficient to procure for these shadows of imagination that willing suspension of disbelief for the moment, which constitutes poetic faith' (Samuel Taylor Coleridge, *Biographia Literaria* (London: Dent, 1906), p 161).

concentration camp at Auschwitz.[21] This is surely Grotowski at his most politically extreme, denying the play's original context and imposing one from close to the time of the 1960s audience to whom his version was presented. Albeit highly politicised, Grotowski's production might be deemed, in Geoffrey Wagner's terms, an adaptation on the basis of 'analogy'. More generally, Grotowski's overriding objective is to present the acted experience in its simplest and starkest form, the audience undistracted by costumes and props which invite them to 'escape' into another world trapped in the historical past. One almost gains the impression that Grotowski might ideally prefer the actor to appear naked if that were not bound, because of current social convention, to prove distracting in itself. At all costs, nothing must be allowed to distract from the text itself and the experience it embodies.

Whether Malle and Gregory can be said to be updating the action and setting of *Uncle Vanya* is a moot point. Certainly no attempt is made via costumes and coiffure to evoke the nineteenth century. The setting of *Vanya on 42nd Street* is hard to assess. Of course it is literally set in 1990s New York, but the New Amsterdam Theater is a building that dates from almost a hundred years before, close to the Chekhov period, and its dilapidated state proves an uncanny 'objective correlative' for a crumbling Russian rural estate. The same emphasis upon the link to the present is highlighted by the fact that the cast appear in what might plausibly be their own casual 1990s clothes. There are no crinolines for the actresses or refined goatee beards and bowties for the actors. At one point Julianne Moore, as Yelena, wears a leather jacket. Larry Pine, in the role of Dr Astrov, wears denim, certainly in contrast with the photographs of Chekhov himself, which show a figure invariably dapper and elegant. The main possible exception to this approach might arguably be said to be George Gaynes, playing Serebriakov, who wears from the outset, as if almost already in character, a full coat which he sports in the introductory minutes of the film, even though not yet taking part in the Chekhov play. In Act III, when pompously announcing his plan to sell the estate, he wears a tie. No heavy, obviously theatrical make-up appears to be worn by the cast. Overall (entirely deliberately) the cast are in most respects indistinguishable from the handful of guests watching that day's rehearsal.

PARALLEL OR ANALOGY: NORTH WALES, NEW SOUTH WALES OR NEW YORK?

In the case of *Vanya on 42nd Street*, Malle does not go anything like as far as Grotowski in *Akropolis*, of course. In a sense, Grotowski's most controversial production is not entirely consistent with the Poverty principle, since it works

---

[21] See Magda Romanska, 'Between History and Memory: Auschwitz in "Akropolis", "Akropolis" in Auschwitz', *Theatre Survey*, 50 (2009), pp. 223–50.

by suggesting an *alternative* setting (Auschwitz) for the classic Polish work which is historically at odds with the original written text. Arguably, *Vanya on 42nd Street*, by playing down traditional period costume, is closer to the vaunted pursuit of minimalism. The point surely being made is that characters in Chekhov's play, though products of a particular historical era, the second half of the nineteenth century, convey a sense of disillusion and hopelessness which might equally well manifest itself in the present day at the date of shooting and in the chosen location (New York). In emphasising that the action is unfolding within a disused theatre, the approach resembles Brechtian *Verfremdungseffekt*, [22] and indeed there are scenes where actors not taking part in a particular scene nevertheless remain visible onstage within the camera shot, as Brecht so often instructs his actors to stand at the back until their next lines in a subsequent scene. Yet in another respect, the fact that the rehearsals are taking place not just in any disused theatre, but in the pre-First World war New Amsterdam Theater, close in historical period to Chekhov's, gives this film many affinities with another genre which was only just entering academic discourse in the 1990s, 'site-specific theatre'.[23]

In a certain sense, it is the cinematic versions already mentioned, by Anthony Hopkins and Michael Blakemore, so near in time to the Louis Malle film, which could be said to be doing something akin to Grotowski in his controversial setting of the *Akropolis* production, for both nevertheless insist (while in no way stressing pervasive minimalism a la Theatre of Poverty or being devoid of political engagement), upon a provocatively alternative setting for the action of their *Vanya*, indeed that is in each case very much their *raison d' être*. Blakemore's film *Country Life* remains close to the era of Chekhov's original, updating it only 20 years to the immediate aftermath of World War I. But the geographical setting is quite distinct, the Russian rural estate becoming an Australian homestead in New South Wales. The protagonists are Anglicised, with Vanya becoming 'Jack', Serebriakov 'Alexander Voysey', an Australian who has made good as a critic in literary London, and Dr Astrov renamed Dr Askey, who, we are told, is treating victims of the 1919 influenza epidemic. The film keeps the broad outlines of the Chekhovian original although there is also amplification, with, for instance, a domineering Irish cook. Moreover,

---

[22] Interviewed by Todd London in *American Theatre*, Gregory said: 'You know, Grotowski is now recognised in Russia as the great disciple of Stanislavsky. And Brecht's work as a director was as close to Strasberg's as you can imagine, except it was simpler. But it came from the same source' (Todd London and André Gregory *This Is Not My Memoir*).

[23] Fiona Wilkie, 'The Production of "Site"', in *Site-Specific Theatre, a Concise Companion to Contemporary British and Irish Drama*, eds Nadine Holdsworth and Mary Luckhurst (London: Wiley-Blackwell, 2008), pp. 87–106.

Blakemore as director exploits the expansive skylines of the Australian outback terrain, with sunsets shown in full-screen silhouettes.

Anthony Hopkins's 1996 film *August* is set, like the original Chekhov, in the late nineteenth century, yet in a North Wales (UK) every bit as verdant as Blakemore's New South Wales is drought-afflicted. Both films add characters and their dialogue is by no means confined to the strict text of Chekhov's play. In each case the film 'describes' and 'elaborates' the reality of aimless provincial life alluded to in Chekhov's play. By McFarlane's yardstick both of these versions constitute film work which adds to the 'mere' text of the stage play. Both films also revolve around actor-directors, Hopkins taking the part of the Welsh Vanya equivalent, and Blakemore taking the role of the Serebriakov counterpart.

Less is More: Propping up the Film. Tea or Coffee?

Grotowski's 'minimalistic' approach goes beyond setting and costume to include stage props. These are almost, but not quite, non-existent in *Vanya on 42nd Street*. This cinematic version can be distinguished from the half dozen or so which preceded it by the absence of that most Chekhovian of stage props, a samovar. Traditional productions, such as the 1957 American film by Blanchot Tone and the 1963 Stuart Burge film, feature a samovar prominently, and it also reliably appears, as if on cue, in the opening frames of Andrei Konchalovsky's 1970 Russian version, even though the director then goes on immediately to a highly 'experimental' use of archive still photographs from the Russian fin-de-siecle, accompanied by a musical score penned by Alfred Schnittke at his most progressive and spiky. Even in a still more radical Chekhov film, such as Nikita Mikhalkov's *An Unfinished Piece for Mechanical Piano* (1976), a reworking of Chekhov's *Platonov*, the samovar appears prominently in the very opening shot, serving there, shiny and silver, as an impromptu looking-glass. The National Theatre/American WNET television joint production starring David Warner and using the same Mamet 'adaptation' of the Chekhov text of *Vanya* which Gregory and Malle work from, likewise focuses very clearly upon the samovar from the earliest moments.

By contrast, in Malle's version, the opening scenes, before Nanny and Astrov start delivering Chekhov's lines from Act I, show us the cast getting coffee, dispensed by a member of the film production team in charge of refreshments. The references in dialogue between the cast members Julianne Moore and Lynn Cohen (at this stage themselves and not yet in character as Yelena and Maman respectively) are definitely to coffee and surely as such to a beverage altogether less idiomatically Russian than tea. This process of eschewal of some of the quintessentially Russian elements does not extend, with Malle and Gregory, to removal of references in the text to vodka, but the vodka is never dispensed

Figure 6.2 Vanya (Wallace Shawn) and Yelena (Julianne Moore). *Vanya on 42nd Street*, directed by Louis Malle, 1994.

from labelled bottles, and thus viewers are not repeatedly reminded of its presence except when it is mentioned in Chekhov's dialogue. Later, during one of Vanya's most heated moments in Act III, the camera shows us neither the samovar nor a vodka bottle. Instead, inescapably in the foreground in the very centre of the plain wooden table top, stands a paper drinking cup bearing the slogan 'I♥NY.' It is perhaps going too far to view this as product placement on a par with James Bond jumping into that most British of sportscars, an Aston Martin, nevertheless it is worth pointing out that this New York slogan is a registered trademark and has a specific author, the commercial graphic designer, Milton Glaser. It was devised in 1976, at the behest of the New York State Department of Design, to promote the city's image. In that respect the slogan, exclusively modern and contemporary in its associations, was successful from the outset and recommended itself to Malle by 1994. If anything, its currency has only increased in more recent decades, having become very popular as a symbol of solidarity with New York City at the time of the 9/11 attacks in 2001.

The slogan's iconographic effect in a Chekhov play is threefold. First and foremost, it counters any inclination in the audience to 'escape' into the past of ornate silver samovars, and forces them onto an altogether different continent from Chekhov's native Russia. Secondly, it appears to evoke American rather than Russian associations. And thirdly, and perhaps of greatest importance, it is not even a generalised American icon. The paper cup does not bear the stars and stripes of the US national flag but specifically evokes New York. In context, this gesture is highly radical, for the most readily quoted line from all of Chekhov's plays (at least beyond the Russian-speaking world) is surely the refrain 'to Moscow' from *Three Sisters*. Time and again, the setting in Chekhov's dramas is the beleaguered rural estate, or the provincial town, whose residents dream of life in the nation's biggest city. Seldom, either in the plays, or for that matter in the short stories, is the setting urban, still less metropolitan. Yet Malle's film emphatically evokes the USA's largest city, New York.

The significance of this gesture is difficult to assess definitively. Despite Grotowski's seminal influence upon André Gregory and through him upon this film, the paper cup New York icon is surely not intended to make the audience think of New York to the exclusion of anything else. Malle and or Gregory are not urging us to think of New York to the exclusion of Russia. Is Vanya's possession, in the depths of the provinces, of a cup proclaiming New York, intended to give the impression that he thinks constantly of a city and a lifestyle which are for him unattainable? In that regard it must be pointed out that the film does retain a traditional glass carafe for the vodka, on its frequent appearances. The final point to be made concerning the significance of the paper cup and the NY logo is that it is a symbol which surely works infinitely better on screen (where Malle's camera can zoom in and linger over it), whereas in anything on a grander scale than the most intimate of fringe theatre performances the logo would be scarcely visible to the many audience members in distant seats.

If the NY cup stands as an icon of the present day of the 1990s, rather than Chekhov's 1890s samovar, in other respects Malle's rendering can be said, in the matter of stage properties, to be closer to the Chekhovian original. In Act III, driven to distraction by Serebriakov's plans for sale of the estate, Vanya goes offstage to fetch a gun. This is first heard fired offstage rather than seen, but when Vanya does rush onstage the gun is specified by the script as a revolver. Malle and Gregory are consistent with Chekhov in this respect, with Shawn wielding a handgun. By contrast, Blakemore and Hopkins both have Vanya firing a shotgun. (This is somewhat counterintuitive – a shotgun would be more easily visible to the audience in a large theatre – Chekhov refers to a rifle when formulating the 'Chekhov's gun' principle – whereas cinema can use close-ups so is not constrained in this way.) The associations which shotguns and handguns evoke are quite different. In Russian culture the handgun (pistol) is especially linked with duelling, most famously in the age of Pushkin, although even at a later date (1861), nearer to Chekhov's time, Tolstoy challenged Turgenev to a duel. (Neither was hit.) Duels are not normally fought using shotguns, whose associations are more with forced marriages. Gregory Mosher, directing David Warner as Vanya for WNET and the BBC in their 1990 television film, remains faithful to the pistol specified in Chekhov's stage directions, and as alluded to in dialogue by Telegin in Act IV, and so do

Blanchot Tone in the 1957 American film of a New York stage production, Andrei Konchalovsky in his 1970 Russian film and Stuart Burge in 1963.

The issue of period authenticity links to another aspect of the film which also involves a degree of collaboration. The version of Chekhov's text used in *Vanya on 42nd Street* is the work of more than one hand. It is based upon a literal translation from the Russian by Vlada Chernomordik, but was then adapted by an American dramatist without access to the Russian language. The American playwright in question is none other than David Mamet, arguably the American dramatist to have enjoyed the most widespread success since the death of Tennessee Williams. Mamet's own plays, such as *Glengarry Glen Ross* (1984) or *American Buffalo* (1975), might lead one to expect an English language version peppered with profanities. However, in this respect, Mamet proves uncharacteristically restrained, at least here, and in general his version has been widely praised for seeming easily comprehensible and yet idiomatic to late twentieth and early twenty-first century ears. The English turns of phrase are indeed generally much more idiomatic in late twentieth century terms than Constance Garnett's 1897 translation, used in Burge's 1963 film. For example, the word employed disparagingly by a local village trader to refer to Telegin in Malle's film is 'freeloader', a word not recorded before the 1930s, according to the *Oxford English Dictionary*.[24] Nonetheless, not all critics agreed. A notable dissenting voice is that of Adam Mars-Jones:

> The language, despite what Mamet's 'adaptation credit' would suggest, has not been brought up to date. A speech like Vanya's 'I'm done. I am silent. Excuse me', has a modern ring only because of Wallace Shawn's definitively New York delivery of 'Excuse me' [. . .] When Nanny says, 'I haven't had simple noodles in the longest time, black with sin as I am,' it isn't the folksy Americana of 'in the longest time' that makes the strongest impression, but the fustiness of the last phrase. And shouldn't those noodles be 'plain'?[25]

Notwithstanding this cavil, Mars-Jones was overall a great enthusiast of Malle's film.

---

[24] Freeloader – An American colloquialism, dating only from the 1930s. *Oxford English Dictionary* <freeloader, n. : Oxford English Dictionary (oed.com)> [accessed 21 August 2021].

[25] Adam Mars-Jones, 'Set Coordinates for the Big Screen, Mr Chekhov', *The Independent*, 22 October 2011 <https://www.independent.co.uk/arts-entertainment/books/features/adam-marsjones-my-writing-is-like-watching-undercoat-dry-2191823.html> [accessed 1 September 2021].

Realising or Contradicting Chekhov?

The question of period detail is also raised by the film's soundtrack. Here Malle seems divided between Russian past and 1990s American present. Telegin, the faithful if aimless family neighbour-cum-hanger on, does indeed strum a guitar, as called for by Chekhov's stage directions in Act II, but the pervasive music of the soundtrack which sets the mood for the film in the opening 1990s 'real life' scenes (returning in the interval scene and at the final 'curtain call') is quite different, comprising contemporary jazz specially composed by Joshua Redman. This is cool jazz, definitely not 1920s Dixieland or 1940s swing or be-bop. It is not, however, surely as cool and melancholy as the celebrated Miles Davis 'blue' jazz chosen for *Lift to the Scaffold* (*Ascenseur pour l'Echafaud,*) with which Malle made his career breakthrough at the end of the 1950s. It is, on the contrary, upbeat and positive, without being frenetic. Whether it is exactly of a piece in historical terms with the outside world of Times Square and 42nd Street depicted in the opening shots before the Chekhov rehearsal gets under way, is debatable. By 1994, hip-hop and rap were probably already established as the contemporary musical idiom of New York. Nonetheless, Redman's score unquestionably evokes African-American culture and as such is far removed from the original world of Chekhov's plays. However, by the same token, it is very much of a piece with the markedly multi-racial crowd scenes with which the film opens. The first faces in the crowd focused on by Malle's camera on 42nd Street and Times Square are Asian, Hispanic and African-American rather than white Caucasians. It is the Redman jazz which also closes the film, stealing into the soundtrack a few moments before Gregory and those members who do not feature in the final scene join Vanya, Sonia and Maman in another instance of Brechtian *Verfremdungseffekt*, taking us back to the 'real life' of the opening New York shots and at the same time doubling as curtain call for the tiny invited audience (who are all but outnumbered by the cast of nine).

The mood created by the late twentieth-century jazz of the musical score, which decisively holds sway over the Chekhovian guitar, and provides both the prelude and postlude, is not, however, allowed altogether to exclude the nineteenth century at one crucial point. After the violent tirade against Serebriakov leads Vanya to fire a gun, albeit missing his brother-in-law, and Elena has persuaded her husband that they must leave without delay, the sound of harness bells is allowed to be heard offstage. Alert viewers will recall that immediately before the film switched from 'real life' to the dialogue between Astrov and Nanny which opens the play, Brooke Smith, who is to take the role of Sonia, is seen, very fleetingly, getting a set of sleighbells out of her rucksack. After in so many respects following the precepts of Grotowski's 'Theatre of Poverty' in the eschewal of all the resources available to the traditional modern theatre, and avoiding the trappings of period drama, Malle and Gregory seem briefly and tellingly content to evoke a bygone age. This is only for three very brief moments, and it underlines to what an extent the crinolines, waistcoats and samovars have been missing during the previous two hours. While gunfire would by no means seem anything much out of the ordinary in 1990s New York, it must indeed have been many decades since horses' harness bells were last heard on the real life 42nd Street, with footage of which Malle's version opens. By its retention, contra Grotowski, this feature both produces a heightened effect and also makes viewers reflect on everything traditionally expected in Chekhov which they have pointedly *not* been confronted with during the performance.

Ultimately, though an undoubted success, and indeed widely considered to be the most persuasive and effective cinematic rendition of any Chekhov play, *Vanya on 42nd Street* remains a paradox, inspired by an avant garde experimental director, yet resulting in one of the versions of a Chekhov play on screen to which viewers return repeatedly and with renewed pleasure. As shown, the film is by no means consistent at all points in rigorously following Grotowski's minimalist principles. It is true that it depends on no single charismatic performance, and it does not reflect an intrusive, interventionist director imposing his or her vision of the work to the exclusion of all else. The film does have moments where it departs from a strict emphasis upon the present day of the production (the bells of the horses' harnesses). At some points Mamet's adaptation is still stuck in the nineteenth century.

To conclude, it is perhaps worth mentioning the words of Vladimir Nabokov in *Lectures on Russian Literature*. Somewhat unusually, Nabokov professed himself an admirer of Chekhov without being able to say precisely why. He concludes that Chekhov persuades in considerable measure thanks to the small details which he uses to convey mood and atmosphere. Nabokov discusses Chekhov's fiction mainly, but his point that Chekhov conveys 'atmosphere' by 'the most concise details'[26] surely applies with equal validity to his drama. It is almost as if the small scale nature of the details (rather than generalised pronouncements) affords the reader greater scope for use of the imagination. Traditionally stage theatre offers the audience greater scope to imagine than the imposed 'realism' possible on film. Alastair Fowler in *Renaissance Realism* makes the point that in the Elizabethan and Jacobean theatre a jail was denoted to the audience by nothing more than a set of keys hanging on a wall at the back of the stage.[27] Perhaps it is the small details of Malle's and Gregory's

---

[26] Vladimir Nabokov, *Lectures on Russian Literature*, ed. F. Bowers (New York: Houghton Mifflin, 1981), p 252.

[27] 'At first stage scenery was limited to a very few props, place being indicated instead by costume. A gaoler's keys, or manacled prisoners, were enough to indicate a prison' (Alastair Fowler, *Renaissance Realism* [Oxford: Oxford University Press, 2003], p. xxviii).

cinematic version, such as the paper cup and the harness bells, which stand out within a generally minimalistic production, and allow viewers freer rein for the imagination than would normally be expected in a cinematic rendering. *Vanya on 42nd Street* is a film which, precisely because based on rehearsals rather than a conventional proscenium performance, and without the distractions of a 'larger than life' man of the theatre like Olivier or Hopkins among the cast, but with a background which is as dark as if one were almost sitting in a theatre, allows the viewer to imagine that is indeed where the last two hours have been spent.

Bibliography

Coleridge, Samuel Taylor, *Biographia Literaria* (London: Dent, 1906).
Fowler, Alastair, *Renaissance Realism* (Oxford: Oxford University Press, 2003).
Goldberg, Leah, *Russian Literature in the Nineteenth Century: Essays* (Jerusalem: Hebrew University, Magnes Press, 1976).
Grotowski, Jerzy, *Towards A Poor Theatre* (New York: Routledge, 2002).
Kendt, Robert Weinert, 'André Gregory: "The Creative Process is Very Mysterious"', *American Theatre*, 3 April 2020 <https://www.americantheatre.org/2020/04/03/andre-gregory-the-creative-process-is-very-mysterious/> [accessed 1 September 2021].
London, Todd and André Gregory *This Is Not My Memoir* (New York: Farrar, Straus and Drew, 2020) <https://books.google.co.uk/books?id=K_2wDwAAQBAJ&q=grotowski#v> [accessed 1 September 2021].
Mars-Jones, Adam, 'Set Coordinates for the Big Screen, Mr Chekhov', *The Independent*, 22 October 2011 <https://www.independent.co.uk/arts-entertainment/books/features/adam-marsjones-my-writing-is-like-watching-undercoat-dry-2191823.html> [accessed 1 September 2021].
McFarlane, Brian, *Novel to Film* (New York: Oxford University Press, 1996).
Miles, Laura Saetveit, 'The Origins and Development of the Virgin Mary's Book at the Annunciation', *Speculum* 89, 3 (2014), pp. 632–69.
My Dinner with André, screenplay, scripts.com <https://www.scripts.com/script/my_dinner_with_andre_14321> [accessed 1 September 2021].
Nabokov, Vladimir, *Lectures on Russian Literature*, ed. F. Bowers (New York: Houghton Mifflin, 1981).
Oxford English Dictionary <freeloader, n. : Oxford English Dictionary (oed.com)> [accessed 21 August 2021].
Romanska, Magda, 'Between History and Memory: Auschwitz in "Akropolis", "Akropolis" in Auschwitz', *Theatre Survey*, 50 (2009), pp. 223–50.
Vanya on 42nd Street, screenplay by David Mamet <https://www.scripts.com/script.php?id=vanya_on_42nd_street_22745&p=11> [accessed 1 September 2021].
Wagner, Geoffrey, *The Novel and the Cinema* (Rutherford: Fairleigh Dickinson University Press, 1975).
Wilkie, Fiona, 'The Production of "Site"', in *Site-Specific Theatre, a Concise Companion to Contemporary British and Irish Drama*, eds Nadine Holdsworth and Mary Luckhurst (London: Wiley-Blackwell, 2008), pp. 87–106.

FILMOGRAPHY

My Dinner with André, directed by Louis Malle (USA, New Yorker Films, 1981).
Vanya on 42nd Street, directed by Louis Malle (USA, Mayfair Entertainment International, 1994).

7. REINVENTING CHEKHOV FOR THE AMERICAN SCREEN: MICHAEL MAYER'S *THE SEAGULL*

Olga Partan

The abundance of Russian and Western cinematic adaptations of Anton Chekhov's plays, short stories and novellas provides a rich collection of cinematic Chekhoviana that deserves methodical critical evaluation.[1] What is the reason for Chekhov's everlasting appeal that goes far beyond geographical or temporal borders? Chekhov's oeuvre, with its multiplicity of comic and dramatic characters, has inspired readers, actors and directors, providing literary and dramatic material for cross-cultural, cross-generational communication. The writer's witty observations on the tragicomic condition of human existence can be easily understood by viewers from a wide variety of cultural and socio-economic backgrounds. As filmmakers transport Chekhovian literary

---

[1] For an overview of screen adaptations of Chekhov's works see Philip French, 'Chekhov on Screen', in *The Cambridge Companion to Chekhov*, eds Vera Gottlieb and Paul Allain (Cambridge: Cambridge University Press, 2000), pp. 149–61. French summarises the Soviet-era adaptations of Chekhov's stories and dramatic works, paying special tribute to Iosif Kheifits's adaptation *The Lady with the Dog* (1960) and Nikita Mikhalkov's *An Unfinished Piece for Mechanical Piano* (1976). In his discussion of the international screen adaptations of Chekhov's plays, French singles out *Vanya on 42nd Street* calling it 'arguably the greatest screen Chekhov' (p. 159). One might add to French's list two of Isidor Annensky's exuberant screen adaptations of one-act comic plays – *The Bear* (1938) and *The Wedding* (1944) – where one can see Stanislavsky and Vsevolod Meyerhold's pupils on screen in these productions that often go under the radar of Western scholars.

and dramatic texts into the film medium, they become co-authors with the nineteenth-century Russian writer, reinterpreting Chekhov's oeuvre by establishing intertextual connections with the originals and adapting their cinematic narratives to the expectations of modern viewers.

Chekhov's celebrated play *The Seagull* (1896) has undergone multiple adaptations on Russian and Western screens, creating a Chekhovian subgenre of its own that is waiting to be fully explored. This chapter is dedicated to the latest 'American *Seagull*' – Michael Mayer's 2018 adaptation that undoubtedly deserves an honourable place in the gallery of screen adaptations of the play. Before plunging into a detailed discussion of Mayer's film, I would like to briefly mention his notable predecessors to emphasise the distinctive features of Mayer's adaptation. One should certainly mention Sidney Lumet's 1968 version with an international cast that included the French movie star Simone Signoret as Arkadina, the English actors Vanessa Redgrave and David Warner as Nina and Treplev respectively, as well as the Hollywood star James Mason as Trigorin. Filmed in the Swedish countryside, this film relies on a group of renowned actors who lack the unity of ensemble acting that had traditionally been fundamental for the overall success of stage or screen adaptations of Chekhov's plays. As Vincent Canby notes: 'Most of the performances are excellent, but all of the actors seem to be on their own.'[2] Lumet's cinematography relies on long shots and close-ups on individual performers while his interpretation is characterised by an absence of humour or a comedic mood, accentuating instead a melodramatic state of affairs as well as boredom and unhappiness. Two more TV adaptations appeared in the 1970s – an American one directed by John J. Desmond that was broadcast as an episode of 'Great Performances' in 1975, and another British one directed by Michael Lindsay-Hogg that was released by BBC Studios in 1978. Despite the fact that nowadays both adaptations are a bit outdated, they have been frequently used as visual teaching tools for English speaking students' exploration of Chekhov's dramaturgy. Both TV versions were produced as theatrical plays slightly modified for a larger TV audience without tangible experimentation with various possibilities of the cinematic medium.

Iulii Karasik's well known 1970 Soviet adaptation relied on movie stars, featuring Alla Demidova as Arkadina and Liudmila Savel'eva (who at that time had received international recognition for her role as Natasha Rostova in Sergei Bondarchuk's 1965–67 film series *War and Peace*[3]) as Nina. The male cast

---

[2] Vincent Canby, '"The Sea Gull" Brought to the Screen by Lumet', *The New York Times*, 24 December 1968.

[3] On Bondarchuk's adaptation of *War and Peace* see Olga Sobolev's contribution to this volume (Chapter 10).

includes such Soviet stage and movie stars as Iurii Iakovlev as Trigorin and Armen Dzhigarkhanian as Shamraev. The musical score written by Alfred Shnitke contributes to the overall gloomy atmosphere of unavoidable catastrophe that dominates this film. Finally, Margarita Terekhova's post-Soviet 2005 version, which marked her debut as a director and screenwriter, was a disappointing adaptation that presented the aging movie star at the end of her career: Terekhova cast herself in the role of Arkadina, and her son and daughter—Anna Terekhova and Alexander Terekhov (Turaev)—as Nina and Treplev respectively. Cinematographically, the production is filmed in a natural setting next to a lake that became the main and the most Chekhovian element of the movie. The adaptation is of interest only as Terekhova's sad farewell to her Russian fans. In her youth, the actress was director Andrei Tarkovsky's muse, starring in his legendary *Mirror* (1974).

While the above-mentioned adaptations present their own artistic achievements and flaws, the main common feature of these films is that, while staying faithful to the Chekhovian text and setting, they overwhelmingly share the quality of being a theatrical play that is filmed for the movie theatre or TV screens. There is no visible attempt to experiment with cinematographic language to convey the mood or create a Chekhovian atmosphere. As a result, viewers have the impression of watching a Chekhov play on screen, observing the nuances of directorial vision and following the artistry of the cast (or sometimes the lack thereof). Reflecting the well-established western directorial perception of what a Chekhovian mood is, Rose Whyman observes that the 'passive and mournful mood of the pre-revolutionary intelligentsia in Russia' became a 'clichéd interpretation, which has persisted in the history of productions'.[4] One might add that the same 'passive and mournful mood' dominates the screen adaptations mentioned above.

How then is Mayer's directorial approach distinct from that of his predecessors? I shall argue that the director and his screenwriter Stephen Karam go against the pre-existing cliché intentionally to create a purely cinematographic version of *The Seagull*, bravely co-authoring this new artifact and successfully establishing an artistic dialogue between the play and the film medium. Modifying the chronology and the denouement of the play, they invite viewers to follow the lead of the ubiquitous presence of a voyeuristic camera eye, replacing the traditional slow pace and long pauses with energetic movement on screen. Most importantly, the main accents are made on modernised Chekhovian women performed by superb female actors whose charismatic screen presence and contrasting life credo enhance the production as a whole.

---

[4] Rose Whyman, *Anton Chekhov* (London: Routledge, 2011), p. 92.

Cinematic Adaptation as Co-authorship

In his influential monograph *The Chekhov Theatre: A Century of the Plays in Performance,* Laurence Senelick remarks: 'For better or worse, Chekhov's plays were written at a time when the stage director was becoming a paramount factor in the theater.'[5] Senelick observes that

> the stage history of Chekhov's drama is a chronicle less of great performers in starring roles than of the success and failure of directors and acting companies in realizing his plays and communicating them to a given audience at a particular moment in history.[6]

Mayer's *The Seagull* displays a similar pattern as it relies on 'ensemble playing' where coordination is 'best achieved under the baton of a single "conductor"'[7] – the film director whose co-authorship re-invents the canonical dramatic text. Mayer's main directorial agenda focuses on the creation of the verisimilitude of the setting where the atmosphere of a magical lake and a country estate full of natural light seems to be as important as the cast of characters. His version of *The Seagull* represents a purely cinematic adaptation using many attributes of the film medium sometimes relying too much on text, instead of the subtext that is quintessential for Chekhov's poetics. Nevertheless, Mayer and his cinematic team succeed in creating the effect of modernity, rendering Chekhov's playwriting universal and understandable to contemporary spectators.

Mayer is known for his stage productions not only on Broadway, off Broadway and in classical opera houses, but in film and television, yet he considers himself first and foremost to be a theatre director. Nevertheless, in his production of *The Seagull* he decided to rely heavily on the versatile possibilities of cinema as a medium that are not feasible in theatre production. 'You want to tell the story cinematographically. Otherwise why bother?' explains the director in one of his interviews.[8] Mayer's aim was to create a version of the play that would reflect all the possibilities of the motion pictures as a visual medium, since theatre is verbal. The film script, written by Karam, underwent several revisions in adapting and shortening the original play for the screen, simplifying the language and truncating the long monologues, making it more appealing and understandable to a larger contemporary audience of moviegoers. Unquestionably, while writing his script, Karam became Chekhov's

---

[5] Laurence Senelick, *The Chekhov Theatre: A Century of the Plays in Performance* (Cambridge: Cambridge University Press, 1997), p. 3.
[6] Ibid., p. 4.
[7] Ibid., p. 3.
[8] Michael Mayer, a video interview on *The Seagull*, YouTube <https://www.youtube.com/watch?v=WLglmW_c9NE> [accessed 15 September 2021].

co-author who significantly changed not only the play's denouement but the whole chronology.

Susan Sontag suggests: 'The success of movie versions of plays is measured by the extent to which the script rearranges and displaces the action and deals less than respectfully with spoken text.'[9] *The Seagull's* screen script is based on exactly the same effect, intentionally moving the play from the theatre domain to the filmic medium. The chronotope of Chekhov's play was significantly changed and, following Mayer's directorial vision, the action on screen represents a circular structure. The film begins with the image of a theatrical curtain, the actors' final bow and the long ovation that depicts yet another stage triumph of Irina Arkadina (Annette Bening). It is behind the stage that Arkadina receives the news that her brother Sorin (Brian Dennehy) is fatally ill. Arkadina immediately leaves Moscow for the country estate, taking her lover with her, the famous writer Trigorin (Corey Stroll) in his formal evening attire. The dark and gloomy atmosphere on screen is achieved by the cinematographer's decision to rely exclusively on candlelight, while being truthful to the period drama setting. The visual and sound effects of rain and thunder effectively contribute to the ominous atmosphere. In the next scene, while most of the play's characters are peacefully playing lotto, the camera switches to Konstantin Treplev (Billy Howle) in his study who encounters the unexpected visit of his beloved Nina Zarechnaia (Saoirse Ronan). Nina knocks on the window and her unhappy face is wet either from raindrops or tears. Only then, after such a long exposition, do the titles start to appear on screen against the background of a drastically different setting full of sunlight. The viewer is transported to the idyllic atmosphere of the country estate with a clear, cloudless summer sky. For those unfamiliar with the original play, this change in sequence offers an opportunity to expect a rather dramatic denouement from the outset, assuming that Nina's and Konstantin's innocent kisses in the next scene would not presage a happy ending.

The whole adaptation is staged as a flashback to a happy past, and the bright setting of the sunny estate with the magical lake creates a stunning visual contrast with the gloomy beginning. The three acts of the play are intentionally filmed with only natural light. The film's finale returns to its beginning as the cinematic narrative replays the opening scenes once again. Unexpectedly for everyone well familiar with the original play, the script completely eliminates Doctor Dorn's original final words to Trigorin after the shot is heard: 'Take Irina Nikolaevna somewhere, away from here. The fact is, Konstantin Gavrilovich has shot himself...'[10] One wonders whether such an intentional open ending with a final close-up on Arkadina's relieved face suggests that Konstantin just wounded

---

[9] Susan Sontag, 'Film and Theater', in *Theater and Film: A Comparative Anthology*, ed. Robert Knopf (New Haven: Yale University Press, 2005), pp. 134–51 (p. 139).

[10] Anton Chekhov, 'The Sea Gull', in *Anton Chekhov's Plays*, trans. and ed. Eugene K. Bristow (New York: Norton & Company, 1977), pp. 1–52 (p. 51).

Figure 7.1 Nina Zarechnaia (Saoirse Ronan), *The Seagull*, directed by Michael Mayer, 2018.

himself once again and the circular structure of life on the estate will go on as usual, or perhaps Dorn's explanation of the shot is not fake and something just burst in his medical case? In her analysis of numerous stage productions of *The Seagull*, Wyman observes: 'The main debate in reading the play has continued to be whether it is ultimately tragic, portraying the futility of the characters' lives, or whether it can be read positively.'[11] Could it be that the filmmakers' decision to conclude the film with such an ambiguous ending follows the trend of positive readings of the play, leaving the viewer with the slight possibility of a happy ending, so cherished by American moviegoers? Such a lack of final resolution in the finale seems to be faithful to Chekhovian poetics, since as a rule the conflicts in his plays are not fully resolved as the tragicomic life journey just enters a new stage, making the circular structure a metaphorical statement. Mayer and Karam's film represents what Geoffrey Wagner defines as a type of adaptation that contains a 'commentary' where an original work is altered for the sake of 're-emphasis or re-structure'.[12] The 're-structure' of the denouement does not contradict what is traditionally defined as Chekhovian stage poetics with a characteristic 'lack of resolution; the absence of definitive conclusion, event, or catharsis; a realisation that events progress but not resolve'.[13]

---

[11] Whyman, p. 92.

[12] Geoffrey Wagner, *The Novel and the Cinema* (Rutherford: Farleigh Dickinson University Press, 1975), p. 223.

[13] Douglas J. Clayton and Yana Meerzon, 'On Chekhov, Adaptation, and Wonders of Writing Plays: Dialogue with Patrice Pavis, J. Douglas Clayton, and Yana Meerzon', pp. 295–304 (p. 295).

The energetic camera movement and the editing based on juxtaposed shots that depict the simultaneity of people's activities on the estate reflect Mayer's signature directing style. The cinematic narration is conveyed at a very rapid pace since the visual form of communication is much faster than the verbal, and the constant camera movements create persistent visual effects of simultaneous action that is happening in different parts of the Sorin country estate. As a result, the camera's voyeuristic eye allows the viewer to see what is happening at the same time on the lake, in the house, in the forest or in Arkadina's bedroom. To recreate the atmosphere of Russian countryside life at the end of the 19th century, the movie was filmed in Monroe in upstate New York. The choice of location and Matthew J. Lloyd's inventive cinematography emphasise the sense of open space, cherishing the natural beauty of the surroundings. As Susan Sontag observes, the main distinction between theatre and cinema lies in the use of space:

> Theater is confined to a logical or *continuous* use of space. Cinema (through editing, that is, through the change of shot – which is the basic unit of film construction) has access to an alogical or discontinuous use of space. In the theater, people are either in the stage space or 'off.' When 'on,' they are always visible or visualizable in contiguity with each other. In the cinema, no such relation is necessarily visible or even visualizable.[14]

The legendary Hollywood costume designer Ann Roth enriched the production with her attention to detail and knowledge of the history of fashion. The whole shooting took only twenty-one days, with rehearsals taking place right before the filming. To produce a special ambience the crew relied on the so-called 'Steadicam' technique, where the cameramen would attach their cameras to their body, closely following the actors. This technique created the effect of the camera being inside the scene and contributed to the overall sense of intimacy for the viewer.

The ensemble of Chekhovian characters with their drama of mutual misunderstanding and unfulfilled dreams and desires needed to rely on performers able to convey the psychological nuances and the changes of mood of the characters they performed. Mayer's film has a well selected cast whose members deliver performances in the tradition of Konstantin Stanislavsky's psychological 'method acting', staying truthful to the genre defined by Chekhov as 'A Comedy in Four Acts'. Chekhovian humour and irony are particularly tangible in the representation of the female characters but Stoll as the egotistic writer Trigorin also delivers a performance full of irony and comedic vanity. Regrettably, the performance of the young inexperienced actor Billy Howle as Konstantin Treplev represents the weakest part of this film, since his acting skills could not match the richness of the artistic palette of the female leads. Howle's approach to his character

---

[14] Sontag, p. 141.

is one-sided, his Konstantin either crying or angry with everyone, exhibiting a rather simplistic interpretation of such a psychologically complex Chekhovian character. As a result, occasionally *The Seagull* lacks the unity of an artistic ensemble, relying perhaps more than necessary on the surface meaning of words, ignoring the significance of the Chekhovian subtext. The fast rhythmical pattern of the film contributes to the sense of action on screen, but at the same time it ignores the importance of the pauses that help spectators get inside the interior worlds of the protagonists.

Mayer's directorial interpretation adds phrases to the film that were not intended for the characters' ears but are overheard by them as if by chance. This technique is applied to Nina and Konstantin, allowing the viewers to better grasp the way other characters are perceiving them. For example, this technique is used when Nina leaves the Sorin's household after the performance of Treplev's play. As she is walking toward the staircase, she seems to overhear Arkadina's comments about her father's marriage and the whole misery of her life. Nina pauses for a moment, hearing everything that was said, and then slowly leaves the house, feeling humiliated. In a similar fashion, at the film's finale when Konstantin is playing piano in his study he seems to overhear Trigorin's comments about his stories being not perfect or fully finished. Playing even more loudly, Konstantin also appears humiliated by such a comment.

The intimacy of frequent close-ups that reveal the characters is camouflaged by the words that often hide the real feelings. Consequently, the viewer can closely follow the facial expressions and nuances of body language that cannot be easily detected in a theatrical setting. The camera eye, therefore, becomes the leading narrator of the story, restating for the medium of film Stanislavsky's conviction that in Chekhov's plays the meaning is 'not conveyed by the words themselves, but by what is hidden behind them or in the pauses, or the way the actors look at each other or in the way they radiate inner feeling'.[15] Despite the period costumes and Russian names, the essential Chekhovian themes such as miscommunication, broken illusions, unrequited love and the spiritual void sound transnational, while the archetypal characters with their social and emotional anxiety sound universal. As the movie proceeds, the depiction of the summer life on the estate displays a striking cross-cultural and cross-temporal parallelism with modernity.

Modernising Chekhovian Women

The performances of Bening as Arkadina, Ronan as Nina, and Moss as Masha, deserve special attention since this superb trio of modernised Chekhovian characters significantly enriches Mayer's production. The female performers

---

[15] Konstantin Stanislavsky, *My Life in Art,* trans. and ed. Jean Benedetti (London: Routledge, 2008), p. 192.

build bridges between fin de siècle Russia and modern day American viewers, enabling viewers to identify themselves with Chekhov's fictional world. Such recurrent universal themes as the search for balance between personal happiness and professional fulfilment; broken illusions and unrequited love; aging and failed motherhood are predominantly embodied in the film by its female characters. Despite their pre-revolutionary era costumes and haircuts, the female characters remain modern in their screen demeanour and understandable in their intentions. Bening as Arkadina sacrifices her motherhood and sisterhood for her successful stage career, and her sarcastic and self-absorbed screen presence seems to be a façade that hides her sense of guilt. Ronan as Nina masterfully builds her role on the gradual transformation from a charming and naïve maiden to her broken self as a result of Trigorin's abandonment, the death of her child and her inability to achieve Arkadina's stage artistry. Moss as Masha is consistently juggling in her performance between comedy and drama as she drinks alcohol from teacups, sniffs tobacco and feels pity for herself in a comic fashion. Being desperately in love with Treplev, a man she cannot get, Masha mirrors Arkadina's failed motherhood as she refuses to go see her own child in order to stay near Treplev even after her marriage to Medvedenko (Michael Zegen), which does not save her from her feelings. In Moss's fabulous interpretation, Masha's consistent self-torture and self-pity appear to be an odd form of guilty pleasure that overshadows the possible life fulfilment with her husband and child.

Starting from its initial planning, *The Seagull* was conceived of as a star-oriented production. Mayer admits that his first directorial decision was to select who was going to play Arkadina – and his first choice was Annette

Figure 7.2   Arkadina (Annette Bening) and Masha (Elisabeth Moss), *The Seagull*, directed by Michael Mayer, 2018.

Bening. As soon as Bening accepted his invitation, the director envisioned a concept for the whole adaptation.[16] At the time of filming, neither Ronan nor Moss had yet achieved movie star status, and despite their impressive performances it is still Bening with her nonchalant ease in front of the camera who gives this adaptation its dynamism, drama and humour. As a result, the film becomes a star-based adaptation with Bening as the epicentre of action on screen. Nevertheless, Ronan and Moss contribute a great deal to their original and fresh interpretations of the Chekhovian heroines' social and emotional anxieties, helping to render this film more modern and relatable to moviegoers.

In his discussion of the transposition of Russian literary texts into film, Alexander Burry argues that cinematic adaptation is a form of cross-cultural communication and when

> a Russian literary text, with all of its embedded cultural meanings, is transported to another country or time or both, these meanings are foreign and must be redefined to correspond with the new spatial and temporal territories. In this process of redefinition, new cultural realities will transform those original semantic meanings.[17]

A similar process occurs with the transposition of Chekhovian women on the American screen, as the original Russian characters acquire novel universal, cross-cultural meaning. From the first scenes of the film, the pure youthful infatuation of Treplev with Nina is contrasted with the erotic nature of the affair between Arkadina and Trigorin. Immediately after the first dialogue between the young couple and their innocent kisses, the camera eye takes us to Arkadina's bedroom, where the actress and the writer share a bed – Arkadina in a negligee and Trigorin half-naked.

The cinematic narrative frequently emphasises the contrast between the freshness of Nina's features and the fading flesh of the aging diva. Nina's youthful charm, her natural beauty with freckles on her face and her floating Botticellian blond curls are juxtaposed to Arkadina's mature beauty that is maintained with make-up and carefully arranged coiffure. The freshness and firmness of Nina's glowing skin is contrasted with Arkadina's wrinkles. At the same time, Nina reciting her monologue from Treplev's experimental play sounds very artificial if not ridiculous, and her lack of stage presence and professional skills make Treplev's play sound ridiculously artificial and pretentious despite its beautiful natural

---

[16] Mayer, on *The Seagull*.

[17] Alexander Burry, 'Introduction: Filming Russian Classics – Challenges and Opportunities', in *Border Crossing: Russian Literature into Film*, eds Alexander Burry and Frederick H. White (Edinburgh: Edinburgh University Press, 2016), pp. 1–16 (p. 7).

setting next to the lake. Unlike many traditional productions where Nina's monologue is performed in a symbolist-mystical fashion, this time it sounds comical as the charming Nina clearly has no stage presence. Mayer accentuates that Nina is at best a mediocre actress who, without the necessary acting training, ended up on the provincial Russian stage. Ronan as Nina is a tragic character who makes the wrong choices in life – a romantic dreamer who has no gift to achieve the fame she is dreaming about, and ruins her reputation by choosing the self-absorbed womaniser Trigorin, rejecting the man who really loves her – Treplev.

In turn, Arkadina's character exhibits many features of the narcissistic stars that populated not only the pre-revolutionary Russian stage, but also modern celebrity culture as they still desire to play the roles of young girls in their mature age, fighting mother nature. Chekhov's original bohemian play touches upon the state of the Imperial theatre industry that preoccupied Stanislavsky and Vladimir Nemirovich-Danchenko at that time. Both theatre practitioners strongly felt the necessity of learning the acting métier step by step, and harshly criticised the Russian Imperial theatre establishment as an institution based on a star system. The camera eye depicts Arkadina as an incarnation of a self-absorbed local celebrity focusing viewers' attention on her posters and photographs in various roles that are hung everywhere around the house. Arkadina's conviction that she has the privilege of being ageless is ridiculed with two consecutive close-ups – one on her aging face and the second on the ironic smile of her own servant who is grinning at her mistress for her attempt to defy nature. Cynthia Marsh observes:

> Chekhov began his mature exploration of the female psyche with two actresses, Arkadina and Nina. Any representation in the theatre has to be viewed in relation to the physicality (use of the body for characterisation and to affect the audience) of the person playing the role. Chekhov is toying with spectacle and physicality in *The Seagull* when he counterpoints the established, mature Arkadina with the aspiring, youthful Nina, and then juxtaposes this Nina with the older and wiser but none the less aspiring Nina at the end of the play.[18]

Echoing Marsh's observations, Mayer's adaptation also explores in depth the psychology, physicality and life journey of the two actresses, contrasting their personality and stage careers.

Bening makes bold acting choices throughout the production, portraying Arkadina as a fascinating, multifaceted and complex personality. Her Arkadina's theatricality on stage and in life is interwoven with her failings as a mother.

---

[18] Cynthia Marsh, 'The Stage Representation of Chekhov's Women', in *The Cambridge Companion to Chekhov*, eds Vera Gottlieb and Paul Allain (Cambridge: Cambridge University Press, 2000), pp. 216–27 (p. 222).

Her stinginess is interwoven with occasional kindness; her hysterical behaviour could be instantaneously replaced with total control of herself. She loves her son Konstantin, but at the same time refuses to support him financially, preferring to pay instead for her own expensive wardrobe. Like her lover Trigorin, Arkadina is a selfish and self-centred celebrity and the two deserve each other. Furthermore, in the case of Arkadina, it is impossible for viewers to grasp where her acting ends and real life begins, just as for Trigorin the boundary between his writing about life and real life is not easily detectable. Arkadina's energy constantly puts her at the centre of events. She sincerely does not understand why Masha does not take care of herself, and gives Masha a lesson in femininity, asking Dorn to answer which of them looks younger, despite the fact that Arkadina is almost twice Masha's age. 'Of course you,' Dorn answers with irony.

The camera focuses on Arkadina, who is observing from her bedroom window a romantic boat ride by Nina and Trigorin. On the boat with Nina, Trigorin is infatuated with her, admiring her natural beauty that becomes an embodiment of the surrounding magical lake. Here indeed the cinematographer's work, utilising the close up, can convey nuances that are simply inaccessible for the stage. The camera here is moving back and forth between Trigorin and Nina's faces – his gaze expresses desire and her gaze expresses admiration. The actors' performance of the dramatic conflict between the two is very convincing in its irony: while Nina dreams of Trigorin's fame and his glamorous lifestyle, he suddenly realises the futility of his life and the vanity of his whole existence and craves the simple life that Nina represents at this particular moment. The screen chemistry between a pure young woman and an experienced womaniser is tangible in the lake scene.

Next, in the scene when Trigorin begs Arkadina to set him free, saying that he finally found what he was looking for, Arkadina is wearing just a corset and her makeup is washed off from her face, after a previous tearful and dramatic scene with Treplev. The camera eye is directed straight at her face covered with fine wrinkles and flabby neck, and her eyes express almost biological fright. When she pronounces 'You are my last page,' she seems to be sincere, but she collects herself and starts her counterattack with superb acting skills and impressive theatricality. She is not going to concede her lover to the younger woman, and it is not clear whether she sincerely loves Trigorin or just hates to lose. Does the aging diva need a lover or does she really believe in his literary genius? In Bening's interpretation, it is both. She skilfully manipulates, seducing him not with her aging flesh but with her unrestrained flattery. The sincerity seems to be replaced by theatrical vocabulary: 'My magician, my pride, my king in all the glory. I am not letting you go.' Arkadina is both pathetic in her attempts to defeat aging and majestic in her artistry. Unlike Nina, she has no illusions about Trigorin's personality and skilfully pushes all the necessary buttons to keep him to herself. When Trigorin gives up, answering 'I am spineless, weak, submissive,' the viewer wonders if he is attracted to Arkadina as a woman or is carried away by her artistry as a great performer. Bening as Arkadina is narcissistic, tragic and funny, aggressive and at the same time defenceless. This trio of female characters, centred around Arkadina and performed by superb actors, represents the spirited force that invigorates the cinematic narrative, creating multiple allusions between 1896 Russia and modernity, and once again demonstrating Chekhov's universality.

Verisimilitude vs Subtext

In his *New York Times* film review, Anthony Scott imposes a harsh verdict on Michael Mayer's 2018 screen adaptation of *The Seagull*: 'The cast is great. The play is great. But this is still a bad movie, because it has no clear or coherent idea of how to be one.'[19] Scott's critique seems to rely on so-called 'fidelity criticism' where critics 'measure the success of the film by its success in capturing the letter or spirit (whatever that may entail) of the source texts'.[20] The critic's main reproaches focus on the lack of a clear directorial concept and the fast camera movements with frequent changes of focus. However, Mayer's adaptation does not deserve such harsh criticism, since it has a clear and coherent directorial agenda as the adaptation meticulously transposes on screen the vital elements of the Russian fin de siècle play, adjusting Chekhovian poetics to the expectations of twentieth-first century American moviegoers.

One wonders whether the novelty of the cinematic language and the critical success of Louis Malle and André Gregory's *Vanya on 42nd Street* (1994) discussed in this volume somehow overshadowed *The Seagull*.[21] In the history of screen adaptations of Chekhov's oeuvre, *Vanya on 42nd Street* represents a unique experiment in creating a harmonious synthesis of theatre and cinematography. As the film critic Steven Vineberg observes, *Vanya* represents 'an astonishing hybrid blurring the boundaries between theater and film, rehearsal and performance, actor and character'.[22] In *Vanya on 42nd Street* where Gregory and Malle created a unique theatrical-cinematic hybrid in which the main emphasis is not on the verisimilitude of the scenery or mise-en-scéne, but instead on the psychological truthfulness of life onscreen produced by a

---

[19] Anthony Scott, 'In "The Seagull," a Great Play, a Great Cast, and Yet', *The New York Times*, 9 May 2018.
[20] Burry, p. 5.
[21] See Angus Wrenn's discussion of this film in Chapter 6 of this volume.
[22] Steve Vineberg, 'Vanya on 42nd Street: An American Vanya', *The Criterion*, 28 February 2012 <https://www.criterion.com/current/posts/2166-vanya-on-42nd-street-an-american-vanya> [accessed 15 September 2021].

harmonious ensemble of actors. In contrast, in *The Seagull* the main directorial accent is on the verisimilitude of the setting where the atmosphere of a magical lake and a country estate full of natural light seem to be as important for Mayer as the cast of characters. *The Seagull* represents a purely cinematic adaptation using many attributes of the filmic medium that were intentionally rejected in *Vanya on 42nd Street*. Moreover, while *Vanya on 42nd Street* largely relies on the Chekhovian subtext, *The Seagull* overwhelmingly relies on text. Despite many dramatic differences, in both cases the filmmakers succeed in creating the effect of modernity, rendering Chekhov's playwriting universal and understandable to contemporary spectators. In their American *Seagull*, Mayer and Karam share their co-authorship with Chekhov, creating a distinctly cinematic version of the play giving priority to the active, energetic movement and verbal expression recreating the exterior atmosphere of a pre-revolutionary Russian country estate on screen. Mayer's clear directorial vision and his faithfulness to the verisimilitude of setting, costumes, and sound effects as well as reliance on a superb ensemble of female actors remain crucial for his transposition of Chekhovian drama into the medium of film.

Bibliography

Burry, Alexander, 'Introduction: Filming Russian Classics – Challenges and Opportunities', in *Border Crossing: Russian Literature into Film*, eds Alexander Burry and Frederick H. White (Edinburgh: Edinburgh University Press, 2016), pp. 1–16.

Chekhov, Anton, *The Sea Gull*, in *Anton Chekhov's Plays*, trans. and ed. Eugene K. Bristow (New York: Norton & Company, 1977), pp. 1–52.

Clayton, J. Douglas and Yana Meerzon, 'On Chekhov, Adaptation, and Wonders of Writing Plays: Dialogue with Patrice Pavis, J. Douglas Clayton, and Yana Meerzon', in *Adapting Chekhov: The Text and Its Mutation*, eds J. Douglas Clayton and Yana Meerzon (London: Routledge, 2013), pp. 295–304.

Canby, Vincent, '"The Sea Gull" Brought to the Screen by Lumet', *The New York Times*, 24 December 1968.

French, Philip, 'Chekhov on Screen', in *The Cambridge Companion to Chekhov*, eds Vera Gottlieb and Paul Allain (Cambridge: Cambridge University Press, 2000), pp. 149–61.

Marsh, Cynthia, 'The Stage Representation of Chekhov's Women', in *The Cambridge Companion to Chekhov*, eds Vera Gottlieb and Paul Allain (Cambridge: Cambridge University Press, 2000), pp. 216–27.

Mayer, Michael, a video interview on *The Seagull*, YouTube <https://www.youtube.com/watch?v=WLglmW_c9NE> [accessed 15 September 2021].

Scott, Anthony, 'In "The Seagull," a Great Play, a Great Cast, and Yet', *The New York Times*, 9 May 2018.

Senelick, Laurence, *The Chekhov Theatre: A Century of the Plays in Performance* (Cambridge: Cambridge University Press, 1997).

Sontag, Susan, 'Film and Theater', in *Theater and Film: A Comparative Anthology*, ed. Robert Knopf (New Haven: Yale University Press, 2005), pp. 134–51.

Stanislavsky, Konstantin, *My Life in Art*, trans. and ed. Jean Benedetti (London: Routledge, 2008).

Vineberg, Steve. 'Vanya on 42nd Street: An American Vanya', *The Criterion*, 28 February 2012 <https://www.criterion.com/current/posts/2166-vanya-on-42nd-street-an-american-vanya> [accessed 15 September 2021].

Wagner, Geoffrey, *The Novel and the Cinema* (Rutherford: Farleigh Dickinson University Press, 1975).

Wyman, Rose, *Anton Chekhov* (London: Routledge, 2011).

Filmography

The Seagull, directed by Michael Mayer (USA, Mar-Key Pictures KGB Media, 2018).

Vanya on 42nd Street, directed by Louis Malle (USA, Mayfair Entertainment International, 1994).

PART FOUR

ENGAGING WITH TOLSTOY

8. THANATOPHOBIA ON THE SOVIET SCREEN: TOLSTOY'S *DEATH OF IVAN IL'ÍCH* AND ALEKSANDR KAIDANOVSKY'S *A SIMPLE DEATH*

Otto Boele

After decades of theorising intertextuality and authorship, the notion of fidelity would seem to have lost all currency as an appropriate criterion for analysing film adaptations. With films often based on literary texts that themselves tend to be adaptations of some other source material, simply comparing a film version to its literary original is considered an unproductive and theoretically flawed operation.[1] Instead of assuming that a film adaptation adapts 'exactly one text a piece',[2] or necessarily seeks to reproduce, on its own terms, some deeper essence of the source text, we are urged to conceive of adaptations in terms of intertextual dialogism, that is as artistic texts that, just like the literary

---

[1] Space does not allow me to elaborate on the concept of fidelity here, but there is general agreement that remaining faithful to each and every aspect of the source text is impossible. Opinions diverge on whether one can remain true to the spirit when adapting a literary text to film. Robert Stam, amongst others, rejects this idea as too vague and speculative, but Colin MacCabe believes that it captures something important. See: Colin MacCabe, 'Introduction. Bazinian Adaptation: *The Butcher Boy as Example*', in *True to the Spirit: Film Adaptation and the Question of Fidelity*, eds Colin MacCabe, Kathleen Murray and Rick Warner (Oxford: Oxford University Press, 2011), pp. 3–26 (p. 8). See also Dudley Andrew's careful handling of the concept of genuine fidelity in Dudley Andrew, 'The Economies of Adaptation', Ibid., pp. 27–39 (p. 38).

[2] Thomas Leitch, 'Twelve Fallacies in Contemporary Adaptation Theory', *Criticism*, 45 (2003), 149–71 (p. 164).

sources on which they are nominally based, are situated in the 'entire matrix of communicative utterances'.[3]

Paradoxically, however, attacks on the fidelity criterion have never stopped, as if the study of film adaptations continues to adhere to a narrowly one-to-one comparative model. Thomas Leitch, for example, lists fidelity as one of the most stubborn fallacies in adaptation studies and explains its persistence as a corollary of the 'appeal to anteriority'. Classical texts are valued more than modern texts, Leitch explains, especially among scholars who received their training in literary studies, and this invites comparisons between film and book in which the former is always found wanting.[4] For this reason even Robert Stam, a proponent of the intertextual approach to film adaptation, has been accused of relapsing into the fidelity argument. According to Leitch, Stam 'fetishises novelists and novels' because he 'wants to use film to look at literature'.[5] Similar comments have been made about Brian MacFarlane's influential study *Novel to Film: An Introduction to the Theory of Adaptation* (1996) and George Bluestone's pioneering *Novels into Film* (1957) even if these authors themselves were highly suspicious of the fidelity criterion.

Perhaps the repetitiveness of this anti-fidelity rhetoric demonstrates that the concept of fidelity itself is not entirely useless. After all, comparing a film adaptation to its literary original is an intuitive thing to do and, as long as we remain alert to other factors that may have shaped the end product and its reception (political context, commercial interests, cultural sensitivities), the (one-to-one) comparative model still has much to offer. Moreover, fidelity is now actually being reconsidered as a criterion for the study of film adaptations, either by scholars interested in questions of artistic value, or by scholars eager to develop a methodology that can serve any kind of theoretical framework.[6] Introducing Mikhail Bakhtin's fundamental idea of dialogism, as well as other concepts from

---

[3] Robert Stam, 'Beyond Fidelity: The Dialogics of Adaptation', in *Film Adaptation*, ed. James Naremore (New Brunswick, NJ: Rutgers University Press, 2000), pp. 54–76 (p. 64).

[4] Leitch, 'Twelve Fallacies in Contemporary Adaptation Theory', p. 150.

[5] Thomas Leitch, 'Everything You Always Wanted to Know About Adaptation', *Literature/Film Quarterly*, 33 (2005), 233–45 (p. 236).

[6] In his contribution to *The Oxford Handbook of Adaptation Studies* Johnson mentions the 2008 collection *In/Fidelity: Essays on Film Adaptation* (edited by David L. Kranz and Nancy C. Mellerski) as an attempt to take fidelity seriously as an analytical tool; the 2011 collection *True to the Spirit: Film Adaptation and the Question of Fidelity* (edited by Colin MacCabe, Kathleen Murray, and Rick Warner) serves as Johnson's example of a more value-driven approach to fidelity in film adaptation: David Johnson, 'Adaptation and Fidelity', *The Oxford Handbook of Adaptation Studies*, ed. Thomas M. Leitch (New York: Oxford University Press, 2017), pp. 87–100.

poststructuralist theory, has certainly enriched adaptation studies, an enrichment the present chapter duly acknowledges by drawing on Stam's concept of intertextual dialogism and his reworking of Gérard Genette's categories of transtextuality. But the 'film-based-on-book' approach is, in my view, perfectly capable of raising questions that can lead us beyond the scope of a narrowly comparative investigation focused only on plot, character and setting.

In this chapter I shall examine *A Simple Death* (*Prostaia smert'*, 1985), a relatively unknown film adaptation of *The Death of Ivan Il'ich*, Lev Tolstoy's famous story about a dying middle-aged judge. Directed by Aleksandr Kaidanovsky and released three years after completion, at first sight the film seems unimaginatively faithful to the source text, especially when compared to critically acclaimed adaptations such as *Ikiru* (Kurosawa, 1952) and *ivans xtc.* (Rose, 2000).[7] In these films the original setting and title character are updated and naturalised to fit the social reality of the immediate target audience (Japanese and American respectively). *A Simple Death* is, by the looks of it, a more straightforward costume drama, set in late nineteenth-century Russia and containing quite a bit of dialogue taken directly from Tolstoy's story. It would seem, then, that the Russian film version violates Frederic Jameson's approach to film adaptation which dictates that a film based on a brilliant literary text can never turn out equally brilliant unless it is 'utterly unfaithful to, [the] original'.[8] And yet, without entering into a discussion of the artistic merits of *A Simple Death*, I hope to show that there is more than meets the eye. Rather than adapting one single story, the film draws on an impressive number of source texts (or 'hypotexts',[9] to use the term Stam borrowed from Julia Kristeva) allowing its director to reinterpret the theme of death and introduce a highly sensitive, almost tabooed topic in Soviet culture: fear of death, or thanatophobia. It is precisely by identifying these hypotexts, analysing their interaction and putting the film in the context of late-Soviet culture, that I seek to demonstrate the relevance of a comparative approach in which fidelity stands out, not as a 'touchstone of value',[10] but as an analytical criterion that can contribute to our

---

[7] For an early comparison between *The Death of Ivan Il'ich* and Kurosawa's *Ikiru* see Thomas Simone, 'The Mythos of "The Sickness Unto Death": Kurosawa's *Ikiru* and Tolstoy's *The Death of Ivan Ilych*', *Literature/Film Quarterly*, 1 (1975), 2–12; a very insightful discussion of Bernard Rose's adaption is provided by Amy Mandelker, 'Out of Breath: Bernard Rose's *ivans xtc.* (2000) and Tolstoy's *The Death of Ivan Il'ich*', in *Tolstoy on Screen*, eds Lorna Fitzsimmons and Michael A. Denner (Evanston: Northwestern University Press, 2014), pp. 217–43.
[8] Frederic Jameson, 'Afterword: Adaptation as a Philosophical Problem', in *True to the Spirit: Film Adaptation and the Question of Fidelity*, eds Colin MacCabe, Kathleen Murray, and Rick War (Oxford: Oxford University Press, 2011), pp. 215–33 (p. 218).
[9] Stam, p. 66.
[10] Leitch, 'Twelve Fallacies in Contemporary Adaptation Theory', p. 162.

understanding of both the source text and the film adaptation (the hypertext). More specifically, I will show how Kaidanovsky's treatment of Tolstoy's work challenges the Soviet myth of immortality and replaces it with a more sober, existentialist vision of death.

TOLSTOY ON THE SOVIET SCREEN: TABOO AND SAFE SOLUTIONS

Well-known as an actor, and particularly admired for his performance as the title character in Andrei Tarkovsky's *Stalker* (1979), Aleksandr Kaidanovsky (1946–1995) turned to directing in the early 1980s when he enrolled in the Higher Courses of Screenplay Writers and Directors at the State Film Institute (VGIK) studying first under Tarkovsky and graduating under Sergei Soloviev. He immediately adopted an uncompromising, slightly absurdist style in which the plot takes a back seat and the mise-en-scène, often underexposed and disorganised, adds to the impression of a chaotic, decaying world. Although some critics took his claim to auteurdom with a pinch of salt,[11] Kaidanovsky regarded each film he made as his personal project, writing the screenplay himself and, on some occasions, even dubbing the leading actor.[12] In the 1980s he directed five films, two shorts and three feature films (including *A Simple Death*), four of which were based on a literary original. His selection of authors is suggestive of his affinity with modern and experimental prose (Jorge Luis Borges, Albert Camus). Especially in *The Guest* (*Gost'*, 1987), inspired by Borges famous short story *The Gospel of St Luke*, and *The Kerosene Seller's Wife* (*Zhena kerosinshchika*, 1989), the only film not based on a literary source, one can sense Kaidanovsky's predilection for intertextual referencing and narrative non-linearity.

Compared to Borges and Camus, Tolstoy stands out as a more traditional writer, whose status as a giant of Russian realism would seem to make any film adaptation of his work a relatively safe project. Yet by Soviet standards, texts written after his spiritual crisis and subsequent conversion were deemed problematic as they took a frank and unorthodox view of sexuality and openly promoted an anarchistic Christian worldview. Before glasnost and perestroika, the only post-crisis texts to be adapted for the screen were *Resurrection* (*Voskresenie*, Shveitser, 1960–61) and *After the Ball* (*Posle bala*, Dudorov, 1961). They were made at the height of the Thaw when the depiction of injustice and state violence against citizens was likely to invite comparisons with Soviet society under Stalin.[13]

---

[11] Lev Karakhan, 'Jobless Prophets', in *Russian Critics on the Cinema of Glasnost*, eds Michael Brashinsky and Andrew Horton (Cambridge: Cambridge University Press, 1994), pp. 30–4 (pp. 32–3).

[12] In *The Death of Ivan Il'ich* the title character is played by Valerii Priyomykhov, but his entire performance was dubbed by Kaidanovsky himself.

[13] David Gillespie, 'Mikhail Shveitser's *Resurrection* (1960, 1962): Film Adaptation as Thaw Narrative', in *Tolstoy on Screen*, eds Lorna Fitzsimmons and Michael A.

When, in the course of the 1960s, the political climate changed and Stalinism became taboo again, the focus shifted back to Tolstoy's pre-crisis period, generating adaptations of *Anna Karenina* (Zarkhi, 1967; Pilikhina, 1974), *Family Happiness* (*Semeinoe schast'e*, Fomenko, 1971), the trilogy *Childhood*, *Boyhood* and *Youth* (*Detstvo. Otrochestvo. Iunost'*, Fomenko, 1973) and the epic blockbuster *War and Peace* (*Voina i mir*, Bondarchuk, 1965–7). As a result, one of Tolstoy's most haunting texts, adapted several times abroad and even in Russia before the Revolution,[14] remained untouched by Soviet filmmakers until 1987 when Mikhail Shveitser made his critically acclaimed film version of *The Kreutzer Sonata*.

The Death of Ivan Il'ich (1886), the first piece of fiction Tolstoy wrote after completing *Confession* (1882), his main conversion text, must have been equally suspicious in Soviet eyes. Even if it hardly touches upon the sexual question and the story could safely be construed as an indictment of the self-centred and pleasure-seeking upper class of late Imperial Russia, from a Soviet perspective there was plenty of reason for concern. Transposing terminal illness from page to screen implied a dramatic departure from the heroic vein in which death was usually visualised in Soviet cinema; and fleshing out physical suffering and decay could easily lead to naturalism, of which Soviet critics were always afraid. When Kaidanovsky completed *A Simple Death* in 1985, this was indeed the kind of criticism he encountered from Goskino, the State Committee for Cinematography. The film's attention to the physiological aspects of death was seen as excessive and even immoral.[15] Yet times were changing quickly. In 1986 Elem Klimov succeeded Lev Kulidzhanov as secretary of the Filmmakers' Union and a Conflict Commission was established that would quickly 'unshelve' over 100 previously banned films.[16] In 1987 *A Simple Death* was shown at the Cannes Film Festival and with the onset of the Black Wave (*chernukha*) in Soviet cinema, films exposing the uglier sides of (Soviet) reality could suddenly be praised for their ruthless honesty.[17] Although few

---

Denner (Evanston: Northwestern University Press, 2014), pp. 75–89. I am grateful to David Gillespie for supplying me with a copy of his chapter when the entire volume proved unavailable to me.

[14] Before the Revolution *The Kreutzer Sonata* was adapted at least twice. See: Lauri Piispa, 'Tolstoy Film Adaptations in Russia, 1909–17', *Tolstoy Studies Journal*, 23 (2011), pp. 44–60.

[15] Andrei Plakhov, 'Iubilei Aleksandra Kaidanovskogo', *Kommersant*, 23 July 1996 <https://www.kommersant.ru/doc/236961> [accessed 11 September 2021].

[16] Birgit Beumers, *A History of Russian Cinema* (Oxford and New York: Berg, 2009), p. 187.

[17] For a good introduction to the phenomenon of *chernukha* see Seth Graham, 'Chernukha and Russian Film' *Studies in Slavic Cultures*, 1 (2000), pp. 9–27; a welcome update is provided by Volha Isakava, 'Reality Excess. Chernukha Cinema in the Late 1980s', in *Ruptures and Continuities in Soviet/Russian Cinema. Styles, Characters and Genres Before and After the Collapse of the USSR*, eds Birgit Beumers and Eugénie Zvonkine (London and New York: Routledge, 2017), pp. 147–65.

people would define *A Simple Death* as *chernukha*, the film has a darker side to it with its focus on physical decay and fear of death. The theme of thanatophobia occupies a crucial place in Tolstoy's writing, but had always been deemed inappropriate for Soviet artists to explore. With Kaidanovsky's film that was about to change.

THE DEATH OF IVAN IL'ÍCH: CONFLICTING INTERPRETATIONS

Traditionally *The Death of Ivan Il'ích* is understood as a story of redemption. Having worked his way up the social ladder to become a highly respected member of the Court of Justice, at forty-five the title character falls fatally ill and he dies only months after the first symptoms of his disease have started to develop. Although he is in great pain and struggles to accept his fate, he eventually comes to understand the moral unsoundness of a life dominated by material comfort and the demands of social respectability. Moments before Ivan Il'ích dies, he is overwhelmed with pity for his wife and son and he draws his last breath thinking: 'Death is finished ... It is no more!'[18] The paradoxical nature of this thought is usually explained as a testament to Ivan Il'ích's last-moment epiphany. Living a bad life he was 'dead,' coming to understand this makes him spiritually 'reborn'.[19]

In Tolstoy's universe fear of death is not so much an emotional or pathological condition, but a signifier of moral corruption. In his essay *On Life*, written only a year after *The Death of Ivan Il'ich*, Tolstoy attributes fear of death to a faulty sense of personal exceptionalism. Only if we stop thinking of ourselves as being more important than our fellow human beings, so that we love and respect them, only then will we be able to overcome our animal-like personality (*zhivotnaia lichnost'*), insatiable hedonism and fear of death.[20] Because the rich always pursue more pleasure and try to amass more material goods, they cling to life more desperately than do simple folk who are usually less afraid of dying.[21] Stephen Lovell has noted that Tolstoy

---

[18] Leo Tolstoy, 'The Death of Ivan Ilych',' trans Aylmer and Louise Maude, in *The Death of Ivan Ilich: An Electronic Study Edition of the Russian Text*, ed. Gary R. Jahn <https://open.lib.umn.edu/ivanilich/part/english-and-russian-texts/> [accessed 11 September 2021].

[19] Gary R. Jahn, 'The Role of the Ending in Lev Tolstoi's *The Death of Ivan Il'ich*', *Canadian Slavonic Papers*, 24 (1982), pp. 229–38 (p. 229). Jahn also quotes Vladimir Nabokov as one of numerous critics who have interpreted *The Death of Ivan Il'ich* as a story of spiritual awakening.

[20] L. N. Tolstoi, 'O zhizni, *Polnoe sobranie sochinenii*, 90 vols (Moscow: Khudozhestvennaia literatura, 1928–58), XXVI, p. 371. Volume and page references are to this edition.

[21] Stephen Lovell, 'Finitude at the Fin de Siècle: Il'ia Mechnikov and Lev Tolstoy on Death and Life', *The Russian Review*, 63 (2004), 296–316 (p. 308).

thought that the goodness of a person would depend on the extent to which he stops fearing death.[22]

This idea found expression in several of Tolstoy's fictional texts including *Three Deaths* (1859) and *Master and Man* (1895). In *The Death of Ivan Il'ích* it is the unruffled peasant servant Gerasim who demonstrates a remarkably level-headed attitude towards death: 'It's God's will. We'll all come to it someday.'[23] Rather than rejoicing in the fact that death has passed him by on this occasion (the common reaction of Ivan Il'ích's colleagues upon learning about his death) or denying his own mortality (as Ivan Il'ích himself used to do), Gerasim soberly acknowledges that death evades no one.

Scholars with a more philosophical approach have taken issue with this redemptive view, arguing that the story's moral purport does not exhaust the question of Ivan Il'ích's struggle. The conclusion he draws on his death bed (that he has lived a shoddy life) is not necessarily a fair assessment of it, nor does it automatically make him a better person. Ivan Il'ích may well be so dismissive about his life to make the prospect of his annihilation more bearable.[24] Reasoning along similar lines, Christopher Cowley proposes the term 'autobiographical despair' to argue that Ivan Il'ích judges himself too harshly and simply lacks someone with whom he could look back on his life in a more forgiving manner.[25]

Of course, one may disagree with these alternative readings on the grounds that they sit uncomfortably with Tolstoy's own views on life and disregard the 'spiritual regeneration' plot structure that so many nineteenth-century texts (including Tolstoy's) share.[26] And yet these readings are indicative of the story's

---

[22] Lovell, p. 307. On 10 August 1904 Tolstoy wrote in his diary: 'The greater one's fear of death, the worse one's life is, and vice versa. [. . .] One can measure a person's goodness by his fear of death' (Tolstoi, Diary, *Polnoe sobranie sochinenii*, LV, p. 74).

[23] Unless stated otherwise, translations from the Russian are mine (O.B.). When quoting from *The Death of Ivan Il'ich* I rely on the translation by Aylmer and Louise Maude as made available in the electronic study edition prepared by Gary R. Jahn (Leo Tolstoy, 'The Death of Ivan Ilych').

[24] Gerald Lang, 'What Does Ivan Ilich Need to Be Rescued From?', *Philosophy*, 89 (2014), 325–47 (p. 346).

[25] Christopher Cowley, 'Ivan Ilych and Autobiographical Despair', *Philosophy and Literature*, 45 (2021), 199–210.

[26] This basic plot structure was described by Iurii Lotman and later by the German scholar Wolf Schmid. A hero is spiritually reborn as a result of some deeper insight (*prozrenie*) he has gained, usually by associating with a representative of the common folk, the *narod* (Iurii Lotman, 'Siuzhetnoe prostranstvo russkogo romana XIX stoletiia', *Izbrannye stat'i*, 3 vols [Tallinn: Aleksandra, 1993], III, pp. 91–106 [p. 102]; Wolf Schmid, 'Problematisierung der Ereignishaftigkeit in Čechovs Erzählungen', *Russiche Literatur an der Wende vom 19. zum 20. Jahrhundert*, ed. R. G. Grübel [Amsterdam and Atlanta: Rodopi, 1993], pp. 41–69 [p. 41]).

potential to provoke questions about the way in which we cope with death, confront our own mortality and become aware of our role as compassionate 'bystanders' who can identify with the suffering of a dying character.[27] It is the philosophical, ethical and even therapeutic aspects of Tolstoy's story that have kept scholars and artists returning to it again and again. We may therefore think of Kaidanovsky's film as yet another critical engagement with *The Death of Ivan Il′ích*, reflecting the doubts and concerns of a late-Soviet filmmaker as obsessed with death as Tolstoy, but not necessarily arriving at the same conclusions.

It has often been argued that for Kaidanovsky personally the making of *A Simple Death* was a kind of therapy that allowed him to overcome his own fear of death. Friends and former colleagues usually adduce as evidence his reckless lifestyle which he refused to give up, even after suffering two heart attacks. Some publications even quote his unpublished diary in which he confirms the healing effect of reading Tolstoy's 'unbearably terrifying story'.[28] Yet whatever the personal significance *The Death of Ivan Il′ích* may have had for Kaidanovsky, *A Simple Death* is a landmark in Russian cinema both in terms of representing terminal illness, and for treating the work of a classical author in such an idiosyncratic way. Rather than taking inspiration from one literary source, Kaidanovsky used a significant part of Tolstoy's later writings to produce a new and self-contained work of art centred on the theme of thanatophobia. For now let us concentrate on the style of the film and the way it represents death and terminal illness, as these were considered its most problematic aspects.

A Simple Death and the Genre of the 'Terminal Illness' Film

Shot in black and white, and set for the most part in the hero's study-turned-bedroom, from the very start *A Simple Death* shows a claustrophobic atmosphere that is missing in the better part of the story. The film almost completely ignores Ivan Il′ích's youth and early career, and the first fifteen years of his marriage is given only in one scene that captures him at the pinnacle of his happiness. Talking to some imagined interlocutor in the living room of his sumptuous house, a self-satisfied Ivan Il′ích briefly states his attitude to life and then sits down with his son to listen to a music box. As he continues to talk, his wife, Praskov'ia Fedorovna, enters the room, followed by their daughter and her fiancé. The butler and the servant Gerasim modestly show up in the

---

[27] Anouk Zuurmond, 'Attending the Dying: Images of Compassion', *Arcadia*, 49 (2014), pp. 74–88 (p. 76).

[28] See, for example, Andrei Shemiakin, '"Prostaia smert′" v god Kaidanovskogo', *Kino-pressa*, 30 September 2016 < http://kinopressa.ru/4320> [accessed 11 September 2021].

background. After Ivan Il'ích has finished his monologue, the characters draw together, look straight into the camera and freeze as if posing for a stately group portrait. Finally, the camera zooms in on Ivan Il'ích, who starts laughing, while a voice-over informs us that he will die within two months.[29]

What we learn from this opening scene is that Ivan Il'ích is unprepared for death precisely because he claims not to be afraid of it ('I don't wish it, but I'm not afraid of it either'[30]). His smugness and posing in front of the camera with his family convey an appropriate sense of petty bourgeois decency, which is in keeping with the 'pleasant lightheartedness and decorum'[31] of Ivan Il'ích's life mentioned in the story. After this scene, which lasts over three minutes, a short flashback shows us the hero as a young child sitting in his cot bed and mimicking the sound of a clock: tick-tock, tick-tock. His dozing nurse looks up and sternly corrects him: not 'tick-tock', but *kto ty, chto ty* ('Who are you? What are you?'). The film then cuts forward again to show Ivan Il'ích as a sick man, emaciated and weak, with a long, ungroomed beard and hardly able to get up. Only ten minutes of screen time have passed (of a total of sixty-five minutes) and we are locked in a stuffy room with a character who knows he is going to die.

If in Tolstoy there is a motivated link between Ivan Il'ích's morally flawed life and his agony as a dying man, Kaidanovsky seems uninterested in making such connections. That the hero is not a particularly likeable character can be inferred from his conceited monologue, but we are more likely to draw this conclusion because we are familiar with the story and may remember the condescending tone in which the narrator describes Ivan Il'ích's life. The film gives no biographical information and never reveals the kind of work with which Ivan Il'ích is involved. By making him an official rather than a judge (thereby undoing Tolstoy's irony),[32] Kaidanovsky turns the hero even more into an everyman than he is in the story. This also affects the role of Gerasim. He can stoically hold his master's legs for hours to alleviate his pain, as he does in the story, and refrain from ostentatiously crossing himself at Ivan Il'ích's final hour (arguably an indication of silent and profound grief), but the camera never picks him out and he does not get to say the resigned words he says in the original: 'We'll all come to it someday.'[33]

---

[29] The entire monologue and the intrusion by a narrator were taken from an earlier draft of the story (Tolstoi, 'Smert' Ivana Il'icha (varianty)', *Polnoe sobranie sochinenii*, XXVI, pp. 523–4).

[30] *A Simple Death* (film), directed by Aleksandr Kaidanovsky, Lenfilm, 1985.

[31] Tolstoy, 'The Death of Ivan Ilych', Chapter 3.

[32] The irony is that Ivan Il'ich feels he is treated by the doctors in the same way in which he used to treat the accused in court (Victor Brombert, 'The Ambiguity of "Ivan Ilich"', *Raritan: A Quarterly Review*, 26 [2006], pp. 152–62 [p. 157]).

[33] Tolstoy, 'The Death of Ivan Ilych', Chapter 1.

A Simple Death, then, is not a film about redemption, but about the very process of dying shown in graphic detail. It abounds in point-of-view shots conveying the hero's morphine-induced and increasingly delirious perception of his surroundings, which enhances the suggestion of utter isolation and loneliness. At one point Ivan Il′ích imagines that he is stormed by a whole army of doctors, who begin to feel, tap and knead his body while making contradictory diagnoses; another scene features his daughter and Praskov′ia Fedorovna holding each other's hand and turning in circles while humming some quaint melody.

Moments of despair are shown in a more realistic manner, as, for example, when Ivan Il′ích studies his face in the mirror and barely recognises himself: it is an uncanny moment, indicative of the pace at which his health is deteriorating.[34] While he never seems to entertain any illusions about his condition, the film contains an invented scene in which he tries to ignore his disease and simply carry on. All dressed up he goes to the living room, lights a cigar and starts listening to the music box, but is distracted by the sound of a mousetrap slamming shut. Initially confused and then disgusted, he orders the butler immediately to remove the convulsing mouse: 'Get this filth out of my sight.' Moments later, however, he collapses and we see him lying on the ground gasping, not unlike the unfortunate mouse the sight of which he could not bear.

In *Death and the Moving Image* Michele Aaron argues that the genre of the 'terminal illness film' tends to be remarkably optimistic and uplifting. Once the main character is fatally diagnosed, he or she often becomes a better person and eventually an inspiring example for others, even from beyond the grave. This triumph-in-tragedy template usually goes hand in hand with a remarkable evasiveness about physical pain, palliative care and the very process of dying. Instead of actually showing the moment of death, terminal illness films prefer flashbacks and freeze frames 'sealing the protagonists in their moments of triumph.'[35] The vacated space (an empty chair or desk) is another popular trope euphemistically indicating that the hero has died.

None of this applies to *A Simple Death*, which is astonishingly direct in showing Ivan Il′ích's death throes (heavy convulsions, incessant groaning) and the hysterical devastation of his son at his bedside. The dying scene lasts for ten torturous minutes forcing us to engage with extreme suffering and taxing our ability to keep watching. A parallel sequence showing from behind a

---

[34] Amelia Defalco uses the term 'uncanny' to describe the conflict between the 'theoretical self and the experiential self' in representations of old age. Although Ivan Il′ích is only middle-aged, his studying himself in the mirror generates a similar collision of the familiar and the unfamiliar: he barely recognises himself (Amelia DeFalco, *Uncanny Subjects: Aging in Contemporary Narrative* (Columbus: The Ohio State University Press, [2009], pp. 6–12).

[35] Michele Aaron, *Death and the Moving Image. Ideology, Iconography and I* (Edinburgh: Edinburgh University Press, 2014), p. 108.

mysterious male figure walking through the house and heading for the exit offers some spectatorial relief, but as soon as the film cuts back to the reality of the living the assault on our senses continues. Many viewers will find the scene unwatchable precisely in the sense in which the editors of an edited volume with that title have recently theorised the term: as a negative qualification of audio-visual material that shows 'the capacities and limits of the human perceptual apparatus'.[36]

The end of the film is ambiguous, offering simultaneously a mystical and an extremely materialistic view of death. Reproducing ad verbatim the very phrases that go through Ivan Il'ích's mind the moment he dies ('What joy!', 'Death is finished . . . It is no more!'[37]), the scene concludes with the triumphant sounds of Franz Schubert's *Deutsche Messe* while the mysterious male figure steps out on the street and a shower of translucent ping-pong balls is unleashed. The next moment we are in Ivan Il'ích's bedroom again, now brightly lit, where two doctors are discussing the blessings of modern life. As they leave the room talking, the camera slowly pans to the left to show the hero's lifeless and almost completely naked body stretched out on his bed. The sight is not particularly gruesome, but it creates a sobering contrast with the sublime splendour of the previous scene and subverts the convention of the vacated space. Instead of focusing on an empty bed, the closing shot shows the hero in a matter-of-fact kind of way, not yet properly dressed and prepared for the funeral service.

By showing Ivan Il'ích's inert body, *A Simple Death* prefigures the even more radical 'objectification' of the corpse in Sokurov's film *The Second Circle* (*Krug vtoroi*, 1990). In this film, according to Mikhail Iampolski, we are not confronted with the 'illusionary triumph over death' through meaningful rituals that turn the 'body-object' into a 'body-sign'; instead, Sokurov shows us death itself, the corpse of the hero's father being mishandled as an unwieldy item by both the apathetic son and a disrespectful undertaker.[38] *A Simple Death* is less drastic in this respect, but like *The Second Circle* it breaks with the established interpretation of death as something meaningful by forcing us to watch the 'unwatchable' (Ivan Il'ích's dying) and showing the hero's corpse as a cold, lifeless object. Significantly, Kaidanovsky entirely omits the funeral service described in Chapter 1 thereby 'missing' an opportunity to show Ivan Il'ích lying in state, that is as a 'simulacrum' of a living body (Iampolski's term).[39]

---

[36] Nicholas Baer et al., 'Introduction. Envisioning the Unwatchable', in *Unwatchable*, eds Nicholas Baer, Maggie Hennefeld, Laura Horak and Gunnar Iversen (New Brunswick, NJ: Rutgers University Press, 2019), pp. 1–29 (p. 7).

[37] Tolstoy, 'The Death of Ivan Ilych', Chapter 12.

[38] Mikhail Iampolski, 'Death in Cinema,' *Re-Entering the Sign. Articulating New Russian Culture* (Ann Arbor: University of Michigan Press, 1995), pp. 270–88 (pp. 272–4). I am grateful to the anonymous reviewer of my chapter for directing me to Iampolski's essay.

[39] Ibid., p. 278.

When the release of *A Simple Death* was finally sanctioned in July 1987, its unvarnished quality was already perceived as less shocking than three years before when the film was completed. Joining the growing army of stagnation-bashing opinion-makers, film critic Viacheslav Shmyrov pointed out the paradox of a country 'only recently celebrating funeral after funeral' (of Party leaders), but producing films in which 'parting with life' was shown in an unrealistically rosy way.[40] Shmyrov commended Kaidanovsky for breaking with this tendency, but found him guilty of aesthetic extremism, which prevented his film from starting a genuine dialogue with the moral extremist Tolstoy. *A Simple Death* was basically a 'crisis phenomenon' (*krizisnoe iavlenie*), a piece of 'solemn penmanship' (*blagorodnoe chistopisanie*) that turned the story of Ivan Il'ích into 'death with a capital letter'.[41]

In accusing Kaidanovsky of aesthetic extremism Shmyrov was not merely referring to the inclusion of Schubert's *Deutsche Messe* or Johann Sebastian Bach's church cantata *I Call to You, Lord Jesus Christ* which we hear in the film twice.[42] Rather he was flagging Kaidanovsky's apparent inability or unwillingness to express his own truth and engage with Tolstoy's moral extremism. Shmyrov may have a point if we consider the relative irrelevance of the redemption plot in *A Simple Death*, yet he seems to be unaware of the extent to which Kaidanovsky drew on Tolstoy's work, selecting quotes and pieces of dialogue from various texts in which death and thanatophobia play a crucial role. The next section will therefore examine on which sources *A Simple Death* is based other than *the Death of Ivan Il'ích*, and describe the function of these sources within the larger framework of the film. Finally, I hope to show the relevance of this analysis with regard to late-Soviet culture and the disintegration of its supporting value system.

The Many Sources of *A Simple Death*

Considering Ivan Il'ích's extreme agony, we may wonder why Kaidanovsky decided to call his film 'a simple death' (*prostaia smert'*) instead of retaining the original title. After all, dying turns out to be anything but simple for the hero,

---

[40] Viacheslav Shmyrov, '"Kakaia smert'"?', *Sovetskii ekran*, 20 (1988), 14. As an example of such rosy films, Shmyrov mentions *And Life, and Tears, and Love* (*I zhizn', i slezy, i liubov'*) by Nikolai Gubenko (1983). Set in a home for the elderly, the film tells the story of a female doctor who is convinced of the concept of positive ageing. She improves the quality of her patients' lives significantly.

[41] Ibid.

[42] Russian film aficionados are likely to associate the cantata *Ich ruf zu dir, Herr Jesu Christ* with the famous 'weightlessness' scene in *Solaris* (1972). Its inclusion in *A Simple Death* and Kaidanovsky's relationship with Tarkovsky may have caused critics, Shmyrov included, to overstate Tarkovsky's influence.

even if he deludes himself into thinking that he is unafraid of it. To be sure the English translation is misleading, inciting us to construe 'simple' as synonymous with 'easy', 'not painful', but in Russian the title may cause similar confusion. In my opinion, a more accurate translation would be 'an ordinary death'[43] which is consistent with the context from which the title was taken. The first time Tolstoy mentions that he is working on *The Death of Ivan Il'ich* is in a personal letter to Leonid Urusov in which he writes: 'I have started finishing and continuing *The Death of Ivan Il'ich*. I think I have told you the plan behind it: it is a description of the ordinary death of an ordinary man (*opisanie prostoi smerti prostogo cheloveka*), told from his point of view.'[44] Clearly, the adjective *prostoi* here does not refer to the *way* in which Ivan Il'ich dies, but to the ordinariness of death and its incongruity with his own sense of exceptionalism.[45] By using only the words *prostaia smert'* and relegating the hero to the subtitle ('from motifs of L.N. Tolstoy's story *The Death of Ivan Il'ich*'), Kaidanovsky puts even more emphasis on death as the film's major theme.

This partial borrowing from a personal letter is a first indication that *A Simple Death* may have considerably more sources than just *The Death of Ivan Il'ich* or any of its earlier drafts. Indeed, the film is not just the last utterance in a whole sequence of texts about death and redemption, starting with the fifteenth-century morality play *Everyman* (*Elckerlijc*)[46] and continuing with Charles Dickens' *A Christmas Carol*, a story Tolstoy admired and was rereading while working on *The Death of Ivan Il'ich*.[47] Identifying this lineage amounts

---

[43] Kaidanovsky's film competed in the section 'Un certain regard' at the Cannes Film Festival of 1987. Various sources mention the title *Une mort simple* or *Une simple mort*. Only the most comprehensive database on French cinema uses *Une mort ordinaire* (<https://www.cinema-francais.fr/cannes/cannes_1987.htm> [accessed 11 September]). Because it is more commonly used, I will stick to the title *A Simple Death*.

[44] Tolstoi, Letter to Urusov, *Polnoe sobranie sochinenii*, LXIII, p. 282.

[45] Ivan Il'ich does not believe that the syllogism from Kiesewetter's Logic ('Caius is a man, men are mortal, therefore Caius is mortal') applies to him and considers himself a 'creature quite, quite separate from all others' (Tolstoy, 'The Death of Ivan Ilych,' Chapter 6).

[46] Although Tolstoy was probably not familiar with the Dutch fifteenth-century morality play, nor with its English translation, the affinity between Everyman and Ivan Il'ich seems obvious (both men have lived bad lives and are unprepared for death), at least to the American novelist Phillip Roth who explicitly identified the intertextual link between the morality play, Tolstoy's story and his own novel *Everyman* from 2006 (Philip Roth, 'Philip Roth Discusses *Everyman*' [8 May 2006], Author Interviews, *NPR* <https://www.npr.org/templates/story/story.php?storyId=5390578&t=1629446802237> [accessed 11 September 2021]).

[47] Philip Rogers, 'Scrooge on the Neva. Dickens and Tolstoi's *Death of Ivan Ilíč*', *Comparative Literature*, 40 (1988), pp. 193–218 (pp.197–8).

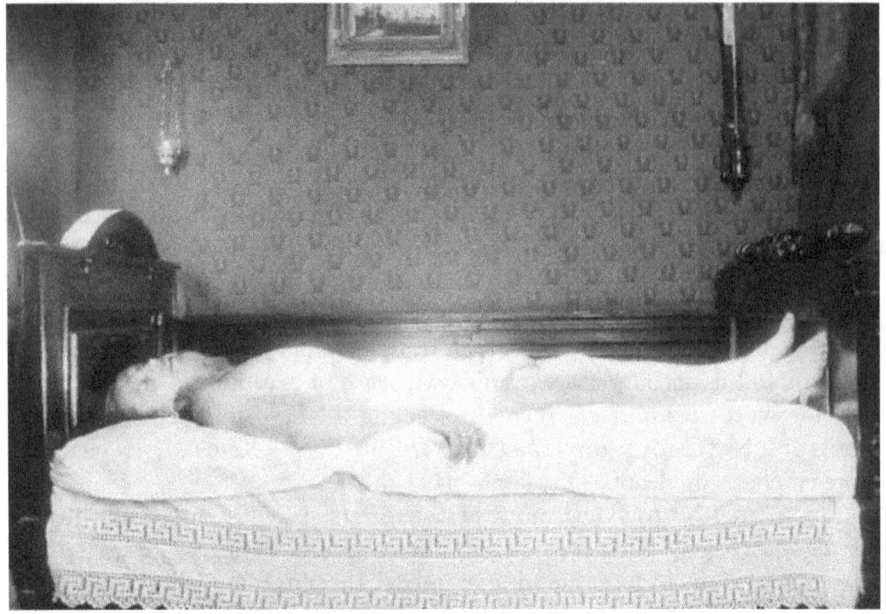

Figure 8.1 Ivan Il'ích (Valerii Priyomykhov) as a corpse. *A Simple Death*, directed by Aleksandr Kaidanovsky, 1985.

to simply providing yet another illustration of the concept of intertextuality. The point is that Kaidanovsky drew on a whole range of Tolstoy texts such as personal letters, essays, stories, diary entries and even other well-known works such as *The Kreutzer Sonata* to produce a film that casts a much wider net than the conventional subtitle suggests. Conceptually *A Simple Death* is similar to *The Overcoat* (1926), the experimental film by Grigorii Kozintsev and Leonid Trauberg for which Iurii Tynianov wrote the screenplay, combining several of Gogol's stories and adding motifs from Pushkin, Tolstoy and Dostoevsky. If Tynianov sought to express the phantasmagoria of Gogol's fictional world with new means that befitted the demands of modern, post-revolutionary art, then Kaidanovsky constructed his film as a mosaic of samplings taken from Tolstoy the artist-cum-thinker-cum-activist. It engages with death and mortality in a new, post-Soviet way. *A Simple Death* signalled the obsolescence of the Soviet myth of immortality, as Nikolai Khrenov has sharply observed.[48] No longer

---

[48] Nikolai Khrenov, 'Kinematograficheskaia tanatologiia', *Otechestvennye zapiski*, 5 (2013) <https://magazines.gorky.media/oz/2013/5/kinematograficheskaya-tanatologiya.html> [accessed 11 September 2021].

subordinated to the collectivist ideals of socialism, death is perceived in an existentialist key, that is as an individual and tragic affair. It is this post-Soviet perception of death that Kaidanovsky sought to express by resorting to the theme of thanatophobia in Tolstoy.

Before discussing the hypotexts to which the film alludes and directly quotes from, let us consider the term thanatophobia in more detail. If Ivan Il'ích suffers from death anxiety, as we have assumed so far, then what exactly is he afraid of? Philosopher Frances Kamm starts her perceptive analysis of Tolstoy's story by distinguishing between three different types of fear: 1) deprivation fear (the fear of no longer being able to enjoy the goods that life has to offer); 2) extinction fear (fear of disappearing, becoming nothing) and 3) fear of waste and rectification (fear that one has wasted one's life and will not be able to rectify it).[49] According to Kamm, Ivan I'lích experiences all of these fears to some extent, easily overcoming the first type, struggling with the second type, but eventually focusing on the third. It is through the realisation that he has lived a bad life that he gains self-understanding and overcomes his fear of death.[50]

Kamm pays relatively little attention to Ivan Il'ích's fear of extinction (the second type). Yet in *A Simple Death* it occupies a central place, precisely as a result of the film's dialogical engagement with other works of Tolstoy, even on a paratextual level. The opening credits, for example, are accompanied by a historical recording of Tolstoy reading a short story (*The Wolf*) in which a boy dreams about getting eaten by a wolf, just like the chickens the boy himself usually has for dinner. When the boy wakes up and ponders the meaning of his dream, he decides he will never eat meat again.[51] Characteristically, in the film the 'vegetarian' punchline of the story is omitted and this makes the boy's fear of death and frantic shouting (mimicked with gusto by Tolstoy) stand out over the story's original message.

The paratext of the Tolstoy recording is followed by a scene that similarly controls our entrance to the story of Ivan Il'ích. It is a re-enactment of an autobiographical episode that inspired Tolstoy to write the short story *Notes of a Madman*. Published two years after his death, the story is yet another variation on the redemption plot, featuring a narrator who, though professionally successful and happily married, is suddenly overwhelmed by severe moral doubt. He resolves this personal crisis by giving away all his possessions to the poor, for which his wife and his friends declare him insane. Again Kaidanovsky seems less interested in the hero's moral purification than in the crisis that precedes it

---

[49] Frances Kamm, 'Rescuing Ivan Ilich: How we Live and How we Die', *Ethics*, 113 (2003), pp. 202–33 (p. 208).
[50] Kamm, 209.
[51] Tolstoi, 'Volk', *Polnoe sobranie sochinenii*, XXXVII, p. 4.

and expresses itself in an acute fit of thanatophobia when he stops at an inn in the middle of the night:

> 'What nonsense', – I said to myself. 'Why am I depressed, what am I afraid of?'—'Me'– death's voice replied quietly. 'I'm here.' A shiver ran down my spine. Yes, death. It's coming, there it is, but it shouldn't be. [. . .] But I wasn't afraid and yet I saw, I felt that death was arriving and at the same time I felt that it shouldn't be. [. . .] And this feeling of being torn apart was terrible.[52]

These feverish lines (and many more) are directly transposed from the story to the film and expressed by the narrator, a rather plump man played by a different actor from the character of Ivan Il'ích. The narrator's monologue sets up a contrast with the next scene, the happy family gathering discussed earlier at which Ivan Il'ích will tell us that he is *not* afraid of death. The film takes great pains to recreate the depressing room in which the narrator of *Notes of a Madman* spends the night: it is painted glaringly white and has a perfectly square shape, which for some reason particularly upsets him. In addition the innkeeper's face is disfigured by an awful birthmark, yet another spooky detail that is not missing in the film. The square-shaped thanatophobia room will reappear once more at the moment of Ivan Il'ích's worst crisis when he turns to God and berates Him for the suffering he has to endure.

In showing this crisis Kaidanovsky hews closely to the original, making sure to include Ivan Il'ích's childhood memories and tormented exclamations. And yet the overall effect is quite different from the original, articulating the existentialist idea that life is essentially meaningless. As in the story, Ivan Il'ích's desperate question 'Why these sufferings?' elicits from his inner voice (a voiceover in the film) an unsatisfying answer: 'For no reason – they just are so.'[53] But if in the story this suffering is an important precondition for him to reconsider his life, in the film it only seems to confirm that human existence is amoral and absurd.

Again it is Tolstoy's later work that provides Kaidanovsky with the necessary material to elaborate this idea. The conversation between the two doctors in the penultimate scene starts with one of them inquiring sarcastically about the purpose of a number of modern conveniences and institutions. It is an all-out attack on contemporary society formulated as a series of rhetorical questions:

> *Doctor-1*: Machines to produce what? Telegraphs, telephones to convey what? Schools, universities, academia to teach what? Meetings to discuss what? Books, newspapers to disseminate information on what?

---

[52] Tolstoi, 'Zapiski sumasshedshego', *Polnoe sobranie sochinenii*, XXVI, p. 469.
[53] Tolstoy, 'The Death of Ivan Ilych', Chapter 10.

Railways to be used by whom and to go where? Millions of people gathered together and subjected to one power to do what?[54]

Expressed by a fictional character in the film, these words are in fact Tolstoy's own, jotted down in his diary on May 10, 1910, six months before his death. They are grouped under the last 'bullet point' in a list of dark meditations on the state of humanity, particularly on the need to preserve absolute chastity and acknowledge the insanity of our lives. The diary entry reads as a rehearsal of many of Tolstoy's controversial ideas on sexuality, family life and religion, some of which found their sharpest expression in *The Kreutzer Sonata*. It is in the spirit of this scandalous story that the discussion between the two doctors then continues, Doctor-1 taking on the role of the embittered hero Pozdnyshev, and Doctor-2 performing as his reasonable interlocutor.

Doctor-2: [If we would listen to you], how would the human race continue?
Doctor-1: But what is the use of its continuing? (. . .).
Doctor-2: What! What is the use? But then we should not exist.
Doctor-1: And why is it necessary that we should exist?
Doctor-2: Why, to live, to be sure.
Doctor-1: And why live? If life is completely without purpose, if life is given for life's sake, then why live? But if there is a purpose to life, then it should stop the moment that purpose has been fulfilled.[55]

In *The Kreutzer Sonata* it is Pozdnyshev's absurd theory of complete sexual abstinence that makes the interlocutor worry about the survival of the human race; in the diary entry we encounter a similar call for chastity as the only means capable of curing the insanity of modern civilisation. Isolated from their original context, however, these two borrowings acquire a more abstract meaning for which the sexual question is no longer relevant. Even if the dialogue remains quite ambiguous, the notion of life's absurdity, its lack of some higher purpose, prevails. Let us not forget that the discussion takes place against the background of Ivan Il'ích's lifeless body and the doctors seem to have

---

[54] Tolstoi, Diary, *Polnoe sobranie sochinenii*, XLVII, p. 580.
[55] Leo Tolstoy, *The Kreutzer Sonata and Other Stories*, trans. Benj. R. Tucker <https://www.gutenberg.org/files/689/689-h/689-h.htm#chap11> [accessed 11 September 2021]. The text between square brackets is unique to the film and was translated by me. The symbol (. . .) indicates that I have omitted the narrator's text in the Maude translation.

completely forgotten about him already. The last shot of the hero shows him reduced to nothing but his earthly frame.

All the Tolstoy texts discussed so far somehow centre on death and extinction, but at least two other sources seem to raise different issues. The film's very last shot shows Ivan Il'ích's nurse again looking straight into the camera, imitating with her arm the movement of a pendulum clock and repeating one of Tolstoy's most vexed questions: 'Who are you? What are you?' In this particular form the question is put to Pierre in the second part of *War and Peace* when he is lectured by the freemason Osip Bazdeev, but in his non-fictional texts, especially in his diary, Tolstoy asked himself the same question many times: 'Who, what am I?' (*Kto, chto ia?*).[56] The first time Ivan Il'ích's nurse starts repeating the words *kto ty, chto ty* she is shown in a reverse shot seemingly looking at us, but directing her words at the young Ivan Il'ích; when she expresses this mantra for the second time, she also looks into the camera, but now she is addressing us directly. Like everyman Ivan Il'ích we are asked to reflect upon who we are, where we stand in life and how we prepare for death.

The very last words in the film are spoken by Tolstoy himself. Again we hear his high-pitched and fragile voice as we are staring at a completely black screen.

Figure 8.2   Ivan Il'ích's nurse (Tamara Timofeeva): '*Kto ty ? Chto ty ?*' ('Who are you?', 'What are you?'). *A Simple Death*, directed by Aleksandr Kaidanovsky, 1985.

[56] Irina Paperno, '*Who, What Am I?*': *Tolstoy Struggles to Narrate the Self* (Ithaca and London: Cornell University Press, 2014), p. 1.

Just like Ivan Il'ích's nurse in the previous scene, Tolstoy seems to address us when he reads a few lines from what would eventually become the long article 'I Cannot Be Silent': 'To live like this is impossible. We cannot live like this, we cannot live like this.'[57] While it is possible to regard these words as an indictment of Ivan Il'ích's life, it is his capacity as some 'everyman' that makes it sound as if Kaidanovsky is appealing to his contemporaries. Far from suggesting that he was trying to teach his audience, as Tolstoy used to do, I would argue that if *A Simple Death* signals the untenability of the Soviet immortality myth, this also has implications for the way in which life is understood and valued. A film as complex and multi-layered as this from Kaidanovsky cannot be reduced to a one-dimensional message on how to live, but it may have provided an incentive for reflection amidst the growing chaos of the late 1980s. In a way the words 'we cannot live like this' even became a slogan expressing both the hope and despair of Soviet society during the final years of its existence. It is no coincidence that Stanislav Govorukhin made an epoch-making documentary in 1990 with a very similar title.[58]

Rejecting as a fallacy the notion that a film adaptation adapts only one text apiece, Thomas Leitch points out that our perception of an adaptation is not only dictated by the source text on which it claims to be based. The distinctive world, style or tone of an entire oeuvre can also be considered when determining whether or not a film is true to the author's spirit. Some texts have been adapted so often that any new adaptation will tend to echo the earlier ones, making the idea of a single precursor text even more problematic. Finally, Leitch urges us to abandon the idea that adaptations are 'intertexts' and their precursors 'simply texts'; any text is also an intertext that 'depends for its interpretation on shared assumptions about language, culture, narrative, and other presentational conventions'.[59]

Leitch's call for 'sensitive and rigorous attention' to the heteroglossia of film adaptations is theoretically justified and useful, as well as being applicable when watching a film like *A Simple Death*. Even viewers who believe that the film adapts only *The Death of Ivan Il'ích* may recognise the relevance of the Book

---

[57] The phrase 'nel'zia tak zhit'' occurs only once in Tolstoi's article 'Ne mogu molchat'' (*Polnoe sobranie sochinenii*, XXXVII, pp. 83–96, [p. 95]), which was published in June 1908. The recording of Tolstoi's voice repeating the phrase a number of times took place on May 11 when he was under the immediate impression of reading a newspaper report casually informing the reader that twenty peasants had been hanged for their involvement in an armed robbery. See 'Ne mogu molchat''. Istoriia pisaniia i pechataniia', *Polnoe sobranie sochinenii*, XXXVII, pp. 425–7.

[58] Govorukhin, *Tak zhit' nel'zia* (1990). The word order in Tolstoy's treatise is slightly different: 'nel'zia tak zhit'' (Tolstoi, 'Ne mogu molchat'', p. 425).

[59] Leitch, 'Twelve Fallacies in Contemporary Adaptation Theory,' pp. 165–7.

of Job or the morality play *Elckerlijck* for both the film and the story. At the same time, Kaidanovsky's film is quite exceptional in that it draws consciously on several texts pertaining to post-conversion Tolstoy, thereby decentring the main text on which it is nominally based. In so doing, *A Simple Death* is on the one hand extremely logocentric, showing remarkable respect for and explicit acknowledgement of the literary sources it uses. At the same time, it is iconoclastic in picking a Tolstoy classic that had never before been adapted for the screen (at least not in Russia), while also taking inspiration from genres that we would normally not associate with film adaptation (diaries, personal letters and treatises).

What I hope to have demonstrated is that the many references to and quotations from Tolstoy in Kaidanovsky's film combine to deconstruct the redemption plot of *The Death of Ivan Il'ích*. Instead of retaining the notion that death can also be a kind of awakening (a notion we find throughout Tolstoy's writing),[60] the film centres almost entirely on death in its immediate and physical manifestations. In the wider context of world cinema *A Simple Death* subverts the conventions of the terminal illness film which is usually reluctant to show the moment of death. In the context of Russian cinema, Kaidanovky's film represents an important step in the dismantling of the immortality myth of Soviet culture and the introduction of a non-teleological view of death in which the individual takes precedence over the collective. I also hope to have shown that a seemingly narrow comparison between a film and its precursor text(s) can yield valuable insights even if they are nothing but intertexts in the 'entire matrix of communicative utterances'.[61]

Bibliography

Aaron, Michele, *Death and the Moving Image. Ideology, Iconography and I* (Edinburgh: Edinburgh University Press, 2014).

Andrew, Dudley, 'The Economies of Adaptation', in *True to the Spirit: Film Adaptation and the Question of Fidelity*, eds Colin MacCabe, Kathleen Murray and Rick Warner (Oxford: Oxford University Press, 2011), pp. 27–39.

Baer, Nicholas, Maggie Hennefeld, Laura Horak and Gunnar Iversen, 'Introduction. Envisioning the Unwatchable', in *Unwatchable*, eds Nicholas Baer, Maggie Hennefeld, Laura Horak and Gunnar Iversen (New Brunswick, NJ: Rutgers University Press, 2019), pp. 1–29.

Beumers, Birgit, *A History of Russian Cinema* (Oxford and New York: Berg, 2009).

Brombert, Victor, 'The Ambiguity of "Ivan Ilich"', *Raritan: A Quarterly Review*, 26 (2006), pp. 152–62.

Cowley, Christopher, 'Ivan Ilych and Autobiographical Despair', *Philosophy and Literature*, 45 (2021), pp. 199–210.

---

[60] Paperno, p. 142.
[61] Stam, p. 64.

Defalco, Amelia, *Uncanny Subjects: Aging in Contemporary Narrative* (Columbus: The Ohio State University Press, 2009).

Gillespie, David, 'Mikhail Shveitser's *Resurrection* (1960, 1962): Film Adaptation as Thaw Narrative', in *Tolstoy on Screen*, eds Lorna Fitzsimmons and Michael A. Denner (Evanston: Northwestern University Press, 2014), pp. 75–89.

Graham, Seth, '*Chernukha* and Russian Film', *Studies in Slavic Cultures*, 1 (2000), pp. 9–27.

Iampolski, Mikhail, 'Death in Cinema,' *Re-Entering the Sign. Articulating New Russian Culture* (Ann Arbor: University of Michigan Press, 1995), pp. 270–88.

Isakava, Volha, 'Reality Excess. Chernukha Cinema in the Late 1980s', in *Ruptures and Continuities in Soviet/Russian Cinema. Styles, Characters and Genres Before and After the Collapse of the USSR*, eds Birgit Beumers and Eugénie Zvonkine (London and New York: Routledge, 2017), pp. 147–65.

Jahn, Gary R., 'The Role of the Ending in Lev Tolstoi's *The Death of Ivan Il'ich*', *Canadian Slavonic Papers*, 24 (1982), pp. 229–38.

Jameson, Frederic, 'Afterword: Adaptation as a Philosophical Problem', in *True to the Spirit: Film Adaptation and the Question of Fidelity*, eds Colin MacCabe, Kathleen Murray and Rick War (Oxford: Oxford University Press, 2011), pp. 215–33.

Johnson, David, 'Adaptation and Fidelity', *The Oxford Handbook of Adaptation Studies*, ed. Thomas M. Leitch (New York: Oxford University Press, 2017), pp. 87–100.

Kamm, Frances, 'Rescuing Ivan Ilich: How we Live and How we Die', *Ethics*, 113 (2003), pp. 202–33.

Karakhan, Lev, 'Jobless Prophets', in *Russian Critics on the Cinema of Glasnost*, eds Michael Brashinsky and Andrew Horton (Cambridge: Cambridge University Press, 1994), pp. 30–4.

Khrenov, Nikolai, 'Kinematograficheskaia tanatologiia', *Otechestvennye zapiski*, 5 (2013) <https://magazines.gorky.media/oz/2013/5/kinematograficheskaya-tanatologiya.html> [accessed 11 September 2021].

Lang, Gerald, 'What Does Ivan Ilich Need to Be Rescued From?', *Philosophy*, 89 (2014), pp. 325–47.

Leitch, Thomas, 'Twelve Fallacies in Contemporary Adaptation Theory', *Criticism*, 45 (2003), pp. 149–71.

———, 'Everything You Always Wanted to Know about Adaptation. Especially if you're looking forward rather than back', *Literature/Film Quarterly*, 33 (2005), pp. 233–45.

Lovell, Stephen, 'Finitude at the Fin de Siècle: Il'ia Mechnikov and Lev Tolstoy on Death and Life', *The Russian Review*, 63 (2004), pp. 296–316.

Lotman, Iurii, 'Siuzhetnoe prostranstvo russkogo romana XIX stoletiia', in *Izbrannye stat'i*, 3 vols (Tallinn: Aleksandra, 1993), III, pp. 91–106.

MacCabe, Colin, 'Introduction. Bazinian Adaptation: *The Butcher Boy* as Example', in *True to the Spirit: Film Adaptation and the Question of Fidelity*, eds Colin MacCabe, Kathleen Murray and Rick Warner (Oxford: Oxford University Press, 2011), pp. 3–26.

Mandelker, Amy, 'Out of Breath: Bernard Rose's *ivans xtc.* (2000) and Tolstoy's *The Death of Ivan Il'ich*', in *Tolstoy on Screen*, eds Lorna Fitzsimmons and Michael A. Denner (Evanston: Northwestern University Press, 2014), pp. 217–43.

Piispa, Lauri, 'Tolstoy Film Adaptations in Russia, 1909–17', *Tolstoy Studies Journal*, 23 (2011), pp. 44–60.

Paperno, Irina, '*Who, What Am I?*' *Tolstoy Struggles to Narrate the Self* (Ithaca and London: Cornell University Press, 2014).

Plakhov, Andrei, 'Iubilei Aleksandra Kaidanovskogo', *Kommersant*, 23 July 1996 <https://www.kommersant.ru/doc/236961> [accessed on 11 September 2021].

Rogers, Philip, 'Scrooge on the Neva. Dickens and Tolstoi's *Death of Ivan Il'ich*', *Comparative Literature*, 40 (1988), pp. 193–218.

Roth, Philip, 'Philip Roth Discusses *Everyman*' (8 May 2006). Author Interviews. *NPR* <https://www.npr.org/templates/story/story.php?storyId=5390578&t=1629446802237> [accessed 11 September 2021].

Schmid, Wolf, 'Problematisierung der Ereignishaftigkeit in Čechovs Erzählungen', in *Russische Literatur an der Wende vom 19. zum 20. Jahrhundert,* ed. R. G. Grübel (Amsterdam and Atlanta: Rodopi, 1993), pp. 41–69.

Shemiakin, Andrei, '"Prostaia smert'" v god Kaidanovskogo', *Kinopressa*, 30 September 2016 <http://kinopressa.ru/4320> [accessed 11 September 2021].

Shmyrov, Viacheslav, '"Kakaia smert'"?', *Sovetskii ekran*, 20 (1988), p. 14.

Simone, Thomas, 'The Mythos of "The Sickness Unto Death": Kurosawa's *Ikiru* and Tolstoy's *The Death of Ivan Ilych*', *Literature/Film Quarterly*, 1 (1975), pp. 2–12.

Stam, Robert, 'Beyond Fidelity: The Dialogics of Adaptation', in *Film Adaptation*, ed. James Naremore (New Brunswick, NJ: Rutgers University Press, 2000), pp. 54–76.

Tolstoi, L. N., *Polnoe sobranie sochinenii,* 90 vols (Moscow: Khudozhestvennaia literature, 1928–58).

Tolstoy, Leo, *The Kreutzer Sonata and Other Stories*, trans. Benj. R. Tucker <https://www.gutenberg.org/files/689/689-h/689-h.htm#chap11> [accessed 11 September 2021].

———, 'The Death of Ivan Ilych', trans Aylmer and Louise Maude, in *The Death of Ivan Ilich: An Electronic Study Edition of the Russian Text*, ed. Gary R. Jahn <https://open.lib.umn.edu/ivanilich/part/english-and-russian-texts/> [accessed 11 September 2021].

Zuurmond, Anouk, 'Attending the Dying: Images of Compassion', *Arcadia*, 49 (2014), pp. 74–88.

Filmography

A Simple Death (*Prostaia smert'*), directed by Aleksandr Kaidanovsky (USSR, Lenfilm, 1985).

The Second Circle (*Krug vtoroi*), directed by Aleksandr Sokurov (USSR, Lenfilm, 1990).

9. FORGED NETWORK NARRATIVES: TOLSTOY'S *THE FORGED COUPON* AND A CYCLE OF ADAPTATIONS IN WORLD CINEMA

Greg Dolgopolov

Did you hear the one about three paranoid film theorists? They were sure someone in a cinema somewhere was watching them. The most significant Soviet semiotician and literary thinker, Iurii Lotman, in a conversation with Iurii Tsivian and Mikhail Iampolski remarked,

> There is a movement towards cinema before cinema. Take Tolstoy's 'The Forged Coupon' and you will see that it is a typical scenario, a screenplay. All literary psychology is discarded, there is psychology, but it is not Tolstoy's meditations, but in the montage of the episodes. In fact, it is something quite amazing. And, apparently, because of this a film based on this novel is impossible to make.[1]

I argue counter to Lotman, not only that it is possible to make a film based on Tolstoy's last story *The Forged Coupon* (*Fal'shivyi kupon*), published posthumously in 1911, but that the story, its structure and its themes have been a source for countless other films. *The Forged Coupon* was a culmination of a lifetime's work, a spiritual and conceptual legacy that has created a complex

---

[1] Iurii Lotman, 'Popytki predskazat' interesny v toi mere v kakoi oni ne opravdyvaiutsia'. Interview with Iurii Lotman by Iurii Tsivian and Mikhail Iampolski, Rezekne, May-June 1986, *Kinovedcheskie zapiski*, 20 (1993–4), 4–11 <http://vivovoco.astronet.ru/VV/PAPERS/LOTMAN/KINO.HTM> [accessed 21 August 2021].

network of cinematic influences – the first emerged in Russia in 1913 as *The Counterfeit Note (Fal'shivyi kupon*, Petr Chardynin); it was followed by a much shorter Italian version in 1914, *The Altered Note (Il falso cupone)*; then in 1926 came a German variation, *The Adventures of a Ten Mark Note (Die Abenteuer eines Zehnmarkscheines*, Berthold Viertel); and this was succeeded by perhaps the best-known adaptation, in France, directed by Robert Bresson, *L'Argent* (1983). This dark interpretation in turn inspired the Finnish director Aki Louhimies's even more miserable 2005 version *Frozen Land (Paha Maa)*. Further unattributed re-imaginings include *Twenty Bucks* (Keva Rosenfeld, 1993); *Pay It Forward* (Mimi Leder, 2000) and *Loot (Bablo*, Konstantin Buslov, 2011). Not all these variations directly attribute Tolstoy's tale, but the distinctive narrative relay structure of *The Forged Coupon* has created the complex 'network narratives' identified by David Bordwell as becoming a remarkably common 'dominant principle of offbeat storytelling'[2] that has spread globally in resistance to mainstream cinema narratives.

However, Lotman was also right. *The Forged Coupon* is remarkably cinematic, with its fast-moving episodic composition; bold character sketches; multi-stranded, circular, highly contingent narrative structure; emblematic situations; and a plot twist leading to an ethical turn focused on a key protagonist's redemption. The novella attempts to capture a pan-Russian scope from a dishevelled peasant all the way to the Tsar in one epic and morally conscious work, highlighting Tolstoy's preoccupation with all-embracing unity and 'the ideal of brotherly love'[3] – a doctrine which serves to unify a series of desperate characters and a variety of diverse cinematic adaptations of the work. Forgery and adaptations are closely connected, involving an alteration of the original that has an impact on the lives of all those with whom it comes into contact. This chapter frames the filmic adaptations, not in the dominant terms of fidelity discourse, but 'biologically' by investigating the story's range of evolutionary adaptations over one hundred years of cinema history. As proponents of this approach, Bortolotti and Hutcheon note, 'biology can celebrate the diversity of life forms, yet at the same time recognise that they come from a common origin',[4] arguing that 'the kind of descriptive rather than evaluative thinking that biology potentially provides [. . .] suggests new ways of thinking about cultural adaptation theory and, beyond that, about the reason for the continuing importance of certain narratives in a given culture'.[5]

---

[2] David Bordwell, *Poetics of Cinema* (London: Routledge, 2007), p. 191.

[3] Ilya Klinger and Nasser Zakariya, 'Poetics of Brotherhood: Organic and Mechanistic Narrative in Late Tolstoi', *Slavic Review*, 70 (2011), pp. 754–72 (p. 754–5).

[4] Gary Bortolotti and Linda Hutcheon, 'On the Origin of Adaptations: Rethinking Fidelity Discourse and "Success" – Biologically', *New Literary History*, 38 (2007), pp. 443–58 (445).

[5] Ibid., p. 446.

The Forged Coupon is a keystone for evolutionary film history with its modular crisscrossing structural model generating a stimulus for a range of relay narratives, anthology films and hand-me-down narratives of objects passing between multiple temporary owners.[6] These objects range from cars (*The Kopeck*, Ivan Dykhovichnyy, 2002) to violins (*Red Violin*, François Girard, 1998) as well as the transitory moments of connections in the films of Altman, Iñárritu, and Shakhnazarov. The common element is that the car, violin, gun or diamond invariably attracts potential owners, but also brings with it a curse or bad luck that is passed on from one person to the next. It is worth noting that there is a distinction between relay objects that bring joy to their temporary hosts and the torment that befalls those that pass on a counterfeit note knowingly creating future trouble.

L'Argent (1983), Bresson's final film, is the best-known adaptation of *The Forged Coupon* and has received considerable critical attention[7]. However, other remarkably provocative adaptations such as *Frozen Land, Loot* and *Pay it Forward* have been largely ignored by film studies. This chapter surveys the legacy of Tolstoy's final story and its phenomenal impact on international cinema narratives and adaptations. I aim to study these three lesser-known cinematic adaptations with a special focus on their narrative structure, thematic universe, and the way in which they examine Tolstoy's key themes of the ideal of brotherly love, evil, fate, choice, contingency, redemption and forgiveness.

TOLSTOY'S *FORGED COUPON*: EVIL AND REDEMPTION

The Forged Coupon is a multi-stranded narrative that starts when two schoolboys forge a bank coupon to repay a small debt of honour, a seemingly harmless caper leading to spiralling consequences. As the forgery is passed on it throws misery and suffering on to the next person, prompting criminality. As Ernest Simmons notes, 'The complexity of its construction is unique for [Tolstoy] in this genre, yet he handles it with superb skill. The motif running through the whole story is the evil-begetting power of evil.'[8] This structure serves to create a

---

[6] In this context one can mention *Diamond Handcuffs* (John P. McCarthy, 1928), *Un carnet de bal* (Julien Duvivier, 1937) and *Red Violin* (François Girard, 1998). Victoria Somoff offers a provocative reading suggesting that Tolstoy produced a literary reworking of the plot drawn from archaic folklore to examine the characters' excesses in relation to ethical norms in 'Nonresistance to Fiction: Archaic Folktale vs Later Tolstoy', *The Slavic and East European Journal*, 60 (2016), pp. 284–306 (p. 285).

[7] Kent Jones in his fine analysis of the film provided much of the initial background detail. Kent Jones, *L'Argent* (London: BFI Film Classics, Bloomsbury Publishing, 1999), pp. 24–34.

[8] Ernest Simmons, *Introduction to Tolstoy's Writings* (Chicago: University of Chicago Press, 1968) <http://www.ourcivilisation.com/smartboard/shop/smmnsej/tolstoy/chap10.htm> [accessed 5 July 2021].

concatenation of factors bringing people together. The connecting relay allows the criminal characters to make choices that eventually lead to personal redemption. Described as one of Tolstoy's 'realistic stories with clear-cut morals'[9] and 'vividly illustrating Tolstoy's ideas of universal brotherhood and non-resistance to evil',[10] the mechanistic narrative shapes this sense of brotherhood to 'offer an alternative vision of social organisation as a whole, one where all individuals are concerned primarily with cultivating in themselves a loving attitude towards others'.[11] This socially positive attitude has been surprisingly minimised in the cinematic adaptations in favour of the focus on criminality and evil.

The Forged Coupon is a vigorous treatise on the iniquities of materialism, corruption, and the power of evil to destroy everything in its path. Part Two claims that the only way of combating evil is through non-resistance, promoting the Tolstoyan pacifist message of brotherly love and forgiveness. The novella also entertains the complex relationship between destiny, chaos, chance and free will, employing an inventive narrative structure that offers divergent pathways, leading eventually in a circular route or an out and back journey to redemption. It is a story of adaptive networks. Tolstoy produced a literary reworking of European folklore into a contemporary Russian epic that minimised the exploration of psychological motivation in favour of presenting a moralising worldview.

The non-psychological, fast-moving, quick-character-sketch, relay-narrative structure remains the story's most prominent feature when it comes to cinematic adaptation. In some ways, this was an innovation for Tolstoy, who was aware that 'structure banishes contingency because each incident must have a purpose, must contribute to the overall plot and pattern or it would not be included in the first place'.[12] Tolstoy adapted the structure from Russian folklore and according to Vladimir Porudominsky he was possibly influenced by Vladimir Dal''s 1867 short story, 'The Grey One' ('Seren'kaia').[13] There are numerous similarities in the structure, characters and narratives: Dal''s story features the crude counterfeiting of a 50 rouble note, not by high school students but by a group of tradesmen and their friends. This thread of deception brings despair and misery to the small number of people who encounter it. Dal''s story is shorter, with far fewer characters than Tolstoy's tale.

---

[9] Donna Orwin, 'Introduction', in *The Cambridge Companion to Tolstoy*, ed. Donna Orwin (Cambridge: Cambridge University Press, 2002), pp. 49–62 (p. 59).
[10] Somoff, p. 285.
[11] Klinger and Zakariya, p. 771.
[12] Gary Saul Morson, *Narrative and Freedom: The Shadows of Time* (New Haven and London: Yale University Press, 1994), p. 158.
[13] Somoff, pp. 284–306; and Vladimir Porudominsky, 'Iz zametok daleveda. Davnii dolg', *Voprosy literatury*, 6 (2001), pp. 132–54.

Tolstoy's story appears to be structured by fate or a causal determinism, with one action leading directly to another and then to another, offering a kind of explanatory logic for social collapses. It starts with a father's grumpiness that leads to a forgery, which in turn creates the circumstances that lead to murder, then jail, before a massive social transformation unravels everything and the story returns to the starting characters who have since been transformed. Gary Saul Morson claims that Tolstoy was a writer of radical contingency: 'In most novels, identification with the character involves sharing a sense of choice while contemplation of structure reveals inevitability; but in Tolstoy's novel, the reverse is the case.'[14] The relay structure of *The Forged Coupon* is rigorous, but unpredictable and the narrative also supports numerous forking paths with considerable moral editorialising. The passing of bad faith leads to a cycle of evil and corruption that escalates, virulently engulfing all of Russia.

The first part of the novella is most frequently adapted in the cinema, with its uncompromising vision of cruelty and deceit (*L'Argent, Frozen Land, Loot*). The second part, focusing on a network of positive and redemptive deeds is less popular, but can be traced in the adaptations of *Pay It Forward* and *Twenty Bucks*. Here, just as the story hits the absolute depths of depravity, the proliferating evil deeds are challenged by a remarkable moment of non-resistance to evil. Tolstoy described his idea in a diary entry of 29 May 1889: 'How good could be a story about a killer, having repented for killing a woman who did not protect herself.'[15] As with most events in this story, the original murder by Stepan Pelageushkin was motivated and in the heat of the moment: his horses were stolen, and the police were utterly unhelpful. His revenge, however, quickly turns into homicidal mania, culminating in the attack on the saintly Maria Semenovna, who by accepting the martyrdom of the defenceless death redeems a series of Stepan's sins. Stepan undergoes a mystical experience that compels him to confess to the police. As a narrative transfiguration, Stepan's asking forgiveness for his sins is the first step to his salvation. The spiritually and morally rehabilitated Stepan becomes involved in activities that help to alter the lives of other evildoers from earlier in the story. Among them is the now grown-up Mitia, the schoolboy who forged a bank coupon at the start of the story. Stepan's goodness, humility, and influence spread as virulently as did the passage of evil. In Tolstoy's reckoning, evil cannot thrive when it is not confronted. He advocated non-resistance to evil through love, humility and peace.

The motif of the multiplying power of evil and the counter-intuitive method of countering its spread serves as the transition point from the first

[14] Morson, p. 10.
[15] Lev Tolstoy, diary entry 29 May 1889; quoted in N.K. Gudzii 'Commentary to *The Forged Coupon*', in L. N. Tolstoi, *Polnoe sobranie sochinenii*, 90 vols (Moscow-Leningrad: Khudozhestvennaia literatura, 1928–1958), XXXVI (1936), p. 557.

to the second section of the novella. Most of the cinematic adaptations simplify Tolstoy's argument to one of a chain of evil events where one deed in bad faith leads to another even more evil act and so on until the interconnected world becomes evil to the core. Tolstoy's argument is more sophisticated if, perhaps, containing less dramatic potential: evil can be countered not with a greater authority or religious institutions, but with the more powerful force of non-resistance and brotherly love. This connects people and saves them from the chasm of meaningless, hierarchical and brutal existence. In the story's first part Tolstoy exposes all the crassness, meanness and criminal tendencies of representatives of several layers of society.

Tolstoy's narrative structure and terse argument about the depraved state of Russian society clearly influenced the logic of montage editing in early cinema. It was employed in the opening sequence of Eisenstein's *Strike* (*Stachka*, 1925), where through dynamic montage an argument is made about the ruthlessness of industrialists in putting down any social unrest. Each shot only requires a stark, forceful image to make the connections for the audience before moving on. Eisenstein understood that the power of montage is the purposeful juxtaposition of images to build an argument. Eisenstein's emphasis on editing as a storytelling device invokes the structure of *The Forged Coupon*. Each causal action of one character receiving and then passing on the thread of evil has a 'blast and counterblast' pattern which emerges when the next character takes over. These issues of choice, evil and redemption, as well as the use of cinematic language, will be explored in various 'impossible' adaptations of Tolstoy's novella, examined in the next section.

A World Relay of Adaptations

Considering the existing film versions of *The Forged Coupon*, all of them are united by a focus on the narrative mechanism of the network and its relay structure. The films can be divided into two groups: those that employ the mechanics of a relay narrative and feature an object passed on from one person to the next, seemingly chaotically yet structured by the progressive networks connecting disparate people into a collective; and the second group closer to Tolstoy's tale, that focus on the tarnished note, the forgery. The emphasis here is on money, its use-value, and the perversion that the falsification creates in the social sphere, upsetting its accepted order.

The story lends itself to a cinematic realisation – a focus on movement, transitions between close-ups and wide shots, a circular narrative, a sense of a broader community, but one unified through the circularity of the narrative into a familial relationship. The redemption storyline of the rarely adapted second part is also important as it has set the standard for Hollywood narratives where the dénouement is based on the hero experiencing life-changing moments in the final act. The cinematic adaptations of *The Forged Coupon* have spread around the world and across many different periods of film history, demonstrating the universality of the narrative, its adaptability and openness for different forms of emphasis.

The first film adaptation of *The Forged Coupon* occurred only three years after Tolstoy's death, two years after the story's publication, and five years after the birth of Russian narrative cinema. The now lost 1913 film, *The Counterfeit Note* (*Fal'shivyi kupon*) at 1183 metres spooled length would have played for approximately 60 minutes. It was adapted and directed by the leading pre-Revolutionary director, Petr Chardynin, for the major Russian film production house, Khanzhonkov & Co. Judging by the other films produced in the same year that do survive, Chardynin's mise-en-scène would've been busy, with little camera movement, simple or staid editing, and performances ranging from the overtly theatrical to modern screen realism. The following year *The Altered Note* (*Il falso cupone*) was released in Italy with a running time of 22 minutes, sadly another lost film with no note as to the director. The relay chain structure appeared in film theorist Béla Balázs' script for *The Adventures of a Ten Mark Note* (*Die Abenteuer eines Zehnmarkscheines*, 1926) directed by Berthold Viertel. This too is a lost film, although snippets of this 60-minute unacknowledged adaptation do remain, as do notes on the plot. Antti Alanen comments, 'from the trailer one can get just an impression of the imagery of this lost film: it starts with a close-up of the banknote, then we see shots from a sewing room, from a bank, newspaper headlines, city streets, [a] dog eating the note'.[16]

According to the programme notes, this film is set during the inflation era and features a young peasant girl, Anna, who has just received her first week's wages in the form of a 10-mark note. She gives it to her mother, who places it in her bible to use later for groceries. Anna's brother steals the money and uses it to buy a knife. The ten-mark note goes on a journey across numerous Berlin locales as it passes through the hands of numerous unrelated characters. Along the way, this banknote generates more trouble than it is actually worth. Anna's brother becomes a murderer. Anna and her mother are about to be ruined. As in Tolstoy's tale, the message appears to be that money is inherently evil and the trouble that it creates far exceeds the good it can do. Maintaining Tolstoy's circular narrative, the 10-mark note eventually returns to Anna at the end of the film. Since losing her money she has met and fallen in love with her neighbour. He has just pawned his bike to try to save some of Anna's furniture from the debt collectors. The note which he receives was Anna's original 10-mark note. As they embrace the banknote flutters to the floor where her dog tears it to shreds! This narrative inflection shares Tolstoy's optimistic conclusion and moralising about the destructiveness of money, but without the forgery and the subsequent process of moral redemption.

---

[16] Antti Alanen, 'Film Diary', 2010 <http://anttialanenfilmdiary.blogspot.com.au/2010/04/k13-513-die-abenteuer-eines.html> [accessed 9 January 2021].

The Adventures of a Ten Mark Note anticipates *Twenty Bucks* (Rosenfeld, 1993) – the connection of a broad cross-section of a city's population through transient currency – which was originally conceived for a 1935 film that was never filmed, that itself was potentially influenced by O. Henry's short story, 'The Tale of the Tainted Tenner' written about New York in the early 1900s that was then made into a television episode in 1957 as part of the *O. Henry Playhouse* series about a shady counterfeiting team that innocently plays good fairy to a group of unusual people. This episode combines the relay narrative and the counterfeiting theme but moves away from the evils of forgery to a positive morality tale. The combination of counterfeit money and its impact on disparate people who connect in an agglomerative plot, but with a black comic twist, can be further seen in Konstantin Buslov's 2011 film *Loot* where a bag containing a million euros is continuously stolen in a long chain of deceit by crooks from cops, who are operating corruptly for some slick businessmen, and then that money is stolen by a different branch of the police from the crooks and so on. All these films share a similar mood and structure and provide a wry commentary on materialist society.

Similarly, *Twenty Bucks* systematically focuses on the enormous social impact of money on a cross-section of American society from a con artist to a millionaire as it follows a $20 bill from its ATM birth to its eventual demise. Along its way, the note weaves in and out of the lives of a variety of characters, with the drama hinging on the disparity of their social levels that range from a stripper to a Saudi millionaire to an aspiring writer. The film shares the melodramatic and sentimental qualities of the earlier work of Balázs and Viertel but avoids the descent into the abyss of the cursed currency. There is an interesting moment early on when a vagrant races to pick up the $20 note as it flies through the street and exclaims to the kids gathered around her, 'There is luck and there is fate. Luck is for you, small-timers. What they used to call miracles.' She raises the $20 note to the sky and proclaims: 'This bill, this bill . . . is my destiny!' Suddenly a kid on a skateboard rides past and snatches it from her grasp. The note then travels across the entire country connecting and disrupting a diverse network of people. It connects people who would never meet otherwise or have any influence on one another. In *Twenty Bucks* the money often stands for far more than its actual value. For every temporary owner it means something different and for everyone it distils a focus on his or her fate and, importantly, unites them in a complex social fabric. Perhaps this is a nod to Tolstoy's all-embracing unity. A determining element of these relay hand-me-down narratives is, as David Scott Diffrient claims, the fact that they 'foreground a hierarchically plotted hand-me-down [. . .] to emphasise the verticality of social relations within a local or national framework'.[17]

---

[17] David Scott Diffrient, 'Stories that Objects Might Live to Tell: The "Hand-Me-Down" Narrative in Film', *Other Voices*, 3 (2007) <http://www.othervoices.org/3.1/sdiffrient/index.php> [accessed 20 August 2021].

A cheery variation on the theme of travelling currency is *The Million Pound Note* (Ronald Neame, 1954). Here the note is real, not counterfeit if some people are suspicious, but it does not actually pass in ownership from one person to another, although there is a moment when the wind catches it, and the note leaves the possession of its new owner and is carried away cheekily by the breeze. The film follows an impoverished American sailor (Gregory Peck), who happens to pass by the house of two rich gentlemen who have conceived the crazy idea of distributing a note worth one million pounds to someone random and in need. They wager that the bearer of the note would meet all sorts of people and travel from the bottom of the social hierarchy to the top with the help of this million-pound note. The sailor finds that whenever he tries to use the note to buy something, people treat him as if he is a King and let him have whatever he likes for free. He cannot exchange or pass the note on. Ultimately, the money proves to be more troublesome than it is worth when it almost destroys his dignity and costs him the woman he loves. This film utilises the social glueyness of money and the way in which it connects disparate social layers in the most hierarchical of societies: London. It also features an episodic narrative, multiple characters and moral redemption when the sailor recognises the extreme burden that a million pounds imposes.

Passing the relay baton on to France, the most famous, yet not the most faithful of the attributed screen adaptations is Bresson's *L'Argent* (1983). The script written by Bresson was inspired by the first part of Tolstoy's tale – avoiding the redemptive, social critique of the second part in favour of a treatise on the communal malaise caused by money and corruption which Kent Jones describes as 'a modern form of indifference that is essentially unconscious'.[18] It is a highly restrained, systematic analysis of evil on an institutional scale where revenge is served cold, with little passion. In *L'Argent* Bresson develops the sparse network narrative initiated in his earlier film, *Au hazard Balthazar* (1966), a tale of a donkey passed from one family to another connecting disparate characters and plotlines – a living being, but one that is treated as an object of use-value. In *L'Argent* as in Tolstoy's tale, the story of the forged banknote acts as an inciting incident, appearing early in the film before disappearing, but remaining as an evil trace throughout the rest of the tale. The forgery highlights contemporary society's obsession with money, while hinting at the power of guilt to offer an interruption to the free fall of destiny in the final moment where Yvon (the French Stepan), having killed the grey-haired woman/Maria Semenovna, gives himself up to the police after enjoying a final quick coffee in a crowded café. Adrian Miles notes that here 'the world is fallen, always fallen, and redemption is never available in or from it'.[19] Bresson removes all pity,

---

[18] Jones, p. 31.

[19] Adrian Miles, '*L'Argent*', *Senses of Cinema*, 7 (2000) <http://www.sensesofcinema.com/2000/cteq/largent-2/> [accessed 25 July 2021].

all forgiveness from his adaptation, leaving just the character's odd quotidian choices for the audience to decipher and touches of theology peppered throughout. There are no solutions offered.

Multi-stranded relay narratives are not common in Russian filmmaking. The rare examples include *12 Chairs* (*Dvenadtsat' stul'ev*, Leonid Gaidai, 1971), *The Day of the Full Moon* (*Den' polnoluniia*, Karen Shakhnazarov, 1998) and *The Kopeck* (*Kopeika*, Ivan Dykhovichnyy, 2002). Of course, the montage connections between unrelated characters across diverse social spheres and in different locales make such films as Eisenstein's *Battleship Potemkin* (*Bronenosets Potemkin*, 1925), *Strike* (*Stachka*, 1925) and Vertov's *Man with a Movie Camera* (*Chelovek s kinoapparatom*, 1928) closely connected to Tolstoy's multi-stranded structure. The most genre-conscious vision of Tolstoy's *The Forged Coupon* is Konstantin Buslov's gangster black comedy, *Loot* (2011). *Loot* does not make a direct attribution as an adaptation, but it features many similarities with Tolstoy's tale as well as some telling differences. The forgery is no longer a quotidian 12.5 rubles, but a dreamy one million euros. In Buslov's treatment this is no longer a moral tale, but a gangster heist comedy that ridicules police corruption and equates it with the squalid activities of regular gangsters – neither grouping exhibiting any noteworthy morality. Tolstoy's themes of redemption and character transformation are absent. Here a thief remains a thief and corruption permeates every aspect of society, uniting rich and poor. The story is about a criminal network's pursuit of a bag of money – and it is hard to tell whether it is the real money or counterfeit notes made by the police to capture the Tax Police's corruption red-handed on behalf of slick but corrupt businessmen. The money escapes and its pursuers chase it with increasing desperation. The positive, redemptive version of the relay passing on forged cash as a cross-section narrative replicates Tolstoy's accusatory social realist critique of the damage done to society by deceit, corruption of the church and State, the depravity of the bourgeoisie, the evils of money and the absence of an all-embracing moral unity. It is described by the director as a 'corruption comedy'.[20] As with Tolstoy's tale, it ultimately does hit that moral moment at the conclusion with its circular structure providing social redemption that re-integrates the money into the community, leaving the hardened criminals empty-handed.

Unlike the other adaptations *Loot* is clearly a genre film and, uncommonly for Russia, abides by the genre rules. Although most adaptations of *The Forged Coupon* examine criminal activity – murder, forgery and injustice – they are not crime genre films. *L'Argent* comes closest in that it deals explicitly with

---

[20] Lidiia Maslova, 'Nastoiashchaia zhizn' fal'shivykh deneg', *Kommersant*, 7 October 2011 <https://www.kommersant.ru/doc/1783017> [accessed 22 November 2021].

Figure 9.1 Kakha (Mishiko Meskhi) and Vazha (Giia Gogishvili), *Loot*, directed by Konstantin Buslov, 2011.

crime and its consequences: the characters do not start off as criminals but become so through circumstance. *Loot* follows the spirit of Tolstoy's narrative, but unlike in Tolstoy's tale, everyone who comes in contact with the money dreams of what good things they will do with the cash before being deceived. Some plan to use the money to open a petrol station, others dream of a hotel in Spain, while yet others just want to grab the money and run. There is no issue of forgiveness as dirty deals, double-crossing and deceit are an integral part of this informal criminal community. They are unrepentant and unashamed. The moment of redemption experienced by the audience rather than the characters is the final scene when the cops and their partners, who are celebrating the return of the million euros, suddenly discover it has disappeared. The audience sees that the briefcase has been taken by the put-upon nameless chauffeur of one of the 'legit' businessmen. The shaven-headed driver smiles as he boards the metro amidst a full carriage – symbolically reintegrating the dirty money back into the community.

All these films – *Twenty Bucks, The Adventures of a Ten Mark Note, Frozen Land, L'Argent, Loot* – share plot structures; the theme of money as a curse; counterfeiting as a crisis of financial order; a circular narrative where money returns and there is no escape from the cycle of corruption; a cross-sectional, anti-hierarchical connection with all social layers; and an energy of contingency that interprets fate and destiny. The forged coupon disappears from Tolstoy's tale at the time when the peasant Ivan Mironov is interned by the police and bribes his way out of jail. He leaves the jail without the forgery. The coupon ends up in the pocket of the arresting policeman, a topic echoed in *Loot* where police are at the centre of the corruption. The coupon is not activated again, but its impact and the connections that it generated continue to influence the characters throughout the rest of the story.

FROZEN LAND: THE TRAUMA OF THE ETERNAL RETURN

Frozen Land (*Paha Maa*, 2005), Finnish director Aku Louhimies' third feature, is an attributed adaptation of *The Forged Coupon* that makes direct in-film references to Tolstoy's source material. It is a film rich in dark existentialist drama. Driving the narrative is the structural logic of Tolstoy's episodic narrative, the counterfeit note, and the notion of passing on evil from one person to the next. But contrary to Tolstoy this film offers an alternative solution to dealing with social evil. At its heart is the cry of existentialist angst in which the chief perpetrator of the initial scam asks in a eulogy that bookends the film:

> NIKO – What's the point of living, if this life is merely hell? But we have to believe that in the end things work out for the best. Otherwise, nothing makes any sense.[21]

Set in a grey, bleak Helsinki, the entire cycle of misery makes perfect sense. The film is peopled by disparate lost souls who criss-cross each other's ill-fated paths as they make their way across the frozen city, and perversely it is the misery created by the forged note that brings people together. Most of the characters are depressives, maniacs, alcoholics and drug addicts. Those who initially appear normal are soon ripped apart. Good people are destroyed by society, the city or their friends and family. In this land, there is little light or hope or community, but all the characters are pre-determined to connect at some unexpected point.

Frozen Land is a consciously existentialist examination of the fraught relationship between contingency and narrative order, authenticity and bad faith, choice and responsibility, and the sense that ultimately death is the only solution to meaningless existence. It plays with Tolstoy's key themes of evil and forgiveness more consciously than *L'Argent*, establishing a three-way dialogue between the two films and the story. Noel Megahey notes that 'more than just adapting the story to the screen, or even remaking Bresson's 1983 film version of the story, *L'Argent*, the director expands the theme and brings it up to date in order to consider the additional social impact of drugs, alcohol, depression,

---

[21] Niko's eulogy from the opening scene of *Frozen Land* (directed by Aku Louhimies, Solar Films, 2005).

and unemployment on the delicate balance of the human psyche'.[22] *Frozen Land* provides an alternative moral commentary on the evil and its process of communication. In this frozen land, evil is not squashed with the shocking recognition of the power of goodness. Evil triumphs. Contrary to Tolstoy's moral teachings that inscribe the second part of the story as an optimistic transfiguration, Louhimies crafts a disturbing tale where the conclusion is one of vengeance and death in the face of meaninglessness.

Unlike Tolstoy's story, the forged €500 note is not the inciting incident, but it does connect the three otherwise disconnected stories and becomes a link in a broader chain of malevolent events. *Frozen Land* starts with a sacking and ends with shooting, going full circle to the initial perpetrator's existential eulogy. Its plot is a disturbing chain reaction of mishaps and mistakes where each character, not through fate, but by choice, passes on their misfortune, their pain and their agony to someone else. Just as Fedor Mikhailovich, in Tolstoy's story, is angered by the Governor's bureaucratic bungle that precipitates his bad mood and leads to his taking his frustration out on his son, so too is the action in *Frozen Land* precipitated by the bureaucratic decision to cut a school's literature programme. A popular literature teacher, Mr Smolander, presents the idea of how evil is passed on from one person to another in Tolstoy's *The Forged Coupon* to his literature class. He draws the scheme on the blackboard: 'Person A shoves it onto person B who cannot help but shove it onto person C.' After the class, Smolander is informed by the principal that he is to be made redundant despite his popularity so that the school can concentrate on more vocational teaching. We meet the new IT teacher, Antti, in the corridor. Smolander turns to alcohol and takes out his frustration on his lazy teenage son, Niko (the Finnish Mitia). In a fit of rage, Smolander kicks his son out of the apartment onto the freezing streets. The now homeless Niko visits his hacker friend Tuomas and asks to stay, but Tuomas's girlfriend, Elina, opposes the idea as she finds Niko disgusting. That night they go to a cocaine- and alcohol-fuelled New Year's Eve party where Niko makes a fool of himself. Stumbling around the fancy apartment he discovers Tuomas's perfectly designed €500 note on a computer and, despite clear instructions to leave the computer alone, Niko prints out the note. He leaves the party and buys a CD player in a pawnshop, thereby passing on the forged note and pocketing the genuine change.

The fake note is then circulated on to the guileless, mullet-headed Isto. When he attempts to pay for dinner with the note, he is apprehended and thrown in jail. After his release Isto finds his car vandalised. So to pass on the negative energy, he breaks into a car yard, steals the most expensive car, and goes on an all-night bender. That evening he meets Teuvo, a door-to-door

---

[22] Noel Megahey, 'Frozen Land DVD Review', *DVD Times*, 10 May 2007 <www.dvd-times.co.uk/content.php?contentid=64821> [accessed 12 July 2021].

Figure 9.2 Niko Smolander (Jasper Pääkkönen) teaching, *Frozen Land*, directed by Aku Louhimies, 2005.

vacuum-cleaner salesman who has just had his car cruelly repossessed by the owner of the car yard that Isto had broken into earlier. Teuvo is a recovering alcoholic, but Isto convinces him to have a drink and the evening spirals out of control. In a fit of jealous rage, Teuvo murders his new friend Isto and his lover, bashing them to death with his vacuum cleaner. He then uses the vacuum to clean up. Teuvo leaves the scene of the crime just as the overworked and depressed policewoman, Hannele, is dispatched to investigate.

When Teuvo sobers up he realises what he has done and attempts to commit suicide. He tries to gas himself unsuccessfully in Isto's stolen 4WD. Meanwhile, Tuomas and his pregnant girlfriend Elina are planning a heist of her father's IT business. They ask Niko to keep watch while Tuomas breaks into the office. But Niko fails to inform Tuomas in time when the police turn up. One of the police officers in pursuit of Tuomas is Hannele. She tracks him to the railway but is knocked down by a train. Tuomas is sent to prison for his part in Hannele's death. The lives of her husband, Antti, and their three children are destroyed, as Antti undergoes a complete breakdown and decides to give their children up to the welfare services. When Tuomas is released from jail a few years later, his world has changed. Elina has raised their son as a single mother with the help of Niko who has been in a relationship with her. Niko now works in his father's old school, teaching Tolstoy's *The Forged Coupon* in the context of a scriptwriting class. Tuomas reconciles with Elina and Niko, meets his son for the first time, and asks Antti for his forgiveness, but his gesture is rejected. We then come full circle, returning to the eulogy that Niko was reading at the start, but with a deeper understanding of the existential horror of the eternal return of the relay chain that offers the characters no escape.

The story begins and ends with the fundamental question as to whether life is worth living and if there is any sense to it all. The discourse of the film suggests otherwise – that narrative order creates chance meetings and suggests that connections make sense, but that life is meaningless and that its end is angst followed by vengeance and death. As in the other film adaptations, the counterfeit €500 passes into social circulation and connects a group of disparate denizens. It disappears relatively early in the plot to allow the connections generated by its power to percolate and take on a life of their own. The film is not about the evil of money, although its absence does precipitate the poor state in which most of the characters find themselves. Unlike Tolstoy's initial stimulus of honour under threat, the precipitating moment is when the principal, acting perhaps in line with state policy, destroys the school's literature programme and dismisses its star teacher. It could be seen that this action, rather than the forgery, led to the ensuing social catastrophe. The scholar Kate Moffat argues that *Frozen Land* makes a case for questioning the egality and function of the Finnish welfare state: 'Finland's small population meant that in order to build a sustainable and egalitarian model, a significant level of cooperation and consensus was required between the state and its citizens.'[23] *Frozen Land* shows just how little cooperation exists, and while it may not be representative of the real situation in Finland, and it may not necessarily exploit a political position, thematically the film challenges the welfare state, the unity of the social contract in a situation in which not all citizens are signing up to the limitations imposed in a system that denies freedom and individuality. It is impossible to ignore a social critique here of the failings of the Finnish welfare state.

The film operates with the theory that one person invariably passes on their misfortune to someone else in an endless cycle without an ability to choose not to pass on their vengeance, to choose freedom from convention. Unlike other adaptations, the characters in the film are largely lower working class and there is no attempt to capture an entire social sphere or a sense of class consciousness – all the characters are equally unhappy. Unlike Tolstoy, Louhimies does not offer an optimistic social alternative or a solution. But each of the characters does have a choice whether to give in to their base impulses or allow reason and civic consciousness to prevail. Like Tolstoy's Stepan, who

---

[23] Kate Moffat, 'Re-thinking Crisis Politics in the Films of Aku Louhimies', in *Cinema of Crisis: Film and Contemporary Europe*, eds Thomas Austin and Angelos Koutsourakis (Edinburgh: Edinburgh University Press, 2020), pp. 93–104 (p. 95).

makes a major effort to transform himself and by his deeds spread goodness as redemption from past sins, so Antti makes an effort to stop the waves of evil from sweeping away his children. Recognising that he is going off the rails, he puts them in foster care.

Frozen Land ignores Tolstoy's themes of repentance and forgiveness. As soon as he is released from jail, Tuomas asks Antti for forgiveness. In response, Antti invites Tuomas to accompany him to the plot of frozen land where five years earlier he and his family scattered his wife's ashes. Over the past five years, Antti, the once bright young man, the future of the school where Niko's father had previously worked, is now broken. Standing by the frozen lake, Antti draws a gun – his wife's former service revolver. We expect that, with his hand quivering, Antti will put away the gun, in that great film cliché of a man with a pointed gun who deliberates but invariably recoils from murder. Against expectations, Antti shoots Tuomas. He shoots the man who has repented, who has served time in jail, who has asked earnestly for his forgiveness. But Antti has not forgiven. He shoots Tuomas and leaves. Is this the moment that evil continues to spread, or did he close the circle with that radical moment of revenge? We do not know what happens to Antti later. He has nothing to give and nothing of value to be taken away. It is not clear whether his burden is lifted with the retribution. We do not know if this sense of evil is passed on. Narratively, that is the end of the chain of evil, but his murderous choice has wide-ranging implications for the rest of the community and does not necessarily bring closure.

This is a significant departure from Tolstoy's tale, but there remains redemption of sorts through a stoic love of fate and suffering. Niko, a latter-day drug-taking slothful Mitia, is responsible for carelessly putting the forgery into circulation. Is he responsible for destroying Tuomas, Isto, and the vacuum-cleaner salesman? He does not seek forgiveness. Rather he tries to destroy, lower, prostitute and punish himself to quench his angst through suffering. But after he has hit rock bottom, we see that he rebuilds his life and carries on the work of his father – lecturing to students at the same school about chaos theory and good and evil. In a deeply structured narrative such as this – there is little chaos – all the characters' paths are bound to crisscross. They interconnect. But what of the future in this pessimistic cycle? How should we comprehend what happens later? Will Niko become a great teacher like his father, repeating a family destiny, but then be forced out for being too popular and the cycle of ill fate begins to repeat itself? There is no response to the existential question of the point of living a hellish life because, apart from Niko's transformation, nothing in that frozen land has changed or defrosted. The answer to the question about the point of living could be the shared audience experience of suffering and of the cinematic exploration of existentialist philosophy. As Robert Solomon asserts, existentialism's attitude recognizes the unresolvable confusion of the human world, yet resists the all-too-human temptation to resolve the confusion by grasping toward whatever appears or can be made to appear firm or familiar – reason, God, nation, authority, history, work, tradition or the 'other-worldly', whether of Plato, Christianity, or utopian fantasy.[24]

In Niko's character, Louhimies' existentialist individual comes through suffering and the experience of his friend's death to contemplate the realisation of self-consciousness and the capacity at least to recognise the trauma of the eternal return.

Pay It Forward: Reversing Tolstoy's Cycle of Degradation

In contrast to the nihilistic *Frozen Land*, the film *Pay It Forward* offers an alternative solution to Tolstoy's problem by offering a folk alternative to the narrative of dystopian vengeance passed on. Close in spirit to the often dismissed second part of Tolstoy's story – the path to redemption of many characters – Mimi Leder's adaptation of Catherine Ryan Hyde's book explores the social impact of a systematised, indirect reciprocity of good deeds as an ever-expanding chain that unites the entire social sphere. It offers a reverse understanding of Tolstoy's cycle of degradation as typical of the modern world.

The film starts with an existential moment of anguish when 11-year-old Trevor realises looking around his backyard that 'everything sucks'. But he does not become apathetic; instead, he starts to think systematically about what he can do to change his life. On the first day of school Trevor's class is set an assignment by their new social studies teacher: 'think of an idea to change our world and put it into action.'[25] Trevor's plan is to do three major favours for people, obligating them to do favours for others, and so on until the whole world is helped by this utopian three favour pyramid scheme. In the process, Trevor helps at least two people: his alcoholic mother and a homeless man with a heroin addiction. But his attempt to help a boy who is being bullied at school ends tragically.

Frederic and Mary Ann Brussat suggest that '*Pay It Forward* dares to point us in a different direction [. . .] It boldly reveals that kindness and putting others first are acts of moral beauty.'[26] Of course, this idealistic system is limited – why

---

[24] Robert Solomon, *From Hegel to Existentialism* (New York: Oxford University Press, 1987), p. 238.

[25] This is said by Eugene Simonet (Kevin Spacey) in encouraging his seventh-grade students with an extra credit assignment that goes all year long in an early scene in *Pay It Forward* (directed by Mimi Leder, Warner, 2000).

[26] Frederic and Mary Ann Brussat, 'Pay It Forward: A Values & Visions Guide', *Spirituality Practice*, 2000 <http://www.spiritualityandpractice.com/films/vvcfeatures.php?id=14967> [accessed 12 August 2021].

only three favours to bring personal contentment? It could be seen as a selfish desire to do good for personal pleasure or a self-centred desire to control the world through a chain of tradable obligations. As a reviewer, Qiu Jin reasons, in a scathing analysis of the film, that:

> the wealthy lawyer in the movie could have sold his Jaguar for maybe $50,000 and donated this to the revolution. Instead, as if on a whim, he just gives the car to the oppressor-nation journalist closest to him, and the audience is left with the impression that suddenly the bourgeoisie doesn't really care about having wealth.[27]

Trevor starts out idealistically committed to his pay-it-forward scheme, but is ultimately forced to admit the pitfalls of his proposition, and that is when he and the audience recognise that the world is inhabited by people who do not all have good intentions. Evil and power reside alongside good deeds and utopian economies. Trevor is not like Tolstoy's Stepan and his endless self-effacing commitment to atoning for his sins. Nonetheless, there is something positive in the idea of 'seeking to change the world one favour at a time'[28] and the film parallels Tolstoy's messianic urge to pass forward goodness in a unified community and not to confront evil with force.

Conclusion by Way of the Opposite of Fate

In a binary world, chaos would be the opposite of fate. Tolstoy's mechanistic narrative, and its rigorous organisation of the relay events that spread evil like a networked contagion across the entire social spectrum, is the opposite of chaos. Everything is planned out. Tolstoy invested considerable attention in the role of fate in his literary works. He denies the possibility of chance, the operation of chaos, or the freedom to choose with a deep commitment to the inevitability of fate. For the American novelist Amy Tan, the opposite of fate, both blind and blessed, is:

> choice, chance, luck, faith, forgiveness, forgetting, freedom of expression, the pursuit of happiness, the balm of love, a sturdy attitude, a strong will, a bevy of good-luck charms, adherence to rituals, appeasement through prayer, trolling for miracles [. . .] and one all-encompassing thing: hope.[29]

---

[27] Qiu Jin, 'Pay It Forward dabbles in sub-reformism and utopianism, and puts down revolutionary young people', *Maoist Internationalist Movement* <http://www.prison-censorship.info/archive/etext/movies/long/payit.html> [accessed 6 March 2021].

[28] Trevor calls for this in *Pay It Forward*.

[29] Amy Tan, *The Opposite of Fate* (London: HarperCollins, 2003), p. 3.

These sentiments resonate with Tolstoy's philosophy, but not his approach to narrative or perception of fate. What motivates the characters in the first part of the novella and in *Frozen Land* is not fate but choice – they choose to shut down the literature department, they choose to start drinking, to forge a banknote, to murder. Perhaps, at that moment, they were free and they did not consider the consequences. Undoubtedly there is a social component and not an individual issue – where the social contract condones this type of behaviour that is far from the brotherhood of man. *Frozen Land* could be seen as a cautionary tale – the interconnectedness of our society means that a thoughtless or even evil deed will come back to haunt the perpetrator. We could, as I have argued in this chapter, reconsider and rehabilitate Tolstoy's notion of evil because in the film adaptations it has a dual meaning: criminal amoral activities and, consequently, a way of bringing people together to combat disenfranchisement and disconnection where the dynamics of evil could be seen as an antidote to loneliness.

What the various adaptations of *The Forged Coupon* have in common is a fascination with evil, chance, fate, order, choice and redemption. The novella and its film versions emphasise structure and its metaphor as a montage. There is no escape from fate as narrative structure and the inevitability of narrative control. Tolstoy set up a tension between fate and chance, amplified the contingency, but created characters who make choices about their lives and are not narrative pawns. Iurii Lotman was wrong when he claimed that it was impossible to adapt *The Forged Coupon* as a film. In over 100 years of cinema, a complex network of films have all in some way passed on an idea, whether by design or by chance, in an uncontrolled relay that connects recent films to the cinematic past. Tolstoy's cinematic novella has emerged and re-emerged as an international cultural influence, whether explicitly quoted and referenced or as a trace element connecting different films from different epochs and cinematic cultures. Even if Tolstoy's final novella remains impossible to adapt, it lends itself to various adaptations that maintain a provocative dialogue with Tolstoy's ideas, oscillating between a mechanistic narrative, fate, choice and a metaphysical unity.

Bibliography

Alanen, Antti, 'Film Diary', 2010 <http://anttialanenfilmdiary.blogspot.com.au/2010/04/k13-513-die-abenteuer-eines.html> [accessed 9 January 2021].

Bordwell, David, *Poetics of Cinema* (London: Routledge, 2007).

Bortolotti, Gary R. and Linda Hutcheon, 'On the Origin of Adaptations: Rethinking Fidelity Discourse and "Success" – Biologically', *New Literary History*, 38 (2007), pp. 443–58.

Brussat, Frederic and Mary Ann Brussat, 'Pay It Forward: A Values & Visions Guide', *Spirituality Practice*, 2000 <http://www.spiritualityandpractice.com/films/vvcfeatures.php?id=14967> [accessed 12 August 2021].

Diffrient, David Scott, 'Stories that Objects Might Live to Tell: The "Hand-Me-Down" Narrative in Film', *Other Voices*, 3 (2007) <http://www.othervoices.org/3.1/sdiffrient/index.php> [accessed 20 August 2021].

Gudzii N.K., 'Commentary to *The Forged Coupon*', in L. N. Tolstoi, *Polnoe sobranie sochinenii*, 90 vols (Moscow-Leningrad: Khudozhestvennaia literatura, 1928–58). XXXVI (1936), p. 557.

Jones, Kent, *L'Argent* (London: BFI Film Classics, Bloomsbury Publishing, 1999).

Kliger, Ilya and Nasser Zakariya, 'Poetics of Brotherhood: Organic and Mechanistic Narrative in Late Tolstoi', *Slavic Review*, 70 (2011), pp. 754–72.

Lotman, Iurii, 'Popytki predskazat' interesny v toi mere v kakoi oni ne opravdyvaiutsia'. Interview with Iurii Lotman by Iurii Tsivian and Mikhail Iampolski, Rezekne, May-June 1986, *Kinovedcheskie zapiski*, 20 (1993/4), pp. 4–11 <http://vivovoco.astronet.ru/VV/PAPERS/LOTMAN/KINO.HTM > [accessed 21 August 2021].

Megahey, Noel, 'Frozen Land DVD Review', *DVD Times*, 10 May 2007 <www.dvdtimes.co.uk/content.php?contentid=64821> [accessed 12 July 2021].

Miles, Adrian, '*L'Argent*', *Senses of Cinema*, 7 (2000) <http://www.sensesofcinema.com/2000/cteq/largent-2/> [accessed 25 July 2021].

Moffat, Kate, 'Re-thinking Crisis Politics in the Films of Aku Louhimies', in *Cinema of Crisis: Film and Contemporary Europe*, eds Thomas Austin and Angelos Koutsourakis (Edinburgh: Edinburgh University Press, 2020), pp. 93–104.

Morson, Gary Saul, *Narrative and Freedom: The Shadows of Time* (New Haven and London: Yale University Press, 1994).

Orwin, Donna, 'Introduction', *The Cambridge Companion to Tolstoy*, ed. Donna Orwin (Cambridge: Cambridge University Press, 2002), pp. 49–62.

Porudominsky, Vladimir, 'Iz zametok daleveda. Davnii dolg', *Voprosy literatury*, 6 (2001), pp. 132–54.

Qiu Jin, 'Pay It Forward dabbles in sub-reformism and utopianism, and puts down revolutionary young people', *Maoist Internationalist Movement* <http://www.prisoncensorship.info/archive/etext/movies/long/payit.html> [accessed 6 March 2021].

Simmons, Ernest, *Introduction to Tolstoy's Writings* (Chicago: University of Chicago Press, 1968) <http://www.ourcivilisation.com/smartboard/shop/smmnsej/tolstoy/chap10.htm> [accessed 5 July 2021].

Solomon, Robert, *From Hegel to Existentialism* (New York: Oxford University Press, 1987).

Somoff, Victoria, 'Nonresistance to Fiction: Archaic Folktale vs Later Tolstoy', *The Slavic and East European Journal*, 60 (2016), pp. 284–306.

Tan, Amy, *The Opposite of Fate* (London: HarperCollins, 2003).

Tolstoy, Leo, *The Forged Coupon and Other Stories*, Project Gutenberg <http://www.gutenberg.org/files/243/243-h/243-h.htm> [accessed May 2020].

Filmography

The Adventures of a Ten Mark Bank Note (*Die Abenteuer eines Zehnmarkscheines*), directed by Berthold Viertel (Germany, Deutsche Vereins-Film AG Defa-Deutsche Fox, 1926).

L'Argent, directed by Robert Bresson (France, Eôs Films, France 3 Cinéma, Marion's Films, 1983).

The Counterfeit Note (*Fal'shivyi kupon*), directed by Petr Chardynin (Russia, A. Khanzhonkov & Co., 1913).

Frozen Land (*Paha Maa*), directed by Aku Louhimies (Finland, Solar Films, 2005).

The Kopeck (*Kopeika*), directed by Ivan Dykhovichnyy (Russia, Etalon Film, 2002).

Loot (*Bablo*), directed by Konstantine Buslov (Russia, CTB Film Company, 2011).

The Million Pound Note, directed by Ronald Neame (UK, Group Film Productions Limited, 1954).

Pay It Forward, directed by Mimi Leder (USA, Warner, 2000).

Twenty Bucks, directed by Keva Rosenfeld (USA, Big Tomorrow Productions, 1993).

10. WAR AND PEACE: A NEW VISUAL DIMENSION

Olga Sobolev

> Literature will not perish in cinematography but will only use its mercenary greed and will come to life in the bright rays of the screen.
>
> – Leo Tolstoy[1]

Tolstoy's relationship with cinema was upbeat from the very first days when the new art of 'motion pictures' made its appearance in the Russian arena. Known for his proverbial dislike of theatre, he developed a lively interest in cinematography, seeing it not as the essence of artifice, but as a fascinating way of rendering the real.[2] The attraction was mutual. During the last years of his life, Tolstoy featured in several documentaries and newsreels; and his works – shorter texts, as well as novels – were adapted for the screen from 1909 onwards.[3] The idea of compressing a large volume of text into a short film did not seem to stop directors, and in 1915 three leading Russian filmmakers, almost in competition with each other, produced three different versions of *War and Peace* (*Natasha*

---

[1] Isaak Teneromo, 'Tolstoi o kinematografe', *Kino: Dvukhnedel'nik Obshchestva kinoizdatelei*, 2 (1922), pp. 3–4 (p. 4).

[2] Isaak Teneromo, who discussed the new art of cinematography with Tolstoy, testifies to the author's enthusiastic comments: 'But I actually like it. This quick change of scenes, the overflow of moods, cascades of experiences – really, it is better than this sticky dragging out of the plot. If you like, it is closer to life [. . .] Cinematography has solved the mystery of movement. And this is great' (Teneromo, p. 3).

[3] In 1909, D. W. Griffith, a founding father of the feature film, produced a twelve-minute-long screen version of Tolstoy's *Resurrection*. The film did not survive, but in principle Tolstoy could have watched it before his death in 1910.

Rostova, directed by Petr Chardynin; *War and Peace*, directed by Vladimir Gardin and Iakov Protazanov; and *War and Peace*, produced by the Drankov company and directed by Anatolii Kamensky). Their interest was not entirely coincidental: given the political context of the day, these screenings were most evidently triggered by the outbreak of the First World War. Since then, for more than a hundred years, Russian and foreign filmmakers have been returning to Tolstoy's 1869 epic; at present, there are five Western and three Russian adaptations of the novel (Table 10.1, excluding silent films).[4]

Table 10.1. Screen Adaptations of Tolstoy's *War and Peace*

Title (year)	Director	Production	Duration
War and Peace (1956)	King Vidor	Ponti-De Laurentiis Cinematografica	3h 28 min
Also People/Tozhe liudi (1959), based on a single episode from the novel	Georgii Daneliia	Mosfilm	14 min
War and Peace (1963)	Silvio Narizzano	Granada Television, TV series	2h 45 min
War and Peace/ Voina i mir (1965–67)	Sergei Bondarchuk	Mosfilm	7h 11 min (4 parts)
War and Peace (1972)	John Davies (script by Jack Pulman)	BBC, TV Series	14h 50 min (20 episodes)
War and Peace (2007)	Robert Dornhelm	Rai 1, RTBF, France 2, TV Mini-Series	6h 34 min (4 episodes)
War and Peace/ Voina i mir (2012), based on 3 short episodes from the novel	Mariia Pankratova, Andrei Grachev	TV Channel Zvezda	32 min (3 episodes)
War and Peace (2016)	Tom Harper (script by Andrew Davies)	BBC, TV series	6h 19 min (6 episodes)

[4] Unsurprisingly (due to the length of the novel), there are more television versions than feature films. Regarding the latter, it is also worth mentioning Woody Allen's comedy *Love and Death* (1975) – a satire on Russian literature, which refers to several nineteenth-century Russian works, including *War and Peace*.

The fact that *War and Peace* remains a popular choice for modern directors prompts a series of questions concerning the very nature of the dialogue implied in the process of text-to-screen adaptation. Can this interest be simply attributed to the inexhaustible potential of Tolstoy's thought, which allows for more and more layers to be discovered by new generations of readers? Or does it bear witness to the overall development of the cinematic means of expression, which allows modern filmmakers to achieve a higher degree of artistry, and thus 'open up' the richness of Tolstoy's text? In this regard, it is worth noting that Western screen adaptations have certain 'advantages', since they are made in the context of a higher degree of estrangement from the original national style, cultural memory and tradition, bringing out the transnational elements of a canonical work. Finally, it is worth taking into account the benefits of commercial success, firmly associated with screening a major classical novel. All these points will constitute the framework of the present discussion. The focus will be on the latest TV version of *War and Peace*, released by the BBC in 2016. Without disregarding other screen adaptations of the novel, the BBC series will be compared to the Russian four-part film directed in 1967 by Sergei Bondarchuk.[5] The latter is commonly regarded as a canonical example of the so-called 'fidelity' approach to the process of adapting for the screen. The chapter will discuss the validity of such an approach within the modern-day social and cultural context. Special emphasis is placed on the role of screen adaptations as an effective means of cultural branding, as well as on the problems of interaction between literature and film in the modern cultural space.

'It's a Good Thing to Chop Out the Boring Bits' from Tolstoy's Text[6]

The adaptation of *War and Peace* was a strategic project for the BBC's public standing. In 2015 the novel had attracted large audiences when it was dramatised on Radio 4.[7] And it is no coincidence that 2016, a year in which the BBC had to agree a new charter and licence fee settlement with the British government, began

---

[5] Bondarchuk's big-screen version of the novel was originally released in a series of four separate parts, with an overall running time of 431 minutes (c. 7 hours). The format of this work (akin to a serialised adaptation) validates its comparison with the 2016 BBC TV series. It also echoes the original serial publication of the novel. It was the first Soviet film to win the Oscar (1968) for the Best Foreign Language Film.

[6] Stephen Smith, '"It's good to chop out the boring bits!": Andrew Davies on adapting War and Peace', *The Spectator* (Australia), 23 January 2016 <https://www.spectator.com.au/2016/01/its-good-to-chop-out-the-boring-bits-andrew-davies-on-adapting-war-and-peace/> [accessed 1 September 2021].

[7] BBC Radio 4 allocated ten hours of its New Year's Day schedule for broadcasting the novel.

with a new televised version of *War and Peace*. A symbolic reference was thus made to the success of the 1972 TV adaptation of the novel, which itself was part of an attempt to boost public confidence in the BBC's reputation. Scripted by Jack Pulman and directed by John Davies, the 1972 series was released at a time when the corporation was emerging from an earlier fight with the government for its autonomy and social standing. It was an award-winning production, which has always been regarded as one of the company's major achievements.

The new 2016 series of *War and Peace* was also an uncontested commercial success. Seven million people – an impressive figure for British television with its dozens of channels – regularly returned to their screens to plunge into the alluring world of Tolstoy's work.[8] The script was written by Andrew Davies, who not unlike Jack Pulman two decades before him,[9] had made a name for

Figure 10.1 Natasha Rostova (Lily James) and Prince Andrei Bolkonsky (James Norton) at Natasha's first ball, *War and Peace*, directed by Tom Harper, BBC TV series, 2016.

---

[8] According to YouGov (a global public opinion and data company), the exact figure was 6.95 million. This was more than tuned into the soap opera *Coronation Street* (6.82 million) and not far behind the talent competition *The Voice* (7.87 million) – the most popular series broadcast during the same month (Will Dahlgreen, '*War and Peace*: the classic Brits are most likely to want to read (but that very few have read)', *YouGov*, 20 January 2016 <https://yougov.co.uk/topics/lifestyle/articles-reports/2016/01/20/war-and-peace-tops-britains-classic-fiction-wishli)> [accessed 1 September 2021]).

[9] Jack Pulman's screen adaptations include *The Portrait of a Lady* (1968), *David Copperfield* (1969), *Jane Eyre* (1970) and *Crime and Punishment* (1979).

himself by adapting capacious classic novels (including an award-winning production of Jane Austen's *Pride and Prejudice* [1995], her *Sense and Sensibility* [2008], Dickens's *Bleak House* [2005] and Pasternak's *Doctor Zhivago* [2002]). His series was carefully thought through, impressively designed, and adjusted to the realities of modern-day culture, concerned simultaneously with education and the attention span of the viewers.

The overall pace assumed in this work was much quicker than that achieved in the series written by Pulman. Viewers of the 1972 version were gradually immersed into the story by watching footmen setting plates on Count Rostov's dinner table practically in real-time – something that is hardly credible by present-day standards. The new BBC series opened with a focused account of the 1805 political context (involving Russia, Austria and France), run across the screen in a set of brief captions. This was followed by the young Pierre Bezukhov's swift stride through the streets of St Petersburg and directly into a ball. The eye-catching display of the latter was effectively permeated by snappy shots of high-society chatter, which left no doubt that Napoleon's conquests in Western Europe had begun to stir fears in Russia as well. By the end of the first episode, Andrew Davies had managed to advance the narrative as far as the 1972 adaptation had done only in week five. All the major characters had been introduced, and their circumstances outlined: the revolutionary romantic Pierre Bezukhov (Paul Dano), the decorous and composed Prince Andrei (James Norton) and the irresistibly charming Natasha Rostova (Lily James).

All dramatic adaptations are a form of cultural appropriation, a declaration of love, a manifestation of the Oedipus complex and a critical statement, which reveals itself, at least partly, through the degree of fidelity to the original work.[10] And the question here is not of whether the adaptor managed to fit in a higher or lower proportion of the content, but of his ability to conduct a creative dialogue with the author, highlighting and refracting the semantic field of the original through the lens of present-day mentalities and concerns.

Such an interpretative dialogue hardly came across as a strong feature of Andrew Davies's adaptation. He was completely transparent regarding his approach to abbreviating Tolstoy's novel (a necessary stage in the process of screening), 'It's a good thing to chop out the boring bits!' from the text, he claimed. 'It contains long passages that shouldn't be in novels: essays about history and philosophy and the theory of war [. . .] And you don't need any of that as long as ideas emerge through characters, and you can make that happen.'[11]

---

[10] As Otto Boele notes in his analysis of the adaptation of Tolstoy's *The Death of Ivan Il'ich* (Chapter 8, p. 184), the repetitiveness of the anti-fidelity rhetoric in modern-day scholarly research 'demonstrates that the concept of fidelity itself is not entirely useless'.

[11] Smith, '"It's good to chop out the boring bits!": Andrew Davies on adapting War and Peace'.

Davies's view undoubtedly offers a valid adaptive strategy for screening an epic. However, it may present certain difficulties when it comes to producing a visual correlative of a novel of such considerable meta-textual complexity as Tolstoy's work. Public opinion typically associates *War and Peace* with intellectual and aesthetic ambition. As an epitome of serious and beautiful prose, the novel offers extensive reflections on human psychology, politics and philosophy, securing its position in the consecrated highbrow regions of the cultural space. According to Simon Schama's account of the novel,

> stylistically, it was also unlike anything anyone else had written before: raw, richly inelegant, sometimes directionless, bursting through the confines of good literary form yet stained on every page with the juice of life [. . .] You emerge from this total immersion with your emotions deepened, vision clarified, [and] exposure to the casual cruelty of the powerful sharpened.[12]

This kind of elevating experience was not on offer for viewers of the 2016 series. Not unlike all previous Western adaptors, Davies structured his script as a triple account of the Bolkonsky and Rostov family chronicles, Pierre's story as an illegitimate child, and the burgeoning romance between Natasha and Prince Andrei. All six episodes were tightly linked; and each of them displayed a neatly shaped dramatic progression, and yet the narrative acquired a sterile and simplistic touch, being refracted through the recognisable clichés of a typical costume drama. Significantly, it bypassed a whole range of the complicating, and at times indeed 'directionless' discursive branches,[13] laying bare the basic scheme of a generic family saga in the novel and creating a popular version of a melodramatic tale at the expense of Tolstoy's work. As Davies claimed in a comment made when beginning his work on the adaptation in 2013, there was absolutely 'no need to dumb it down for the mass modern audiences':[14] the interaction between characters and their families would be 'very familiar' to fans of BBC1's soap *EastEnders*, but with 'not so much yelling and nobody on the dole'.[15]

---

[12] Simon Schama, 'What Tolstoy's "War and Peace" can teach us', *Financial Times*, 8 January 2016 <https://www.ft.com/content/8a003e2c-b497-11e5-8358-9a82b43f6b2f> [accessed 1 September 2021].

[13] Ibid.

[14] John Plunkett, 'BBC Returns to Tolstoy's War and Peace', *The Guardian*, 18 February 2013 <https://www.theguardian.com/media/2013/feb/18/bbc-returns-tolstoy-war-peace> [accessed 1 September 2021].

[15] Plunkett, 'BBC Returns to Tolstoy's War and Peace'.

The same kind of 'straightening out' formula was applied to characterisation. There are certain discursive features of Tolstoy's novel that effectively lend it to the format of screening. The text contains numerous remarks that can be read as script directions. The author specifies the characters' positions in the room, their entrances and their exits, the tone of their voices, their facial expressions, and even gestures performed in the process of interaction. The effect thus created is the remarkable (almost incomparable) *multifacetedness* of Tolstoy's characters. From the very first moments, the reader cannot but notice that his personalities tend to function in several psychological modes, saying one thing, being driven by a completely different set of motives, and at the same time trying to tune in to a further type of intention, burgeoning somewhere deeper in their souls. Tolstoy uses a highly sophisticated palette of colours and shades to portray his characters. By contrast, Davies's figures are essentially monochrome, sketched with primary colours and devoid of any nuanced undertones or shades (with some rare exceptions, as for instance, in Paul Dano's interpretation of Pierre). As a model of sanity, prudent optimism and corrected mistakes, their lives are tinted with neither self-destructive doubt nor existential search. To use a snappy phrase, coined by Lev Anninsky (a prominent cultural critic) in connection with his review of King Vidor's 1956 version of the novel, the interaction of such characters is akin to that of snooker balls on the table: 'Hard and polished, they tend to collide, but invariably bounce back unscratched and unaffected by the collision.'[16] The unparalleled contrapuntal complexity so characteristic of Tolstoy's figures, tormented by the forces of cupidity, vanity and ambition, was completely effaced from Davies's adaptation. And without this meta-textual dimension, it was hardly possible to conduct a meaningful dialogue with Tolstoy.

Cinematic Drama or Melodrama?

In her examination of screen versions of *Anna Karenina* – a novel which presents a similar set of challenges to its adaptors, Irina Makoveeva offers an effective summary of contemporary approaches to cinematic translation.[17] Basing her work on studies by Neia Zorkaia, Geoffrey Wagner and Brian McFarlane,[18] she distinguishes between four types of cinematic adaptation. The first one is *kinolubok* – a type of transposition, which effaces all the individuality of the

---

[16] Lev Anninsky, *Okhota na L'va* (Moscow: Shar, 1998), p. 174.
[17] Irina Makoveeva, 'Cinematic Adaptations of *Anna Karenina*', *Studies in Slavic Cultures*, 2 (2001), pp. 111–33 (pp. 113–14).
[18] Neia Zorkaia, 'Russkaia shkola ekranizatsii', in *Ekrannye iskusstva i literatura. Nemoe kino* (Moscow: Nauka, 1991), pp. 105–30; Geoffrey Wagner, *The Novel and the Cinema* (Rutherford: Fairleigh Dickinson University Press, 1975), pp. 219–31; Brian McFarlane, *Novel to Film* (New York: Oxford University Press, 1996), pp. 1–37.

original work, reducing it to a stock pattern of a love-, murder- or jealousy-story. An *illustration*, on the contrary, is a faithful and obedient rendering of a source text, characterised by meticulous attention to its cinematic correlatives and visual analogies (such as, for instance, portraits, scenery or historical setting). *Interpretation* differs from the first two, as 'it consists of the cinematic embodiment of a literary work, an interpretation of the author's style, and a conception of the original to be achieved through cinematic means'.[19] Geoffrey Wagner supplements this list with an extra type, the, so to speak, *analogy-transposition*,[20] which decontextualises the source-text in order to create a new work of art in a different form (as an example of this type of adaptation, one can mention Louis Malle's *Vanya on 42nd Street*, from 1994[21]). By focusing on the structural features of text-to-screen transposition, Brian McFarlane rationalises the scheme by presenting it as a two-fold process, which for him is based on various degrees of transferring and adapting.[22] Thus, an *illustrative*-type adaptation transfers whatever is possible while blurring or leaving out the elements that resist direct transposition (for instance, characters' inner lives and psychological transformations); *interpretation* 'transfers the most, and modestly adapts those elements that call for it; [and] *analogy* adapts the original and transfers the least'.[23] *Interpretation* or a *commentary*-type adaptation goes further than *illustration* in interpreting the conceptual scheme of the novel, but in distinction to *kinolubok* and *analogy* never violates or disfigures the source-text.

Considering its cliched features of a typical historical melodrama, the BBC series, arguably, falls into the category of *kinolubok* (though not without some elements of an *illustration* – to be discussed later). It affirms all the stereotypes and patterns of 'a story of life and love during the time of conflict' (as Faith Penhale, executive producer of the series, characterised their work),[24] defying

---

[19] Makoveeva, p. 113.
[20] Wagner, pp. 219–31.
[21] For a detailed analysis see Angus Wrenn's account of this film in Chapter 6 of this volume.
[22] Brian McFarlane, p. 21.
[23] Makoveeva, p. 114.
[24] Plunkett, 'BBC Returns to Tolstoy's War and Peace'.

   To bring the series even closer to the standards of a soap-opera, Andrew Davies furnished several provocative scenes for Tolstoy. Critics were frankly puzzled (not to say dismayed) by the overtly incestual moments between Anatole and Helene Kuragin (Tuppence Middleton and Callum Turner), certain piquant details of her terminal illness, as well as some other episodes in the spirit of *Fanny Hill* by John Cleland (Davies adapted this text for the TV screen in 2007) or *Dangerous Liaisons* by Choderlos de Laclos.

expectations that cinema's progression as an artform would eventually efface its initial adherence to the sensational and melodramatic.[25]

This aspect of the production becomes even more pronounced when the BBC series is viewed alongside the *commentary* or *interpretative* type adaptation of *War and Peace* created by Bondarchuk (1967).[26] The two versions are comparable in length (respectively 379 and 431 minutes), as well as in the scope and mastery of their depiction of massive historical battles.[27] The Soviet film, however, was clearly different in its intention, designed to project not only the dramatic impulse, but also the philosophical frame of Tolstoy's work. As Georgii Daneliia – an eminent Russian director, and himself the author of *Tozhe liudi* (*Also People*, 1959), a short film based on a single episode from *War and Peace* – put it:

> Of all the possible ways of working on the film, Sergei Bondarchuk and Vasily Soloviev [the author of the script] have chosen, perhaps, the most difficult, but, from my point of view, the most correct way. In their screening, they tried to convey Tolstoy's thought.[28]

---

[25] In this context, it is worth mentioning that in her examination of the 2007 TV series of *War and Peace* directed by Robert Dornhelm, Christine Engel also centres her argument on the melodramatic nature of this work (Christine Engel, 'Tolstoy Transnational: Dornhelm's Adaptation of *War and Peace* for Television (2007)', in *Tolstoy on Screen*, eds Lorna Fitzsimmons and Michael A. Denner [Evanston: Northwestern University Press, 2015], pp. 179–97).

[26] For a more detailed account of Bondarchuk's adaptation see Denise J. Youngblood, *Bondarchuk's War and Peace: Literary Classic to Soviet Cinematic Epic* (Lawrence, KA: University of Kansas Press, 2014).

[27] The budget of Bondarchuk's film amounted to a hitherto unheard-of sum of 8,165,200 roubles (approximately £50 million today) not to mention the contribution of the Soviet Ministry of Defence which funded the shooting of the battle scenes (Valeriia Gorelova, '"Voina i mir": samyi masshtabnyi kinoproekt XX veka', *Zhivaia istoriia*, 13 March 2018 <http://lhistory.ru/statyi/vojna-i-mir)> [accessed 1 September 2021]).

As regards the BBC series, the costs were in the region of £2 million per episode (Sarah Doran, 'How War and Peace Finally Found Its Stride', *Radio Times*, 17 January 2016 <https://www.radiotimes.com/tv/drama/how-war-and-peace-finally-found-its-stride/> [accessed 1 September 2021]). This was a relatively cost-effective production (in comparison, the budget for *The Crown* was £9 million per episode), achieved through the BBC's extensive use of the latest filming technology such as drone cameras and computer generated effects ('Five Reasons Why You Should Watch (or Rewatch) BBC's 2016 War and Peace', *Lost in Drama*, 20 August, 2017 <http://www.lostindrama.com/2017/08/20/5-reasons-why-you-should-watch-or-rewatch-bbcs-2016-war-and-peace/> [accessed 1 September 2021]).

[28] Georgii Daneliia, 'Ne boias' literatury', *Iskusstvo kino*, 9 (1965), pp. 10–11.

Daneliia saw Bondarchuk's film as an exemplar of the director's dialogue with and fidelity to Tolstoy's novel. 'Generally, we have a habit of affirming our respect and love for literature in every possible way', he wrote. 'But at times, we also tend to fear this very literature [. . .] We are afraid to bore our viewers; and therefore, remove from our screen-versions everything which is not immediately connected to the plot.'[29] This, according to Daneliia, renders the work simplistic and sterile, for it loses the very reason for which it had been originally created by the author. Contrary to this approach, Bondarchuk worked Tolstoy's vision into the palatable episodic structure of his screen version. He was 'not afraid that the viewer would be bored'.[30]

The film intended to bring out Tolstoy's pantheistic reflections on the world as an expression of the unifying life-force that reveals itself in all manifestations of the real; on the poetic sense of the divine within and around all human beings; and, consequently, on the blurred boundaries of one's personal existence. As articulated by Pierre in the novel:

> Don't I feel in my soul that I am part of this vast harmonious whole? Don't I feel that I form one link, one step, between the lower and higher beings, in this vast harmonious multitude of beings in whom the Deity – the Supreme Power if you prefer the term – is manifest? If I see, clearly see, that ladder leading from plant to man, why should I suppose it breaks off at me and does not go farther and farther?[31]

In his attempt to merge dramatic action with the philosophical meditations of Tolstoy, Bondarchuk placed emphasis on the latter, which defined the overall structure and expressive means of his work. Among cinematic effects used to underscore the idea of an all-embracing life-flow, one can mention 'soft' editing (allowing a gradual transition between the frames as opposed to a 'straight cut'), and the extensive use of the 'subjective camera viewpoint'. The effect thus created was that of a fused polyphony of inner voices and perspectives – hence the deliberations of the old oak tree at the Bolkonskys' manor, or the hunt presented through the eyes of a wolf. In the same vein, Lev Anninsky calls attention to the discrete (delineated in semi-tones) performances of all secondary figures. The critic saw it as yet another trope intended to project the notion of an uninterrupted historical flow (rather than the singularity of one's life), 'as if they meant to merge with, or dissolve in the interior of their own era'.[32] The reference was

---

[29] Daneliia, p.10.
[30] Ibid.
[31] Leo Tolstoy, *War and Peace*, trans Louise and Aylmer Maude (Chicago, London and Toronto: Encyclopaedia Britannica Inc., 1952), p. 217.
[32] Anninsky, p. 204.

unmissable, as this toned-down performance was completely uncharacteristic of such eye-catching actors as Oleg Efremov (Dolokhov) and Oleg Tabakov (Nikolai Rostov).[33]

In one of his creative seminars, the award-winning television writer and producer Morgan Gendel[34] made a point concerning the much-discussed difference between cinematic drama and melodrama. In his view, the main difference consists in the fact that in melodrama the plot drives the characters; while in cinematic drama it is the characters who drive the plot. Bondarchuk's *War and Peace* undoubtedly complies with the latter, which distinguishes it from all other screenings of Tolstoy's work. At times he did not even try to find cinematic equivalents for the novel's numerous philosophical digressions. They were rendered directly through the characters' dialogue or the comments of an off-screen narrator. This evidently slowed down the overall pace of dramatic progression, but the film made a clear point that the personalities of Tolstoy's epic would not have been so authentic and alluring if in the mud and confusion of battle they did not meditate on the transcendental nature of human existence (as Pierre, Captain Tushin, and Prince Andrei all do).

In accordance with Tolstoy's metaphysics, a man has little control over his circumstances, and even less over the stream of social and political events. He is completely absorbed by this flow, drawn and carried away by its power like an ant or a grain of sand. 'It is [. . .] necessary to renounce a freedom that does not exist, and to recognise a dependence of which we are not conscious',[35] asserts the author in the very last phrase of his epic. An ability to merge with the life flow, or at least to feel the vectors of its currents, was, in his view, one of the most significant talents to be mastered during one's earthly existence. In the novel, such an ability is granted to General Kutuzov, who defeats Napoleon against all strategic and rational odds (Bondarchuk makes a distinct feature of this point, showing Kutuzov [Boris Zakhava] sleeping all the way through the debate during the military council at Fili). Being in direct opposition to Thomas Carlyle's view of history as driven by heroes pursuing a goal,[36] Tolstoy in *War and Peace* places many more constraints on the heroic power of the leaders.

---

[33] Anninsky, pp. 203–4.

[34] Ken Miyamoto, 'The Single Difference Between Cinematic Drama and Melodrama', *Screencraft*, 10 March 2020 <https://screencraft.org/2020/03/10/the-single-difference-between-cinematic-drama-and-melodrama/> [accessed 1 September 2021].

Morgan Gendel has written for such television shows as *Drop Dead Diva*, *Nash Bridges*, *Law & Order*, *Star Trek: The Next Generation*, *Star Trek: Deep Space Nine*, *Wiseguy*, and *21 Jump Street*. He is best known for winning a Hugo Award for *The Inner Light*, one of the most popular and lauded episodes of *Star Trek: The Next Generation*.

[35] Tolstoy, p. 696.

[36] Ilia Stambler, 'Heroic Power in Thomas Carlyle and Leo Tolstoy', *The European Legacy*, 11 (2006), pp. 737–51.

There is a certain sense of egalitarianism that lies at the core of his a-heroic philosophy and artistic representation – a highly liberal concept, giving each person equal weight in shaping cultural and historical events (in this context, it is sufficient to mention such figures as Platon Karataev or Captain Tushin). This aspect of Tolstoy's views ties in well (and therefore was always aligned) with the Soviet paradigmatic emphasis on the collective; however, it acquired some original and context-specific undertones in Bondarchuk's work.

Another prominent feature of Bondarchuk's adaptation consisted in the fact that it was deeply anchored in the realities of his own time, showing why Soviet society of the 1960s was in desperate need of these ideas of Tolstoy.[37] It is worth bearing in mind that *War and Peace* was conceived as a novel about the formation of Russian society, unified and solidified by the spirit of patriotism, seen by the author as a specific realisation of the flow of the life-force. Drawing upon Tolstoy's concept of identity, and above all the belief that identity makes sense only when appreciated as a part of the bigger whole, Bondarchuk was trying to reassemble a world shattered by the Second World War and the atrocities of the Stalin era. In each of Tolstoy's characters, he was looking for an opening through which he could re-establish and affirm this unity and this link with the outside world. And it was not the link to an abstract existential notion of being, 'but a concrete connection with other people, with their family, tradition, and the national myth'.[38]

This double-edged and multi-layered approach to *interpretative* (or in other words 'fidelity') text-to-screen transposition is deeply ingrained in the Russian tradition. Going back to Grigorii Kozintsev's *Hamlet* (1964) and *King Lear* (1971), it is still traceable now in such works as Sergei Soloviev's *Anna Karenina* (2009) or Vladimir Khotinenko's TV adaptation of Dostoevsky's *Demons* (2014). The battle scenes and pivotal points of the plot (such as for instance Natasha's first ball, Pierre and Dolokhov's duel, and the sky of Austerlitz that opened up to Andrei), must be configured through a conceptually solid perspective, which says something meaningful about the relevance and the novelty of the adaptation itself. The dominance and the very existence of this canon partly account for the absence of new versions of *War and Peace* by present-day Russian directors.[39] The factors under consideration are in no way connected to fearful reverence for

---

See also Tolstoy's excursions into biology and atomism in 'The First Epilogue' (Tolstoy, pp. 680–3), and into engineering, physics, astronomy, and mathematics in 'The Second Epilogue', where he enlists scientific principles in support of the a-heroic, pantheistic worldview (Tolstoy, pp. 647–9; pp. 655–7; pp. 657–9; pp. 662–3, respectively).

[37] According to Denise Youngblood, in this sense the film exemplifies all 'the intimacy of the Thaw-era cinema' (Youngblood, p. 7).

[38] Anninsky, p. 214.

[39] Though in 2015, declared a Year of Literature, a sixty-hour continuous public reading of the book was broadcast live on television, radio and the internet. Leading artists, critics

the classics (even less to the problems of funding, which should not present much difficulty for such well-established directors as for instance Valerii Todorovsky or Nikita Mikhalkov), but rather to a certain set of socio-cultural issues and the changing balance in the text-and-film interaction in the modern cultural space. The main question here is what exactly the adaptor has to say about the current *status quo* of the Russian idea and issues of national identity, or at least those of some significant social concern. Russian directors evidently doubt whether *War and Peace* would offer an adequate medium for this kind of conversation with today's viewers; how far viewers will be able to identify themselves with early nineteenth-century culture; and, ultimately, to what extent Russian aristocratic grace could be used as a lens for the discussion of present-day morals.[40]

Bringing Tolstoy Closer to British Viewers: From Efferent to Aesthetic Reading

Coming from a different starting point and tradition, the authors of the BBC series were presented with a different set of objectives and concerns. Firstly, it is worth bearing in mind that the majority of BBC viewers were not familiar with Tolstoy's writings (in distinction to Russia, where *War and Peace* remains part of the school curriculum).[41] This was also the case for the entire cast of British and American actors. None of them had read Tolstoy's work prior to filming, and some did not master the 1200-page epic even in the process of no less than two years of shooting.[42] Shocking as it may seem, but for all its fame,

---

and public figures took part in the project ('1 300 chelovek chitaiut "Voinu i mir" za 60 chasov', *Moscow-24* <https://www.m24.ru/articles/literatura/12122015/91875> [accessed 1 September 2021]).

[40] Recent films such as Aleksei Mizgirev's *The Duellist* (*Dueliant*, 2016), set in 1860, and Andrei Kravchuk's *The Union of Salvation* (*Soiuz spaseniia*, 2019), concerning the Decembrist revolt, show that these attempts are mainly unsuccessful.

[41] In an interview Andrew Davies affirmed that his target audience consisted of those who were not familiar with Tolstoy; and that it was their reception that he relied upon in his work. For instance, he was quite moved by the genuine expressions of alarm that appeared on Twitter after the episode showing Natasha's affair with Anatole: 'No, no, Natasha, don't go with him! He's a bastard' (Alla Mironenko, '"Voina i mir" glazami angliiskogo romantika', *Revizor*, 29 December 2016 <http://www.rewizor.ru/cinema/special-projects/epoha-kino/intervu/voyna-i-mir-glazami-angliyskogo-romantika/> [accessed 1 September 2021]).

[42] To give but a few examples, in the words of James Norton (Prince Andrei), he once tried to read *War and Peace* but did not get further than a dozen pages. He read the novel in its entirety only when he got the part in this adaptation (Alexander Kan, '"Voina i mir" na ekranakh: pervye otkliki', *BBC Russian Service*, 7 January 2016 <https://www.bbc.com/

War and Peace has long since passed into that category of literary masterpieces, like Greek tragedies, *Don Quixote,* or even Dickens, the content of which is known to the majority from TV and film adaptations rather than from the original text. This lends further importance to the production of these widely accessible screen versions. Yes, the richness and the philosophical depth of the work most likely will be lost. However, in the hands of a skilful director it may gain an arresting visual dimension, stimulating a potential inquiry into the original source.

The transnational success of the BBC's *War and Peace* (the series was broadcast in twenty-nine countries, including Russia) bears witness to the fact that its authors managed to respond to a wide range of interests and demands of today's viewers. Two further points should be considered in relation to this observation. The first concerns the set of elements of this project that may contribute to the general mind-map of cultural branding – a modern-day phenomenon with a dual social and aesthetic function. On the one hand, it operates in the field of cultural consumers, drawing upon the socio-cultural particularities of viewers' reception. At the same time, it falls into the realm of cultural diplomacy, promoting a wider range of human values, cultural rapprochement and communication. The second point is related specifically to the aesthetic qualities of the BBC adaptation. By looking closer into the role and function of this element in the art of cinematic translation, the objective is to examine whether the BBC screen-version of the novel can be characterised in terms other than *kinolubok*.

Among those factors that had a definitive bearing on audience reception of this production, its visual dimension should be placed at the top of the list. Tom Harper as director, and George Steel as cinematographer, were known to audiences for their stunning production of the first series of the TV gangster drama series *Peaky Blinders* (2013); and their engagement in the project, unanticipated for many, suggested that the visual element would be under the spotlight from the start. Their work met the audience's expectations: massive scenes showing computer-generated battlefields and virtual armies made a strong impression on viewers, especially when combined with high-tech shooting from flying drone devices that are more powerful and less cumbersome than the helicopter cameras used at the time of Bondarchuk.

russian/society/2016/01/160106_war_and_peace_kan> [accessed 1 September 2021]). Likewise, Lily James testifies that she got to know the work only after she had accepted the part of Natasha. Due to lack of time, she had to do the reading right on the set of *Downton Abbey* (Kristina Desiatova, 'Voina i mir na BBC: sem′ faktov o s″emkakh', wday.ru, 3 March 2016 <https://www.wday.ru/stil-zhizny/novosty/voyna-i-mir-na-bbc-7-faktov-o-syemkah/> [accessed 1 September 2021]).

Leaving aside the sheer scope and sophistication of these digital gimmicks, special mention goes to the state-of-the-art camera work produced for the series by George Steel. When working with actors, he often resorted to the utmost extremes of, so to speak, 'direct close shooting', invading the private space of an actor and conducting a visual narrative from inside this very intimate space. These unexpected and almost out of proportion close-ups were used as an effective means of 'opening up' the characters for the viewers, evoking intimacy and a feeling of confidence and compassion. The examples are many and include the camera focusing on Natasha's eyes when she is bewildered by Anatole's courting; or Pierre recovering from the explosion of an ammunition cart at the Battle of Borodino. He slowly brings his hand to the forehead of a dead officer, as if trying to understand – very much in line with Tolstoy's narrative meditations – where and how the person's life went out of this body, which a second ago was still a man.[43]

Another effective choice made by the producers was the young cast of actors engaged in the screening. At the beginning of *War and Peace*, Pierre is about

Figure 10.2 Pierre Bezukhov (Paul Dano) at the Battle of Borodino, *War and Peace*, directed by Tom Harper, BBC TV series, 2016.

[43] Though the difference is that it is a mortally wounded horse, not an officer, that features in the novel: 'When he came to himself he was sitting on the ground leaning on his hands; the ammunition wagons he had been approaching no longer existed, only charred green boards and rags littered the scorched grass, and a horse, dangling fragments of its shaft behind it, galloped past, while another horse lay, like Pierre, on the ground, uttering prolonged and piercing cries' (Tolstoy, p. 383).

twenty years old, while Andrei Bolkonsky is twenty-seven.[44] Traditionally, and to ensure high revenues guaranteed by casting major stars in leading roles, Pierre and Andrei were performed by actors approaching or already well into their forties.[45] In the Soviet adaptation, their age difference was even inverted; and Viacheslav Tikhonov (Andrei) had to conjure an 'older' demeanour by acting with extreme restraint and speaking in a lower and deeper voice. Unlike all earlier adaptations, the age of the actors in the BBC series was, or at least appeared to be, fairly close to that mentioned in the novel. Visually, this added an extra layer of authenticity to Tolstoy's characters, making it easier for the audience to relate to their motives and actions. This was particularly the case for the younger generation of viewers, brought up on the straightforward and explicit language of Hollywood culture.

According to critics, Paul Dano turned out to be the youngest (aged thirty at the time of filming) and the best of all the Pierres that have ever appeared in screen adaptations.[46] Pierre is a notably difficult part to dramatise – a character who does not know himself at all and a misfit, which most leading actors tend not to be. As a symbolic seeker of enlightenment (often regarded as a projection of Tolstoy's own yearnings), Pierre represents the younger generation of the modern era, more liberal and more open to the surrounding world than the austere generation of Prince Andrei. There are certain elements of Pierre's idealism and impulsive decisions (becoming a Freemason or suddenly joining the army in his casual dress) that appear more credible when enacted by a young person. Not to mention Pierre's proverbial childlike smile, which had escaped all Dano's predecessors, adding an ineffable touch of authenticity to his forthcoming and endearing Pierre: 'His smile was unlike the half-smile of other people. When he smiled, his grave, even rather gloomy, look was instantaneously replaced by another, a childlike, kindly, even rather silly look, which seemed to ask forgiveness.'[47]

---

[44] 'Pierre at the age of ten had been sent abroad with an abbé as tutor and had remained away till he was twenty' (Tolstoy, p. 12). Regarding the age of Andrei, the narrative takes place in 1809 when he affirms that 'life is not over at thirty-one!' (Tolstoy, p. 237).

[45] In King Vidor's 1956 adaptation, Henry Fonda (Pierre) was 51, and Mel Ferrer (Andrei) 39; in the 1972 series, Anthony Hopkins (Pierre) was nearly 35; while Alan Dobie (Andrei) had reached 40. At the time when the Soviet film was released, Sergei Bondarchuk (Pierre) was 45, and Viacheslav Tikhonov (Andrei) was 37.

[46] Hannah Ellis-Petersen, 'Paul Dano: a resolutely hexagonal peg in the square hole of showbusiness', *The Guardian*, 6 February 2016 <https://www.theguardian.com/film/2016/feb/06/guardian-profile-paul-dano-war-and-peace> [accessed 1 September 2021]; Tat'iana Ershova, 'Russkaia voina, angliiskii mir', *Meduza*, 12 January 2016 <https://meduza.io/feature/2016/01/12/russkaya-voyna-angliyskiy-mir> [accessed 1 September 2021].

[47] Tolstoy, p. 11.

To add to the factors that brought Tolstoy's characters closer to British viewers one should mention a number of references that the series made to the characters of Jane Austen, especially those versions of them known to the public from Davies's now almost canonical TV adaptation of *Pride and Prejudice* of 1995. Although Austen's work was published in 1811, and Tolstoy's *War and Peace* first appeared in *The Russian Messenger* only in 1865, both novels start in 1805. Among the set of Tolstoy's nobles, the production team skilfully italicised a lot of commonalities with their counterparts delineated by Austen. Not unlike Mrs Bennet, Countess Rostova is anxious about the marriages of her children, hoping that through this she can improve the family fortune. After her attempt to elope with Anatole Kuragin, Natasha finds herself in the same compromised position as Lydia Bennet or, more likely, Georgiana Darcy; and the analogies go on.

From the perspective of social psychology and the theories of identity construction, people are more willing to ally themselves with other cultures when, firstly, there are some positive common characteristics to share; and, secondly, when the 'other' culture appears different on a positively valued scale.[48] Both considerations are essential for the aims of cultural branding, and both found their thorough realisation in the BBC's work. Notes of Britishness, as discussed, were manifestly present in the BBC's vision of the novel. These overtones were further enhanced by the fact that Lily James – Natasha – was firmly associated with the *echt*-British spirit of *Downton Abbey* (a highly popular upper-class family saga that dominated the country's screens in 2010–15), in which she played Lady Rose MacClare. As regards the colour of Russianness in this adaptation of *War and Peace*, it was projected with a considerable degree of attractiveness and insight into its idiomatic, illustrative and aesthetic dimensions.

The production gained greatly from the use of Russian or near-Russian landscapes and locations, especially as compared to the artificial studio sets of the 1972 BBC series and the Hollywood adaptation of 1956. Most of the film was shot in St Petersburg, while Moscow settings were represented by the old town area of Vilnius. Suitable aristocratic estates were found in Latvia (like Vilnius too once a part of the Russian Empire[49]), and the battle scenes were filmed near Novgorod in *plein-air*.

All three key households of the novel, the Rostovs, the Bolkonskys, and the Bezukhov-Kuragins, were represented by meticulously constructed artistic spaces, designed with an appreciable input from the Lenfilm studio's (St Petersburg)

---

[48] John C. Turner, 'Towards A Cognitive Redefinition of the Social Group', in *Social Identity and Intergroup Relations*, ed. Henri Tajfel (Cambridge: Cambridge University Press, 1982), pp. 15–40 (p. 26).

[49] By the end of the 18th century the whole of Latvia and Lithuania had been annexed by expansionist Russia.

props collection.⁵⁰ This helped to create an aesthetically idiomatic entourage for the action and facilitated finding an appropriate visual language for the narrative of Tolstoy's world. For instance, the interior of the Rostovs' house recalled that of a cosy flea market. Everyone brought in something to his/her liking (though completely impractical); and the rooms were piled with embroidered napkins, snuffboxes, ribbons and bonbonnieres scattered over the armchairs and tables. By contrast, The Bolkonskys' manor in Bald Hills (as well as their Moscow residence) looked grand, orderly, and austere. Filled with echoes resonating in the high vaults of its empty galleries and halls, the house appeared as the epitome of the bygone eighteenth-century era. Princess Maria (Jesse Buckley) was often filmed passing through the enfilades of these empty spaces, as if she did not have a place in her big and alien ancestral home. The interior of old Prince Bolkonsky's office, on the contrary, represented the comfort zone of its master: walls covered with numerous neatly assembled artefacts of the past, his emblematic lathe in the foreground.

This carefully thought-through descriptive aspect certainly distinguished the BBC series from a typical example of a *kinolubok*. And its faithful attempt to recreate *byt*, and to fill the screen with cinematic analogies of literary narrative render this production entirely characteristic of an *illustrative* approach to screening. As regards certain elements of an *interpretative* adaptation, it is worth looking closer into the very notion of this term and its evolving function within the frame of the modern-day context.

Back in the early twentieth century Martin Heidegger examined questions of formal philosophical analysis versus personal interpretations of aesthetic experience, referencing the immediate subjective experience of a work of art as essential for aesthetic interpretation.⁵¹ His ideas have been further developed by modern scholars. In this context, it is worth mentioning the studies of Louise Rosenblatt,⁵² a leading specialist in the process of reading, who draws attention to the dichotomy of objectives that underpin people's engagement in

---

⁵⁰ 'Lenfil'm odevaet akterov v britanskom seriale "Voina i mir"', *Lenfilm*, 23 January 2015 <https://www.lenfilm.ru/news/2015/01/Lenfilm_odevaet_akterov_v_britanskom_seriale_Voyna_i_mir> [accessed 1 September 2021].
  Since October 2012 (covering the entire duration of the BBC project), the Chairman of the board of directors of Lenfilm has been Fyodor Bondarchuk, the son of Sergei Bondarchuk, the director of the Soviet film-version of *War and Peace*.

⁵¹ Martin Heidegger, 'On the Origin of the Work of Art', in Martin Heidegger, *Basic Writings*, ed. David Farrell Krell (New York: HarperCollins, 2008), pp. 143–212.

⁵² Louise M. Rosenblatt, 'The Transactional Theory of Reading and Writing', in *Theoretical Models and Processes of Reading*, eds Robert Ruddell, Martha Rapp Ruddell and Harry Singer (Newark, DE: International Reading Association, 1994), pp. 1057–92; Louise Rosenblatt, *Literature as Exploration* (New York: The Modern Language Association of America, 1995), p. 32.

reading. Rosenblatt distinguishes between two modes of reading that occupy diametrically polar ends of a spectrum. *Aesthetic* reading differs from *efferent* reading in that the former is characteristic of a reader expecting to get an affective or emotionally charged experience from this process, being moved by the text's prosody, imagery and impressionistic sensations. *Efferent* reading, on the other hand, refers to someone reading for knowledge, focusing on the text's semantics, and expecting to 'carry away information' as from a textbook or a similar source.[53] Rosenblatt argues that

> The transaction with any text stirs up both referential and affective aspects of consciousness, and the proportion of attention given to these will determine where the reading will fall on a continuum from predominantly efferent to predominantly aesthetic. [. . .] From this mixture of sensations, feelings, images, and ideas is structured the experience that constitutes the story or poem or play.[54]

An aesthetic interpretation expresses a particular emotional or experiential understanding, most often referring to one's interaction with a poem or a piece of music, but equally applicable to the domain of performance or film. In this sense, one can also talk about an *aesthetic*, rather than *efferent*, interpretation arising in the process of text-to-screen transposition. An adaptation, arguably, may not offer any message to be 'carried away' by the viewer but the sheer pleasure of an experience to be taken part in actively – aesthetically. This claim is supported by modern studies in the psychology of perception. Informed by the rapid advancement of digital culture, these studies see virtual reality and immersive experience as the very essence of the *aesthetic* interpretation.[55] Given its dynamic multi-layered cultural framing, its cinematic plasticity and its gripping aesthetic dimension, the BBC series clearly offered this interpretative 'lived through' experience to viewers.

Despite a degree of awkwardness, the BBC project can least of all be accused of frivolity, ignorance or misunderstanding of the artistic and cultural significance of the Russian novel. At a time of economic sanctions and the noticeable worsening of British-Russian relations, such a token of cultural diplomacy could not but be welcomed by the international community of filmmakers and critics.[56]

---

[53] Rosenblatt, 1995, p. 32.
[54] Rosenblatt, 1995, p. 33.
[55] Grant Tavinor, *The Aesthetics of Virtual Reality* (Abingdon: Routledge, 2021).
[56] Alexander Kan, 'Britanskie kritiki: "Voina i mir" – triumf BBC', *BBC Russian Service*, 8 February 2016 <https://www.bbc.com/russian/society/2016/02/160208_war_and_peace_final_reviews> [accessed 1 September 2021]; Schama, 'What Tolstoy's "War and Peace" can teach us'; Maksim Kaziuchits, 'Voina i mir: sinteticheskii variant', *Iskusstvo kino*, 5 (2016) <http://old.kinoart.ru/archive/2016/05/vojna-i-mir-sinteticheskij-variant-vojna-i-mir-rezhisser-rezhisser-tom-kharperю> [accessed 1 September 2021].

The overwhelming majority saw it as a significant step in intercultural communication, raising artistic dialogue above the level of political tension and disputes. One has to admit that over the past twenty years, Russian culture has largely fallen under the radar of the British public, and the image of the country is now associated with nothing but a series of political scandals. The vast tide of interest evoked by this production of *War and Peace* may be regarded as a long-awaited positive harbinger, though not without a mixture of some bittersweet notes. For all its worth, one is left with the feeling that of all things Russian, the only one suitable for 'export' is the world of the Russian past. On the other hand, it is difficult to deny that the series does work as an instructive example of cultural branding, capitalising on the timeless identity of Russian attainments. With its arresting imagery and coherent illustrative aspect, it also offers an attractive introduction to Tolstoy, underscoring the importance of the symbolisation and visualisation of this type of information in the modern world of cultural consumers. As Davies noted in an interview with Russian reporters:

> After the BBC series, *War and Peace* appeared for the first time among the top fifty best-selling novels in the UK. And deep down, I do hope that people did not buy it just to put it on the shelf [. . .] It is good to know that it was our film that became the main stimulus for people's closer acquaintance with your literature.[57]

Bibliography

Anninsky, Lev, *Okhota na L'va* (Moscow: Shar, 1998).

Dahlgreen, Will, 'War and Peace: the classic Brits are most likely to want to read (but that very few have read)', *YouGov*, 20 January 2016 <https://yougov.co.uk/topics/lifestyle/articles-reports/2016/01/20/war-and-peace-tops-britains-classic-fiction-wishli.> [accessed 1 September 2021].

Daneliia, Georgii, 'Ne boias' literatury', *Iskusstvo kino*, 9 (1965), pp. 10–11.

Desiatova, Kristina, 'Voina i mir na BBC: sem' faktov o s"emkakh', wday.ru, 3 March 2016 <https://www.wday.ru/stil-zhizny/novosty/voyna-i-mir-na-bbc-7-faktov-o-syemkah/> [accessed 1 September 2021].

Doran, Sarah, 'How War and Peace Finally Found Its Stride', *Radio Times*, 17 January 2016 <https://www.radiotimes.com/tv/drama/how-war-and-peace-finally-found-its-stride/> [accessed 1 September 2021].

Though there were mixed reviews by some Russian cultural figures; see Ershova, 'Russkaia voina, angliiskii mir'.

[57] Mironenko, '"Voina i mir" glazami angliiskogo romantika'. See also 'War and Peace enters top 50 for first time', *Bookseller*, 15 February 2016 <https://www.thebookseller.com/news/tolstoy-scores-first-nielsen-top-50-hit-322498> [accessed 1 September 2021].

YouGov research reveals *War and Peace* 'tops the list of 25 19th Century classic novels British people say they would most like to read if they had the time and the patience' (Dahlgreen, '*War and Peace*').

Ellis-Petersen, Hannah, 'Paul Dano: a resolutely hexagonal peg in the square hole of show-business', *The Guardian*, 6 February 2016 <https://www.theguardian.com/film/2016/feb/06/guardian-profile-paul-dano-war-and-peace> [accessed 1 September 2021].

Engel, Christine, 'Tolstoy Transnational: Dornhelm's Adaptation of *War and Peace* for Television (2007)', in *Tolstoy on Screen*, eds Lorna Fitzsimmons and Michael A. Denner (Evanston: Northwestern University Press, 2015), pp. 179–97.

Ershova, Tat'iana, 'Russkaia voina, angliiskii mir', *Meduza*, 12 January 2016 <https://meduza.io/feature/2016/01/12/russkaya-voyna-angliyskiy-mir > [accessed 1 September 2021].

'Five Reasons Why You Should Watch (or Rewatch) BBC's 2016 War and Peace', *Lost in Drama*, 20 August 2017 <http://www.lostindrama.com/2017/08/20/5-reasons-why-you-should-watch-or-rewatch-bbcs-2016-war-and-peace/> [accessed 1 September 2021].

Gorelova, Valeriia, '"Voina i mir": samyi masshtabnyi kinoproekt XX veka', *Zhivaia istoriia*, 13 March 2018 <http://lhistory.ru/statyi/vojna-i-mir)> [accessed 1 September 2021].

Heidegger, Martin, 'On the Origin of the Work of Art', in Martin Heidegger, *Basic Writings*, ed. David Farrell Krell (New York: HarperCollins, 2008).

Kan, Alexander, '"Voina i mir" na ekranakh: pervye otkliki', *BBC Russian Service*, 7 January 2016 <https://www.bbc.com/russian/society/2016/01/160106_war_and_peace_kan> [accessed 1 September 2021].

——, 'Britanskie kritiki: "Voina i mir" – triumf BBC', *BBC Russian Service*, 8 February 2016 <https://www.bbc.com/russian/society/2016/02/160208_war_and_peace_final_reviews> [accessed 1 September 2021].

'Lenfil'm odevaet akterov v britanskom seriale "Voina i mir"', *Lenfilm*, 23 January 2015 <https://www.lenfilm.ru/news/2015/01/Lenfilm_odevaet_akterov_v_britanskom_seriale_Voyna_i_mir> [accessed 1 September 2021].

Kaziuchits, Maksim, 'Voina i mir: sinteticheskii variant', *Iskusstvo kino*, 5 (2016) <http://old.kinoart.ru/archive/2016/05/vojna-i-mir-sinteticheskij-variant-vojna-i-mir-rezhisser-rezhisser-tom-kharperю> [accessed 1 September 2021].

Makoveeva, Irina, 'Cinematic Adaptations of *Anna Karenina*', *Studies in Slavic Cultures*, 2 (2001), pp. 111–33.

McFarlane, Brian, *Novel to Film* (New York: Oxford University Press, 1996).

Mironenko, Alla, '"Voina i mir" glazami angliiskogo romantika', *Revizor*, 29 December 2016 <http://www.rewizor.ru/cinema/special-projects/epoha-kino/intervu/voyna-i-mir-glazami-angliyskogo-romantika/> [accessed 1 September 2021].

Miyamoto, Ken, 'The Single Difference Between Cinematic Drama and Melodrama', *Screencraft*, 10 March 2020 <https://screencraft.org/2020/03/10/the-single-difference-between-cinematic-drama-and-melodrama/> [accessed 1 September 2021].

Plunkett, John, 'BBC Returns to Tolstoy's War and Peace', *The Guardian*, 18 February 2013 <https://www.theguardian.com/media/2013/feb/18/bbc-returns-tolstoy-war-peace> [accessed 1 September 2021].

Rosenblatt, Louise M., 'The Transactional Theory of Reading and Writing', in *Theoretical Models and Processes of Reading*, eds Robert Ruddell, Martha Rapp Ruddell and Harry Singer (Newark, DE: International Reading Association, 1994), pp. 1057–92.

——, *Literature as Exploration* (New York: The Modern Language Association of America, 1995).

Schama, Simon, 'What Tolstoy's "War and Peace" can teach us', *Financial Times*, 8 January 2016 < https://www.ft.com/content/8a003e2c-b497-11e5-8358-9a82b43f6b2f> [accessed 1 September 2021].
Smith, Stephen, '"It's good to chop out the boring bits!": Andrew Davies on adapting War and Peace', *The Spectator* (Australia), 23 January 2016 <https://www.spectator.com.au/2016/01/its-good-to-chop-out-the-boring-bits-andrew-davies-on-adapting-war-and-peace/> [accessed 1 September 2021].
Stambler, Ilia, 'Heroic Power in Thomas Carlyle and Leo Tolstoy', *The European Legacy*, 11 (2006), pp. 737–51.
Tavinor, Grant, *The Aesthetics of Virtual Reality* (Abingdon: Routledge, 2021).
Teneromo, Isaak, 'Tolstoi o kinematografe', *Kino: Dvukhnedel'nik Obshchestva kinoizdatelei*, 2 (1922), pp. 3–4.
Tolstoy, Leo, *War and Peace*, trans Louise and Aylmer Maude (Chicago, London and Toronto: Encyclopaedia Britannica Inc., 1952).
Turner, John C., 'Towards A Cognitive Redefinition of the Social Group', in *Social Identity and Intergroup Relations*, ed. Henri Tajfel (Cambridge: Cambridge University Press, 1982), pp. 15–40.
Wagner, Geoffrey, *The Novel and the Cinema* (Rutherford: Fairleigh Dickinson University Press, 1975).
'War and Peace enters top 50 for first time', *Bookseller*, 15 February 2016 <https://www.thebookseller.com/news/tolstoy-scores-first-nielsen-top-50-hit-322498> [accessed 1 September 2021].
Youngblood, Denise J., *Bondarchuk's War and Peace: Literary Classic to Soviet Cinematic Epic* (Lawrence, KA: University of Kansas Press, 2014).
Zorkaia, Neia, 'Russkaia shkola ekranizatsii', in *Ekrannye iskusstva i literatura. Nemoe kino* (Moscow: Nauka, 1991), pp. 105–30.
'1 300 chelovek chitaiut "Voinu i mir" za 60 chasov', *Moscow-24* <https://www.m24.ru/articles/literatura/12122015/91875> [accessed 1 September 2021].

FILMOGRAPHY

War and Peace, directed by King Vidor (USA, Ponti-De Laurentiis Cinematografica, 1956).
War and Peace (*Voina i mir*), directed by Sergei Bondarchuk (USSR, Mosfilm, 1965–7).
War and Peace, directed by John Davies (UK, BBC TV series, 1972).
War and Peace, directed by Tom Harper (UK, BBC TV series, 2016).

INDEX

Adabashian, Aleksandr, 61, 62, 66, 71
adaptation theory, 1, 3, 206
adaptation type
   analogy, 3, 72, 134, 145, 146, 154, 155, 233
   commentary (interpretative), 3, 34, 36, 59, 88, 170, 212, 217, 233, 234, 237
   kinolubok, 232, 233, 239, 243
   transposition (illustrative), 3, 4, 23, 233, 242, 243, 245
Adorno, Theodor, 134
Altman, Robert, 128, 207
   Boogie Nights, 128
   Happy Endings, 128
   Magnolia, 128
   Short Cuts, 128, 129, 130, 131
anamorphic discourse, 3
Annensky, Isidor, 165
Anninsky, Lev, 232, 235, 236, 237
Ayoade, Richard, 22, 100, 101, 105, 107, 108, 109, 110, 111, 112, 113, 114, 115, 116, 117
   The Double, 22, 100, 101, 103, 104, 105, 106, 108, 110, 112, 113, 114, 117

Bakhtin, Mikhail, 5, 42, 104, 105, 106, 184
Barthes, Roland, 22
Bauer, Evgenii, 9, 54
Bening, Annette, 169, 172, 173, 174, 175, 176, 177
Beumers, Birgit, 37, 45, 48, 187
Blakemore, Michael, 145, 146, 147, 148, 156, 157, 159
   Country Life, 145, 147, 156
Boele, Otto, 9, 23, 54, 183, 230
Bogatyrev, Iurii, 40
Bondarchuk, Sergei, 21, 166, 187, 227, 228, 234, 235, 236, 237, 239, 241, 243
Bourdieu, Pierre, 17
branding (cultural), 7, 8, 13, 14, 17, 23, 24, 228, 239, 242, 245
Brecht, Bertolt, 154, 156
Bresson, Robert, 22, 79, 80, 81, 82, 83, 84, 85, 86, 87, 88, 89, 90, 91, 92, 93, 94, 95, 96, 97, 98, 206, 207, 213, 216
   L'Argent, 206, 207, 209, 213, 214, 215, 216

Pickpocket, 83, 91
Quatre nuits d'un rêveur, 83
Une femme douce, 22, 79, 80, 81, 82, 83, 85, 86, 87, 88, 90, 91, 92, 94, 96, 97, 98
Brodsky, Joseph, 35
Bunin, Ivan, 50
Burry, Alexander, 6, 7, 18, 22, 49, 79, 80, 83, 139, 140, 174, 177
Buslov, Konstantin, 206, 212, 214, 215

Cardwell, Sarah, 1, 2
Cartmell, Deborah, 1, 11, 53
Chardynin, Petr, 206, 211, 227
Chekhov, Anton, 5, 9, 10, 18, 21, 22, 59, 123, 124, 125, 126, 127, 128, 129, 130, 131, 132, 133, 134, 135, 136, 137, 138, 139, 140, 141, 142, 145, 146, 147, 148, 149, 150, 151, 152, 153, 154, 155, 156, 157, 158, 159, 160, 161, 162, 165, 166, 167, 168, 169, 170, 171, 172, 173, 175, 177, 178
   'Grief', 124, 126, 127, 130
   Motley Stories, 130
   Platonov, 72, 150, 157
   'The Bear', 125, 165
   The Cherry Orchard, 150
   'The Cossack', 125, 126
   'The Father', 124, 126
   The Lady with the Dog, 10, 165
   The Seagull, 23, 124, 165, 166, 167, 168, 169, 170, 172, 173, 174, 175, 177, 178
   'The Wedding', 165
   Three Sisters, 131, 133, 134, 159
   Uncle Vanya, 131, 145, 146, 147, 149, 150, 151, 153, 155
   Ward No. 6, 135
cultural diplomacy, 13, 14, 24, 66, 239, 244

Daneliia, Georgii, 227, 234, 235
Dano, Paul, 230, 232, 240, 241
Davies, Andrew, 61, 227, 228, 229, 230, 231, 232, 233, 238, 242, 245
   Bleak House, 230
   Doctor Zhivago, 230
   Pride and Prejudice, 230, 242
   Sense and Sensibility, 230
Davies, John, 227, 229
Denner, Michael, 9, 18, 185, 187, 234
Diaghilev seasons, 14
Dickens, Charles, 11, 61, 114, 195, 230, 239
Dolgopolov, Greg, 23, 205
Dornhelm, Robert, 227, 234
Dostoevsky, Fedor, 7, 9, 12, 13, 15, 16, 18, 21, 22, 36, 79, 80, 81, 83, 84, 85, 86, 87, 88, 89, 90, 91, 92, 93, 94, 95, 96, 97, 98, 100, 101, 103, 104, 105, 106, 107, 108, 109, 110, 112, 113, 114, 115, 116, 117, 151, 196, 237
   'A Meek Creature', 22, 79, 80, 81, 84, 85, 86, 87, 88, 89, 91, 93, 94, 97, 98
   Demons, 13, 16, 237
   Netochka Nezvanova, 12
   The Brothers Karamazov, 10, 15
   The Diary of a Writer, 86
   The Double, 101, 103, 104, 106, 107, 110, 113, 114, 116
   The House of the Dead, 12
   'White Nights', 12, 83

Eisenstein, Sergei, 210, 214

Fedorova, Liudmila, 18, 22
Fitzsimmons, Lorna, 9, 18, 185, 186, 234
French, Philip, 18, 165

Geal, Robert, 3, 4, 11
Gillespie, David, 9, 10, 11, 186, 187
Ginzburg, Lidiia, 7
Goethe, Johann Wolfgang, 17, 67, 88
Gogol, Nikolai, 5, 9, 67, 103, 104, 106, 110, 113, 114, 115, 196
   Diary of a Madman, 104
   Petersburg Tales, 103, 106
   'The Nose', 104
   'The Overcoat', 110, 196

Goncharov, Ivan, 21, 31, 32, 33, 34, 35, 36, 37, 38, 42, 43, 45, 46, 47, 49, 67
  Oblomov, 21, 31, 32, 33, 34, 36, 37, 38, 39, 40, 41, 42, 43, 44, 45, 46, 47, 48, 49, 50, 66, 67
Gorky, Maxim, 14
Gregory, André, 146, 147, 148, 149, 150, 151, 152, 153, 154, 155, 156, 157, 159, 161, 162, 177, 213
Grotowski, Jerzy, 146, 152, 153, 154, 155, 156, 157, 159, 161, 162

Harper, Tom, 222, 227, 229, 239, 240
Hasty, Olga, 22, 79, 80
Heidegger, Martin, 243
Hopkins, Anthony, 1, 145, 146, 147, 156, 157, 159, 163, 241
  August, 157
Hutcheon, Linda, 6, 206
Hutchings, Stephen, 5, 18, 37, 59
hypertext, 7, 50, 80, 186
hypotext, 50, 80, 135

Iampolski, Mikhail, 131, 193, 205
identity (Russian, national), 8, 11, 14, 24, 44, 61, 66, 69, 70, 71, 72, 93, 100, 101, 106, 108, 109, 110, 113, 114, 115, 116, 117, 237, 238, 242, 245
interpretation *efferent* vs *aesthetic*, 24, 244
Iutkevich, Sergei, 83
Ivanovsky, Alexander, 9

James, Lily, 229, 230, 239, 242
jazz, 124, 128
Jefferson, Thomas, 13, 128

Kaidanovsky, Aleksandr, 23, 183, 185, 186, 187, 188, 190, 191, 193, 194, 195, 196, 197, 198, 200, 201, 202
Kantor, Vladimir, 34, 42, 47, 49
Kheifits, Iosif, 10, 165
Kirov (Mariinskii) Ballet, 15
Konchalovsky, Andrei, 10, 44, 157, 160
Kozintsev, Grigorii, 12, 196, 237
Kristeva, Julie, 6, 185
Kurosawa, Akira, 185

Lapushin, Radislav, 22, 123, 134
Leder, Mimi, 206, 221
Leitch, Thomas, 1, 3, 16, 183, 184, 185, 201
Lenfilm, 56, 70, 191, 242, 243
literary-cinematic space, 18, 20, 24
Loshchits, Iurii, 33, 34, 35, 36, 37, 42, 44, 45, 49
Lotman, Iurii, 189, 205, 206, 223
Louhimies, Aki, 206, 216, 217, 218, 219, 221
Lyotard, Jean-François, 7

MacCabe, Colin, 37, 183, 184, 185
McFarlane, Brian, 145, 146, 157, 232, 233
Maiakovsky, Vladimir, 54, 55, 57
Makoveeva, Irina, 232, 233
Malle, Louis
  Au Revoir Les Enfants, 149
  Lift to the Scaffold (Ascenseur pour l'Echafaud), 161
  May Fools (Milou en mai), 149
  My Dinner with André, 148, 149, 150, 151, 152, 153
  Vanya on 42nd Street, 23, 144, 146, 147, 148, 149, 150, 151, 152, 154, 155, 158, 160, 162, 177, 178, 233
Mamet, David, 149, 157, 160, 162
Mayer, Michael, 23, 165, 166, 167, 168, 169, 170, 171, 172, 173, 174, 175, 177, 178
Meredith, Michael, 123, 124, 126, 141
  Three Days of Rain, 124, 127, 128, 129, 130, 131, 141
Meyerhold, Vsevolod, 54, 55, 165
Mikhalkov, Nikita, 10, 21, 31, 33, 34, 35, 37, 38, 39, 40, 42, 43, 44, 45, 46, 47, 48, 49, 50, 66, 157, 165, 238
  A Few Days from the Life of I. I. Oblomov, 31, 40, 48
  An Unfinished Piece for Mechanical Piano, 157, 165
  Anna from 6 to 18, 50
Mikhalkov-Konchalovsky, Andrei *see* Konchalovsky, Andrei
Mil'don, Valerii, 18, 19

Mill, John Stuart, 79, 86
Mondry, Henrietta, 21, 31, 66
Mosfilm, 62, 227
Moss, Elisabeth, 172, 173, 174
Muratova, Kira, 5

neo-modernist, 7
New Amsterdam Theater, 147, 150, 155, 156
Norton, James, 126, 169, 229, 230, 238
Nye, Joseph, 13

oblomovshchina, 31, 32, 33, 34, 45, 49
Olivier, Laurence, 147, 148, 163

Partan, Olga, 23, 165
Pasternak, Boris, 15, 129, 230
  Doctor Zhivago, 15, 230
Paterson, Don, 124
postmodernist, 7, 20, 22
post-Soviet, 5, 21, 49, 50, 53, 59, 62, 63, 64, 65, 66, 69, 70, 137, 139, 167, 196, 197
Pulman, Jack, 227, 229, 230
Pushkin, Alexander, 5, 9, 67, 106, 123, 159, 196
  Dubrovsky, 9
  The Bronze Horseman, 106

Redgrave, Michael, 147, 166
Ronan, Saoirse, 169, 170, 172, 173, 174, 175
Rosenfeld, Keva, 206, 212

Schiller, Friedrich (von), 17
Schubert, Franz, 58, 193, 194
Seidelman, Arthur Allan, 123, 131, 132, 134, 141
  The Sisters, 123, 131, 132, 133, 141
Senelick, Laurence, 168
Shakespeare, William, 3, 81, 91, 92, 93, 94
  Hamlet, 81, 91, 92, 93, 94, 96, 98, 237
  King Lear, 237

Shakhnazarov, Karen, 123, 136, 137, 138, 139, 140, 141, 207, 214
  Ward No. 6, 123, 135, 136, 137, 139, 140, 141
Shawn, Wallace, 148, 149, 150, 151, 152, 158, 159, 160
Shklovsky, Viktor, 12
Shveitser, Mikhail, 130, 186, 187
Smirnova, Avdotya, 21, 52, 53, 59, 60, 61, 62, 63, 64, 65, 66, 67, 68, 69, 70, 71, 72
Smith, Alexandra, 21, 52, 134, 161, 228, 230
Sobolev, Olga, 23, 61, 134, 166, 226
Sokurov, Alexander, 23, 193
Sontag, Susan, 169, 171
Soviet Union, 4, 10, 12, 31, 33, 35, 36, 50, 54, 56
Stam, Robert, 4, 6, 131, 183, 184, 185
Stanislavsky, Konstantin, 150, 156, 165, 171, 172, 175
Strasberg, Lee, 147, 150, 156

Tabakov, Oleg, 40, 44, 45, 236
Tarkovsky, Andrei, 23, 82, 167, 186, 194
The Death of Ivan Il'ich (screen adaptations)
  A Simple Death (*Prostaia smert'*, 1985), 23, 183, 185, 186, 187, 188, 190, 191, 192, 193, 194, 195, 196, 197, 200, 201, 202
  Ikiru (1952), 185
  ivans xtc (2000), 185
The Forged Coupon (screen adaptations)
  Counterfeit Note (*Fal'shivyi kupon*, 1913), 206
  Frozen Land (*Paha Maa*, 2005), 207, 209, 216, 217, 218, 219, 220, 221, 223
  L'Argent (1983) *see* Bresson, Robert
  Loot (*Bablo*, 2011), 206, 207, 209, 212, 214, 215, 216
  Pay It Forward (2000), 206, 209, 221, 222

The Forged Coupon (Cont.)
  The Adventures of a Ten Mark Note (*Die Abenteuer eines Zehnmarkscheines*, 1926), 206, 212, 215
  The Altered Note (*Il falso cupone*, 1914), 206
  Twenty Bucks (1993), 206, 212, 215
Theatre of Poverty, 146, 152, 153, 154, 156, 161
Tolstoy, Lev, 5, 7, 8, 9, 15, 16, 18, 21, 23, 24, 83, 114, 159, 183, 185, 186, 187, 188, 189, 190, 191, 193, 194, 195, 196, 197, 198, 199, 200, 201, 202, 205, 206, 207, 208, 209, 210, 211, 212, 213, 214, 215, 216, 217, 218, 219, 220, 221, 222, 223, 226, 227, 228, 229, 230, 231, 232, 233, 234, 235, 236, 237, 238, 240, 241, 242, 243, 244, 245
  'After the Ball', 186
  Anna Karenina, 10, 11, 15, 16, 187, 232, 237
  Childhood, Boyhood and Youth, 187
  Family Happiness, 130, 187
  Resurrection, 186, 226
  The Death of Ivan Il'ich, 185, 187, 188, 189, 190, 195, 201, 202
  The Forged Coupon, 23, 205, 206, 207, 208, 209, 210, 211, 214, 216, 217, 218, 223
  The Kreutzer Sonata, 187, 196, 199
  War and Peace, 8, 9, 10, 15, 16, 21, 23, 24, 61, 166, 187, 200, 226, 227, 228, 229, 231, 233, 234, 235, 237, 238, 239, 240, 242, 243, 245
Trauberg, Leonid, 196
Tsivian, Iurii, 205

Turgenev, Ivan, 5, 7, 8, 9, 10, 21, 52, 53, 54, 55, 56, 57, 58, 59, 60, 61, 62, 63, 64, 65, 66, 67, 68, 69, 70, 71, 72, 159
  A Nest of Gentlefolk, 10
  Fathers and Sons, 9, 21, 52, 53, 54, 55, 56, 57, 59, 60, 61, 63, 64, 65, 66, 67, 71, 72
  Klara Milich, 54
Tynianov, Iurii, 196

Verfremdungseffekt, 154, 156, 161
Vernitski, Anat, 5, 18, 37
Vidor, King, 10, 227, 232, 241
Viertel, Berthold, 206, 211, 212
Village Prose, 33, 35, 36, 37, 39, 45, 46, 47, 48, 49
  derevenshchiki, 33, 34, 35, 48

Wagner, Geoffrey, 3, 145, 155, 170, 232, 233
War and Peace (screen adaptations), 227
  War and Peace (1956) *see* Vidor, King
  War and Peace (1972) *see* Davies, John and Pulman Jack
  War and Peace (2007) *see* Dornhelm, Robert
  War and Peace (2016) *see* Davies, Andrew and Harper, Tom
  War and Peace/ Voina i mir (1965–7) *see* Bondarchuk, Sergei
White, Frederick H., 6, 7, 12, 18, 49, 80, 83, 139, 174
Widdis, Emma, 47, 72
Woolf, Virginia, 8, 66, 145
  'The Russian Point of View', 8, 66
Wrenn, Angus, 23, 131, 144, 177, 233

Youngblood, Denise, 9, 44, 234, 237

Žižek, Slavoj, 20, 21

EU representative:
Easy Access System Europe
Mustamäe tee 50, 10621 Tallinn, Estonia
Gpsr.requests@easproject.com

www.ingramcontent.com/pod-product-compliance
Lightning Source LLC
Chambersburg PA
CBHW050845230426
43667CB00012B/2159